MITCHELL
BEAZLEY
WINE
GUIDES

WINES OF
Italy

BURTON ANDERSON

Wines of Italy
by Burton Anderson

Edited and designed by Mitchell Beazley, an imprint of Octopus Publishing Group Ltd, 2–4 Heron Quays, London E14 4JP

First published in 1983 as *The Mitchell Beazley Pocket Guide to Italian Wines* by Burton Anderson. This edition, revised, updated, and expanded 2004

Revised editions 1988, 1992, 1998, 2000, 2002, 2004

A CIP catalogue record of this book is available from the British Library.

ISBN 1 84000 861 X

Mitchell Beazley would like to thank Maureen Ashley MW for her assistance in the update for the 2004 edition.

Commissioning Editor: Hilary Lumsden
Executive Art Editor: Yasia Williams
Editor: Juanne Branquinho
Design: Peter Gerrish, Tim Pattinson
Index: Hilary Bird
Production: Gilbert Francourt

Typeset in Veljovic
Printed and bound in China

Contents

Key to Symbols

r	red
p	rosé
w	white
am	amber
mc	*metodo classico* (for bottle-fermented sparkling wine)
s/sw	semi-sweet
sw	sweet
fz	*frizzante*
sp	sparkling
dr	dry

The above in parentheses means relatively unimportant.

☆	everyday wine
☆☆	above average
☆☆☆	superior in its category
☆☆☆☆	outstanding

IGT	wine typical of its geographical indication
DOC	name and origin controlled
DOCG	name and origin controlled and guaranteed
Age: 1 yr etc	ageing required under DOC
96, 99, etc	recommended years
DYA	drink youngest available
CS	*Cantina Sociale* (co-operative cellar)

See pages 6–7 for more information.

Introduction

Italy's winemakers seem filled by an unstoppable sense of optimism. New estates, new wines, and new money being invested into emerging areas, not to mention continuous improvements in wines already on the market place have created a buoyant scene light-years away from the prolific supplier of light-hearted wines at bargain-basement prices that typified the country two decades ago.

Developments have been at their most striking in the Asti zone in Piedmont in the northwest, long tired of playing second fiddle to the more renowned production of nearby Alba, and in the Maremma in southern Tuscany, which has seen unprecedented levels of vineyard land being bought by producers from the region's more famous zones and elsewhere.

Yet this surge of enthusiasm may harbour a negative side. It is telling that the vast majority of producers listed in this guide have come out with at least one or two new wines in the past two years and few have withdrawn any from the market. The so-called international varieties – Chardonnay, Cabernet, Merlot, Syrah, Sauvignon Blanc – have staked an important place in the vineyards and even more significant achievements have come from the many native varieties which yield wines of unique personality and style. Blends of the two have given some fascinating wines of great class, but the number of international-indigenous combinations seems endless and while noone can blame Italy's winemakers for wanting to exploit the possibilities to the full, maybe the country is heading to the point where it explodes from an abundance of wines, drowning the spectator in a sea of names.

Each of Italy's twenty regions produces wine in vineyards that grace hillsides from the Alps to the Mediterranean islands. It seems unlikely that anyone will ever manage to compute, let alone categorize, all the types. The aim of this compact volume is to single out the wines and winemakers that really count.The country is the champion of diversity. Wine-lovers could spend a lifetime exploring its vineyards and still not taste everything while to casual drinkers, the scope is staggering. The profusion of colours, scents, and flavours that make Italian wines so fascinating is reflected by labels which abound with place names, grape varieties, estates, vineyards, brands, and terms for various types and styles of vinifying and ageing. Explanations through the text may help to allay any confusion.

While Italy's weather, despite common preconceptions, is anything but stable, and there are often significant variations from vintage to vintage (which this guide indicates), producers are now well equipped to coax their grapes to ripeness and far bolder at eliminating imperfect grapes. It is therefore becoming ever more the case that a "poor" vintage will result in a reduction in the quantity of many wines produced rather than their quality.

The country's classified wines are designated DOC or DOCG. In some cases this refers to the wine-growing hectarage of an entire region; in other instances the DOC only refers to a few selected vineyards. Many of these denominations are famous worldwide while others are hardly known, even in their place of origin. And while DOC(G) wines continue to increase in number, only a minority of the country's total production is classed in this (theoretically, at least) cream-of-the-crop category. Today, ever more producers of high-quality wine in Italy prefer to market some or all of their range under the more liberal "lesser" IGT designation.

The most important wines and producers are dealt with in separate chapters which cover all twenty regions in a geographical sequence moving generally from north to south. After basic observations and vintage information, each region is surveyed through alphabetical listings, first of classified wines and vines, then of wineries with notes on production. At the end are entries on regional foods and wines and recommended restaurants. The book follows a region-by-region format because Italy's wines come into context only when related to their places of origin – to the terrains, climates, customs, foods, and people that give them local character.

This volume may serve as a tour guide providing outline maps of key regions, travel tips, and suggested restaurants to help visitors discover the intricacies of Italian wine at first hand. For consumers abroad, it is designed to be used as a buyer's guide, compact enough to take along to a shop or restaurant, or as a quick reference in determining a top vintage or deciding on the right wine to serve with dinner.

How to Read an Entry

The top line of each entry indicates in abbreviated form:

1   If it is DOC, DOCG, or IGT.
2   Whether it is red, pink, white, amber, dry, semi-sweet, sweet, slightly fizzy (*frizzante*), sparkling, or several of these.
3   Rating of general quality:

☆	everyday wine
☆☆	normally good quality
☆☆☆	superior in its category
☆☆☆☆	outstanding

These ratings are personal assessments weighed against opinions of other critics and experts. One star indicates the ordinary, but many of Italy's everyday wines are more than drinkable. Four stars (these are used sparingly in the book) refer to wines of the highest quality. Some of these are not well known abroad, though a growing number have gained international prestige. Some DOC or DOCG categories cover wines of different sub-zones, vine varieties, types, and colours; as some are made by a multitude of producers, the quality within a single denomination (DOC/DOCG) can vary considerably. This explains how, for instance, the assessment of the nineteen South Tyrolean wine types of the DOC Alto Adige range from ☆ to ☆☆☆☆.

4   Most entries indicate the period when the wines are at their best for consumption. DYA means that wines are normally best soon after bottles are released, though that doesn't exclude some that would hold well for a couple of years or more. For wines for ageing, recommended vintages often have a note in the text on when they should be at their prime. So if 1997 is recommended and the prime is four to seven years, the wine should be at its best between 2001 and 2004. Vintage recommendations for wines that require long ageing may include recent harvests, even though they won't be released until later. For example, Barolo 2001, like Brunello di Montalcino 2000, may not be sold before 2005. Vintage assessments are always somewhat arbitrary. Wines from some vintages age much better than wines from others. Some producers make good wines even in off years. Some consumers prefer longer-aged wines than

others. So no matter what the charts say, personal taste and experience are the best determinants of when a wine is at its prime.

5   If a wine is subjected to ageing of a year or more under DOC, the required time is mentioned. Special designations, such as *riserva,* signify an additional maturation, indicated where relevant under wine entries.

Following the wine entries are listings of producers by region, giving locations by town and province with mention of wines made, sometimes noting grape varieties and names of vineyards or special bottlings. Producers mentioned have been screened for reliability against available sources, but lists are not complete. Italy has thousands of registered wine-bottlers, including many emerging estates and winemakers, so inevitably some worthy names will not have been included.

Some Italian wines sold abroad are labelled with the bottler's, shipper's, or importer's brand name, names that are used only in the countries where sold. Most such wines, however qualified, are not considered here. The focus is on wines whose origins are verifiable in Italy.

The information under Wine & Food at the end of each regional section is intended to aid travellers in Italy, though home cooks and diners in Italian restaurants in other lands may also find it useful. Wine suggestions with each speciality are intended to be indicators, not requisites. Readers may prefer to make their own choices.

Glossary

These terms may help you to read a wine label or be of use when you are travelling through a wine zone.

abboccato lightly sweet, literally "mouth-filling"
acidità acidity
alcool alcohol
amabile semi-sweet, literally "amiable"; a shade sweeter than *abboccato*
amaro bitter
amarognolo the almond-like, lightly bitter undertone detectable in certain wines, usually on the aftertaste
ambrato amber hue noted in many dessert or apéritif wines
annata year of vintage
aroma the scent of a wine
asciutto bone-dry
assemblaggio wine made from two or more grapes, blended after fermentation
azienda agricola/agraria/viticola estate producing wine from its own grapes
azienda vinicola estate producing wine from bought-in grapes
barrique small barrel, usually of new, French oak
bianc de blancs white wine made only from white grapes, refers usually to sparkling wines
bianco white
bicchiere drinking glass
botte cask
bottiglia bottle
brut dry when referring to sparkling wine
cantina wine cellar or winery
cantina sociale or **cooperativa** co-op winery (abbreviated to CS in listings)
casa vinicola c.f. *azienda vinicola*
cascina farm or estate, usually in northern Italy
cerasuolo cherry-red, used to describe certain deepish-coloured rosés

Charmat method whereby wine is made sparkling by refermenting in sealed, pressure-resistant vats

chiaretto term referring to certain lightish-coloured rosé wines

classico classic, used to define heartland zones of tradition and particular quality within a DOC(G), *eg.* Chianti Classico, Orvieto Classico

consorzio voluntary consortium of growers and producers set up to oversee production and/or promote the wines of an area

coltivatore grower

degustazione wine tasting

denominazione di origini controllata/e garantita (DOC/DOCG). *See* under Laws & Labels

dolce sweet

enologia oenology, the study of winemaking

enologo oenologist, winemaker with a degree

enotecnico winemaking technician with a further education diploma

enoteca literally wine library, but also wine shop and wine bar

etichetta label

ettaro hectare (2.471 acres); the standard European measure of land area

ettolitro hectolitre, or 100 litres, the standard European measure of wine volume

extra term to describe certain fortified wines of very high alcohol

extra dry term used to describe sparkling wine that is dry, but less so than brut

fattoria farm or estate, usually in central Italy

fermentazione fermentation

fermentazione naturale wine made lightly bubbly without a second fermentation

frizzante lightly bubbly, *pétillant*, but not fully sparkling

frizzantino refers to wine with a barely noticeable prickle

fusto cask, barrel

gradazione alcoolica alcohol percentages by volume

gusto flavour (not in the English sense of "gusto", however)

imbottigliato da bottled by

indicazione geografica tipica (IGT) *See* under Laws & Labels

invecchiato aged

liquoroso high alcohol, fortified wine

litro litre, equivalent to 1.056 US quarts

marchio depositato registered brand name or trademark

marsalato or **maderizzato** refers to wines that through oxidation take on flavours reminiscent of marsala or madeira

metodo classico term for sparkling wine made by the classic, Champagne method with a refermentation in bottle. (*Metodo classico* is abbreviated to mc in text)

millesimato sparkling wine from a stated vintage year

passito/a partially dried grapes and the wines, usually sweet, sometimes strong, made from them

pastoso full, round, mouth-filling

podere small farm or estate

produttore producer

profumo odour or scent

quintale quintal, 100 kilograms

riserva reserve, applied only to DOC or DOCG wines that have undergone specified ageing

rosato rosé

rosso red

rubino ruby colour

sapore flavour

secco dry (but medium dry when referring to sparkling wine)

semi-secco medium-sweet, *demi-sec*, usually used to describe
    sparkling wine

spumante sparkling wine, whether bone dry or fully sweet

superiore term for DOC wine usually indicating higher alcohol

tappo di sughero cork top

tenuta farm or estate

uva grape

uvaggio wine made from two or more grapes blended before fermentation

vecchio old, describing certain aged wines

stravecchio very old, applies to the longest-aged marsala and to some spirits

vendemmia the grape harvest, often also in the sense of vintage

vendemmia tardiva late-harvest, wines from grapes left to overripen on
    the vine

vigna, vigneto vineyard

vignaiolo grape-grower

vino da meditazione wine, often strong, sweet, or particularly concentrated
    for sipping meditatively

vino da taglio strong wine used for blending

vino da tavola table wine. *See* under Laws & Labels

vino novello new wine, usually red, in the beaujolais nouveau style. By law,
    novello wines are sold from 6 November in the year of harvest

vite vine

viticoltore grape-grower

vitigno vine or grape variety

vivace lively, as in lightly bubbly wines

VQPRD, VSQPRD *See* under Laws & Labels

Laws & Labels

The ancient Romans may have been the first people to formulate wine laws,
setting production codes for sixteen appellations on the Italian peninsula and
Sicily. In 1716, the Grand Duchy of Tuscany set a precedent by delimiting the
production zones for some important wines. Yet it wasn't until the mid-1960s
that Italy introduced the laws of controlled origin that brought much-needed
discipline and a new sense of dignity to modern wine production.

The laws cover the main classifications of *denominazione di origine
controllata* (DOC) *e garantita* (DOCG), as well as the category of *indicazione
geografica tipica* (IGT), which classifies wines from larger geographical
areas and from vine varieties that are not covered under DOC/DOCG. There
are heading up to 350 approved DOC zones in Italy, including twenty-eight
DOCGs. Even though well over 2,000 types of wine are defined under
the many denominations – and the percentage continues to increase –
DOC/DOCG still applies to national production. The mandate is to raise
the total, including IGT, to more than half.

DOCs, which always specify a delimited zone on the label, apply to wines
from specified vine varieties (alone or blended) produced with limited yields
and vinified, and aged, to meet prescribed standards of colour, odour,
flavour, alcohol content, acidity, and so on. DOC wines may be defined by
colour or type (still, *frizzante*, or sparkling; dry, semi-sweet, or sweet; natural
or fortified), or by grape variety. Some DOCs apply to multiple types (Friuli-
Venezia Giulia's Collio, for example, has nineteen types, including seventeen
varietals). Wines may be defined further by age (young as *novello* or aged as

vecchio, stravecchio, or *riserva*), or by a special sub-zone as *classico.* The term *superiore* may apply to wine with a higher degree of alcohol than the norm or, occasionally, a longer period of ageing.

Details of each DOC region are determined by the producers in the zone, who sometimes join together to form a consortium (*consorzio*), which acts as a monitoring and promoting body. The *consorzio* passes on suggestions for changes in the production regulations to the national DOC committee in Rome, which may either sanction them or turn them down. Despite a few dubious choices and disappointing results from some denominations, DOC has been a major factor in the improved status of Italian wine worldwide.

DOCG, which guarantees the authenticity of wines of "particular esteem", has expanded from the original four – Barbaresco, Barolo, Brunello di Montalcino, Vino Nobile di Montepulciano – to cover Chianti, Chianti Classico, Asti, Brachetto d'Acqui, Gattinara, Gavi, Ghemme, Franciacorta, Valtellina Superiore, Sfursat della Valtellina, Ramandolo, Soave Superiore, Bardolino Superiore, Recioto di Soave, Albana di Romagna, Carmignano, Vernaccia di San Gimignano, Montefalco Sagrantino, Torgiano Rosso Riserva, Montepulciano d'Abruzzo Colline Teramane, Taurasi, Greco di Tufo, Fiano di Avellino, and Vermentino di Gallura. Although some question the use of the term "guaranteed", DOCG has improved quality, and made counterfeiting more difficult, by imposing more stringent quality specifications on producers, such as strict control of the amounts produced and obligatory tasting checks by expert tasters. DOCG wines must have the official strip seal at the top of each bottle.

Vino da tavola applies to anonymous wine that, if bottled, may not specify grape variety, vintage, or place of origin. Everything else is IGT, a category that classifies wines from specific regions, provinces, or general areas by colour, grape variety, or typology. There are over eighty, many subdivided into numerous varietal versions. A curious fact is that some of Italy's top modern wines are made by producers who – by chance or by choice – are working outside the DOC/DOCG norms and fall into the IGT category.

Labelling of all wines, DOC and otherwise, is restricted to pertinent data in which the wording, and in some cases even the type sizes, are controlled. Required on all labels are the wine name and category (DOC, IGT etc); the producer's or bottler's name and commune of bottling; the quantity of wine contained; and the alcohol percentage by volume. Labels may also carry a vintage (obligatory for most DOCG and many DOC wines), its sweetness category and colour, plus a trademark, coat of arms, and consortium seal. Other information may be given on back labels or attached cards or scrolls, but this should be verifiable and cannot include such terms as *riserva, speciale,* or *superiore,* unless the wine officially qualifies for them.

Anatomy of Italian Wine

Over the last quarter-century Italy's wine industry has undergone the most radical transformation ever witnessed by a single nation. There has emerged a whole new class of premium wines, both red and white, as well as highly attractive light and bubbly styles for popular consumption. But perhaps the most important change has come from the greater class found in Italy's traditional wines, led by the classic reds of Piedmont and Tuscany, and the elegant whites of Friuli. Yet Italy still has considerable unrealized quality potential. Additionally, the fact that there is such a variety of wines from so many sources does not assist effective marketing.

In the 1990s, Italy produced an average of some fifty-eight million hectolitres a year – about a fifth of the world's wine, or nearly as much as the combined output of all nations outside Europe. Yet, after the record crops of the early 1980s that flooded what was known as Europe's "wine lake", production has diminished so much in some Italian regions that supplies of premium wine no longer meets demands.

Much of Italy's land mass is intrinsically suited to grape growing. Most (four-fifths) is hilly or mountainous. The Alps shield the northern regions from the damp cold of northern Europe, and the Apennines temper the Mediterranean climates of the centre and south. But there can be no generalizing about conditions. High vineyards in the south may be cooler and damper than those in the plains and valleys of the north. What makes Italy's vineyards all the more complex is the way that myriad microclimates interact with different types of soil.

All twenty regions have favourable conditions for vine growth, but some have exploited them better than others. The eight northern regions, set in the vast arc formed by the Alps and Apennines, and bordered by the broad Po valley which almost bisects the country, opening out into the Adriatic, make more than half of the country's DOC(G) wine. The Veneto, with Soave and Valpolicella, produces more delimited wine than any other region, while neighbouring Trentino-Alto Adige and Friuli-Venezia Giulia have built up enviable status for their varietals, especially the whites, and Piedmont's reds, led by Barolo and Barbaresco, have justified renown.

Change has reverberated through in central Italy, too, where Tuscany has surged to the forefront with dramatically improved Chianti, Brunello di Montalcino, Vino Nobile di Montepulciano, and others, as well as the vaunted "Super Tuscans" that have given the renaissance a modern spirit. White wines too are revealing ever more their intrinsic character, most notably Verdicchio from the Marches, Orvieto from Umbria, and Frascati from Lazio.

The revolution in the south has been possibly even more sweeping, with the focus having moved swiftly, in less than a decade, from bulk to good-quality bottled wine. The Puglian, Sicilian, and Campanian wines on the market, in particular, have increased markedly in both quantity and quality.

In order to liquidate the wine lake of the 1980s, the EU (European Union) had required distillation of wine into alcohol, while banning the planting of new vineyards and paying premiums to growers to uproot old vines. As a result the wine-growing area of Italy reduced from over 1.2 million hectares (2.97 milllion acres) in the 1980s to less than 800,000 hectares (1.98 million acres), and production decreased from roughly eighty-five million hectolitres to a level that fluctuates between fifty and fifty-five million hectolitres or so. Nevertheless Italy continues to vie with France as the world's leading wine producer. It is only recently that wine-growers have once more been allowed to plant new vineyards in DOC(G) regions where demand exceeds supply.

Italy also vies with France as the world's largest wine exporter, although much of this is blending wine that is sold mainly to France and Germany. With the higher quality wines, new markets in the Pacific Basin have helped to offset the general decline in wine drinking in Europe. Meanwhile, wine consumption in Italy remains the second highest worldwide, even though it has halved in the past thirty years to little over fifty litres per head.

The vine varieties that thrive in a wine-producing country depend not only on soil, climate, and the lie of the land but also on people, eating styles, and fashion. The latter, in particular, led to the rapid diffusion of the so-called international varieties throughout Italy in the last decade of the twentieth century, most notably Cabernet Sauvignon, Merlot, Syrah, Chardonnay, and Sauvignon Blanc. This trend is now thankfully on the decline with a marked

Temperature

Wine expresses its best only when it is served at the right temperature, although there is always considerable leeway for personal preference. No other factor – letting it breathe, decanting it, serving from the proper glasses, etc. – has quite as much impact. The chart shown below indicates the suggested serving temperature for each type of wine.

Left	°F • °C	Right
		Big, aged reds:
	66 • 19	Barolo, Brunello,
Chianti Classico,		Amarone, Taurasi,
Cabernet,	64 • 18	Torgiano Riserva
Montepulciano		
d'Abruzzo, Teroldego	63 • 17	Barbera, Merlot,
		Valpolicella, Sangiovese
		di Romagna
Bardolino *rosso*,	61 • 16	
Dolcetto, Grignolino,		
Santa Maddalena,	59 • 15	Lambrusco, *vin santo*,
Marsala Vergine		Marsala Superiore,
	57 • 14	Recioto della
		Valpolicella
Most rosés and new	55 • 13	
wines: Bardolino		
Chiaretto, Ramandolo	54 • 12	
	52 • 11	Delicate, fruity whites:
		Fiano, oaked Chardonnay,
		Picolit, Moscato d'Asti,
	50 • 10	Recioto di Soave
Most dry whites: Soave,	48 • 9	
Gavi, Frascati, Pinot Grigio;		
best sparkling wines	46 • 8	Most dry and semi-sweet
		sparkling wines: Asti
	45 • 7	
Fortified dessert wines:	43 • 6	
Moscato Passito di		
Pantelleria	41 • 5	
	39 • 4	
	37 • 3	Room temp
	35 • 2	Ideal cellar
	33 • 1	Domestic refrigerator

return to the use of indigenous varieties, thereby assisting the specificity and individuality of Italian wine styles.

Another trend is the wine market's move towards red wine, strengthened by favourable reports on its supposed health benefits Whites in Italy are usually drunk while still youthfully fresh and crisp which can seem at odds with markets that prefer more pronounced, developed flavours. Nevertheless there are ever more whites being made with depth and personality, dispelling the myth that Italy cannot produce great, world-class, dry white wines. In addition, the pre-eminence of Italy's sweet wines in combining luscious sweetness with a zippy freshness that leaves the palate beautifully clean should not be overlooked.

Grape Varieties

Italy grows an impressive range of grape varieties, despite drastic reductions since the vine scourges of oidium and phylloxera struck in the nineteenth century. There are more than 1,000 grape vines still recorded in Italy, of which around 400 are recommended or approved in one or more regions. These include varieties that are either indigenous or have become so well adjusted to a habitat that they may be considered as such, carrying a local name. There is also a virtually complete array of Europe's major vines. Listed are all the more commonly found varieties as well as local varieties that are of more than passing interst.

Abbuoto Outcrops of this rare red are scattered around south Lazio and north Campania, where it is used in Cecubo, the modern version of the ancient Caecubum.

Aglianico An aristocrat of Greek origin, epitomized in Campania's Taurasi and Basilicata's Aglianico del Vulture. Together with the Piedmontese Nebbiolo, Aglianico is one of the best grape varieties in Italy, producing firm, tannic, long-lasting reds of power and refinement.

Albana Native to Romagna's hills, where it makes both dry and semi-sweet wines, still, or bubbly.

Aleatico Makes perfumed, richly sweet, strongly fruited, red dessert wines in Lazio, Puglia, Tuscany, and Umbria.

Ansonica *See* Inzolia.

Arneis Elegant, delicate white found mostly in Piedmont's Roero hills.

Asprinio Campanian white making light, refreshing, uncomplicated but fairly acidic wines, often with a slight fizz.

Barbera Native of Piedmont, of outstanding class. Produces some everyday wines, too, sometimes lightly sparkling or semi-sweet. Excellent blended with Nebbiolo. Italy's most widely planted red after Sangiovese.

Biancolella White Campanian vine prominent on Ischia both as a varietal and blended with Forastera.

Bombino Bianco High-quality white grape grown predominantly in Abruzzo, Molise, and northern Puglia. Main grape of Puglia's San Severo Bianco.

Bombino Nero Red grown mainly in northern Puglia, where prized for Castel del Monte Rosato.

Bonarda Prominent in the Oltrepò Pavese (Lombardy) and adjacent Colli Piacentini (Emilia) where it makes supple, livley reds. Also known as Croatina. The Bonarda Piemontese is not the same variety and of lesser importance.

Bosco Prime ingredient of Cinqueterre in Liguria.

Brachetto Makes bubbly, usually sweet, red wines in Piedmont with strawberry-like flavours.

Cabernet Franc *See* Carmenère.

Cabernet Sauvignon Bordeaux native initially prominent in the northeast but now widespread throughout Italy. Produced as a varietal and in blends, both of high quality, although interest in the variety is on the wane.

Cagnina *See* Terrano.

Calabarese *See* Nero d'Avola.

Canaiolo Nero Mostly found in Tuscany and used with Sangiovese in Vino Nobile di Montepulciano and some Chianti. Opinions on its qualities vary.

Cannonau Sardinia's main red variety used for dry and, sometimes, sweet wines. The same vine as Spain's Garnacha and France's Grenache, it is found in Ligura as Granaccia, in the south as Guarnaccia and Alicante, and in the Veneto as Tocai Rosso.

Carignano The Carignan of France and Cariñena of Spain, grown in Sardinia, where it can make reds of real interest.

Carmenère It now appears that nearly all the Cabernet Franc of Northern Italy is in fact the ancient variety Carmenère.

Carricante Chief grape of Etna Bianco in Sicily, making firm, lean whites with ageing potential.

Catarratto Widespread in Sicily, where it figures in many whites as well as marsala. Gives freshness, body, but little aroma unless grown at altitude.

Cesanese Native of Lazio producing tannic and slightly rustic reds. Best when blended.

Chardonnay This aristocratic Burgundian has high stature in Italy. Used to produce still and sparkling wines, especially in the northeast, its popularity peak has now passed.

Ciliegiolo This variety, once prominent in central Italy, has been revived in blended and varietal reds.

Cortese Piedmont's more structured whites, most notably Gavi, are made from this variety, which is also native to Oltrepò Pavese.

Corvina Leading grape variety in Valpolicella and Bardolino along with Rondinella, Molinara, Negrara, and Rossignola; grown throughout Verona and around Lake Garda.

Croatina *See* Bonarda.

Dolcetto Much admired in the winelands of southern Piedmont, where it makes supple, mouth-filling, succulent red wines, usually drunk youngish. Also found in Valle d'Aosta and Liguria, where it is called Ormeasco.

Erbaluce Firm but perfumed white found in northern Piedmont. Makes dry wines and sweet Caluso Passito.

Falanghina Increasingly popular variety, vine of Greek origin, making both stylish and simple whites in Campania and elsewhere in the south.

Favorita Lightweight but attractive white grown mainly in Piedmont's Roero.

Fiano Known as Apianum to the ancient Romans, grown mainly in central Campania, it makes fine whtes which can develop nutty characteristics.

Freisa Makes original, light but firm, often sparkling, reds in its native Piedmont.

Gaglioppo Worthy source of most Calabrian reds, including Cirò, potential not yet fully exploited.

Gamay This beaujolais grape grows in Valle d'Aosta and sparsely elsewhere.

Garganega Admirable mainstay of white Soave and Gambellara, in the Veneto.

Gewürztraminer Also known as Traminer Aromatico. Developed in Alsace, cultivated to great effect in Alto Adige where it makes spicily aromatic wines of real character.

Grechetto Respected source of Umbrian whites, may be of Greek origin; also known as Pignoletto.

Greco Of Greek origin, middle-ranking vine family, with red and white versions, although whites more common. Grown quite widely but mainly in Campania and Calabria.

Grignolino Once prominent Piedmontese variety, centered around Asti, needs careful handling for its lightish red wines to develop style.

Grillo The grape giving class and style to marsala. Also used in Sicilian white wines, often with Catarratto.

Groppello Makes strightforward reds chiefly around Lake Garda.

Inzolia Sicilian native where it makes elegant, respected whites. Known as Ansonica in coastal Tuscany. There it makes ever-improving rich, powerful wines.

Lagrein Used in Alto Adige to make punchy, characterful red wines and gentle rosés.

Lambrusco Prolific, much sniffed-at variety abounding in the plains of Emilia, with several sub-varieties making light reds, often sweetish and bubbly. Turned into pink and white wines too.

Magliocco Recently rediscovered variety now making highly lauded reds in Cirò in Calabria.

Malvasia Name applied to a vast range of southern European vines, also known as Malvoisie and malmsey, making wines of all types but frequently dry. White sub-varieties are grown throughout Italy, especially in Lazio, Friuli, and Sicily. Reds are concentrated in Puglia (where it is prominent), Piedmont, Alto Adige, and the centre.

Marzemino Popular variety producing easy-drinking reds in Trentino and Lombardy.

Merlot The Bordeaux native is extremely popular in northeast Italy as a source of varietals and elsewhere for highly impressive reds. One of the nation's most heavily planted vines.

Monica Of Spanish origin, it makes dry and sweet wines in Sardinia.

Montepulciano Dominant dark variety of Abruzzo, versatile, and richly fruited. Favoured in other regions, too, for varietals and blends.

Moscato Muscat vines are grown throughout Italy. White versions are most common, often with some sweetness and a characteristic grapey aroma. Most frequent styles are light, sparkling, or *frizzante* – as in Piedmont's Asti Spumante and Moscato d'Asti (from Moscato Bianco) – and richly sweet, as in Sicily (Moscato d'Alessandria, also called Zibibbo). Moscato Rosa makes fragrant rosé in the Veneto; Moscato Nero is rare but makes sweet reds in Piedmont.

Müller-Thurgau A cross from Switzerland; produces wines of good quality, elegant aromatic wines in Trentino-Alto Adige and Friuli.

Nebbiolo Very high-quality variety. In southern Piedmont (Barolo, Barbaresco) it makes long-lived, powerful reds of supreme stature. In northern Piedmont (Gattinara, Ghemme), Lombardy (Valtellina), and Aosta, its wines are as individual but less intense. Sometimes blended, blends with Barbera are particularly effective. Spanna, Chiavennasca, and Picutener are synonyms.

Negroamaro This variety's full, strapping, yet approachable, reds and fresh, fruity rosés domiante Puglia's Salento peninsula.

Nerello Mascalese Worthy Sicilian grape giving lightish coloured, firm, fruited wines, especially on Mount Etna. Usually blended.

Nero d'Avola or **Calabrese** Sicily's most esteemed source of red wines with intense berried fruit, power, and attack.

Nosiola Curious Trentino native; dry whites and *vin santo*.

Nuragus Ancient Sardinian vine making uncomplicated whites around Cagliari and Oristano.

Ortrugo Full-bodied, lean reds come from this rare Emilian (Colli Piacentini) variety.

Perricone or **Pignatello** Sicilian variety; lends vigour to reds.

Petit Rouge Used in some of Valle d'Aosta's finer reds.

Picolit Difficult to ripen but produces a highly prized, delicate, honeyed dessert wine in Friuli's Colli Orientali.

Piedirosso or **Per'e Palummo** Prominent in Campanian reds, notably those of Ischia.

Pigato Grown only in southwest Liguria. Produces fine dry whites.

Pinot Bianco (Pinot Blanc in France and **Weissburgunder** in Alto Adige), grows primarily in northeastern Italy and makes elegant, creamy whites, often drunk young but with good ageing potential, that have occasional similarities to Chardonnay.

Pinot Grigio (Pinot Gris in France and **Ruländer** in Alto Adige) is exceedingly popular and grows widely in Friuli, Trentino-Alto Adige, the Veneto, and Lombardy. Quality of this white ranges from ordinary to rather good.

Pinot Nero (Pinot Noir in France, **Blauburgunder** in Alto Adige) remains the holy grail for many nothern and central Italian winemakers. Fine examples are now more numerous but not yet common. Best results overall are in Alto Adige. It also makes successful white and rosé sparklers.

Primitivo Puglian source of powerful, ripe, rich red wines, sometimes sweet, often quite alcoholic. This is the same variety as California's Zinfandel.

Prosecco Grown mainly in eastern Veneto's Colli Trevigiani, it makes sparkling, semi-sparkling, and still, dry, semi-dry, and sweet wines. The best, lightly sparkling, and off-dry are gradually being overtaken by fully sparkling versions.

Prugnolo Secondary Tuscan red grape used with Sangiovese, also found in northern Italy.

Raboso Makes chunky reds in its native Veneto.

Rebo Idiosyncratic Trentino red, derived from a Merlot-Teroldego cross.

Refosco Friulian variety, fully titled Refosco dal Peduncolo Rosso; making sturdy reds. Refosco del Carso is a different variety, also known as Terrano.

Ribolla Gialla Underrated vine from Friuli makes lively, buttery whites, also often used in blends.

Riesling Italico (**Welschriesling** in Alto Adige) Not a true Riesling, nor native to Italy. Produces attractive but undistinguished wines in the central north.

Riesling Renano (**Rheinriesling** in Alto Adige) The Johannisberg or White Riesling of Germany and Alsace shows its steely, incisive class in northern Italy only when from particular terrains and in skilled hands, otherwise the style is still fragrant but lighter.

Rossese Produces softish red wines in Liguria.

Sagrantino Gives pep to Sangiovese and makes vibrant varietals, some very powerful in Umbria's Montefalco. Strong, sweet (*passito*) versions also made.

Sangiovese Italy's most widely planted variety is most at home in Tuscany where it sets the stamp of Chianti, Brunello di Montalcino, Vino Nobile di Montepulciano, Morellino di Scansano (all from different clones), and others. Plummy but assertive wines range from simple and refreshing to intense, long-lived, star performers.

Sauvignon Blanc The grassy, gooseberry, uncompromising character of Sauvignon Blanc is commonly realized in northern Italy and sometimes further south, too, although many producers opt for a more muted, yet still distinctive style.

Schiava (**Vernatsch** in Alto Adige) Widespread family of vines in Trentino-Alto Adige, producing light, raspberryish reds, most notably from Santa Maddalena and Caldaro. It is now in decline.

Schioppettino Also known as **Ribolla Nera**. Grows only sporadically in eastern Friuli making incisive, dense, powerful reds of great personality.

Semidano Attention in Sardinia is now reuturning to this intriguing white.

Sylvaner Northern Alto Adige sees good, firm, perfumed whites from this Germanic variety.

Syrah The vine, prominent in France's Rhône Valley and Australia, makes impressive reds in much of Italy, although it is not widely diffused.

Tazzelenghe Rare, high-acidity red from Friuli.

Teroldego Grown almost exclusively on Trentino's Rotaliano plain, giving occasionally distinguished reds of high potential.

Tocai Friulano Friuli is under orders form the EU to chande Tocai's name to avoid confusion with the Hungarian region of Tokaji. The vine, actually Sauvignonasse or Sauvignon Vert of French origin, is Friuli's pride with its classy, elegant, apply, nut-cream character. It is not the same variety as France's Tokay (which is Pinot Gris).

Tocai Italico Considered to be the same variety as Tocai Friulano but, grown in various parts of Veneto and Lombardy, makes less compelling wines.

Tocai Rosso *See* Cannonau.

Torbato Spanish native which makes fine white in Sardinia's Alghero area.

Traminer Native of Asia but developed at Tramin in Alto Adige, this toned down, more productive relative of Gewürztraminer appeals to those who find the latter too intensely perfumed and spicy.

Trebbiano Toscano Widely diffused – Italy's most widespread white – but often unprepossessing variety; known as Ugni Blanc in France.

Trebbiano di Lugana *See* Verdicchio.

Trebbiano di Romagna A distinct Trebbiano strain grown throughout Romagna which often lacks character.

Uva di Troia Respected red variety from northern Puglia.

Uva Rara Often confused with Bonarda but a distinct red variety, grown mainly in northern Piedmont. Almost always used in blends.

Verdeca Important Puglian grape, used with Bianco d'Alessano in Locorotondo, Martina Franca, and other north Puglian whites.

Verdicchio Predominant variety of the Marches where it once made pleasant but innocuous whites but now produces a wealth of crisp yet deep wines of growing stature. Also grown on the south shores of Lake Garda where it is called Trebbiano di Lugana.

Verduzzo Grape from Friuli used for stylish dry whites and dessert wines. Also found in the Veneto.

Vermentino Believed to be of Spanish origin, arriving in Sardinia and Liguria, and thence to Tuscany, from Corsica. Makes firm whites of increasing renown.

Vernaccia di Oristano Grown exclusively around Oristano in Sardinia, giving a sherry-like dessert wine.

Vernaccia di San Gimignano Ancient vine used for the rapidly improving, fleshy white of Tuscany's famous towered town.

Vernaccia di Serrapetrona Gives a red wine, often sweet or sparkling, in the Marche.

Vespaiola Makes dry white and rich golden dessert wines in the Veneto.

Vespolina A red variety usually blended with Nebbiolo and others in Piedmont's Novara and Vercelli hills.

Viognier A white variety from France's Rhône, with many admirers in Italy.

Zibibbo *See* Moscato.

Valle d'Aosta *Valle d'Aosta*

Italy's smallest region, tucked into Piedmont's northwestern corner with mountainous borders on France and Switzerland, and officially Italian/French bilingual, has little space for vineyards amid its massive Alps. Most vines grow over *pergolas* on terraces hewn out of stone on south-facing slopes along the Dora Baltea River, which flows from Mont Blanc's glaciers through its sole city of Aosta and on into Piedmont. Wine production of fewer than three million litres a year (Italy's lowest rate) isn't nearly enough to supply the region's 114,000 citizens.

The limited number of wines from the Valle d'Aosta are made by plucky and persevering *vignerons*, including those who work Europe's highest-altitude classified vineyards at Morgex. They take in a little galaxy of *crus*, drawing some lustre from Piedmontese and French varieties, although the most intriguing wines come from vines Aostans claim as their own: Blanc de Valdigne, Petit Rouge, the mutation of Pinot Gris known locally as Malvoisie, and Vien de Nus.

A comprehensive regionwide DOC, known as Valle d'Aosta/Vallée d'Aoste, includes twenty-five types of wine. An ambitious programme to upgrade winemaking techniques has improved quality, but Aostan wines could never be more than curiosities to be savoured close to home by visitors who come to ski, climb, or take in the scenery of castles and chalets amid some of Europe's highest peaks. The region's well-marked *Route des Vins* follows the Dora Baltea River from Piedmont to Morgex. Aosta's *Cave Valdotaine* is a great place to shop for wine.

Recent Vintages

Recommended years of wines for ageing appear with each entry.

Wines

VALLE D'AOSTA/VALLÉE D'AOSTE *DOC*

Comprehensive appellation taking in nearly all of the region's vineyards, and accounting for nearly 85% of the wine in the 25 types and variations. Italian or French names and labels.

Arnad Montjovet *r dr* ✩✩ *98 99 00 01 02*
From at least 70% Nebbiolo with Dolcetto, Pinot Noir or other varieties grown around the towns of Arnad and Montjovet, this shows character similar to the historic Donnaz. Age: *superiore/supérieur* 1 yr

Bianco/Blanc *w dr (fz)* ✩ *DYA* From various white varieties grown along the Dora Baltea, this is designed to be light (min 9%) and possibly fizzy.

Blanc de Morgex et de La Salle *w dr (fz)* ✩✩ *DYA* From the indigenous Blanc de Valdigne, grapes for this wine grow in mountain meadows at heights of 1,000 to 1,300 metres (3,280 to 4,265 feet) above sea level at the villages of Morgex and La Salle near Courmayeur. With rarefied aroma and delicately dry, crisp flavour; may be some *pétillance*.

Chambave Moscato/Muscat *w dr (sw)* ✩✩ *DYA* The basic Moscato grown around Chambave is surprisingly dry, perfumed and grapey, to drink inside a year.

Chambave Moscato Passito/Muscat Fletri *w dr (sw)* ✩✩→✩✩✩✩ *91 93 95 97 98 99 00 01 02* The vaunted Passito (or Flétri) comes from semi-dried Moscato grapes in a richly aromatic, deep-golden wine that has been known to keep for decades, becoming drier and deeper. Age: 1 yr in barrel.

Chambave Rosso/Rouge *r dr* ☆☆ *99 00 01 02* From Petit Rouge with other varieties grown around Chambave, this pleasant red has a ruby-garnet colour, dry, subtle flavour and bouquet taking on hints of violets with age.

Chardonnay *vdt w dr* ☆☆ *00 01 02* Both oaked and non-oaked versions show great promise.

Donnaz/Donnas *r dr* ☆☆ *98 99 00 01* This established red from Nebbiolo, grown at Donnaz in the southeast, has never matched its Piedmontese neighbour Carema. Refined, with understated Nebbiolo character but impressive bouquet, it can age beyond 5 to 6 years. Age: 2 yrs.

Enfer d'Arvier *r dr* ☆☆ *99 00 01 02* Petit Rouge grown in restricted yields on rocky slopes at Arvier where torrid climate prompted the reference to *l'Enfer* (the inferno). Ruby to medium garnet, a rather sharp, grapey flavour in its youth.

Fumin *vdt r dr* ☆☆ *99 00 01 02* Curious robust red from the rare Fumin vine.

Gamay *r dr* ☆☆ *00 01 02* The beaujolais grape puts on its Alpine act here in hearty wines, sometimes a bit rustic and restrained, but with a likeable folksiness about them.

Müller-Thurgau *w dr* ☆☆ *DYA* This does nicely on the sunny side of the Alps giving aromatic whites of zesty flavour.

Nus Malvoisie *w dr* ☆☆ *DYA* Fruity white wine from a strain of Pinot Gris known as Malvoisie in the village of Nus.

Nus Malvoisie Passito *am sw* ☆☆ *93 95 96 97 98 00 01* The *passito* is a curio that can last for decades. Age: 1 yr.

Nus Rosso/Rouge *r dr* ☆☆ *99 00 01 02* From Vien de Nus with Petit Rouge and Pinot Noir, can show distinction.

Petit Rouge *r dr* ☆☆ *97 98 01 02* Zesty red from the admirable local variety.

Petite Arvine *w dr* ☆☆ *97 98 01 02* Tasty white from a local variety which can retain its style for several years.

Pinot Grigio/Pinot Gris *w dr* ☆☆ *DYA* Fresh, fruity white from the popular French variety.

Pinot Nero/Pinot Noir *r (w) dr* ☆☆ *97 98 99 00 01* Impressive bottlings from various sources indicate the suitability of the burgundy variety to these Alpine climes – usually red, though a white version is permitted.

Premetta *vdt r dr* ☆☆ *01 02* Tasty light red from local grape variety Premetta (or Primaticcio).

Rosato/Rosé *p dr* ☆ *DYA* From approved red varieties grown throughout the region.

Rosso/Rouge *r dr* ☆ *DYA* From approved red varieties grown throughout the region, it may also be a *vino novello*.

Torrette *r dr* ☆☆–☆☆☆ *97 98 99 00 01 02* Worthy red from Petit Rouge, with other varieties grown on either side of Aosta, notably to the west at St-Pierre, Sarre, and Aymavilles. This graceful ruby red gains bouquet with age (sometimes over a decade) as the early robust flavour becomes more delicate. Age: *superiore/supérieur* 8 mths in barrels.

VIN DE LA SABLA

vdt r dr ☆☆☆ *97 98 99 00 01 02* One of region's best reds from Petit Rouge, Fumin, and others made by Costantino Charrère at Aymavilles.

Producers

Anselmet, Villeneuve, Torrette, Petit Rouge, Chardonnay, Müler-Thurgau, and experimental dried-grape wines.

Di Barrò, Villeneuve, Torette specialists.

La Cave du Vin Blanc de Morgex et de La Salle, Morgex. DOC Blanc de Morgex et de La Salle including new *cru* Rayon and an "ice vintage".

Caves Coopératives de Donnaz, Donnaz. DOC Donnaz, Rosso Barmet (Nebbiolo).

Costantino Charrère, Aymavilles. Admirable producer of Vin de La Sabla and Grenache-based Vin Les Fourches. Also DOC Premetta and Torrette.

Les Cretes, Aymavilles. Costantino Charrère's large and impressive range is topped by fine DOC Chardonnay Coteau La Tour and Cuvée Frissonière Les Cretes, Fumin Vigne La Tour, and Syrah Coteau La Tour.

La Crotta di Vegneron, Chambave. Admirable co-op makes DOC from Chambave and Nus. Outstanding Chambave Moscato Passito. Intruiging sparkler Refrain.

Fratelli Grosjean, Quart. Fine Pinot Nero and Fumin plus good Petite Arvine and Torrette.

Institut Agricole Régional, Aosta. The agricultural school run by canons of the St Bernard order continues to set the pace in Aosta. A large range of wines is split into non-oaked and oaked lines. Pinot *crus* leads the former, Chardonnay the latter.

La Triolet, Introd. Small estate specializing in Pinot Grigio.

Albert Vevey, Morgex. Leading DOC Blanc de Morgex et de La Salle.

Marziano Vevey, Morgex. DOC Blanc de Morgex et de La Salle.

Ezio Voyat, Chambave. Respected veteran makes only unclassified La Gazella (dry Moscato), Passito Le Muraglie (Moscato for ageing) and Rosso Le Muraglie (from Petit Rouge, Gros Vien and Dolcetto).

Wine & Food

Aostans thrive on rustic fare; few specialities, but dishes shared with Piedmont taste unmistakably Aostan. No pasta here, but polenta, thick soups, rye bread, and butter are. Meat is the essence of this hearty diet, with salami, sausages, mountain prosciutto, the rare *mocetta* (air-dried chamois meat), and tasty stews and game dishes cooked with wine. Cheeses are *fontina* and *toma* (ewe's milk). After cooked fruit and biscuits, the *grolla* (a pot with spouts filled with coffee and grappa) ensues.

Wines to accompany each dish are suggested below in italics.

Boudins Blood sausages, a speciality of Morgex. *Petit Rouge*

Capriolo alla valdostana Venison stewed with vegetables, wine, grappa, and cream. *Torrette*

Carbonade Salted beef cooked with wine in a rich stew served with polenta. *Chambave Rouge*

Costoletta alla valdostana Breaded veal cutlets with *fontina*, and possibly truffles. *Donnaz*

Polenta cùns a polenta with *fontina*, *toma*, melted butter, and Parmesan. *Pinot Noir*

Tegole Crunchy almond biscuits. *Chambave Moscato Passito*

Trota Trout from mountain streams cooked in butter. *Blanc de Morgex et de La Salle*

Zuppa valpellinentze *Fontina*, ham, black bread, cabbage, herbs, and spice in a kind of soup. *Gamay*

Restaurants

Recommended in the region: *Vecchio Ristoro* at Aosta; *Grand Baou* at Avise; *Hotel Royal e Golf Grill* at Courmayeur; *Maison de Filippo* at Entreves de Courmayeur; *Casale* at St Cristophe; *La Tour* at Saint Pierre; *Nuovo Batezar da Renato* at Saint Vincent; *Da Pierre* at Verres.

Piedmont *Piemonte*

In terms of craftsmanship, sense of tradition, and respect for native vines
in their traditional habitat, Piedmont has no equal outside of the most
venerated wine zones of France, or so it would seem. There is something
reminiscent of Burgundy in the Langhe hills near Alba, where Barolo
and Barbaresco are grown: manicured vineyards fragmented into single-
owner plots on every south-facing slope, trim villages, where the lusty
odour of fermenting grapes perfumes the autumn air, and the self-assured
way in which the *vignaiolo* hands you a glass of his best. In the Langhe,
as in the Côte d'Or, wine is a way of life. And yet, below the surface, there
is as much, if not more, frenzy and uncertainty as in most other parts
of the country.

Piedmontese wines are so distinctive that they are often not
comprehended at a first encounter. Most of the region's classified wines
derive from native vines and single varietals predominate, though not all
carry variety names. Nebbiolo, source of Barolo and Barbaresco, plus
Gattinara, Ghemme, Carema, Lessona, Nebbiolo d'Alba, and other eminent

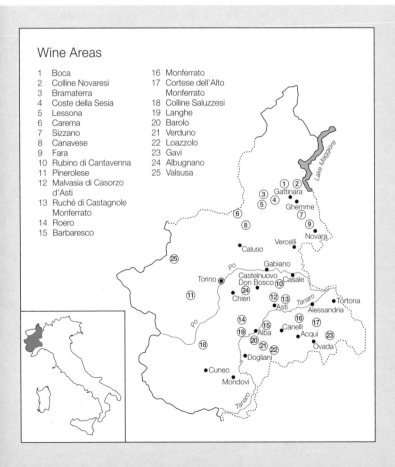

Wine Areas

1   Boca
2   Colline Novaresi
3   Bramaterra
4   Coste della Sesia
5   Lessona
6   Carema
7   Sizzano
8   Canavese
9   Fara
10 Rubino di Cantavenna
11 Pinerolese
12 Malvasia di Casorzo
    d'Asti
13 Ruché di Castagnole
    Monferrato
14 Roero
15 Barbaresco
16 Monferrato
17 Cortese dell'Alto
    Monferrato
18 Colline Saluzzesi
19 Langhe
20 Barolo
21 Verduno
22 Loazzolo
23 Gavi
24 Albugnano
25 Valsusa

reds is by far the noblest vine. But it is wine made from the once derided Barbera variety that are now setting the pace.

Piedmont ranks only seventh among Italy's twenty regions in volume of production but its fifty-two DOC(G) zones, including the comprehensive Piemonte denomiation, are the most of any region. There are seven DOCG wines: Barbaresco, Barolo, Gattinara, Asti, Brachetto d'Acqui, Ghemme, and Gavi. DOC wines form eighty per cent of production and are the mainstay of the respected producers; even new wines, whether from indigenous or foreign grape varieties usually come under DOC – mostly Piemonte DOC, Langhe DOC or Monferrato DOC – because the region has avoided the introduction of IGTs.

Barolo and Barbaresco have undergone changes in style that have divided progressive winemakers from traditionalists. The best modern interpretations of Barolo and Barberesco maintain their ample dimensions, but are better balanced and more approachable than before. The less successful leave an excessive note of oak that risks smothering these noble wines. But even the traditionally styled Barolo and Barbaresco have responded to modern know-how and are more impressive.

The lively, fruity Dolcetto, meanwhile, remains as popular as ever, both in Italy and abroad. Wine specialists appreciate the uncomplicated but not simplistic nature of the wine, which is a perfect accompaniment to a wide range of dishes. The Piedmontese drink more red wine than white, and about half of the red is Barbera. The wine has plentiful fruit and acidity but lacks supporting tannin, a combination that gives wonderful vibrancy and lift when made from good quality grapes. Yet many producers seek to give additional balance and complexity to the wine through ageing in small, new oak casks, which can give a classy but indistinct style. Others use oak less liberally, probably to better effect. Grignolino and Freisa are so unusual that they remain little more than local curiosities, but deserve greater attention.

Among whites, Asti, from the Moscato Bianco grape, is the world's most popular sweet sparkling wine yet is often, unjustifiably, looked down on by connoisseurs who prefer the gently bubbly Moscato d'Asti. The native varieties Arneis, from the Roero hills near Alba, and Cortese, at its best in Gavi, make increasingly stylish dry whites.

Viticulture is most intense in the Langhe and Monferrato hills around Alba, Asti, and Alessandria, where thousands of growers work vineyards that are often little larger than a hectare (2,47 acres). Many sell grapes to wineries producing vermouth, Asti, and other sparkling wines and are centred around Canelli, Alba, and Turin, but more and more the urge to make one's own wine is taking over and there has been an explosion of new estates and new labels emerging. Piedmont's other outstanding wine district is the Alpine foothills between Valle d'Aosta and Lake Maggiore in the provinces of Vercelli and Novara. Cultivation is much more spasmodic here but Nebbiolo still prevails with Gattinara, Ghemme, and Lessona the leading wines.

Piedmont is by far the best-organized Italian region for wine tourism. Focal points for travellers include the Langhe and Monferrato hills and the town of Alba, reachable by car in just over two hours from Milan, and in even less time from Turin and Genoa. Well-marked wine roads cover a score of production zones. Signs from Alba lead to vineyards and cellars of Barolo, Barbaresco, Dolcetto d'Alba, Barbera d'Alba, Nebbiolo d'Alba, and Moscato d'Asti. Public *enoteche* provide places to taste and buy the wines: at the towns of Barolo, Barbaresco, La Morra, Canale, Dogliani, and Grinzane Cavour (Alba and Roero wines); Acqui Terme, Canelli, Costigliole d'Asti Mango and Vignale Monferrato (Asti and Monferrato wines); Gattinara and Roppolo (northern Piedmontese wines). Interesting wine museums include *Abbazia dell' Annunziata* at La Morra, *Bersano* at Nizza

Monferrato, and *Martini & Rossi* at Pessione. Good wine shops in the region include *Del Santo* and *Il Vinaio* at Turin, *La Mia Crota* at Biella, *Ferrando* at Ivrea, *Vivian* at Novara, *Bava* and *Conca d'Oro* at Cannobio, *Al Nido della Cinciallegra* at Neive, *I Piaceri del Gusto* at Alba.

Recent Vintages

ALBA: BAROLO, BARBARESCO, BARBERA, DOLCETTO

As a rule, Barbaresco from an average-to-good harvest rounds into approachable form at four to six years and Barolo at five to eight, after which they hold well for several more years. From the best vintages, a couple of years more are needed. Among Alba's other DOC reds, Dolcetto is often best within a year or two of harvest, as is Nebbiolo from Roero, but the finest Barbera can improve for five to six years or more. Barbera from neighbouring Asti province and the Monferrato hills can equal Alba's in class and durability.

2002 A poor summer and occasional hailstorms made this a difficult vintage with most producers harvesting very selectivley to achieve quality at the expense of quantity. The late-ripening Nebbiolo fared better than most.

2001 A remarkably fine vintage across the board with perfectly ripened grapes.

2000 Another excellent harvest.

1999 The fifth of an uninterrupted series of perfect vintages.

1998 An outstanding vintage; many winemakers lean towards 1998 as the best of all for Nebbiolo and Barbera wines. Excellent for Dolcetto and whites.

1997 Superb rich, balanced Barolo, Barbaresco, and Barbera for ageing. Fine weather also benefited Dolcetto and white wines.

1996 This fine vintage could have been even better if rains hadn't marred the late stages of the Nebbiolo harvest. Barolo, Barbaresco, and Barbera of full structure and good balance should age well.

1995 Small crop of generally good quality, except in spots where torrential rains and hail damaged vineyards. Wines from Nebbiolo and Barbera show full structure and good ageing potential.

1990 A great vintage for Barolo and Barbaresco, similar to 1989, extraordinary depth and harmony; equally favourable for Barbera.

1989 A hot, dry summer made southern Piedmont one of the few places in Italy where reds showed power and durability in an outstanding vintage rated about even with 1990 and a shade superior to 1988. First-rate Barbera.

Notes on earlier vintages: 1988 Good wines from a limited crop. 85 Excellent year. 1982 A fine year. 1979 also should now be drunk. 1978, the "miracle vintage" seems overrated. Only 1974 stood out between 1978 and the extraordinary 1971 vintage, the latter overshadowing the excellent 1970 crop. Other fine Piedmontese harvests were 1967, 1965 (especially Barolo), 1964 (especially Barbaresco), 1962, 1961. Even wines that should already have been drunk can prove quite unforgettable.

NOVARA-VERCELLI HILLS AND CAREMA

Although Nebbiolo is often mixed with Bonarda and Vespaiola in these Alpine foothills, there are some wines able to equal Barolo in longevity. Gattinara, Carema, Lessona, Ghemme, and choice Spanna need four to six years or more to reach prime. Wines containing less Nebbiolo – Boca, Fara, Sizzano, Bramaterra – usually mature sooner. This unique series of good vintages since 1995 has breathed new life into Piedmont's wine-growing industry, which had experienced difficult times because of the supremacy of Barolo, and a series of bad vintages, as a result of which their wines risked falling into oblivion.

2002 A rainy summer compromised quality but a sunny spell in September benefited the late-ripening Nebbiolo.

2001 Excellent year giving a good crop of wines with fine ageing potential.
2000 Very good year, smaller yield than usual because a spell of bad weather in the middle of October interrupted harvest.
1999 Great year, better than 1998: a rainy summer and beautiful autumn led to intense colour and mature tannin, well-balanced concentrated wines.
1998 A very good year, not enormous concentration but well-balanced harmonious wines.
1997 An exceptional vintage for Nebbiolo wines, with almost perfect conditions through the season.
1996 A very good to excellent vintage for Nebbiolo-based wines of full structure and good balance.
1995 Very small yields because of late frosts, but a very good year. Nebbiolo ripened well due to a warm, sunny autumn.
1994 A challenging harvest in the autumn due to a period of rain; average year.
1993 Because of rain during the harvest, there were few outstanding wines.
1992 Mediocre.
1991 A disappointment after the great 1990 vintage. Few capable of ageing.
1990 The best of recent vintages for reds of outstanding structure, balance and ageing potential.
1989 Good to very good Nebbiolo wines of better-than-average life expectancy.
1988 Excellent quality from a small crop.

Wines

ALBUGNANO
DOC r p dr (fz) (sw)
Recent appellation for red and rosé based on Nebbiolo with Freisa, Barbera, and Uva rara in a zone between Asti and Turin in the communes of Albugnano, Castelnuovo Don Bosco, Passerano Marmorito, and Pino d'Asti. The *rosso* can be dry or *abboccato* and lively, as can the *rosato* which is best young.

ALTA LANGA
DOC wp sp
New denomination for sparkling, white, and *rosato* wines, produced from Pinot Nero and Chardonnay in the parts of the provinces of Cuneo, Asti, and Alessandria lying on the right bank of the River Tanaro.

ARNEIS
DOC in Roero (*See* below).

ASTI *DOCG*
Popular appellation, elevated to DOCG in 1995. Covers two types: aromatically sweet Asti Spumante, Italy's best-known sparkling wine, and the lightly bubbly, grapey Moscato d'Asti, which is even more admired by cognoscenti. Both derive from Moscato Bianco or di Canelli grapes, grown on steep hillsides in a vast zone of the southern Monferrato and eastern Langhe in the provinces of Asti, Cuneo, and Alessandria. Production of about 60 million litres a year is second to Chianti in volume among Italy's classified wines.

Asti or Asti Spumante *w sw sp*
☆☆→☆☆☆ *DYA* Sparkling Asti is produced mainly by large wineries centred in the town of Canelli and equipped to process delicate Moscato grapes *en masse*. Techniques involve slow fermentation of purified musts at low temperature in sealed tanks until the balance between alcohol (7–9°) and residual sugars (3–5%) is right in a fully sparkling wine of buoyant aroma, refreshing sweetness and moderate strength. Some Asti houses show personalized styles, but quality is admirably consistent due to strict controls by producers and their consortium under the auspices of

DOCG. Some 75% of production is exported – mainly to the USA, UK, and Germany – where such names as Cinzano, Gancia, Contratto, Fontanafredda, Martini & Rossi, and Riccadonna are well known. Recently Asti has made a comeback in Italy as its former reputation as the "poor man's Champagne" has been replaced by an image as a unique and sophisticated sweet sparkling wine.

Moscato d'Asti *w s/sw sw fz* ☆☆→☆☆☆ *DYA* Made mainly in the high Langhe hills between Alba and Canelli, this Moscato has a cult following, building demand well beyond supply. Though the base is the same as for Asti Spumante, the musts are usually only lightly filtered to retain greater aroma and flavour, and fermentation is arrested when alcohol reaches 5 to 6 degrees. This method creates a sweeter wine, with less carbon dioxide – at levels between *frizzante* and crémant. The soaring Moscato aroma and vibrant, fresh flavour combined with almost creamy texture can be sensational

BARBARESCO
DOCG r dr ☆☆→☆☆☆☆ *82 85 86 88 89 90 93 94 95 96 97 98 99 00* One of Italy's great red wines. Made from Nebbiolo grown around the villages of Barbaresco, Neive, and Treiso, adjacent to Alba, Barbaresco production is around 3 million bottles per year. With its neighbour Barolo, it shares the robust, austere, dramatic elegance of great Nebbiolo. Though Barbaresco rarely equals the sheer power of the biggest Barolo and requires less maturing in barrel and bottle to develop bouquet (4 to 8 years), it often has greater finesse and more consistent quality. Certain bottlings command prices at the top for Italian wines from recent vintages. The progressive modernist Angelo Gaja and the traditionalist Bruno Giacosa have won the highest praise, though Produttori del Barbaresco, Marchesi di Gresy, and a growing number of small but significant producers are greatly admired. Much Barbaresco is selected from single vineyards on the slopes south of Tanaro. Age: 2 yrs (1 in wood); *riserva* 4 yrs.

BARBERA
About half of Piedmont's red wine derives from Barbera, most of it DOC. Most is at least attractive, with many bottles giving excellent drinking and an increasing share is unexpectedly refined, with a propensity for ageing in oak barrels.

BARBERA D'ALBA
DOC r dr ☆☆→☆☆☆☆ *97 98 99 00 01* Rich in colour and body, smooth in scent and flavour, slightly tannic, mostly aged in small oak casks, this is often the longest-lived Barbera and is often vinified to ensure a good ageing potential. Although still overshadowed by Barolo and Barbaresco, it is no longer all that far behind them in prestige. Age: *superiore* 1 yr.

BARBERA D'ASTI
DOC r dr ☆☆→☆☆☆☆ *97 98 99 00 01* The best wines are robust and full-bodied, with good acidity, and are fruitier and livelier than Barbera d'Alba. At its best Barbera d'Asti is hard to beat. Most is drunk fairly young. Also makes fruity *novello*. Some producers' rich, structured wines will age a decade or more, though styles vary greatly in this vast zone of abundant production. Age: *superiore* 1 yr.

BARBERA D'ASTI SUPERIORE NIZZA
DOC r dr New sub-denomination launched with much enthusiasm to highlight the improved profile of Barbera from Nizza Monferrato.

BARBERA DEL MONFERRATO
DOC r dr (fz) ☆→☆☆☆ *98 99 00 01* Barbera from Monferrato hills north and south of Asti and

Alessandria may include up to 15% Freisa, Grignolino, or Dolcetto, making it lighter than those from Asti and Alba. It can be *frizzante* and is usually best when under 4 years old. Age: *superiore* 1 yr.

BAROLO

DOCG r dr ☆☆→☆☆☆☆ *82 85 86 88 89 90 93 94 95 96 97 98 99 00 01 02*
"King of wine and wine of kings," as the Piedmontese defined it in the 19th century, Barolo is historically the most honoured red of Italy. Made from Nebbiolo grown in the Langhe southeast of Alba, it takes the name of the village of Barolo. For decades Barolo remained aloof, almost a cult wine to Italian drinkers. Traditional Barolo needed years to lose its initial tannic hardness, yet its austere robustness and intense concentration of fruit and extract could remain largely intact for well over a decade as colour evolved from deep ruby-garnet towards brick red, and bouquet became increasingly refined. Now a new breed of winemaker has emerged, using studied techniques to achieve a more approachable style and the wine has gained new converts to its aristocratic style. Modern Barolo is often identified with single vineyards although the zone has recognized the value of terrains for well over a century. Production is centred in the villages of Castiglione Falletto, Monforte d'Alba, and Serralunga d'Alba (where the firmest wines are made), and Barolo and La Morra (producing more graceful wines), and is increasing rapidly: already 8 million bottles of the 2000 vintage have been produced. It is expected to rise to 10 million in 3 to 4 years. Regularly twinned with Barbaresco, it surpasses the latter in dimension and longevity. Most of Barolo's more than 400 producers enjoy a good reputation but some newcomers are trying to leap on the bandwaggon without the same

quality-directed underpinning. Age: 3 yrs (2 in wood); *riserva* 5 yrs.

BAROLO CHINATO

A few producers of Barolo make a tonic wine by steeping *china* (quinine, the bark of the chinchona tree) in the wine to give an exotic bitter taste. This fine *amaro* style is confined mainly to wine makers' homes.

BOCA

DOC r dr ☆☆ *88 99 90 91 93 94 95 96 97 98 99 00 01 02*
Rare red from 45–70% Nebbiolo (here called Spanna) blended with Vespolina and Uva Rara grown in the Novara hills around the villages of Boca and Maggiora. Robust and aggressive when young, the wine grows smooth, with violet tones, after 4 to 5 years' ageing. Podere ai Valloni and La Meridiana lead the pace. Age: 3 yrs (2 in barrel).

UVA RARA (OR BONARDA PIEMONTESE)

A variety often blended with Nebbiolo in reds of northern Piedmont; a DOC varietal under Colline Novaresi and Coste della Sesia.

BRACHETTO

The Brachetto grape variety is generally used for apppealing, strawberry-coloured, sweet, bubbly wines produced in the Monferrato hills, as in Brachetto d'Acqui DOCG. But it also makes for dry reds, most notably in the Roero hills and Monferrato, where Scarpa's Brachetto di Moirano is enticingly drinkable in its youth.

BRACHETTO D'ACQUI

DOCG r s/sw sw fz sp ☆☆→☆☆☆☆ *DYA*
This sweet, bubbly red of great popularity was promoted to DOCG in 1996, as producers struggled to protect it against widespread imitations. Made from Brachetto grapes in the Acqui Terme-Strevi area of the

Monferrato hills, it has a brilliant ruby colour and may be either *frizzante* or sparkling. With delicate Muscat-like fragrance and moderate strawberry-like sweetness, it is served cool with pastry, fruit, and even sausages.

BRAMATERRA
DOC r dr ☆☆ *88 89 90 91 93 94 95 96 97 98 99 00*
DOC area in north Piedmont for wine made from 50–70% Nebbiolo (Spanna) with Croatina Uva Rara and Vespolina grapes. Full-bodied and sturdy, it gains harmony and grace with 4 to 8 years. Age: 2 yrs (in wood); *riserva* 3 yrs.

CABERNET SAUVIGNON
New plantings of the bordeaux vine in a region where it had once thrived are exemplified by Gaja's excellent Darmagi, which has influenced other growers to follow. But, fine as Cabernet can be here, either alone or in blends, it is not challenging the supremacy of Nebbiolo and Barbera.

CALUSO PASSITO
See Erbaluce di Caluso DOC.

CANAVESE
DOC r p w dr
Recent DOC for a zone in the Canavese hills covering 1998 communes in the provinces of Torino, Biella, and Vercelli. The wines include a *bianco* (Erbaluce), *rosato* and *rosso* (Nebbiolo/Barbera/Uva Rara/Freisa/Neretto), and varietal reds from Barbera and Nebbiolo. The *rosso* may also be produced as a *novello*.

CAREMA
DOC r dr ☆☆→☆☆☆ *88 89 90 91 93 94 95 96 97 98 99 00*
Tiny wine-growing area on the border of Valle d'Aosta where vines are trained over trellises on rocky terraces. The wine is made from

Nebbiolo (here called Picutener). Carema is garnet-hued with less body and durability than other Nebbiolo wines, but harsh climate and stony terrain account for its unique refinement in bouquet and flavour, developed through long barrel- and bottle-ageing. The wine needs 5 to 6 years or more. Ferrando's black-label wine and the Produttori Nebbiolo di Carema's Carema di Carema stand out. Age: 4 yrs (2 in barrel).

CHARDONNAY
A boom in planting of this noble French vine has resulted in some impressive wines in oaked styles ranging from Burgundian to Californian. Now DOC under Langhe and Piemonte.

CISTERNA D'ASTI
DOC r dr
New DOC for lightish reds made mainly (80–100%) from Croatina in the Roero and the Basso Monferrato of Asti.

COLLI TORTONESI
DOC r w p dr ☆☆ *DYA*
Zone near the town of Tortona in southeast Piedmont with varietal reds from Barbera and Dolcetto (also *novello*) and white Cortese (usually *frizzante* or *spumante*), as well as *bianco*, *rosso*, and *chiaretto*. Barbera Superiore best at 1 to 3 years after harvest.

COLLINE NOVARESI
DOC r w dr ☆→☆☆ *DYA*
Appellation for the hills of Novara province in northern Piedmont created to cover a *bianco* from Erbaluce and the varietal reds of Barbera, Croatina, Nebbiolo , Uva Rara, and Vespolina; all can be used to make a basic *rosso* that may also be *novello*.

COLLINE SALUZZESI
DOC r w dr (sp)
Obscure DOC for hills around the town of Saluzzo, south of Turin,

for the rare varietals of Pelaverga, which makes a pale, tasty red, and Quagliano, which makes a zesty white, also *spumante*. A *rosso* is made from Pelaverga, Nebbiolo, and/or Barbera.

CORTESE DELL'ALTO MONFERRATO
DOC w dr (fz) (sp) ☆☆ *DYA*
Fresh, palish green wine made from at least 85% Cortese from a large area of the Alto Monferrato hills. Sometimes *frizzante*.

CORTESE DI GAVI
See Gavi DOCG.

COSTE DELLA SESIA
DOC r p w dr ☆→☆☆ *DYA*
Zone in the hills of Vercelli province near the Sesia River in northern Piedmont created to cover a *bianco* from Erbaluce and the varietal reds of Uva Rara, Croatina, Nebbiolo (or Spanna), and Vespolina. Often fresh fruity wines for everyday consumption.

CROATINA
Red variety of northern Piedmont traditionally used in blends but now also in varietal wines under the DOCs of Colline Novaresi and Coste della Sesia.

DIANO
Another name for Dolcetto di Diano d'Alba DOC.

DOLCETTO
Dolcetto makes wines that are quite full yet soft with a grapey, mouth-filling, bittersweet flavour. They are DOC in many zones of Piedmont.

DOLCETTO D'ACQUI
DOC r dr ☆☆→☆☆☆ *99 00 01*
Styles in this zone along the Bormida River around Acqui Terme and Strevi range from soft and fruity to sturdily tannic and durable. Age: *superiore* 1 yr.

DOLCETTO D'ALBA
DOC r dr ☆☆→☆☆☆☆ *00 01*
Improvements in wine making techniques have enabled producers to achieve Dolcetto of great appeal in the zone that produces more than half of the wine from this popular variety. Styles naturally vary from producer to producer, but the norm is balanced, smooth, gracefully grapey, mouth-filling wine to drink within 1 to 3 years. Age: *superiore* 1 yr.

DOLCETTO D'ASTI
DOC r dr ☆☆ *DYA*
Easy-drinking but often light Dolcetto made in limited quantity from vineyards centred in Asti's Langhe hills. Age: *superiore* 1 yr.

DOLCETTO DELLE LANGHE MONREGALESI
DOC r dr ☆☆→☆☆☆ *BV*
Made in minute quantities in the Langhe between Dogliani and Mondovi. Though lighter than others, it is noted for special bouquet. Age: *superiore* 1 yr.

DOLCETTO DI DIANO D'ALBA OR DIANO
DOC r dr ☆☆→☆☆☆ *99 00 01*
The commune of Diano is just south of Alba and is distinguished by its Dolcetto from 77 approved plots or *sorì* – the first official vineyard designations in Italy. The wine compares with Dolcetto d'Alba, meaning that it ranks with the finest of Piedmont. Age: *superiore* 1 yr.

DOLCETTO DI DOGLIANI
DOC r dr ☆☆→☆☆☆ *99 00 01*
Dolcetto reputedly originated at Dogliani, where it makes wine of firm tone, depth, and length of flavours that are rarely matched elsewhere. Age: *superiore* 1 yr.

DOLCETTO DI OVADA
DOC r dr ☆☆→☆☆☆ *95 96 97 98 99 00 01*
Dolcetto from hills around Ovada in southeast Piedmont rivals the

best of Alba in terms of class. With its robustness, it keeps well; some big vintages have been known to hold their class for up to a decade, though the trend is toward younger, fresher wines. Age: *superiore* 1 yr.

DOUX D'HENRY

Rare variety used for a red under Pinerolese DOC.

ERBALUCE

Native variety used for white wines in northern Piedmont, notably as Erbaluce di Caluso DOC.

ERBALUCE DI CALUSO

DOC w dr (sp) ☆☆ DYA

The Erbaluce grape can make good, broad, crisp dry white. Most noted are those from Luigi Ferrando, Cieck, Favaro, and Orsolani. The sweet Caluso Passito was the strong point of the appellation when it was made by Vittorio Boratto, but it is rarely seen today. Age: *passi to* 5 yrs.

FARA

DOC r dr ☆☆→☆☆☆ 90 93 95 96 97 98 99 00 01

Noteworthy red from Nebbiolo, Vespolina and Uva Rara grown in the Novara hills. Robust and well scented, it improves over 4 to 8 years, or longer. Age: 3 yrs (2 in wood).

FAVORITA

New interest in the once-forgotten Favorita grown in the Roero and Langhe hills near Alba has led to a modest comeback. Bone-dry and light, when well made it is not as simplistic as it may seem on first sip. DOC under Langhe.

FREISA

Once popular in central Piedmont as a rustic, bubbly wine with unique sweet-acidic flavour, Freisa had been losing ground. But lately producers have resumed making dry Freisa of good balance (fizzy and still). With an enticing ruby-cherry colour and raspberry-like aroma, they show enough class to herald a revival under the DOC Langhe. Uniquely noteworthy is Coppo's barrique-aged Mondaccione.

FREISA D'ASTI

DOC r dr s/sw fz sp ☆☆ 00 01

Dry or *amabile*, still, *frizzante,* or *spumante*; bright cherry-garnet; lively acidic flavour with berry-like undertones. Age: *superiore* 1 yr.

FREISA DI CHIERI

DOC r (dr) s/sw fz sp ☆☆

Limited production zone at the doorstep of Turin is usually sweet and bubbly. Age: *superiore* 1 yr.

GABIANO

DOC r dr ☆☆ 99 00 01

Red based on Barbera from the village of Gabiano in the Monferrato Casalese hills. Wine from Castello di Gabiano was noted in the past for its longevity, but this wine is now rarely seen.

GATTINARA

DOCG r dr ☆☆☆→☆☆☆☆ 85 86 88 89 90 93 95 96 97 98 99 00 01 02

At its best, this red from Nebbiolo (here called Spanna), grown around Gattinara in the hills north of Vercelli can reach notable heights of grandeur and its long-standing fame is beginning to seem justified even though many examples fail to impress overwhelmingly. With 10% Uva rara theoretically permitted with the Nebbiolo, it develops distinct nuances in the glacial moraine north of the town of Gattinara. There is a hint more of violets and tar on the nose, and a softer texture and sense of bitter almond at the finish that set it apart. Antoniolo, Nervi, and Travaglini remain the standard bearers but with a total production of less than 300,000 bottles a year the number of disappointments is possibly still disproportionate. Age: 3 yrs (2 in barrel); *riserva* 4 yrs.

GAVI OR CORTESE DI GAVI

DOC w dr (fz) (sp) ☆☆→☆☆☆ *00 01 02*
The most prestigious wines from Cortese grapes come from the hills around the town of Gavi in southeast Piedmont. One of Italy's most fashionable whites, it is noted for acute dryness and fresh, flinty acidity when young, although those who let it mature a little may be rewarded by greater depth, roundness, and fleshiness. Despite a tendency to use oak unnecessarily standards are generally high, confirmed by promotion to DOCG from the 1998 vintage. La Scolca was the standard-bearer for years, with a wine of unusual depth of aroma and flavours, though the competition has caught up. Wines from Gavi commune were once called Gavi di Gavi, now Gavi del Comune di Gavi, though neighbouring Tassarolo makes wine of comparable class. *Frizzante* and *spumante* versions must be made exclusively from Cortese grapes.

GHEMME

DOCG r dr ☆☆→☆☆☆☆ *85 86 88 89 90 93 95 96 97 98 99 00*
Among Nebbiolo-based wines of northern Piedmont, Ghemme ranks second to Gattinara in status but can certainly equal it in class. Made from 75–100% Nebbiolo with the addition of Vespolina and Uva Rara. Ghemme's sturdy, robust qualities smooth out with age as it develops an elegant bouquet, notably from Antichi Vigneti di Cantalupo and Novellolti. Age: 4 yrs (3 in wood).

GRIGNOLINO

Once widely planted, Grignolino has been reduced to secondary status in Piedmont, a victim of shy yields and pale, delicate wines that seem out of step with the region's bold reds. But admirers – in the Basso Monferrato hills north of Asti and Alessandria – find its almost rosy colour and dry, vaguely bitter, gritty flavour unmatchable.

GRIGNOLINO D'ASTI

DOC r dr ☆→☆☆ *DYA*
The largest DOC zone permits 10% Freisa in usually light Grignolino to drink young and fairly cool, though some wines show more depth and complexity.

GRIGNOLINO DEL MONFERRATO CASALESE

DOC r dr ☆→☆☆☆ *00 01*
Grown in the hills around Casale Monferrato, Grignolino (with 10% Freisa) is light ruby-orange, refreshing yet fairly tannic, and can be quite stylish. The classic Grignolino zone is in the hills around Olivola, Terruggia, Treville, and especially Vignale Monferrato.

LANGHE

DOC r w dr ☆☆→☆☆☆☆ *96 97 98 99 00 01*
Wines made in the Langhe and Roero hills around Alba fall into this umbrella denomination. They include red Nebbiolo, Dolcetto, and Freisa, and white Arneis, Favorita, and Chardonnay, and *bianco* from approved white varieties and *rosso* from approved red varieties. Although designed to bring wines not covered by an established denomination into the DOC net or DOCG, Langhe embraces some first-rate single-vineyard bottlings, including several inspired red wines, often Nebbiolo/Barbera blends, and some of Italy's finest Chardonnay.

LESSONA

DOC r dr ☆☆→☆☆☆ *89 90 93 95 96 97 98 99 00 01*
Tiny zone in the Vercelli hills making refined red wine from Nebbiolo with up to 25% Vespolina and Uva Rara. Rich in bouquet and flavour, robust and lightly tannic, Lessona usually needs 6 to 8 years or more. Age: 2 yrs (1 in wood).

LOAZZOLO

DOC w sw ☆☆→☆☆☆ *98 99 00 01*
A model appellation for Moscato

from high vineyards around the village of Loazzolo, south of Canelli, where Giancarlo Scaglione created a golden sweet wine using a mixture of ancient and modern methods: the grapes are both late-harvest and dried after picking (*passito*). His artistically bottled Loazzolo from Forteto della Luja is exquisitely sweet and formidably expensive. Age: 2 yrs (6 mths in small barrels).

MALVASIA DI CASORZO D'ASTI

DOC r s/sw sw fz sp ☆☆ *DYA*
Usually sweet and sparkling, this cherry-hued wine comes from the dark-skinned Malvasia vine grown around Casorzo, northeast of Asti, and is appreciated for its fragrant, grapey fruitness.

MALVASIA DI CASTELNUOVO DON BOSCO

DOC r sw sp ☆☆ *DYA*
This wine, from the town of Castelnuovo Don Bosco between Asti and Turin, is similar to Malvasia di Casorzo and somewhat easier to find, thanks to producers Bava and Grili.

MONFERRATO

DOC r p w dr
The vast Monferrato range of hills lying between the Po River and the Apennines in the provinces of Asti and Alessandria produces more than half of Piedmont's wine, much of it DOC, including Barbera del Monferrato, Grignolino del Monferrato Casalese, and Cortese dell'Alto Monferrato. The comprehensive Monferrato DOC applies to reds, whites, and rosé (called *chiaretto* or *ciaret*) in an abundance of types and styles.

Bianco *w dr* ☆☆ *00 01 02* Can be made from any of the recommended white varieties of the region, so ranges from light and fresh to oaky and complex.

Bianco Casalese *w dr* ☆☆ *DYA* This zesty white is based on Cortese, which may be cited on labels when 85% of the variety is included.

Rosato or Chiaretto or Ciaret *p dr* ☆→☆☆ *DYA* This can be made from any of the recommended red varieties of the zone; designed to drink young and fresh, also as *novello*.

Rosso *r dr* ☆→☆☆☆ *95 96 97 98 99 00 01* This can be made from any of the many recommended red varieties of the region, so wines range from as light and fresh as *novello* through varying degrees of flavours, colours, and styles depending on the varieties used and ageing techniques. They include numerous so-called "Super Piedmontese" blends of Barbera with other varieties, mainly Cabernet, Merlot, and Pinot Nero – intended to compete with the "Super Tuscans".

Dolcetto *r dr* ☆→☆☆ *98 99 00* The vine can do well in certain parts of the Monferrato range. It may also be *novello*.

Freisa *r dr fz* ☆→☆☆ *BV* Freisa makes mainly zesty young wines here, also as *novello*.

MOSCATO D'ASTI

See Asti DOC.

NEBBIOLO D'ALBA

DOC r dr (s/sw) (fz) (sp) ☆☆→☆☆☆
98 99 00 01 02
Vineyards around the town of Alba (but not in the Barolo or Barbaresco zones) produce this often impressive but varied DOC with lightly sweet and/or bubbly wines to drink young, occasionally seen). The still dry version can show the nobility of more vaunted Nebbiolo wines, with the advantage of being softer, easier, and less expensive. Prime is often reached at 3 to 6 years, but some vintages can last a decade. Wines made in the Roero hills, the traditional centre of production, may take either DOC Roero or Nebbiolo d'Alba, which can cause confusion. Age: 1 yr (*secco*).

PELAVERGA

The revived Pelaverga variety makes pale red wines under

the DOCs of Colline Saluzzesi and Verduno.

PIEMONTE

DOC r w dr (sw) (sp)

Broad appellation designed to classify a range of varietal wines not covered by the region's other DOC(G)s, as well as sparkling wines from PinoT and/or Chardonnay grapes grown in the region. The red varietals are Barbera, Uva Rara, and Grignolino (all of which may also be *novello*), and Brachetto, which may be *novello* or sparkling. The white varietals are Chardonnay, Cortese, Pinot Bianco, and Pinot Grigio, all of which may also be sparkling, as well as Moscato, which may also be a richly sweet *passito* if aged a year. The DOC also covers Pinot Nero vinified as white wine (still or sparkling) and sparkling blends of Pinot and Chardonnay.

PINEROLESE

DOC r p dr

This zone around the town of Pinerolo southwest of Turin covers reds from Barbera, Uva Rara, Dolcetto, and Freisa, as well as the rarities of Doux d'Henry, a varietal rosé, and Ramiè, a red from Avana, Avarengo, and Neretto. The list also covers a *rosso* and *rosato* from blends of local varieties. Interesting wines in theory, but rarely seen.

PINOT

Both red and white Pinot wines were once well known in Piedmont, but only recently have they been replanted mainly for sparkling wines. Piemonte DOC applies to Pinot Bianco, Pinot Grigio, and Pinot Nero alone or blended in both still and sparkling versions.

QUAGLIANO

Rare variety used for a white wine, also sparkling, under Colline Saluzzesi DOC.

ROERO

DOC r dr ☆☆→☆☆☆ *97 98 99 00 01*

The name Roero alone on the label refers to a red wine made from Nebbiolo grapes from the Roero hills. The appellation also includes Roero Arneis, the white wine that has surged to prominence over the last decade. The Roero hills are noted for Nebbiolo of medium weight and easy drinkability that had previously come under Nebbiolo d'Alba DOC. Producers now may opt for one or the other, which seems only to have complicated matters. *Superiore* is slightly stronger.

Roero Arneis or **Arneis di Roero**

w dr (sp) ☆→☆☆☆ *DYA* Arneis is an ancient white variety whose grapes were often blended with red Nebbiolo, but has recently blossomed as the source of Alba's leading white wines. They range between modest and full of character, sometimes with the complexity associated with other varieties. Quality standards continue to improve. *Spumante* is rare. Sweet *passito* versions – though not sanctioned by DOC – can be impressive.

RUBINO DI CANTAVENNA

DOC r dr ☆→☆☆ *99 00 01*

Obscure red of Barbera with Grignolino and Freisa grown in the Monferrato Casalese hills at Cantavenna.

RUCHE DI CASTAGNOLE MONFERRATO

DOC r dr ☆☆ *97 98 99 00 01*

Rare and inimitable red from a vine of mysterious origin known as Ruchè, Rochè, or Rouchet, grown in vineyards above Castagnole Monferrato. Its few producers aim for a youthful style in a ruby-violet wine of blossomy bouquet. But Scarpa's Rouchet Briccorosa (☆☆☆) has more structure than the norm, developing a peculiar elegance after 4 to 5 years.

SIZZANO

DOC r dr ☆☆→☆☆☆ *95 96 97 98 99 00 01*

Red of limited production made from 40–60% Nebbiolo, with Vespolina and Uva Rara grown around Sizzano in the Novara hills. Robust, with fine Nebbiolo bouquet; good vintages can keep 10 years. Age: 3 yrs (2 in barrel).

SPANNA

The local name for Nebbiolo in the Novara-Vercelli hills applies to red wines under the recently created DOCs of Colline Novaresi and Coste della Sesia. Spanna was long used to describe unclassified wines, some mediocre, some superb, with life spans that could range beyond two decades, notably those from Antonio Vallana & Figlio whose cellars provided unsurpassed bargains in aged wines. Though they could be made of Spanna alone, they may have included varieties from southern Italy giving body, strength, colour, and longevity even to wines from medium vintages. Some such Spanna rivalled Gattinara in every way except authenticity.

SPUMANTE

Piedmont produces a dazzling array of sparkling wines from its native varieties: the Moscato of Asti, Brachetto, Cortese, Malvasia, Erbaluce, Arneis, and even Nebbiolo. Riesling and Sauvignon Blanc are also used but today many of Piedmont's sparklers – whether made in bottle or tank – come from Pinot or Chardonnay. Most of these would qualify under the recent Piemonte DOC. In the past, the large industrial producers relied on Lombardy's Oltrepò Pavese or Trentino-Alto Adige to supply the Pinot and Chardonnay, but as these varieties are now prominent in the Langhe and Monferrato hills, locally sourced *metodo classico* wines can be first rate. Large wineries such as Banfi, Cinzano, Contratto, Fontanafredda, Gancia, and Martini & Rossi may market such wines under the collective appellation of Talento. The other noteworthy sparkling wines are Bruno Giacosa Extra Brut and Valentino Brut Zero from Rocche dei Manzoni.

VERDUNO OR VERDUNO PELAVERGA

DOC r dr ☆☆ *DYA*

The Pelaverga variety produces prickly, pale-ruby wines with a scent of currants and spices. It grows around the town of Verduno in the Barolo zone.

VERMOUTH

Piedmont is the world leader in vermouth, which by law must contain at least 70% wine, in intricate and often secret blends with herbs, spices, and other natural flavourings, along with sweetening components and grape spirits to bring alcohol to 16%. The industry, based in Turin, Asti, and Canelli, now usually uses wines from other regions. Martini & Rossi, Cinzano, Carpano, Gancia, Riccadonna, and Cora are leading names.

VESPOLINA

A variety used in blends of red wines in northern Piedmont as well as for a varietal wine under the Colline Novaresi DOC.

Producers

Provinces: Alessandria (AL), Asti (AT), Biella (BI), Cuneo (CN), Novara (NO), Torino (TO), Vercelli (VC).

Abbazia di Vallechiara, Dolcetto di Ovada, known primarily because made by Italian actress Ornella Muti.

Marziano e Enrico Abbona, Dogliani (CN), leading producer of Dolcetto di Dogliani (Papà Celso), also good

Langhe Rosso, Langhe Chardonnay, and others.

Anna Maria Abbona, Farigliano (CN). Well made Dolcetto di Dogliani (Maioli, Sorì dij But), Langhe Rosso Cadò (Dolcetto/Barbera).

Orlando Abrigo, Treiso (CN). Promising DOCG Barbaresco (Montersino, Rongallo), Barbera d'Alba, and Merlot-based Liuraie.

Giovanni Accomasso e Fislio, La Morra (CN). Barolo Crus Rocchette, Rocche).

Alario, Diano d'Alba (CN). DOC Diano (Costa Fiore and Montagrillo, Nebbiolo d'Alba Cascinotto).

Antica Casa Vinicola Scarpa, Nizza Monferrato (AT). Mario Pesce and Carlo Castino excel with Barolo (Le Coste di Monforte, Tettimora), Barbaresco (Barberis, Tettineive); Asti DOCs Barbera (Banin dell'Annunziata, Bogliona, Possabreno), Grignolino (San Defendente), Dolcetto (Selva di Moirano), Nebbiolo d'Alba (Moirane); plus singular Monferrato Freisa (Selva di Moirano) and vdt Rouchet Briccorosa .

Antichi Vigneti di Cantalupo, Ghemme (NO). The Arlunno family leads in Ghemme (Collis Breclemae, Collis Carellae, Signore di Bayard), their reds being among best of northern Piedmont.

Antoniolo, Gattinara (VC). Excellent Gattinara (Osso San Grato, San Francesco, Vigneto Castelle).

Anzivino, Gattinara (VC). Newcomer to Gattinara, Bramaterra.

Fratelli Alessandria, Verduno (CN). Elegant structured Barolo (Monvigliero, S. Lorenzo), Verduno Pelaverga.

Giovanni Almondo, Montà (CN). Fine Roero, Arneis, and Barbera d'Alba.

Elio Altare, La Morra (CN). Passionate *vignaiolo* with Barolo (Vigneto Arborina), Dolcetto d'Alba (La Pria), as well as outstanding Langhe Vigna Larigi and Vigna Arborina.

Giacomo Ascheri, Bra (CN). Revitalized family firm with huge range and good reliability across the board from top Barolo (Sorano, Vigna dei Pola) to experimental Montalupa white (Viognier) and red (Syrah).

Azelia, Castiglione Falletto (CN). Modern Barolo (Bricco Fiasco, San Rocco); Dolcetto d'Alba (Bricco dell'Oriolo).

Pietro Barbero, Moasca (AT). Good Barbera d'Asti (La Vignassa, Bricco Verlenga, Camparò) and Monferrato Bianco (Sivoy) and Rosso (Piage').

Barni, Brusnengo (BI). Small estate with good Coste delle Sesia (Torrearsa, Mesolone), promising Bramaterra

Batasiolo, La Morra (CN). Large winery with major vineyards for Barolo (Boscareto, Cordadella, Briccolina, Bofani, Cerequio); Dolcetto d'Alba (Bricco di Vergne), Moscato d'Asti, and Langhe Chardonnay (Morino).

Bava, Cocconato d'Asti (AT). Active family house with wide range of quality and individuality especially in Barbera d'Asti (Arbest, Libera, Piano Alto, Stradivario), Piemonte Chardonnay (Thou Blanc), Monferrato Bianco (Alteserre) Ruchè di Castagnole Monferrato, Malvasia di Castelnuovo Don Bosco. The firm also owns the sparkling wine house Giulio Cocchi (*q.v.*).

Bel Colle, Verduno (CN). Barolo (Monvigliero); Alba Dolcetto (Madonna di Como, Borgo Castagni), Nebbiolo (Monvijé), Roero Arneis; Verduno Pelaverga and Langhe Favorita.

Carlo Benotto, Costigliole d'Asti. Barbera d'Asti (Rupestris, Balau) and the rarely seen varietal Gamba di Pernice.

Fratelli Bera, Neviglie (CN). Fine Moscato (Su Reimond) and Asti Spumante, Barbera and Dolcetto d'Alba, Langhe (Sassisto).

Nicola Bergaglio, Rovereto di Gavi (AL). Good Gavi (La Minaia).

Bersano Riccadonna, Nizza Monferrato (AT). Good Barbera d'Asti (Generala), Brachetto d'Acqui top a large range.

Bertelli, Costigliole d'Asti (AT). Carefully crafted wines of personality from Barbera (Giarone,

Montetusa), Grignolino, Traminer (Plissé), Chardonnay, Cabernet, Syrah (St Marsan), Sauvignon (Mon Mayor), and others.

Giuseppe Bianchi, Sizzano (NO). Sizzano, Ghemme, Galtihera, white Oloise (Chardonnay and Erbaluce)

Fratelli Biletta, Casorzo d'Asti (AT). Grignolino d'Asti, Maluasia di Casorzo.

Gabutti-Boasso, Serralunga d'Alba (CN). Barolo (Gabutti, Serralunga), Dolcetto d'Alba (Meriame).

Alfiero Boffa, San Marzano Oliveto (AT). Characterful series of Barbera d'Asti.

Carlo Boffa & Figli, Barbaresco (CN). Barbaresco (Casot, Vitalotti); Barbera and Dolcetto d'Alba.

Enzo Boglietti, La Morra (CN). Rising star in the Langhe with Barolo (Brunate, Fossati), Barbera d'Alba (Vigna dei Romani), Dolcetto.

Borgo Maragliano, Loazzolo (AT). Attractive Loazzolo *vendemmia tardiva*, Moscato d'Asti (La Calliera). Also dry, Chardonnay-based still and sparkling wines.

Giacomo Borgogno & Figli, Barolo (CN). Traditional, long-lived Barolo, from excellent sites. Also single-vineyard Liste.

Francesco Boschis, Dogliani (CN). Good Dolcetto di Dogliani (Sorì San Martino Pianezzo, Vigna dei Prey).

Gianfranco Bovio, La Morra (CN). Fine range of Barolo (Arborina, Gattera, Nocchettevino); Langhe Chardonnay (La Villa), Barbera d'Alba (Parussi, Negiaveja).

Braida-Giacomo Bologna, Rochetta Tanaro (AT). Bricco dell'Uccellone was the pioneering barriqued Barbera and still one of the best. Also excellent Barbera d'Asti, Bricco della Bigotta, Ai Suma, and light, zesty La Monella. Grignolino and Moscato d'Asti (Vigna Senza Nome).

Brema, Incisa Scapaccino (AT). Barbera d'Asti specialists (Bricco Volpettona, Bricconizza, Cascina Croce), Brachetto, Grignolino, Moscato.

Brezza, Barolo (CN). Giacomo Brezza and family make fine Barolo (Bricco Sarmassa, Cannubi, Castellero), Barbera (Cannubi), and Dolcetto d'Alba (San Lorenzo) for their family restaurant in Barolo.

Bricco del Cucù, Bastia Mondovì (CN). Rapidly improving Dolcetto from Dogliani and Langhe.

Bricco Maiolica, Diano d'Alba (CN). First-rate Dolcetto (Sorrì Bricco Maiolica), along with Barbera and Nebbiolo d'Alba.

Bricco Mondalino, Vignale Monferrato (AL). Mauro Gaudio makes leading Grignolino (Bricco Mondalino) and Barbera, Monferrato, Barbera d'Asti (Il Bergantino Caudium Magnum, Zerolegno), Malvasia di Casorzo.

Luciano Brigatti, Suno (NO). DOC Colline Novaresi Möt Ziflon, Uva rara, Vespolina, Bianco (Erbaluce).

Gian Piero Broglia, Gavi (AL). Stylish Gavi (Bruno Broglia, la Meirana, Villa Broglia).

Fratelli Brovia, Castiglione Falletto (CN). Firm, classic Barolo (La Mia, Rocche dei Brovia, Monprivato); Dolcetto (Solatio), and Barbera d'Alba (Brea).

GB Burlotto, Verduno (CN). Barolo (Cannubi, Monvigliero); Barbera d'Alba (Aves), Pelaverga, Langhe Mores.

Bussia Soprana, Monforte d'Alba (CN). Barolo (Bussia, Mosconi, Vigna Colonello).

Piero Busso, Neive (CN). Very good Barbaresco (Vigna Borgese Bricco Mondino).

Ca' Bianca, Alice Bel Colle (AL). Owned by giant Gruppo Italiano Uini. Exemplary Barbera d'Asti (Cherzi), Cavi, good Dolcetto d'Acqui, Barolo.

Ca' del Baio, Treiso (CN). Barbaresco (Asili, Marcarini, Valgrande) and others.

Ca' Romé, Barbaresco (CN). Romano Marengo makes fine Barbaresco (Maria di Brun, Sorì Rio Sordo) and Barolo (Rapet).

Ca' Viola, Dogliani (CN). Highly impressive Langhe versions of DOC

Dolcetto (Barturot) and Langhe Rosso (Bric du Luv, Rangone).

Cabutto-Tenuta La Volta, Barolo (CN). Promising Barolo (La Volta, Riserva del Fondatore); Barbera (Bricco delle Viole), Dolcetto d'Alba.

Cantina del Glicine, Neive (CN). Barbaresco (Marcorino, Curà), Barbera, Dolcetto d'Alba.

Cantina del Pino, Barbaresco (CN). Outstanding Barbaresco, fine Langhe Freisa; Barbera, Dolcetto d'Alba.

Cantine Sant'Agata, Scurzolengo (AT). Largish Monferrato estate with wide range dominated by Barbera and the unusual Ruché.

Cantina Vignaioli Elvio Pertinace, Treiso (CN). Cooperative producing good Barbaresco (Casotto, Castellizzano, Marcarini, Nervo), and DOC Dolcetto d'Alba, Langhe Pertinace, and more.

Cantine Volpi, Tortona (AL). Fine Colli Tortonesi and Monferrato. Large range.

Cappellano, Serralunga d'Alba (CN). Traditional Barolo (Otin Fiorin Collina Gabutti, plus fine Barolo Chinato); Barbera, Dolcetto (d'Alba).

Carlotta, Borgone Valsusa (TO). Respected producer of Valsusa (Costadoro, Rocca del Lupo, Vignacombe).

Giorgio Carnevale, Cerro Tanaro (AT). Veteran producer of Asti DOCs, led by Barbera Il Crottino.

Cascina Ballarin, La Morra (CN). Barolo (Bricco Rosso, Bussia); Alba and Langhe DOCs.

Cascina La Barbatella, Nizza Monferrato (AT). Leading Monferrato estate Barbera d'Asti (Vigna dell'Angelo), and outstanding Monferrato Rosso Sonvico (Cabernet/Barbera) lead range.

Cascina Barisel, Canelli (AT). Admired organic Barbera (La Cappelletta), Moscato d'Asti.

Cascina Bertolotto, Spigno Monferrato (AL). Barbera, Brachetto, and Dolcetto d'Acqui.

Cascina Bongiovanni, Castiglione Falletto (CN). Stylish, modernist

Barolo (Pernanno); Barbera, Dolcetto d'Alba; Langhe Rosso.

Cascina Ca' Rossa, Canale (CN). Outstanding Roero wines, including Arneis and red Vigna Audinaggio.

Cascina Castlét, Costigliole d'Asti (AT). Joyous Barbera d'Asti runing from the lively Goj to barrique Policalpo and Passum (Fine Moscato from semi-dried grapes).

Cascina Chicco, Canale (CN). Large estate, with fine Barbera (Bric Loira), Nebbiolo d'Alba (Mompissano); Roero (Valmaggiore).

Cascina degli Ulivi, Novi Ligure (AL). Organic Gavi (Filagnotti), Piemonte Barbera.

Cascina Fonda-Barbero, Mango (CN). Moscato d'Asti, Moscato Passito.

Cascina Gilli, Castelnuovo Don Bosco (AT). Delicious Freisa d'Asti (Vigna del Forno), Malvasia Don Bosio, Barbera d'Asti (More).

Cascina Luisin, Barbaresco (CN). Excellent Barbera d'Asti (Asili), traditional-style Barbaresco (single vineyards Rabajà, Sorì Paolin), Barbera, Dolcetto d'Alba, Langhe Nebbiolo.

Cascina Pellerino, Monteu Roero (CN). Good Roero Arneis (Bonŗeur, Pòch Ma Bon *passito*), Roero (Vicot), Barbera d'Alba.

Cascina Pian d'Or-Barbero, Mango (CN). Moscato d'Asti.

Cascina Roera, Costigliole d'Asti. Barbera specialists.

Cascina Scarsi Olive, Rocca Grimalda (AL). Distinctive Dolcetto di Ovada.

Castellari Bergaglio, Rovereto di Gavi (AL). Distinctive Gavi (Pilìn, Rolona, Vignavecchia, Fornaci).

Castello di Neive, Neive (CN). Leading Barbaresco producer (Santo Stefano, Messoirano, Gallina). Also Moscato d'Asti (Marcorino); Dolcetto d'Alba (Basarin, Messoirano); Langhe Arneis, and numerous others.

Castello del Poggio, Portacomaro (AT). Owned by Zonin group. Noted Grignolino, Barbera, and Dolcetto d'Asti.

Castello di Razzano, Alfiano Natta (AL). Fine Barbera d'Asti Crus.

Castello di Tagliolo, Tagliolo Monferrato (AL). Large range led by Classic Dolcetto di Ovada, Barbera, and Cortese Alto Monferrato.

Castello di Tassarolo, Tassarolo (AL). Stylish Gavi (Vigneto Arborina, Castello di Tassarolo).

Cascina Val del Prete, Priocca (CN). Estate concentrating on Nebbiolo: d'Alba and Roero.

Cascina Vano, Neive (CN). Barbaresco (Canova), Barbera d'Alba, Langhe Rosso.

Castello di Verduno, Verduno (CN). Barolo (Massara), Barbaresco (Rabajà, Faset); Barbera (Bricco del Cuculo) and Dolcetto d'Alba, Verduno Pelaverga.

Caudrina Dogliotti, Castiglione Tinella (CN). Excellent Moscato d'Asti (La Caudrina, La Galeisa).

Cavallotto, Castiglione Falletto (CN). Vineyards at Bricco Boschis and Vignolo give fine traditional Barolo (Bricco Boschis Vignolo, San Giuseppe); Barbera (Cuculo), and Dolcetto (Mellera, Scot) d'Alba.

Ceretto, Alba (CN). Brothers Bruno and Marcello Ceretto are pace-setters in Alba with established wines from estates of Bricco Rocche, Bricco Asili, and innovations from La Bernardina on the edge of Alba. Barolo (Bricco Rocche, Prapò, Brunate), Barbaresco (Bricco Asili, Faset), Barbera (Piana), Dolcetto (Rossana), Nebbiolo (Lantasco) d'Alba and Langhe Arneis (Blangé) and Chardonnay, Cabernet, and Pinot Nero (La Bernardina); plus reliable brut (Chardonnay/Pinot Nero sparkling wine).

Pio Cesare, Alba (CN). Renowned, long-standing company with convincing modern styles in DOCG Barolo (Ornato) and Barbaresco (Il Bricco), as well as Dolcetto and Nebbiolo d'Alba (Il Nebbio), Langhe Chardonnay (Piodilei and L'Altro), and others.

Michele Chiarlo, Calamandrana (AT). Chiarlo produces a wide range of well-structured wines. Barolo (Cerequio and Cannubi), Barbaresco (Rabajà Asili); Barbera, Grignolino and Moscato d'Asti, Asti Spumante and Gavi; also Monferrato Bianco (Plenilunio), Rosso (Countacci), and more.

Quinto Chionetti & Figlio, Dogliani (CN). Leading producer of traditional Dolcetto di Dogliani (Briccolero, San Luigi).

Cieck, Agliè (TO). Erbaluce di Caluso (Misobolo), *passito* (Alladium) and sparkling Erbaluce made by the traditional method.

Fratelli Cigliuti, Neive (CN). Superb, firm Barbaresco Barbera and Dolcetto d'Alba from vineyards at Serraboella.

Cinzano, Torino. Major producer of vermouth with cellars in Santa Vittoria d'Alba; also Asti and *spumante* and sparkling *metodo classico* (Cinzano Brut, Marone Cinzano Pas Dosé) and Charmat (Pinot Chardonnay, Principe di Piemonte Riserva). The company is now owned by Campari.

Clerico, Monforte d'Alba (CN). Refined, modern-style Barolo (Ciabot Mentin Ginestra, Pajana); Barbera and Dolcetto d'Alba, and a fine Langhe DOC Arte (Nebbiolo in barrique).

Giulio Cocchi, Asti. Sparkling wine house. Range includes a rare *metodo classico* Asti and Barolo Chinato. Owned by Bava (*q.v.*).

Elvio Cogno, Novello (CN). Classy Barolo (Ravera, Vigna Elena); Alba DOC Barbera (Bricco dei Merli), and Dolcetto (Vigna del Mandorlo) d'Alba, Langhe Rosso (Montegrilli), and white Nas-cetta.

Colle Manora, Quargnento (AL). Good Barbera del Monferrato (Pais), also Manora Collezione (Barbera/Cabernet Sauvignon), Mimosa Collezione (Sauvignon Blanc), Mimosa Diane (Chardonnay/Sauvignon), and Palo Alto (Pinot Nero/Merlot/Cabernet/Barbera).

Il Colombo-Barone Riccati, Mondovì (CN). Small quantities of exemplary Dolcetto delle

Langhe Monregalesi (Il Colombo, Monteregale Vigna Chiesetta).

Aldo Conterno, Monforte d'Alba (CN). Superb tradionalist Barolo (Cicala, Colonello, Gran Bussia, Romirasco); Barbera (Conca Tre Pile), Dolcetto (Bussia Soprana) d'Alba Rosso (Quartetto); Langhe DOC Bianco (Printanié), Chardonnay (Bussiador), and Nebbiolo (Favot).

Giacomo Conterno, Monforte d'Alba (CN). Legendary Barolo (Monfortino Riserva, Cascina Franca), and Barbera d'Alba.

Paolo Conterno, Monforte d'Alba (CN). Good Barolo, Dolcetto d'Alba, Langhe Nebbiolo from Ginestra.

Conterno-Fantino, Monforte d'Alba (CN). Reliable class with Barolo (Sorì Ginestra, Vigna del Gris Parussi); Barbera (Vignota) and Dolcetto (Bricco Bastia) d'Alba, and Langhe Chardonnay (Bastia) and Rosso (Monprà).

Contratto, Canelli (AT). Historic house now owned by Bocchino makes outstanding *metodo classico* Asti (De Miranda), sparkling Giuseppe Contratto Brut Riserva, plus Barolo (Cerequio Tenuta Secolo), Barbera d'Asti (Solus Ad), and Piedmont Chardonnay (La Sabauda).

Luigi Coppo & Figli, Canelli (AT). Enterprising Coppo brothers are noted for Barbera (Pomorosso, Camp du Rouss, Riserva della Famiglia), Grignolino (Il Rotondino), and Moscato d'Asti (Moncalvina), and Asti, Brachetto d'Acqui, as well as Piemonte Chardonnay (Monteriolo, Riserva della Famiglia), Mondaccione (Freisa), and sparkling Piero Coppo Riserva Brut.

Corino, La Morra (CN). Stylish Barolo (Rocche dell'Annunziata, Giachini Vecchie Vigne), Barbera (Vigna Pozzo), and Dolcetto (Giachini) d'Alba.

Matteo Correggia, Canale d'Alba (CN). Correggia's inspired winemaking produced Barbera (Bricco Marum), and Nebbiolo (La Val dei Preti) d'Alba plus Roero (Ròche d'Ampsèj), Arneis and

Langhe Bianco (Sauvignon), all of absolute splendour. It is hoped his descendants show equal talent.

Giuseppe Cortese, Barbaresco (CN). Barbaresco (Rabajà) tops the range.

Teo Costa, Castellinaldo (CN). Arneis, Barbera, and Nebbiolo vines do best here.

Alessandria Crissante, La Morra (CN). Softish Barolo (Otin Capalot, Roggeri), Dolcetto d'Alba, Monferrato Barbera.

CS di Rubino, Cantavenna di Gabiano (AL). Rare Rubino di Cantavenna.

CS di Vinchio e Vaglio Serra, Vinchio d'Asti (AT). Very good Barbera d'Asti (Nizza Vigne Vecchie).

Dacapo, Agliano Terme (AT). New estate concentrating on Barbera d'Asti in various styles.

Damilano, Barolo (CN). New outlook brings new interest to Barolos (Cannubi, Liste).

Sergio Degiorgis, Mango (CN). Lively Moscato d'Asti (Sorì del Re) and *passito* Essenza. Good reds from Dolcetto, Barbera; Chardonnay-based Accordo Bianco.

Deltetto, Canale d'Alba (CN). Good Roero (Braja, Madonna dei Boschi), Arneis (San Michele), and Barbera d'Alba, plus new Barolo (Bussia).

Luigi Dessilani, Fara Novarese (NO). Refined Fara (Caramino), Ghemme, and Nebbiolo.

Destafanis, Montelupo Albese (CN). Up-and-coming estate working with Dolcetto (Monia Bassa), Barbera, Nebbiolo d'Alba, and Chardonnay.

Domenico Ghio e Figli, Bosio (AL). Promising developments with Dolcetto di Ovada and Gavi.

Dosio, La Morra (CN). Finely honed Barolo (Fossati); Barbera, Docetto, and Nebbiolo d'Alba; Langhe Freisa and Eventi (Merlot).

Luigi Einaudi, Dogliani (CN). House founded by former Italian president Luigi Einaudi makes excellent Barolo (Cannubi, Costa Grimaldi), Dolcetto di Dogliani (I Filari, Vigna Tecc), and Langhe Rosso (four-grape blend).

Giacomo Fenocchio, Monforte d'Alba (CN). Admired Barolo (Bussia, Sottana, Cannubi), Barbera and Dolcetto d'Alba.

Luigi Ferrando, Ivrea (TO). Leader in northern Piedmont with Carema (black-label *riserva*) Erbaluce di Caluso (Vigneto Cariola, Solativa, and sparkling brut).

Roberto Ferraris, Agliano (AT). Barbera d'Asti (La Cricca Nobbio).

Fontanabianca, Neive (CN). Excellent Barbaresco (Sorì Burdin, Brunet); Barbera, Dolcetto d'Alba.

Fontanafredda, Serralunga d'Alba (CN). Former Savoy cellars are centre of large estate producing full range of Alba wines: Barolo (Gattinera, La Rosa, La Delizia, Lazzarito, La Villa, and others), Barbaresco; Barbera (Vigna Raimondo), Diano (Vigna La Lepre), Nebbiolo d'Alba, and Asti; as well as first-rate *spumante classico* (Contessa Rosa Brut and Rosé, Gattinera Brut).

Forteto della Luja, Loazzolo (AT). Renowned oenologist Giancarlo Scaglione created the rich, sweet *passito* Moscato (Piasa Rischei) that defines the Loazzolo DOC. Also Piemonte Brachetto (Forteto Pian dei Sogni) and Monterrato Rosso (Le Grive).

Fratelli Fantino, Monforte d'Alba (CN). Barolo, Barbera d'Alba (both Vigna dei Dardi), Nepas Rosso (Nebbiolo Passito).

Fratelli Mossio, Rodello (CN). Characterful Dolcetto d'Alba (Bricco Caramelli, Piano delli Perdoni); Langhe Rosso.

Fratelli Revello, La Morra (CN). Fine Barolo (Rocche dell'Annunziata, Conca, Giachini), Barbera d'Alba (Ciabot du Re).

Funtanin, Canale (CN). Reliable range of wines from Roero, Barbera most in evidence.

Gaja, Barbaresco (CN). Charismatic Angelo Gaja is Piedmont's undisputed leader with outstanding wines. Barbaresco (Sorì Tildin, Sorì San Lorenzo, Costa Russi), Barolo (Sperss) and Langhe Darmagi (Cabernet Sauvignon), Gaia & Rey and Rossj-Bass (both Chardonnay), Alteni di Brassica (Sauvignon). Also Langhe Dolcetto (Cremes) and Piemonte Barbera (Sitorey). He also owns the Gromis winery for Barolo Cerequio.

Filippo Gallino, Canale (CN). Impressive Barbera d'Alba and Roero.

Gancia, Canelli (AT). Family firm that pioneered Asti's sparkling wine industry in 1860s makes DOC Asti and various *spumanti*, both *classico* (Vallarino Gancia Gran Crémant Riserva) and Charmat (Pinot di Pinot, Gancia dei Gancia, Castello Gancia), as well as vermouth.

Gastaldi, Neive (CN). Superb Dolcetto d'Alba (Moriolo), and Langhe Rosso Gastaldi (Nebbiolo). Also Bianco Gastaldi (Sauvignon Blanc/Chardonnay).

Gatti, Santo Stefano Belbo (CN). Good Moscato and Verbeia (Barbera/Freisa).

Giacomo Grimaldi, Barolo (CN). New estate with individual Barolo (Le Coste), Barbera, Dolcetto, Nebbiolo d'Alba.

Gianfranco Alessandria, Monforte d'Alba (CN). Exceptional Barolo (San Giovanni), Barbera (Vittoria), Dolcetto d'Alba.

Gianluigi Lano, San Rocco Seno d'Elvio (CN). Young winemaker developing lively Barbaresco, Barbera d'Alba (Fondo Prà).

Gianni Gagliardo, La Morra (CN). Barolo Barbera and Dolcetto d'Alba. Langhe Favorita, Barolo Chinato.

Giulio Accornero, Vignale Monferrato (AL). Good Monferrato Barbera, Grignolino, Malvasia *passito*.

Ettore Germano, Serralunga d'Alba (CN). Distinguished Barolo (Cerretta) leads theusual Alba spread.

Attilio Ghisolfi, Monforte d'Alba (CN). Classy Langhe Rosso Alta Bussia (Barbera/Nebbiolo) and Carlin (Nebbiolo/Freisa), and Barolo (Bricco Visette).

Bruno Giacosa, Neive (CN). Leading traditionalist Giacosa makes exceptional Barbaresco (Sànto Stefano, Gallina, Rio Sordo) and Barolo (Bussia, Rocche di Castiglione, Villero, Falletto); Alba DOC Barbera (Altavilla), Dolcetto (Basarin) and Nebbiolo (Valmaggiore), Roero Arneis, Grignolino d'Asti and Freisa d'Asti, along with fine *spumante classico* Bruno Giacosa Extra Brut.

Carlo Giacosa, Barbaresco (CN). DOCG Barbaresco (Montefico, Narin).

Fratelli Giacosa, Neive (CN). DOCG Barbaresco (Rio Sordo) and Barolo (Mandorlo) lead large, rapidly improving range.

Raffaele Gili, Castellinaldo (CN). New, small, modernist estate working mainly with Nebbiolo (Roero, d'Alba) and Barbera (d'Alba).

Gillardi, Farigliano (CN). Highly admired Harys (Syrah/Cabernet Sauvignon) overshadows Dolcetto di Dogliani (Cursalet, Maestra) and others.

La Giustiniana, Rovereto di Gavi (AL). Distinguished Gavi (Lugarara, Montessora, Centurionetta, Vignaclara). Also Moscato, Branchetto, Dolcetto. Just Bianco (Cortese).

Elio Grasso, Monforte d'Alba (CN). Prized Barolo (Runcot, Chiniera, Ginestra Case Matè). Also good Barbera (Vigna Martina) and Dolcetto (Vigna dei Grassi) d'Alba, and Langhe Chardonnay (Educato).

Fratelli Grasso, Treiso (CN). Barbaresco (Sorì Valgrande), Moscato d'Alba.

Silvio Grasso, La Morra (CN). Fine Barolo (Bricco Luciani, Ciabot Manzoni, Pèvigne), Barbera, Dolcetto, and Nebbiolo .

Sergio Grimaldi, Santo Stefano Belbo (CN). Deep Moscato d'Asti (Ca' du Sindic) from old vines.

Gromis, La Morra (CN). Gaja's winery for Barolo Cerequio.

La Guardia, Morsasco (AL). Monferrato Barbera (Dante, Ornovo), Rosso Innominato (Dolcetto/Cabernet) Dolcetto di Ovada (Delfini).

Hastae, Calamandrana (AT). Intriguing project: Barbera d'Asti (Quorum) comes from vineyards (1 hectare each) belonging to 6 leading producers.

Hilberg–Pasquero, Priocca (CN). Admired Nebbiolo, Barbera d'Alba, Langhe Rosso.

Icardi, Castiglione Tinella (CN). Large estate, large range headed by Moscato d'Asti (La Rosa Selvatica) and Barbera d'Alba (Surì di Mù, Vigna dei Gelsi).

Liedholm, Cuccaro Monferrato (AL). Legendary Swedish soccer coach Nils Liedholm's son Carlo makes good Barbera d'Asti and Monferrato Grignolino, and innovative Bianco della Boemia (Cortese/Pinot Bianco) and Rosso della Boemia (Barbera/Cabernet/ Pinot Nero).

Luigi Baudana, Serralunga d'Alba (CN). Well-honed Barbaresco and Alba/Langhe DOCs from this small estate.

Luigi Boveri, Costa Vescovato (AL). Impressive Colli Tortonesi Barbera (Vignalunga, Poggio delle Amarene), Cortese (Vigna del Prete), and Bianco from the rare Timorasso.

Luigi Pira, Serralunga d'Alba (CN). Barolo (Vigneto Marenca).

Malvirà, Canale (CN). High-ranking Roero (Trinità, Mombeltramo) and Arneis (Renesio, Saglietto, Trinità). Also Langhe Bianco (Tre Uve), Rosso (San Guglielmo), and Favorita.

Giovanni Manzone, Monforte d'Alba (CN). Barolo (Le Gramolere), Langhe Tris (Nebbiolo/Barbera/Dolcetto).

Marcarini, La Morra (CN). Long-standing, re-emerging winery. Barolo (Brunate, La Serra); Dolcetto d'Alba (Boschi di Berri, Fontanazza).

Marchesi Alfieri, San Martino Alfieri (AT). Outstanding Barbera d'Asti (La Tota, Alfiera). Good Grignolino (Sansoero), Monferrato Rosso San Germano (Pinot Nero), Rosso dei Marchesi (Barbera/ Pinot Nero), Bianco dei Marchesi/Riesling Italico.

Marchesi di Barolo, Barolo (CN). Wide range, all of reliable quality, led by Stalwart Barolo from Cannubi and Sarmassa.

Marenco, Strevi (AL). Characterful Barbera d'Asti (Ciresa), Brachetto d'Acqui (Pineto), Dolcetto d'Acqui (Marchesa), Moscato d'Asti (Scrapona) and *passito* (Passrì).

Mario Marengo, La Morra (CN). Barolo (Brunate, Bricco Viole), Dolcetto d'Alba and Nebbiolo (Valmaggiore).

Franco M. Martinetti, Turin. Wines from several locations. Outstanding Monferrato Rosso Sul Bric (Barbera/Cabernet), Barbera d'Asti (Montruc and Bric dei Banditi), Gavi (Minaia) and Colli from Tortonesi Martin (Timorasso).

Martini & Rossi, Torino. Well-known vermouth house is a major producer of sparkling wines in cellars at Pessione and Santo Stefano Belbo with Asti Spumante, Riesling Oltrepò Pavese, and refined Riserva Montelera Brut.

Bartolo Mascarello, Barolo (CN). Living legend with Barolo from vineyards at Cannubi, Ruè, San Lorenzo and Torriglione. Also Barbera and Dolcetto d'Alba, and others.

Giuseppe Mascarello & Figlio, Monchiero (CN). Masterful Barolo (Monprivato) leads impressive range recently enhanced by Langhe Rosso Status (Nebbiolo/Barbera/Freisa).

Mauro Molino, La Morra (CN). Superb Barolo (Vigna Conca, Vigna Gattere), Barbera d'Alba (Gattere). Langhe Chardonnay (Livrot) and Rosso (Acanzio).

Mauro Sebaste, Alba (CN). Stylish Barolo (Monvigliero, Prapò), leads Barbera, Dolcetto, Nebbiolo d'Alba, Langhe Rosso, Roero Arneis.

La Meridiana, Montegrosso d'Asti (AT). Barbera d'Asti (Bricco Sereno).

Moccagatta, Barbaresco (CN). Great Barbaresco (Basarin, Bric Balin, Cole); good Barbera d'Alba (Basarin); Langhe Chardonnay (Bric Buschet), and Freisa.

Monchiero Carbone, Canale (CN). Estate owned by noted oenologist Marco Monchiero. Roero (Priniti,

Srü) and Arneis (Recit), Barbera d'Alba (Mon Birone), and Langhe Bianco (Tamardi).

Fratelli Monchiero, Castiglione Falletto (CN). Good Barolo (Le Rocche, Montanello, Roere), Barbera and Dolcetto d'Alba.

Monfalletto-Cordero di Montezemolo, La Morra (CN). Firm, refined Barolo (Enrico VI, Monfalletto, Villero) lead consistently good range.

Il Mongetto, Vignale Monferrato (AL). Monferrato Barbera, Cortese, and Grignolino; Barbera d'Asti (Guera).

La Morandina, Castiglione Tinella (CN). Incisive Barbera (Varmat), Moscato d'Asti, Costa del Sole (Moscato/Riesling Italico).

Musso, Barbaresco (CN). Barbaresco (Rio Sordo, Pora, Ronchi); Barbera and Dolcetto d'Alba.

Mutti, Sarezzano (AL). Reliable estate from Colli Tortonesi, rare Timorasso especially good.

Fiorenzo Nada, Treiso (CN). Dense Barbaresco (Rombone), Barbera and Dolcetto d'Alba, and Langhe Rosso Seifile (Barbera/Nebbiolo).

Marco Negri, Costigliole d'Asti (AT). Moscato d'Asti.

Angelo Negro & Figli, Monteu Roero (CN). Roero (Sodisfà, Prachiosso), Arneis (Perdaudin), also *passito*. Barbera d'Alba.

Nervi, Gattinara (VC). Respected Gattinara (Molsino).

Nuova Cappelletta, Vignale Monferrato (AL). Monferrato Barbera leads Grignolino, Freisa, Cortese, and others.

Andrea Oberto, La Morra (CN). Praised Barolo (Albarella, Rocche); Barbera (Giada, Boiolo), and Dolcetto (San Francesco, Vantrino Albarella) d'Alba; Langhe Rosso Fabio.

Fratelli Oddero, La Morra (CN). Powerful Barolo (Mondoca di Bussia Soprana, Rocche di Castiglione, Vigna Rionda), and others.

Orsolani, San Giorgio Canavese (TO). Leading Erbaluce di Caluso, plus *passito* (La Rustia), and *spumante* made from Erbaluce grapes.

I Paglieri, Barbaresco (CN). Reliable Barbaresco (Pajé) and Barolo (La

Rocca e La Pira); Dolcetto d'Alba, Langhe Bianco and Rosso (Soleo); Crichët Pajé (Nebbiolo), Opera Prima (Nebbiolo/Barbera).

Paitin, Neive (CN). Fine Barbaresco (Sorì Paitin) plus Barbera, Dolcetto, Nebbiolo d'Alba, Langhe Rosso (Paitin), Bianco Campolive, Roero Arneis.

Parroco di Neive, Neive (CN). Barbaresco (Gallina); Barbera and Dolcetto (Basarin) d'Alba.

Armando Parusso, Monforte d'Alba (CN). Series of modern Barolos from vineyards on Bussia Cru (Munie, Rocche, Fiurin) and Mariondino, Piccole Vigne. Also Barbara, Docetto, Langhe Rosso, and Bianco.

Livio Pavese, Treville Monferrato (AL). Noted Monferrato producer.

Agostino Pavia, Agliano (AT). Barbera d'Asti (Bricco Blina, La Marescialla, Moliss) specialist.

Fratelli Pecchenino, Dogliani (CN). Modern, rich Dolcetto di Dogliani (Bricco Botti, Sirì, d'Yermu S. Luigi).

Giorgio e Luigi Pelissero, Treiso (CN). Stylish Barbaresco (Vanotu); Barbera (Casot, Piani) and Dolcetto (Augenta, Mun'frina), Langhe Nebbiolo, Favorita, Piemonte Grignolino.

Luigi Perazzi, Roasio (BI). Bramaterra.

Elio Perrone, Castiglione Tinella (CN). Good Barbera, Moscato d'Asti.

Fabrizio Pinsoglio, Castellinaldo (CN). New, small estate. Barbera d'Alba (Bric La Rondolina), Roero, and others.

Pira, Dogliani (CN). Impressive Barbera (Vigna Fornaci, vendemmia tardiva) and Dolcetto (Vigna Fornaci) d'Alba, DOC Dolcetto di Dogliani (Bricco dei Botti, Vigna Landes), and others.

Enrico Pira & Figli, Barolo (CN). Chiara Boschis has resurrected this once renowned winery with newly outstanding Barolo (Cannubi).

Podere ai Valloni, Boca (NO). Boca (Vigna Cristiana).

Poderi Colla, San Rocco Seno d'Elvio (CN). Vines at Cascina Drago and Monforte give classy Langhe Bricco del Drago (Dolcetto/Nebbiolo) and Barolo (Bussia Dardi Le Rose) plus Barbaresco (Tenuta Roncaglia), and Alba DOC Barbera, Dolcetto and Nebbiolo d'Alba, and Langhe Bianco Sanrocco.

Poderi Sinaglio, Alba (CN). New estate working mainly with Barbera, Dolcetto, Nebbiolo, Moscato, Chardonnay, Sauvignon, to good effect.

Principiano, Monforte d'Alba (CN). Newish estate. Barolo (Boscareto, Le Coste) and Barbera d'Alba (Pian Romualdo), and Docetto d'Alba.

Produttori del Barbaresco, Barbaresco (CN). Nine crus of outstanding co-op making Barbaresco (Asili, Montefico, Montestefano, Rio Sordo, Ovello, Pajé Rabajà, Moccagatta, Pora); Langhe Nebbiolo.

Produttori Dianesi, Diano d'Alba (CN). Co-op making reliable Dolcetto.

Produttori del Gavi, Gavi (AL). Co-op making Gavi versions from decent to very good. Also sparkling Gavi Brut, Piemonte Cortese.

Produttori di Nebbiolo e di Carema, Carema (TO). Co-op producing sound Carema.

Alfredo Prunotto, Alba (CN). Admired house owned by Antinori of Tuscany makes good Barolo (Bussia), Barbaresco (Bric Turot); Barbera (Pian Romualdo), Dolcetto (Mosesco), Nebbiolo (Occhetti) d'Alba, Barbera d'Asti (Costamiole, Fiulòt).

Punset, Neive (CN). Organic Barbaresco (Campo Quadro); Barbera and Dolcetto d'Alba.

Carlo Quarello, Cossombrato (AT). Small traditionalist with notable Grignolino del Monferrato Casalese (Cré Marcaleone), Monterrato Rosso Crebarné.

Renato Rabezzana, San Desiderio d'Asti (AT). Barbera (Il Bricco) and Grignolino d'Asti.

Renato Ratti, La Morra (CN). Noted Barolo (Marcenasco, Rocche di Marcenasco, Conca di Marcenasco) and others; Alba and Monferrato DOCs.

Riccadonna, Canelli (AT). Large producer of Asti Spumante; metodo classico Conte Balduino

Extra Brut and Riserva Privata Angelo Riccadonna, Charmat President Reserve. Also vermouth.

Francesco Rinaldi & Figli, Alba (CN). Barolo (Cannubio).

Giuseppe Citrico Rinaldi, Barolo (CN). Although still young, this veterinary surgeon has already become a legendary producer of traditional Barolo (Brunate Le Coste, Cannula Ravera San Lorenzo).

Albino Rocca, Barbaresco (CN). Devoted producer of increasingly admired Barbaresco (Brich Ronchi, Vigneto Loreto), Barbera (Gepin), Dolcetto (Vignalunga) d'Alba, and Langhe Bianco (La Rocca).

Bruno Rocca, Barbaresco (CN). Modern Barbaresco (Rabajà, Coparossa). Barbera and Dolcetto (Trifolè) d'Alba, Langhe Rosso, and Chardonnay.

Rocche Costamagna, La Morra (CN). Barolo (Rocche dell'Annunziata, Bricco Francesco), plus Alba and Langhe DOCs.

Rocche dei Manzoni, Monforte d'Alba (CN). Bricco Manzoni was the first Nebbiolo/Barbera blend to gain fame. Large range now topped by Langhe Rosso Quatr Nas (Nebbiolo, Cabernet, Merlot, Pinot Nero), Barolo (Cappella di Santo Stefano, Big'd Big, d'la Roul), and sparkler Valentino Brut Zero.

Flavio Roddolo, Monforte d'Alba (CN). Powerful Bricco Appiani (Cabernet); Barolo (Ravera); Nebbiolo, Barbera, Dolcetto d'Alba.

Carlo Romana, Dogliani (CN). Dolcetto di Dogliani (Bric dij Nor, Rumanot Surì Vinsant).

Gigi Rosso, Castiglione Falletto (CN). Barolo (Cascina Arione) and wide range from Mebbiolo, Barbera, Docetto, Freisa, Arneis.

Rovellotti, Ghemme (NO). Admired Ghemme; Colline Novarese Nebbiolo, Vespolina, and Bianco (Erbaluce); Erbaluce *passito* Valdenrico.

Fratelli Rovero, San Marzanotto d'Asti (AT). Organic Barbera (Rouvé), Grignolino (Casalina) d'Asti and Monferrato reds and whites from.

San Fereolo, Dogliani (CN). Great Dolcetto di Dogliani (San Fereolo, Valdibà) and good Langhe Rosso Brumaio (Barbera).

San Romano, Dogliani (CN). Dolcetto di Dogliani specialist (Dolianum, Vigna del Pilone).

Sandrone, Barolo (CN). Superb, modernist Barolo (Cannubi Boschis, Le Vigne); Barbera, Dolcetto, Nebbiolo (Valmaggiore) d'Alba.

Santa Seraffa, Colombara di Gavi (AL). Impressive Gavi (Le Colombare).

Saracco, Castiglione Tinella (CN). Fine Moscato delle Langhe plus Langhe Chardonnay (Prasuè, Bianch del Luv), and Bianco Grattagno (Sauvgnon/Riesling).

Fratelli Savigliano, Diano d'Alba (CN). Dolcetto (Autin Grand, Sorì del Söt) and others.

Scagliola, Calosso (AT). Moscato d'Asti (Volo di Farfalle), Barbera d'Asti (SanSì), Langhe Dolcetto Busiord.

La Scamuzza, Vignale Monferrato (AT). Admired Monferrato Barbera, Grignolino, Rosso (Barbera/Cabernet).

Giorgio Scarzello, Barolo (CN). Barolo (Vigna Merenda), Barbera d'Alba.

Paolo Scavino, Castiglione Falletto (CN). Superb Barolo (Bric dël Fiasc, Cannubi, Rocche dell'Annunziata); Dolcetto (Vigneto dël Fiasc) and stunningly rich Barbera d'Alba, plus Langhe Rosso, Bianco.

Sciorio, Costigliole d'Asti. Barbera d'Asti for traditionalists (Sciorio) and modernists (Beneficio, Reginal); Monferrato Rosso (Antico Vitigno – Cabernet!, Reginal – Cabernet/Barbera).

La Scolca, Rovereto di Gavi (AL). The estate that glorified Gavi in the 1950s still makes notable Gavi and fine *spumante* Brut Soldati La Scolca.

Scrimaglio, Nizza Monferrato (AT). Good Barbera d'Asti (Bricco Sant'Ippolito, Croutin, Acsé Il Sogno, Monferrato, Rosso, Bianco.

Sylla Sebaste, Barolo (CN). Sound Barolo (Brunate, Bussia) leads varietals from Barbera, Dolcetto, Freisa, Arnesis, and Barbera/

Nebbiolo, Chardonnay/
Favorita blends.

Aldo e Riccardo Seghesio, Monforte
d'Alba (CN). Respected DOCG
Barolo (La Villa); Alba DOC Barbera
(Vigneto della Chiesa), and Dolcetto.

Renzo Seghesio, Monforte d'Alba
(CN). Barolo (La Villa), Barbera,
Dolcetto d'Alba (both Vigneto
della Chiesa), Langhe Rosso.

Sella, Lessona (BI). Classic Lessona,
plus Bramaterra, Coste della
Sesia (Orbello, Piccone).

Sottimano, Neive (CN). Beautifully
crafted Barbaresco (Cottà, Currà,
Fausoni, Pajoré) lead range.

Luigi Spertino, Mombercelli (AT).
Barbera and late-harvested
Grignolino d'Asti.

La Spinetta, Castagnole Lanze
(AT). Giorgio and Carlo Rivetti,
leaders in Moscato d'Asti (Bricco
Quaglia, San Rümu, Bric Lapasot,
Biancospino, Muscatel Vej), also
excel with new reds: Barbaresco
(Vigneto Gallina Vürzù, Vigneti
Staderi), Barbera d'Alba (Vigneto
Gallina), Barbera d'Asti (Ca' di
Pian), and Monferrato Rosso (Pin).

La Spinona, Barbaresco (CN).
Traditional Barbaresco Alba DOCs.

Oreste Stroppiana, La Morra
(CN). Barolo (San Giacomo),
Dolcetto d'Alba.

La Tenaglia, Serralunga di Crea (AL).
Fine Barbera d'Asti (Emozioni) and
Grignolino di Monferrato Casalese;
Giorgio Tenaglia (Barbera),
Paradiso (Syrah), and Chardonnay.

Tenuta dell'Arbiola, San Marzano
Oliveto (AT). Solid Monferrato
estate with wide range including
new Barbera d'Asti sub-zone Nizza.

Tenuta Carretta, Piobesi d'Alba (CN).
Barolo (Cannubi); Barbaresco
(Cascina Bordino); Roero (Bric
Paradiso) and Arneis (Vigna
Canorei), Langhe Rosso Bric
Quercia, plus Alba DOCs.

Tenuta dei Fiori, Calosso (AT). Barbera
d'Asti (Vigneto del Tulipano Nero),
Monferrato Rosso (Cabernet),
and others.

Tenuta Gaiano, Camino (AL). Barbera
del Monferrato (Vigna della Torretta,

Gallianum) from old vines; lively
Grignolino del Monferrato Casalese.

Tenuta Garetto, Agliano Terme (AT).
Newly revived estate. Barbera
d'Asti in three styles (Favà, In
Pectore, Tra Neuit e Dì).

Tenuta San Pietro, Tassarolo (AL).
Admired Gavi (Il Gaio, Bricco
del Mandorlo).

**Tenute Cisa Asinari dei Marchesi di
Gresy**, Barbaresco (CN).Elegant
Barbaresco (La Martinenga, Gajun,
Camp Gros); Dolcetto d'Alba
(Monte Aribaldo), Langhe
Chardonnay (Gresy), Sauvignon
and Rosso (Villa Martis); Moscato
d'Asti (La Serra), Villa Giulia
(Chardonnay/Sauvignon).

Terralba, Berzano di Tortona (AL). New
estate making Colli Tortonesi Bianco
(Stato from rare Timorasso, La Vetta
from Cortese), *rosso* (Terralba from
Barbera, Monleale mainly Barbera,
Montegrande mainly Croatina, Strà
Loja from Dolcetto).

Terre del Barolo, Castiglione Falletto
(CN). Co-op producing reliable
Barolo (Castello di Grinzane,
Rocche, Codana, Baudana,
Monvigliero), and the full range
of Alba and Langhe DOCs.

Terre da Vino, Barolo (CN). Co-op
producing most Piedmont DOC(G)s
of good quality and value.

Travaglini, Gattinara (VC). Reliable
Gattinara, and *riserva* Tre Vigne.

Traversa, Neive (CN). Tre Vigne.
Barbaresco (Sorì Ciabot), Moscato
d'Asti; and numerous Alba and
Langhe DOCs.

Fratelli Trinchero, Agliano (AT). Prized
Barbera d'Asti (Vigna del Noce).
Good Freisa, Dolcetto.

Ugo Lequio, Neive (CN). Traditional
Barbaresco (Gallina). Also Barbera,
Dolcetto d'Alba, Arneis.

GD Vajra, Barolo (CN). Outstanding
Barolo (Bricco delle Viole, Fossati);
Barbera (Bricco delle Viole) and
Dolcetto (Coste & Fossati) d'Alba,
Langhe Freisa (San Ponzio),
Moscato d'Asti.

Valfieri, Costigliole d'Asti. Three
versions of Barbera d'Asti, all
stylish, and others.

Rino Varaldo, Barbaresco (CN). Firm Barbaresco (Bricco Libero, Vigna di Alda); intriguing Barolo (Vigna di Aldo). Also Barbera, Dolcetto d'Alba, Langhe Freisa, Nebbiolo.

Giovanni Veglio & Figlio, Diano d'Alba (CN). Diano (Sorì Ubart, Puncia d'lBric).

Mauro Veglio, La Morra (CN). Emerging producer with fine Barolo (Vigneto Arborina, Rocche), Castelletto, Gattera Barbera (Cascina Nuova), and Dolcetto d'Alba.

Eraldo Viberti, La Morra (CN). Fine Barolo and Barbera (Vigna Clara) and Dolcetto d'Alba.

Vietti, Castiglione Falletto (CN). A wide range of small lots of superb Barolo (Rocche di Castiglione, Lazzarito, Bussia, Brunate, Villero), Barbaresco (Masseria, Rabajà); Dolcetto (Lazzarito, Tre Vigne), Barbera (Bussia, Pian Romualdo, Scarrone, Vigna Vecchia) and Nebbiolo (San Michele), d'Alba, Arneis, Moscato d'Asti.

Vigna Rionda-Massolino, Serralunga d'Alba (CN). Classy Barolo (Margheria, Parafada, Vigna Rionda), and range of Alba and Langhe DOCs.

Il Vignale, Novi Ligure (AL). Admirable Gavi Vigne Alte.

Vigne Regali, Strevi (AL). The Piedmontese branch of the American-owned Banfi winery makes a decent range of Asti Spumante, Brachetto d'Acqui (La Rosa), Dolcetto d'Acqui (Argusto), DOCG Gavi (Principessa Gavia, Vigna Regale); Spumante Classico Banfi Brut, Charmat Brut Pinot.

I Vignaioli di Santo Stefano, Santo Stefano Belbo (CN). Archetypal Asti, Moscato d'Asti, and Piemonte Moscato Passito (IL).

Vigne del Pareto, Novi Ligure (AL). Lively Gavi.

Vigneti Massa, Monleale (AL). Individual, ever-evolving wine styles. From Colli Tortonesi come Cerreta, Monleale, and Bigolla (all Barbera baseo), Barbera, Croatina, Freisa, and the rare white Timorasso. Also Piemonte Barbera, Cortese, and white Muscaté.

Villa Fiorita, Castello d'Annone (AT). Barbera (Giorgione) and Grignolino d'Asti, Monferrato Rosso.

Villa Ile, Treiso (CN). Barbaresco and others.

Villa Sparina, Monterotondo di Gavi (AL). Pace-setting Gavi (La Villa), sparkling Villa Sparina Brut, Monferrato Rosso (Rivalta, Sampò), Dolcetto d'Acqui (Bric Maioli), and Monferrato Bianco (Müller Thurgau).

Viticoltori Associati di Rodello, Rodello (CN). Good range of Dolcetto d'Alba.

Viticoltori dell'Acquese, Acqui Terme (AL). Good value in Brachetto, Dolcetto d'Acqui, Barbera, Grignolino, Moscato d'Asti.

Gianni Voerzio, La Morra (CN). Elegant Barolo (La Serra). Barbera (Ciabot della Luna) and Dolcetto (Rocchettevino) d'Alba; Langhe Rosso Serrapiù; Roero Arneis (Bricco Cappellina), Langhe Freisa and Nebbiolo, Moscato d'Asti (Vignasergente).

Roberto Voerzio, La Morra (CN). Fabulous Barolo (Brunate, La Serra, Sarmassa, Capalot, Cerequio), and Barbera d'Alba (Pozzo dell Anunziata).

Wine & Food

Piedmontese cooking, like robust red wine, comes into its own in the autumn. Hearty, almost chauvinistically traditional, it is refined country cooking that follows the seasons, and autumn provides the bounty. There is game from the mountainsides; hams, cheeses, and salami matured to perfection, and a bright array of garden vegetables augmented by what is found in the woods and fields. The multitude of *antipasti*, the ample pastas and risottos, thick soups and stews, and roast and boiled meats are the kind of fare that requires generous red wines. But the heartiness can be deceptive, for Piedmontese cooking has touches of grace distinct from, but equal to, the artistry of the provincial cooking of Burgundy and Lyons. The ultimate luxury is the white truffle, sniffed out by dogs in the Langhe and shaved raw over pastas, risottos, meats, and fondues. Some of the best restaurants are found where the best wines are. The best time to visit is when the grapes and truffles are coming in.

Wines to accompany each dish are suggested below in italics.

Bagna caôda "Hot bath" of oil, garlic, and anchovies, bubbling over a burner, into which raw vegetables – such as peppers, cardoons, fennel, celery, etc. – are dipped. *Young Barbera* or *Freisa d'Asti*

Brasato al Barolo Beef stewed very slowly in Barolo. *Barolo,* mature

Bollito misto alla piemontese Boiled veal and beef with *bagnet piemontese* (a garlicky green sauce). *Barbera d'Asti*

Camoscio alla piemontese Chamois in a savoury stew. *Carema* or *Lessona*

Capretto arrosto Richly seasoned roast kid. *Barbaresco*

Finanziera Stew or sauce including veal brains, sweetbreads, chicken livers, and cockscombs. *Nebbiolo d'Alba*

Fonduta Steaming mass of cheese fondue best topped with shaved truffles. *Dolcetto d'Alba* or *Diano*

Fritto misto or fricia Delicacies – brains, sweetbreads, lamb cutlets, chicken breasts, aubergines, courgettes, frogs' legs, sweet pastes, etc. – dipped in batter and fried. *Freisa d'Asti*

Insalata di carne cruda Minced fillet of beef marinated with oil, lemon, and pepper, sometimes served with mushrooms, Parmesan, or truffles. *Dolcetto di Dogliano*

Lepre al sivè "Jugged hare", marinated in wine and spices and stewed to rich tenderness. *Gattinara* or *Ghemme*

Panna cotta Fresh cream moulded with burnt sugar, like a crème caramel but more luxurious. *Asti or Moscato d'Asti*

Tajarin al tartufo Hand-cut egg noddles with butter, Parmesan, and shaved truffles. *Arneis di Roero*

Tapulon Ground donkey meat cooked with red wine, cabbage and seasonings. *Ghemme* or *Gattinara*

Tome or **tume** Small, round cheeses from the Langhe, mild when young, sharp when aged. *Dolcetto* (young cheese), *Nebbiolo* (aged cheese)

Zabaglione Egg yolks whipped with marsala, other sweet wine, or Barolo. *Caluso Passito* or *Asti*

Restaurants

Recommended in or near wine zones:

Alba-Langhe-Roero *Osteria dell'Arco* and *Il Vicoletto* at Alba; *Cesare* at Alberetto Torre; *Borgo Antico* and *Brezza* at Barolo; *Boccondivino* at Bra; *Moderno* at Carrù; *Trattoria Enoteca del Castello* at Grinzane Cavour; *Bel Sit* and *Belvedere* at La Morra; *Il Giardino di Felicin* and *Osteria della Posta* at Monforte; *La Contea* at Neive; *La Ciau del Tornavento* and *Osteria dell'Unione* at Treiso; *Falstaff* and *Real Castello* at Verduno; *La Pergola* at Vezza d'Alba.

Asti-Monferrato *L'Angolo del Beato, Da Dirce* and *Gener Neuv* at Asti; *Violetta* at Calamandrana; *San Marco* at Canelli; *I Caffi* at Cassinasco; *Torre* at Casale; *Da Beppe* at Cioccaro di Penango; *Da Guido* at

Costigliole d'Asti; *Il Cascinalenuovo* at Isola d'Asti; *I Bologna* at Rocchetta Tanaro; *Castello di San Giorgio* at San Giorgio Monferrato; *Da Bardon* at San Marzano Oliveto; *Vittoria* at Tigliole.
Gavi-Ovada *I Cacciatori* at

Cartosio; *Bel Soggiorno* at Cremolino; *Cantine del Gavi* at Gavi; *Italia* at Ovada; *Locanda San Martino* at Pasturana; *Pace* at San Cristoforo.
Novara-Vercelli *Pinocchio* at Borgomanero; *Cascina dei Fiori* at Borgo Vercelli; *Angiulli* at Candelo.

Liguria *Liguria*

Wine is a minor item in the economy of the Italian Riviera. Still, more than one hundred types of vine are grown on the rocky hillsides of this slender crescent, which arches along the Ligurian Sea from France past the capital Genoa to Tuscany. Liguria's wine production is among the lowest in the country (only Valle d'Aosta trails). The region is known to be rather introspective, which may help to explain the obscurity of Liguria's myriad local wines. The exception, though, is Cinqueterre, from the eastern coast, the Riviera di Levante, whose reputation derives more from past than present achievements – though the sweet Cinqueterre Sciacchetrà has been revived.

Other wines merit more attention: under the Riviere Ligure di Ponente DOC of the western coast are the intriguing red varieties Rossese and Ormeasco (a clone of Dolcetto), the unique white Pigato, and the leading white Vermentino, a variety gaining prominence everywhere, most notably in the Colli di Luni DOC to the east. Rossese also has its own DOC, Rosseso di Dolceacqua, in a small area near the French border. Wines from Ligura's other DOCs – Colline di Levanto, Golfo del Tigullio, and Val Polcevera (with its sub-zone Coronata) – are rarely seen.

Tracking down local wines can be fascinating. Most are white and go well with fish and the local *pesto* (basil and garlic sauce) and can seem divine when sipped on a terrace at Portofino or Portovenere. Whether they'd taste as good back home probably doesn't matter. The region has few IGTs: Colline Savonesi, Golfo dei Poeti, and Colline del Genovesato. Most other wine is called simply *nostrano* (ours) – but proudly.

Visitors may find the rusticity of the westerly Dolceacqua zone a relaxing counterpoint to the crowds of nearby San Remo and Monaco. The stunning vineyards of Cinqueterre, just northwest of La Spezia, are poised dramatically on precipitous cliffs above the sea. The *Vinoteca Sola* in Genoa provides an intelligent choice of Ligurian wines with the best from elsewhere. Also recommended are *Enoteca Bisson* at Chiavari, *Enoteca Lupi* at Imperia, *Enoteca Baroni* at Lerici and *Enoteca Bacchus* at San Remo. Francesco Giusti's *Enoteca Internazionale* at Monterosso is the reference point for Cinqueterre.

Recent Vintages

Recommended vintages appear with each entry for the few Ligurian wines capable of ageing.

Wines

CINQUETERRE

DOC w dr ☆→☆☆☆ *DYA*
Cinqueterre's romantic history alone is worthy of respect, but there are only a few hands overcoming the challenges of making fine wine on the steep slopes above the "Five Lands" – the coastal villages of

Monterosso, Vernazza, Corniglia, Manarola, and Riomaggiore. From Bosco grapes with Albarola and Vermentino, the wine is (ideally) straw-green, dry, fresh, and delicately scented.

Sciacchetrà *am s/sw sw* ☆→☆☆☆ *95 96 97 98 99 00 01* Cinqueterre dessert wine from the same grapes but dried; often remarkably good but difficult to get; at least 13.5% alcohol and 3.5% potential alcohol as residual sugar. Golden brown, mellow, often good as an apéritif, and can keep for years.

COLLI DI LUNI *DOC*

The Luni hills near La Spezia, where vines were planted by a revival with some of the best wines of Liguria, notably the white Vermentino. The zone extends into Tuscany's province of Massa Carrara.

Bianco *w dr* ☆→☆☆ *DYA* Refreshing white from Vermentino and Trebbiano Toscano.

Rosso *r dr* ☆→☆☆☆ *98 99 00 01 02* Plump and tasty red from Sangiovese, Canaiolo, Ciliegiolo, and others.

Vermentino *w dr* ☆→☆☆☆ *DYA* Some of the most impressive wines of the Colli di Luni, crisp yet succulently fruited.

COLLINE DI LEVANTO

DOC r w dr DYA
Rather like a continuation of Cinqueterre along the hills of La Spezia province. The *bianco* comes from Vermentino with Albarola and Bosco. The less common Rosso (which can also be *novello*) is mostly from Sangiovese and Ciliegiolo.

GOLFO DEL TIGULLIO *DOC*

Covers various types of red and white wines from vineyards in hills facing the gulf of Tigullio between Portofino and Sestri Levante, southeast of Genoa.

Bianco *w dr (fz) (sp) (sw)* ☆→☆☆ *DYA* Vermentino and Bianchetta make an easy, often bubbly wine for summer sipping. A sweet *passito* version is also approved, from semi-dried grapes.

Rosso *w dr (fz)* ☆→☆☆☆ *00 01 02* Dolcetto and Ciliegiolo combine to give reds that may be light and fizzy, also *novello*, or full and round.

Bianchetta Genovese *w dr (fz) (sp)* ☆☆ *DYA* Refined and attractively fruity white.

Ciliegiolo *w dr (fz)* ☆→☆☆ *00 01* Varietal red of cherry-pink colour and fresh tone, also *novello*.

Moscato *w s/sw sw (fz) (sp)* ☆→☆☆ *DYA* Moscato Bianco makes a pleasantly fragrant dessert wine, whether fresh and fruity or in a *passito* version of richer tone.

Vermentino *w dr (fz) (sp)* ☆→☆☆☆ *DYA* This can match Vermentino from Colli di Luni or Riviera di Ponente.

RIVIERA LIGURE DI PONENTE

DOC
Groups four wines grown along the western Riviera from near Genoa to the French border. There are sub-zones: Albenga or Albenganese for Pigato and Rossese; Finale or Finalese for Vermentino, and Riviera dei Fiori for all types within Imperia province in the west.

Ormeasco *r dr (p)* ☆☆→☆☆☆ *98 01 02* From a sub-zone centred in upper Arroscio Valley, this Dolcetto can outlast many Piedmontese versions as ruby turns to garnet, and texture and bouquet become rich and velvety. There is also a rare, Sciacchetrà version from dried grapes which can reach impressive heights. Age: *superiore* 1 yr.

Pigato *w dr* ☆☆→☆☆☆ *DYA* This white variety thrives around Albenga but does well near Imperia, too. Amply structured and rich in flavour, best a year or 2 after harvest.

Rossese *r dr* ☆→☆☆ *DYA* Though it pales in comparison to the best of Dolceacqua, Rossese around Albenga can be zesty in its youth.

Vermentino *w dr* ☆→☆☆☆ *DYA* Pale yellow in colour, with fragrant delicacy but firm body and flavour.

Often preferred to Pigato around Finale and Imperia.

ROSSESE DI DOLCEACQUA OR DOLCEACQUA
DOC r dr ☆→☆☆☆ *98 00 01*
Rustic and seductive, from Rossese grown in a hilly enclave around the town of Dolceacqua within the Rivrera Ligure di Porente zone. It is bright ruby to deep violet, as flowery on the nose as it is fruity on the palate, with warmth and plushness after 2 to 3 years, sometimes more in the *superiore*.

VAL POLCEVERA *DOC*
Recent appellation for several red, white, and rosé wines from hills surrounding the city of Genoa.

Bianco *w dr (sw) (fz) sp DYA* Made from any or all of Vermentino, Bianchetta Genovese, and Albarola with others. A sweet *passito* version is sometimes made.

Rosso/Rosato *r (p) dr (fr)* Any or all of Dolcetto, Sangiovese, and Ciliegiolo combine with Barbera to give fruity wines.

Bianchetta Genovese *w dr DYA* Lively, fruity white.

Vermentino *w dr DYA* Vermentino's inherent class shows here too.

CORONATA *w dr DYA*
Sub-zone for whites grown around the village of Coronata, at the southernmost part of Genoa and almost absorbed into the city.

Producers

Provinces: Genova (GE), Imperia (IM), La Spezia (SP), Savona (SV).

Alessandri, Ranzo (IM). New estate specialising in Riviera Ponente Pigato.

Anfossi, Bastia di Albenga (SV). Riviera Ponente Pigato, Rossese.

Laura Aschero, Pontedassio (IM). Reliable Riviera Ponente Pigato, Vermentino.

W. De Batté, Riomaggiore (SP). Superb Cinqueterre of full fruit flavours and smooth texture mainly from Bosco. Also Sciacchetrà.

Bisson, Chiavari (GE). Large but reducing range from Cinqueterre and Golfo del Tugullio includes Aeini Ravi Passito from Vermentino.

Riccardo Bruna, Ranzo (IM). Impressive Riviera Ponente Pigato (Le Russeghine, U Baccan, Villa Torracchetta). IGT Granaccia/ Rossese/Barbera blend.

Buranco, Monterosso al Mare (SP). New, organic estate with fine Cinqueterre, lustrous Sciacchetrà.

Giovan Battista Mandino Cane, Dolceacqua (IM). Fine Rossese (Vigneto Arcagna, Vigneto Morghe).

Calleri, Albenga (SV). Reliably good Riviera Ponente Pigato, Vermentino.

Forlini Capellini, Manarola (SP). Good, reliable Cinqueterre.

Cascina Fèipu du Massaretti, Bastia di Albenga (SV). Leading Riviera Ponente Pigato.

Colle dei Bardellini, Imperia. Notable Riviera Ponente Vermentino (U Munte) Pigato (Vigna La Torretta).

La Colombiera, Castelnuovo Magra (SP). Good Colli di Luni Vermentino (Vignale Paterno) and Rosso (Terizzo).

Cooperativa Agricola di Cinqueterre, Riomaggiore (SP). High-standing co-op responsible for most of Cinqueterre's output. Three vineyard selections and good Sciacchetrà alongside reliable basic Cinqueterre.

Maria Donata Bianchi, Diano Castello (IM). Riviera Ponente Pigato, Vermentino.

Durin, Ortovero (SV). Antonio Basso makes good Riviera Ponente from all four varieties and IGT from Granaccia.

Felice Foresti, Camporosso (IM). Estate on the rise with fine Rossese di Dolceacqua (Luvaira, Morghe), Riviera Ponente Pigato (I Solì), and Vermentino (Selvadolce I Solì).

Ottaviano Lambruschi, Castelnuovo Magra (SP). Fine Colli di Luni Vermentino (Costa Marina, Sarticola).

Lupi, Pieve di Teco (IM). Leading producer with grapes selected from choice plots. Riviera Ponente Ormeasco, Pigato (Le Petraie), Vermentino (Le Serre); IGT white Vignamare (barrel-aged Vermentino/Pigato), and more.

Il Monticello, Sarzana (SP). Fine Colli di Luni Vermentino (Podere Paterno), Sangiovese-based Rosso (Rupestro, Poggio dei Magni)

Picedi Benettini, Sarzana (SP). Colli di Luni, including impressive Vermentino (Il Chioso, Stemma).

La Pietra del Focolare, Ortonovo (SP). Small, new estate. Good Colli di Luni Vermentino.

La Rocca di San Nicolao, Chiusanico (IM). Emerging Riviera Ponente estate. Pigato, Vermentino lead.

Santa Caterina, Sarzana (SP). Emerging Colli di Luni estate with good Vermentino.

Tenuta Giuncheo, Camporosso (IM). Good Rossese di Dolceacqua DOC, Vermentino IGT syrah.

Terre Bianche, Dolceacqua (IM). Admired Rossese di Dolceacqua, Riviera Pone nte Pigato, Vermentino, IGT blends.

Terre Rosse, Finale Ligure (SV). Riviera Ponente Pigato, Vermentino, classy IGT blends.

Il Torchio, Castelnuovo Magra (SP). New Colli di Luni estate with fine Vermentino; *rosso* from Sangiovese/Merlot.

La Vecchia Cantina, Albenga (SV). Riviera Ponente Pigato, Vermentio; intriguing *passito*.

Claudio Vio, Vendone (SV). Riviera Ponente DOC Pigato, Vermentino.

Wine & Food

The Ligurians rely on fish prepared in artistic and savoury ways. There are tiny white *bianchetti* (whitebait), *datteri* (sea dates), *tartufi del mare* (oyster-like sea truffles), prawns, squid, octopus, mullet, sea bass, and dozens of others, many of which appear in the fish soups known as *buridda* or *ciuppin*. Ligurians also work magic on their terraced gardens, orchards, and herb-scented hillsides. Basil is highly revered, nuts, herbs, mushrooms, and spices are features of the exotic sauces and dressings for pasta and other dishes, so deftly delicious that they are called *tocchi* (touches). Meat is secondary, though rabbit braised with olives is adored along the western Riviera. Ligurians like the elaborate on special occasions, expresssed in dishes such as *cima alla genovese*, *torta pasqualina*, and, the epitome of indulgence, *cappon magro*.

Wines to accompany each dish are suggested below in italics.

Branzino in tegame Sumptuous sea bass cooked with white wine, tomato, and seasonings. *Vignamare*

Cappon magro At least 12 types of fish are piled pyramid-style on a base of sea biscuits and topped with oysters and lobsters. *Vermentino*

Capponada is a simpler version, containing preserved fish. *Pigato*

Castagnaccio Crunchy chestnut cake with raisins and pine nuts. *Cinqueterre Sciacchetrà*

Cima alla genovese Veal breast rolled with vegetables, nuts, herbs, spices, eggs, and cheese. *Riviera di Ponente Rossese*

Coniglio al Rossese Rabbit braised in Rossese with tomato, garlic, rosemary, and olives. *Rossese di Dolceacqua*

Farinata Irresistible chick pea paste cooked in oil and served in crisp slabs like pizza, known as *panissa*, and served with onions. *Vermentino*

Pansôti Type of ravioli filled with ricotta and chard and topped with a walnut cream sauce. *Pigato*

Torta pasqualina Monumental Easter tart, its multitude of ingredients spread through 33 layers. *Vermentino*

Trenette al pesto Slender ribbon noodles topped with Genoa's sauce of basil, cheese, nuts, oil, and garlic. *Lumassina*

Restaurants

Recommended in or near wine zones: **Riviera di Levante**, **Cinqueterre** and **Colli di Luni** *Locanda delle Tamerici* and *Paracucchi-Locanda Dell'Angelo* at Ameglia; *Hotel Lido* at Deiva Marina; *Ca' Peo* at Leivi; *Taverna del Corsaro* at Portovenere. **Riviera di Ponente** and **Dolceacqua** *Palma* at Alassio; *La Conchiglia* at Arma di Taggia; *Mistral* at Bordighera; *Doc* at Borgio Verezzi; *La Meridiana* at Garlenda; *Baia Beniamin* at Grimaldi Inferiore di Imperia; *Balzi Rossi* at Ponte San Ludovico di Imperia; *Lanterna Blu* at Porto Maurzio-Imperia; *Paolo & Barbara* at San Remo; *Giappun* at Vallecrosia.

Lombardy *Lombardia*

Lombardy is a moderate wine producer if compared to its neighbours of Piedmont, the Veneto and Emilia-Romagna. But as consumers, Lombardians are second to none. Milan, capital of industry and finance, is also the most active wine market, the pace-setter in food and drink. This influence has contributed to Lombardy's lead in production of classic method sparkling wine, of which Franciacorta and Oltrepò Pavese are the centres. But otherwise, the Milanese show a cosmopolitan nonchalance about wines from their home region, often turning to regions such as Piedmont, Tuscany, or Bordeaux for premium reds; Friuli, Trentino Alto-Adige, or Burgundy for premium whites, and for special occasions, Champagne.

Still, Italy's most populous and industrialized region does have hillsides between the Alps and Apennines and the hot Po valley floor where vines excel. To the southwest is the Oltrepò Pavese, where the luxuriant vineyards are Lombardy's most productive. As a perennial supplier of everyday wines to Milan and of Pinot grapes to sparkling wine producers elsewhere, the Oltrepò has never enjoyed much prestige, despite vastly improved wines. To the north is the Valtellina, where vines grow on a south-facing hill overlooking the Adda river and whose sub-zones of Grumello, Inferno, Sassella, and Valgella are covered by the Valtellina Superiore DOCG. Its apogee is the powerful *sfursat*, from semi-dried grapes, it too DOCG. Valtellina is the prime source, after Barolo for red wines from Nebbiolo, though the main market is across the border in Switzerland.

To the east are the provinces of Brescia, Bergamo, and Mantova (Mantua), with thirteen of the region's eighteen DOC zones. Franciacorta, which lies not far from Brescia, produces Italy's best sparkling wine by a long chalk. To the east along Lake Garda is the old Riviera del Garda Bresciano zone lying within the province of Brescia and Garda Colli Mantovani, covering the adjacent province of Mantova. The small zone of Lugana nestles under the south shores of the lake. There is also an umbrella DOC, Garda, which spreads over all the winegrowing territories under the lake's climatic influence, in both Lombardy and the Veneto, but its *classico* sub-zone is restricted to lands in Brescia province.

Visitors to the Lombardy lake country can take in Garda, Lugana, and Franciacorta, which touches on pretty Lake Iseo. The Valtellina is a gorgeous valley in the Alps with steeply terraced vineyards overlooking

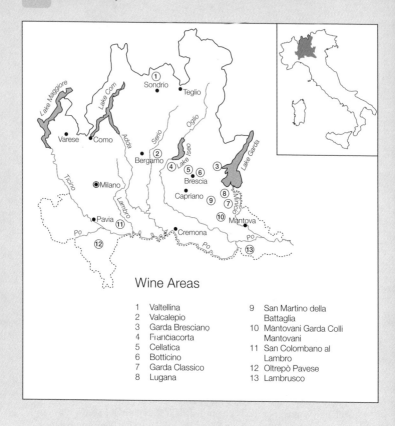

Wine Areas

1	Valtellina	9	San Martino della Battaglia
2	Valcalepio	10	Mantovani Garda Colli Mantovani
3	Garda Bresciano	11	San Colombano al Lambro
4	Franciacorta	12	Oltrepò Pavese
5	Cellatica	13	Lambrusco
6	Botticino		
7	Garda Classico		
8	Lugana		

the Adda River. The Oltrepò Pavese lies in rustically scenic hills south of Pavia. Oltrepò wines are screened at the *enoteca* in Certosa di Pavia. Lombardy has some of Italy's best-stocked *enoteche*. Milan: *Emporio Solci, Cotti, Ronchi, N'Ombra de Vin, Peck, Vino Vino,* and nearby *Longo* at Legnano, *Enoteca 77* at Meda, and *Meregalli* at Monza. The provinces: *Delizie di Bacco* at Como, *Castelletti* at Ponte San Pietro (Bergamo), *Il Carato* and *Creminati* at Brescia, *Marino* at Chiavenna (Sondrio), *Malinverno* at Isola Dovarese (Cremona), *Re Carlo Alberto* at Mantua, *L'Enoteca* at Voghera (Pavia).

Recent Vintages

Lombardy's longest-lived wines are the reds from Valtellina, which may mature and improve for a decade or more. In Oltrepò Pavese, Brescia, and other eastern zones of the region, most reds are made with a view to drinking within six or seven years.

2002 A wet summer with widespread hailstorms followed by a fine autumn resulted in variable grape quality but very good results for the more assiduous producers who selected stringently. The notable exception was Valtellina which escaped the worst of the weather and gained excellent wines.

2001 A rainy spring followed by a hot summer brought gratifyingly good wines throughout the region with whites especially excelling.

2000 Very good throughout, except in Lugana where hail struck, particularly good for reds.

1999 Good vintage for Valtellina thanks to cold nights and sunny days in autumn; excellent Chardonnay wines in Franciacorta.

1998 Small crop with some wines rated at levels of 1997.

1997 Outstanding vintage in Valtellina and Brescia area, very good in Oltrepò Pavese.

1996 Good to excellent harvest for reds throughout the region.

1995 Small crop of generally good quality; Valtellina reds show fairly full structure.

Notes on earlier vintages: Earlier good vintages in Valtellina include 94, 93, 92, 90, 89, 88, 86, 85, 83, 80, 79, 78, 71, 70.

Wines

BARBACARLO
See Oltrepò Pavese DOC Rosso.

BARBERA
Lombardy's most prominent vine, with a DOC under Garda and Oltrepò Pavese. It is prominent in blends of red wines throughout the region.

BOTTICINO
DOC r dr ☆→☆☆ *99 00 01*
Bright garnet-red wine from Barbera, Marzemino, Schiava, and Sangiovese grown at village of Botticino east of Brescia. Warm, fairly robust, and lightly tannic, it develops some grace in 3 or 4 years.

BUTTAFUOCO
See Oltrepò Pavese DOC.

CABERNET
Cabernet Franc, grown in eastern Lombardy for decades, has been upstaged by Cabernet Sauvignon. This is sometimes used alone but more often combined with Merlot as, for instance, in Valcalepio Rosso and in some highly regarded Franciacorta reds.

CAPRIANO DEL COLLE
DOC r w dr ☆ *97 98 00 01*
Little-known wines from Capriano del Colle south of Brescia. *rosso* (Sangiovese,

Marzemino) is bright and lively when young. Trebbiano is pale straw-green and tart.

CELLATICA
DOC r dr ☆→☆☆ *98 99 00 01*
From Schiava Gentile, Barbera, and Marzemino grapes grown at the village of Cellatica, northwest of Brescia, this tasty, scented, ruby red is good in 2 to 4 years. Age: *superiore* 1 yr.

COLLI GARDA MANTOVANI
DOC ☆→☆☆ *DYA*
Localized area between Mantova and Lake Garda.

Bianco *w dr* This comes from Trebbiano, Garganega, and Chardonnay with, optionally, some aromatic Sauvignon, Riesling Renano, or Riesling Italico.

Cabernet *r dr* From Cabernet Franc and/or Cabernet Sauvignon. Age: *riserva* 1 yr.

Rosato *p dr* This comes from the same grapes as the *rosso*, pale cherry in colour and delicate, may be called *chiaretto*.

Rosso *r dr* This comes predominantly from any or all of Merlot, Rondinella, and Cabernet, and is lightweight and dry; it may be called *rubino*.

Chardonnay *w dr*
Merlot *r dr* Age: *riserva* 1 yr.
Pinot Bianco *r dr*
Pinot Grigio *r dr*
Sauvignon *r dr*

FRANCIACORTA

DOCG w p dr sp ☆☆→☆☆☆☆

The low, rolling hills west of Brescia fronting on Lake Iseo were once noted for rustic reds, but over the last two decades Franciacorta has gained a reputation as a miniature Champagne. Although still wines are also produced (*see* Terre di Frnaciacorta DOC) Franciacorta DOCG applies only to its classic method sparkling wines. Its requirements are strict: the label does not allow mention of the terms *metodo classico, metodo tradizionale* or *spumante* and, like Champagne, the wine is identified only by a place-name. Ageing requirements for Franciacorta are more demanding than for Champagne. The non-vintage must age at least 25 months from the latest vintage in the *cuvée* before being sold, and this includes a minimum of 18 months in bottle after the second fermentation. Vintage Franciacorta (*millesimato*) must age for 37 months, of which 30 must be in bottle. The better wines all age for at least 3 years in bottle.

Franciacorta is produced from any or all of: Chardonnay, Pinot Bianco, and Pinot Nero. Chardonnay, noted for its finesse, often dominates blends or stands alone as blanc de blancs. Franciacorta Rosé must contain at least 15% of Pinot Nero. This variety cannot be used in the growingly esteemed *satèn*, the registered term for crémant, whose "creamy" texture and gentle *perlage* come from lower CO_2 pressure. Typology covers a range of tastes, from brut (dry) to extra dry (lightly sweet), *demi-sec* (medium-sweet) and *sec* (quite sweet). However, the vast majority of Franciacorta is brut. This includes the wines that receive no final *dosage* or *liqueur d'expédition* and may be described as extra brut, *pas dosé, dosage zéro,* etc. Production has surpassed 3 million bottles annually and quality overall is remarkably fine.

GARDA *DOC*

Covers 16 varietals, a blended rosé, and a lightly sparkling *frizzante* from a large area on both sides of Lake Garda in the provinces of Brescia, Mantova, and Verona. Garda Classico concerns a much more limited area within the province of Brescia and more carefully honed wine styles with just one varietal and a white, red, and rosé offering restricted varietal freedom.

Garda Barbera *r dr*

Garda Cabernet *r dr* Little-known. From Cabernet Sauvignon and/or Cabernet Franc and/or Carmenère.

Garda Cabernet Sauvignon *r dr*

Garda Chardonnay *w dr (sp)*

Garda Cortese *w dr*

Garda Corvina *w dr*

Garda Frizzante *w fr* From Chardonnay and/or Garganega.

Garda Garganega *w dr*

Garda Marzemino *r dr*

Garda Merlot *r dr*

Garda Pinot Bianco *w dr (sp)*

Garda Pinot Grigio *w dr*

Garda Pinot Nero *r dr*

Garda Riesling (Renano) *w dr (sp)*

Garda Riesling Italico *w dr*

Garda Rosato *p dr* From Gropello, Sangiovese, Marzemino, and Barbera.

Garda Sauvignon *w dr*

Garda Tocai *w dr*

Garda Classico Bianco *w dr* ☆→☆☆ *DYA* From minimum 70% Riesling Italico and/or Renano.

Garda Classico Rosso *r dr* ☆→☆☆☆ *00 01* Groppello gives the style to this blend which also contains Marzemino, Sangiovese, and Barbera. Wines best enjoyed fresh and fruity, within 1 to 3 years, but some wood-aged examples can show style. Age: *superiore* 1 yr.

Garda Classico Chiaretto *p dr* ☆→☆☆☆ *DYA* From the same grapes as *rosso*, this enlivening cherry-pink wine is a summer feature along the lake and can be quite classy.

Garda Classico Groppello *r dr* ☆→☆☆☆ *00 01* Groppello in its Gentile, Groppellone, and

Mocasina sub-varieties gives wines that can show distinct character after 3 to 4 years of age, when they develop bouquet and a rich, round flavour with a hint of a bitter finish. Age: *riserva* 2 yrs.

RIVIERA DEL GARDA BRESCIANO OR GARDA BRESCIANO *DOC*

This zone lies west and southwest of Lake Garda in the Brescia province and, long denominated, remains the emblematic Garda zone.

Bianco *w dr ☆ DYA* Riesling Italico and Renano combine in a white of little character.

Rosso *r dr ☆→☆☆ 00 01 02* The blend of Groppello, Sangiovese, Marzemino, and Barbera can make a bright, clean, tasty red; usually best within 1 to 3 yrs. Age: *superiore* 1 yr.

Chiaretto *p dr ☆→☆☆* From the same varieties as Rosso, this buoyant, cherry-pink wine is popular locally.

Groppello *r dr ☆→☆☆ 00 01 02* Groppello sub-varieties, Gentile, Santo Stefano, and Mucasina go into this lively red although Garda Classico DOC versions can be better.

GRUMELLO

See Valtellina Superiore DOC.

INFERNO

See Valtellina Superiore DOC.

MANTOVANO

DOC r dr fz ☆→☆☆ DYA
Lambrusco grapes from the flatlands of Mantua make wines that occasionally match their more famous neigbours in Emilia-Romagna.

LUGANA

DOC w dr (sp) ☆→☆☆☆ DYA
This is a fine dry white from the Trebbiano di Lugana variety, believed to be a clone of Verdicchio, grown to the south of Lake Garda in a small zone which straddles the Veneto. Straw-green to sunny yellow in colour and with a delicately flowery aroma, its considerable grace and personality make it one of the most consistent whites of the Garda-Verona area. Good young, some Lugana develops depth with a year or more in bottle. A passable *spumante* is made, usually by Charmat method.

MOSCATO DI SCANZO

DOC r sw ☆☆
Once a sub-zone of Valcalepio DOC, this rustic, sweet *passito* wine from semi-dried grapes, now has a DOC all its own. Produced in tiny quantities, and only around the town of Scarzorosciate, from the dark Metera sub-variety of Moscato, it has aromas recalling dried flowers, spices, and exotic fruits. Age: 2 yrs.

OLTREPO PAVESE *DOC*

The hills across the Po from Pavia in southwest Lombardy account for over half the region's production, and a major share of the DOCs in an array of 17 types with variations. Yet this potential giant of Italian wine is only now starting to find its identity. The Oltrepò is the nation's largest source of Pinot Nero, most often used in *spumante*, which as *metodo classico* qualifies for the (infrequently used) collective name of Talento. A great deal of this Pinot, though, is sold to *spumante* producers elsewhere, who do not indicate the origin of the grapes. The best of the Oltrepò, though is its punchy varietal reds from Barbera and Uva rara (Croatina), which go together with Bonarda and Ughetta in the blended Rosso. The special categories of Buttafuoco and Sangue di Giuda are also of interest. But there are still producers growing for quantity and selling in bulk.

Barbera *r dr (fz) ☆→☆☆☆☆ 96 97 98 99 00 01 02* Whether drunk young, when its tannic robustness is inviting, or after 7 or 8 years, when it can develop bouquet and composure, this can rank highly with its counterparts in Piedmont.

Bonarda *r (dr) s/sw fz* ☆→☆☆☆ 98 99 00 01 02 Lively Uva rara epitomizes the fruity zest of Oltrepò reds. Usually light, sweetish, strawberry-like, and very drinkable, some styles are dryer, fuller, and age to give succulence with firmness, and great pleasure.

Buttafuoco *r dr (fz)* ☆→☆☆☆ 99 00 01 Colourfully named ("sparks like fire"), this inky, generous, dry, often bubbly wine can have distinctive personality from Valenti. Good after 3 to 4 years, or longer in particularly good vintages.

Cabernet Sauvignon *r dr* ☆→☆☆☆ 98 99 00 01 Fine quality examples increasingly seen.

Chardonnay *w dr (fz) (sp)* Varietal rapidly on the rise for both still and sparkling wines.

Cortese *w dr (fz) (sp)* ☆→☆☆ DYA Light, crisp wines, sometimes bubbly, from the variety making Piedmont's Gavi.

Malvasia *w dr s/sw fz sp* ☆→☆☆ DYA Bubbly Malvasia, dry or sweet, can be crisply refreshing.

Moscato *w s/sw sw fz sp* ☆☆ DYA Rare dessert wines, nearly always bubbly, occasionally match those of Asti. Also permitted are a *passito* from semi-dried grapes and a rare *liquoroso*, fortified, in both *secco* (semi-sweet) and *dolce naturale* (very sweet) versions with up to 22% alcohol.

Pinot Grigio *w dr (fz) (sp)* ☆☆ DYA Usually still, this can outclass Pinot Grigio from the Veneto. Colour ranges from light to coppery.

Pinot Nero *r (p) (w) dr (fz) (sp)* ☆→☆☆☆ 97 98 99 00 01 This name applies to red, still wines which can attain the class of middling burgundy, as well as pink and white wines, also fizzy and sparkling, made from at least 85% Pinot Nero topped up with Pinot Bianco or Chardonnay. Pinot Nero sparkling wines may be either tank-fermented or made by *metodo classico*. Age: *metodo classico* 18 months, *millesimato* 2 yrs.

Riesling Italico *w dr (fz)* ☆→☆☆ DYA Inconspicuous, simple whites of fresh tone.

Riesling Renano *w dr (fz)* ☆→☆☆ 98 99 00 01 02 Simple, light, and very drinkable. Few growers wrestle with this variety but those who do may achieve refined, steely, long-lived wines that recall Alsace.

Rosato *p dr (fz)* ☆→☆☆ DYA From the basic *rosso* grapes, this can be a zesty, cherry-hued rosé.

Rosso *r dr (fz)* ☆→☆☆☆☆ 95 96 97 98 99 00 01 02 Made in different styles from a blend in which the sinewy strength of Barbera is enveloped by the softer Uva rara and given added nuances by Bonarda and Ughetta. Some wines are fairly light and lively, others are in the medium range, but some are wines of impressive depth of character with *riservas* that last a decade or more. Also coming under the DOC is Barbacarlo, a fizzy red of character made exclusively by Lino Maga. Age: *riserva* 2 yrs.

Sangue di Giuda *r dr fz s/sw sw* ☆→☆☆ 99 00 01 Usually the fizziest of the Oltrepò reds, "Judas's Blood" is made in limited quantities from a restricted zone near Broni. Lively, soft, sometimes with a hint of sweetness, it is dominated by Uva rara. Best inside three years.

Sauvignon *w dr (sp)* ☆→☆☆ DYA Promising as a still white, less so as *spumante*.

Spumante Bianco or Rosato *w (p) dr sp* ☆☆→☆☆☆ Sparkling wines, only *metodo classico*, may be white or rosé, made from at least 70% Pinot Nero with up to 30% of white Pinots or Chardonnay. Age: 18 mths, *millesimato* 2 yrs.

SAN COLOMBANO AL LAMBRO OR SAN COLOMBANO

DOC r dr ☆→☆☆ 98 99 00 01 Hearty red from Barbera and Bonarda grown on the gentle rises around San Colombano southeast of Milan. Best in 2 to 4 years.

SANGUE DI GIUDA

See Oltrepo Pavese DOC.

SAN MARTINO DELLA BATTAGLIA

DOC w dr (am) (sw) ☆→☆☆ *DYA*
Tocai Friulano alone is the base for both a dry white and a sweet, amber *liquoroso* (of at least 16% alcohol) from a zone in the lower Garda basin around San Martino, a noted battle site.

SASSELLA

See Valtellina Superiore DOC.

SEBINO *IGT*

Reds from Cabernet Franc, Cabernet Sauvignon, Merlot, Pinot Nero; whites from Pinot Grigio and Riesling mostly used by producers in Terre di Franciacorta for wines that do not come under the DOC.

SFURSAT (OR SFURZAT, SFORZATO)

See Valtellina DOC.

SPUMANTE

Lombardy is a major producer of sparkling wine by both classical and Charmat methods, coming mainly from of Oltrepò Pavese from Pinot grapes (where DOC wines qualify under the name of Talento) and from Franciacorta (where DOCG covers wines from Chardonnay and Pinot grapes).

TERRE DI FRANCIACORTA *DOC*

This DOC covers the still white and red wines grown in the Franciacorta (*q.v.*) territory. They can be highly impressive, particularly those that carry the names of single vineyards although their frequently international styling does not suit some Italophiles. Other wines in the zone – particularly those from Cabernet Sauvignon, Merlot, and Pinot Nero – may be classified as Sebino IGT and can be impressive.

Bianco *w dr* ☆☆→☆☆☆ *98 00 01 02*
From Pinot Bianco and/or Chardonnay and/or Pinot Nero, this may be a pleasantly fruity white to drink young or an amply proportioned wood-aged wine that gains complexity with age. Standards in the zone are admirable, with some wines among the finest of Italy.

Rosso *r dr* ☆☆→☆☆☆☆ *98 99 00*
The bizarre but effective blend of Cabernet Franc/Cabernet/Merlot/ Barbera/Nebbio – accounts for a diversity of interesting styles, although some estates keep the proportions of the latter two varieties to their minimun (10% each) for a more "international" patina. Overall quality is high and value relatively good in a place where the concept of cheap no longer exists.

VALCALEPIO *DOC*

This hilly zone extends from the south shores of Lake Iseo west across much of Bergamo province. Promising quality in wines from French varieties.

Bianco *w dr* ☆→☆☆☆ *99 00 01*
From Pinot Bianco, Chardonnay, and Pinot Grigio, this is usually straw-yellow, delicate, dry, light, and good young, though some producers are making wines of more weight and complexity.

Rosso *r dr* ☆→☆☆☆ *97 98 99 00 01*
From Merlot and Cabernet Sauvignon, this is dark ruby with a dry, robust flavour and herb-like bouquet. Some wines show elegance after 2 to 5 years. Age: *riserva* 3 yrs.

VALGELLA

See Valtellina Superiore DOC.

VALTELLINA *DOC*

Dramatically scenic Alpine zone around Sondrio near the Swiss border. Praised since Roman times, Valtellina is one of the few places outside of Piedmont where the Nebbiolo variety (here called Chiavennasca) thrives, on south-facing slopes receiving reflected light and warmth from the Adda river. From a peak of 6 million bottles a year, second only to Barolo, production now only amounts to 4 million bottles a year.

After the collapse of the export boom in Switzerland at the beginning of the 1990s, wine-growing in Valtellina went through a serious crisis until winemakers invested massively in the high quality production, thus leading to a series of oustanding wines. Because of their quality, Valtellina is now in a position to reclaim its reputation as a producer at the top level.

Valtellina r dr ☆☆ 97 98 00 01 02 The basic Valtellina red can be made throughout the zone from at least 70% Nebbiolo, with other dark varieties permitted. It has a lively red colour, delicate scent, and somewhat tannic flavour. Good in 3 to 5 years.

Sforzato (or Sfursat) Di Valtellina DOCG r dr ☆☆→☆☆☆☆ 90 93 94 95 96 97 98 99 00 01 02 The names are dialect versions of the vinification process that semi-dries the Valtellina grapes to bring alcohol to a minimum of 14%. Ample in body, with a rich, ruby-garnet colour, it becomes warm and perfumed after 4 to 5 years and can age for a decade or more. It is considered by many as Valtellina's best wine. Age: 2 yr.

VALTELLINA SUPERIORE
DOCG r ☆☆→☆☆☆☆ 93 94 95 96 97 98 99 00 01 02

DOCG for four wines from sub-regions within Valtellina. All must contain at least 90% Nebbiolo. Though there are differences between them, basic traits are similar: ruby-red colour, which tends to garnet with age, the bouquet becoming complex and the dry, tannic taste more mellow and rounder (very good vintages will keep for a long time). First-class Valtellina has an ageing potential which compares favourably with that of Barolo and Barbaresco. Age: 2 yrs (1 in barrel); riserva 3 yrs.

Grumello The excellent region takes its name from the 13th century castle between Sondrio and Montagna.

Inferno This superbly positioned region is adjacent to Grumello to the east around Poggiridenti. Inferno is the hottest of the sub-districts but also weather-dependent, so not as good as Sassella and Grumello in some years but unequalled in the good ones.

Sassella Considered the best of the four, the stony-soiled zone lies west of Sondrio toward Castione Andevenno and makes powerful but refined wines.

Valgella Between towns of Chiuro and Teglio; most voluminous of the four.

Producers

Provinces: Bergamo (BG), Brescia (BS), Como (CO), Cremona (CR), Lodi (LO), Mantova (MN), Milano (MI), Pavia (PV), Sondrio (SO), Varese (VA).

Fratelli Agnes, Rovescala (PV). Oltrepò Uva rara in an array of styles.

Albani, Casteggio (PV). Top notch Oltrepò estate sensibly avoiding the temptation to produce innumerable labels – or over-oak. Impeccable, long-lived Rosso Vigna della Casona, exhilarating Rosso Costa del Morone, refined Riesling Renano and Pinot Nero, both for ageing.

Anteo, Rocca de' Giorgi (PV). Notable Oltrepò Pinot Nero: red and white

Cà del Oca, sparkling Brut Anteo, Anteo Nature.

Antica Cantina Fratta, Monticelli Brusati (BS). Franciacorta and Terre di Fanciacorta produced by Guido Berlucchi (q.v.).

Bellaria, Casteggio (PV). Low-cropping Barbera, Bonarda, Chardonnay, Cabernet Sauvignon, Merlot in Oltrepò.

Bellavista, Erbusco (BS). Vittorio Outstanding Franciacorta Cuvée Bellavista, Gran Cuvée Millesimato (brut, satèn, pas opéré, rosé), and Riserva Vittorio Moretti. Also perfectly honed Terre di Franciacorta Bianco (Uccellanda, Convento dell'Annunciata) and Rosso, IGT Rosso del Sebino, Solesine (Cabernet/ Merlot), and Casotte (Pinot Nero).

Fratelli Berlucchi, Borgonato di Cortefranca (BS). Fine range of Franciacorta. Good Terre di Franciacorta red and white.

Guido Berlucchi, Borgonato di Cortefranca (BS). Italy's largest *metodo classico* sparkling wine house (nearly 5 million bottles annually). Good quality but not made under the Franciacora DOCG.

Bersi Serlini, Prouaglio d'Iseo (BS). Good range of Franciacortas and red and white Terre.

Bonaldi-Cascina del Bosco, Sorisole (BG). Good red and white Valcalepio and IGT Cantoalto.

La Boscaiola, Cologne (BS). Emerging Franciacorta Brut, Terre red and white.

Ca' del Bosco, Erbusco (BS). Now a joint venture with Santa Margherita, there is an outstanding array of Franciacorta (brut, rosé, *satèn*, *dosage zero, brut millesimato*, and the superb Cuvée Anna Maria Clemente). Still wines earn similar praise: Terre di Franciacorta Chardonnay and Curtefranca Rosso and Bianco blends; Sebino IGT Pinèro (Pinot Nero) and Carmenèro (Carmenère) plus the signature red Maurizio Zanella (Cabernet Sauvignon/ Cabernet Franc/Merlot).

Tenuta Il Bosco, Zenevredo (PV). The large company here Zonin concentrates on sparkling and *frizzante* Oltrepò DOCs, to good effect.

Ca' di Frara, Mornico Losana (PV). Range of Oltrepò DOCs, including unusual late-harvest Pinot Grigio.

Ca' Lojera, Sirmione (BS). Lively Lugana (normal, oak-fermented superiore, Vigna Silva).

Ca' Montebello, Cigognola (PV). Large range of Oltrepò DOCs.

Cabanon, Godiasco (PV). Good range of Oltrepò DOC, especially Barbera.

Il Calepio, Castelli Calepio (BG). Valcalepio red and white sometimes eclipsed by brut and extra brut *metodo classico* sparklers.

Cascina La Pertica, Picedo di Polpenazze (BS). Emerging producer of Garda (*classico*) DOCs. Impressive Cabernet (Le Zalte) leads range.

Castel Faglia, Cazzago San Martino (BS). Sound Franciacorta; red and white Terre.

Castello di Luzzano, Rovescala (PV). Fine range of characterful, individualist Oltrepò DOCs from lands bordering Emilia.

Tenuta Castellino, Coccaglio (BS). Franciacorta Terre, fine brut, *satèn*.

Castelveder, Monticelli Brusati (BS). Franciacorta brut, extra brut, *millesimato*.

Cavalleri, Erbusco (BS). Beautifully refined Franciacorta (brut, *pas dosé, satèn*, Collezione Rosé, and the acclaimed Collezione Brut), together with Terre Bianco (Rampaneto, Seradina), Rosso (Tajardino), and IGT Sebino Corniole (Merlot).

Cola, Adro (BS). Franciacorta and Terre Bianco and Rosso.

Monzio Compagnoni, Cenate Sotto (BG). Valcalepio Bianco di Luna, *rosso* and *bianco* (Colle di Luna); IGT Rosso di Luna Moscato di Scanzo Passito Don Quijote. Further estate at Cortefranca for Franciacorta (brut, extra brut, *satèn*) and Terre white and red.

Contadi Castaldi, Adro (BS). Impressive and reasonably priced range of Franciacorta. Also Terre.

Cornaleto, Adro (BS). Distinguished Terre di Franciacorta, *bianco* (Saline), and *rosso* (Poligono). Also elegant Franciacorta.

La Cornasella, Grumello del Monte (BG). Valcalepio Rosso, Moscato di Scanzo (Rubente).

Costaripa, Moniga del Garda (BS). Garda Classico Rosso, Groppello, and, unusually, oaked *chiaretto* shine among others.

CS Bergamasco, San Paolo d'Aragon (BG). Reliable Valcalepio Rosso.

CS La Versa, Santa Maria della Versa (PV). Large Oltrepò co-op now revamping its huge range giving an exponential shift to the quality.

Ricci Curbastro, Capriolo (BS). Increasingly classy Franciacorta (*satèn*, extra brut, brut) and Terre red and white, plus Sebino IGT Pinot Nero.

Doria, Respected Oltrepò DOCs from Pinot Nero, Bonarda, Riesling, and others. Plus IGT "A.D." (Nebbiolo).

Lorenzo Faccoli, Coccaglio (BS). Textbook Franciacorta (brut, extra brut). Also Terre Bianco, Rosso.

Sandro Fay, San Giacomo di Teglio (SO). Modern Valtellina Superiore Sassella (Il Glicine) and Valgella (Ca' Moréi); Valtellina Sforzato (Ronco del Picchio).

La Ferghettina, Erbusco (BS). Franciacorta good Terre red and white, IGT Merlot, all at attractive prices.

Le Fracce, Casteggio (PV). Good Oltrepò DOCs, Bonarda, Pinot Grigio, Pinot Nero, Riesling Renano, and *rosso*.

Francesco Quaquarini, Canneto Pavese (PV). Easy-going Oltrepò Sangue di Giuda, Buttafuoco, Bonarda, Barbera.

Emilio Franzoni, Botticino (BS). Smallish estate but producing 80% of the rare Botticino DOC.

Fratelli Giorgi, Canneto Pavese (PV). Well-delineated spread of Oltrepò DOCs, including Buttafuoco, Sangue di Giuda.

Ca' dei Frati, Sirmione (BS). Inspired Lugana including long ageing Brolettino and sparkling Brut. Also Garda Chiaretto; IGT Benacco Bresciano, white Pratto, and excellent, sweet Tre Filer.

Frecciarossa, Casteggio (PV). Rapidly improving Otrepò DOCs, reliably good across the board.

Enrico Gatti, Erbusco (BS). Admired Franciacorta (brut, *satèn*) Terre Bianco, and Rosso, and Sebino IGT Gatti Rosso.

Guarischi, Cazzago San Martino (BS). Franciacorta Brut (Contessa Matilde Maggi), under the management of Antinori.

Giuseppe Vezzoli, Erbusco (BS). Brand new Franciacorta estate promising well.

Castello di Grumello, Grumello del Monte (BG). Variable Valcalepio Rosso (Colle del Calvario), IDT Chardonnay (Aurito) and others.

Isimbarda, Santa Giuletta (PV). Sound Oltrepò DOCs.

Longhi-De Carli, Erbusco (BS). Brut, *satèn* Franciacorta; Terre red and white.

Lino Maga, Broni (PV). Sole producer of Barbacarlo Oltrepò Rosso.

Majolini, Ome (BS). Fine range of Franciacortas led by Electo Brut. Terre Bianco (Ronchello) and Rosso (Dordaro, Ruc di Gnoc).

Mamete Prevostini, Mese (SO). Emerging Valtellina producer. Great Sforzato, good Superiore Sassella, Corte di Cama from part-dried grapes.

Marangona, Pozzolengo (BS). Carefully honed Garda Classico, Lugana.

Tenuta Mazzolino, Corvino San Quirico (PV). Large range of reliable Oltrepò varietals, topped by Pinot Nero.

Mirabella, Rodengo Saiano (BS). Franciacorta; red and white.

Monsupello, Torricella Verzate (PV). Comprehensive range of elegant Oltrepò DOCs.

Monte Cicogna, Moniga del Garda (BS). Garda Classico DOCs, rich IGT Malvasia Passita.

Monte Rossa, Cazzago San Martino (BS). All efforts, finely repaid, on Franciacorta: brut, *extra brut millesimato*, *satèn*, and especially *brut cabochon*.

Montelio, Codevilla (PV). Long-noted Oltrepò estate.

Monterucco, Cigognola (PV). Range of Oltrepò DOCs, including enjoyable Buttafuoco and Sangue di Giuda.

La Montina, Monticelli Brusati (BS). Improving Franciacorta and Terre.

Il Mosnel, Camignone di Passirano (BS). Re-emergent Franciacorta (brut, extra brut, *satèn*, *millesimato*); Terre.

Nino Negri, Chiuro (SO). Part of the Gruppo Italiano Vini. Stunning Valtellina Sfursat 5 Stelle, impressive Valtellina Superiore Inferno Sassella, Grumello, and Vigneto Fracia.

Nera, Chiuro (SO). Valtellina Superiore including *sfursat*.

Antonio Panigada, San Colombano al Lambro (MI). Rare San Colombano.

Mario Pasolini, Brescia. Fine IGT Ronco di Mompiano (Marzemino/Merlot) and Nebbiolo, Chardonnay, brut grown on lands on the edge of Brescia.

Pasini Produttori, Puegnago sul Garda (BS). Garda wines worth watching.

Tenuta Pegazzera, Casteggio (PV). Re-emerging estate with Oltrepò DOCs of individual style.

Provenza, Desenzano del Garda (BS). Lugana, from simple (Ca' Maiol) to oak-aged (Ca' Molin), to oak-fermented (Fabio Contato) and sparkling. Also Garda Classico Rosso (Fabio Contato).

Piccolo Bacco dei Quaroni, Montù Beccaria (PV). Oltrepò DOCs.

Carlo Pietrasanta, San Colombano al Lambro (MI). Rare San Colombano.

Barone Pizzini, Corte Franca (BS). Smartly styled Franciacorta (brut, extra brut, *satèn*), Terre red and white, Sebino San Carlo (Pinot Nero).

Premiovini, Brescia. Reliable wines from Italy's leading wine areas.

La Prendina, Monzambano (MN). Emerging line of Garda varietals.

Provenza, Rivoltella del Garda (BS). Lugana, Garda Classico, and IGTs.

Rainoldi, Chiuro (SO). Finely crafted Valtellina Superiore: Grumello, Sassella, *sfursat* (Fruitaio), modern Crespino.

Ronco Calino, Erbusco (BS). Promising Franciacorta and Terre.

Tenuta Roveglia, Pozzolengo (BS). Lugana (Vigna di Catullo).

Ruiz de Cardenas, Casteggio (PV). Individual Pinot Nero, Chardonnay, and sparklers from Oltrepò.

San Cristoforo, Erbusco (BS). Emerging Franciacorta Terre estate with admirable pricing.

Conti Sertoli Salis, Tirano (SO). Admired Valtellina Superiore, starry Sforzato.

Lo Sparviere, Monticelli Brusati (BS). Owned by the wife of Ugo Gussalli Beretta (of the gunmakers). Admired Franciacorta (brut, extra brut) Terre red and white.

Spia d'Italia, Lonato (BS). San Martino della Battaglia, Garda, and Garda Bresciano.

Stefano Spezia, Mariana Mantovana (MN). Tasty bottle-fermented Lambrusco and Ancellotta.

Travaglino, Calvignano (PV). Consistently sound Oltrepò DOCs, especially whites.

La Tordela, Torre de' Roveri (BG). Emerging Valcalepio estate.

Fratelli Triacca, Villa di Tirano (SO). Outstanding Valtellina, especially *sfursat*, Prestigio, and *superiore riserva*.

Uberti, Erbusco (BS). Good Terre white, exceptional Franciacorta (Brut Comari del Salem, Brut Francesco 1, extra brut, rosé, and the starry *satèn magnificentia*).

Vercesi del Castellazzo, Montù Beccaria (PV). Impressive red Oltrepò DOCs.

Bruno Verdi, Canneto Pavese (PV). Oltrepò DOCs including lively Buttafuoco and Sangue di Giuda, led by *rosso riserva* (Cavariola).

Villa, Monticelli Brusati (BS). Ever-improving Franciacorta (brut, extra brut, *satèn*, rosé, *demi-sec*, and extra dry cuvette), Terre red and white.

Visconti, Desenzano (BS). Lugana and Garda Classico.

Wine & Food

Natural opulence is reflected in Lombardy's multifarious diet. Milan, unavoidably, instigates food forms called "fast", "international", "*nouvelle*", but the city also has more fine "Italian" restaurants than any other. Gourmets still relish their *ossobuco*, *costoletta*, and *risotto alla milanese* in the city that deserves recognition as Italy's rice capital. The outlying seven provinces have so clung to tradition that Lombardian cooking is more accurately described as provincial than regional. Still, everybody eats veal, beef, pork, (though cuts and cooking differ) and cheese (besides blue-veined Gorgonzola there are Grana Padano to rival Parmigiano Reggiano, Stracchino, Taleggio, Robiola, and Bitto). Risotto reigns in the flatlands, polenta and pasta in the hills, though there is plenty of crossover. In Pavia, they eat frogs and snails, in Bergamo small birds, in Mantua pasta with pumpkin, in Cremona candied fruit with mustard. Perhaps the leading preserve of provincial cooking is the Valtellina around Sondrio where, among other nutritious eccentricities, buckwheat is used for pasta and polenta.

Wines to accompany each dish are suggested below in italics.
Bresaola Beef cured much as prosciutto and served in paper-thin slices. *Valtellina*
Busecca A richly flavoured Milanese tripe soup. *Terre di Franciacorta Rosso* or *Oltrepò Pavese Rosso*
Casonsei Ravioli of Brescia and Bergamo filled with sausage, cheese, and bread. *Valcalepio Rosso* or *Garda Chiaretto*
Cassoeula Various cuts of pork cooked with cabbage, celery, and

carrots and often served with polenta. *San Colombano*
Costoletta alla milanese Breaded veal cutlet with mashed potatoes. *Oltrepò Pinot Nero*
Ossobuco e risotto alla milanese Braised veal shank with saffron risotto, the pride of Milan. *Oltrepò Barbera*
Panettone Milan's dome-shaped Christmas cake. *Oltrepò Moscato*
Pizzoccheri Rustic buckwheat noodles served with boiled potatoes, cabbage, and melted cheese in the Valtellina. *Valtellina*, fairly young.
Polenta e osei alla bergamasca Polenta with small game birds cooked with butter and sage, a speciality. *Valcalepio Rosso*
Risotto alla certosina Risotto with freshwater prawns, frogs, perch, and vegetables, cooked in white wine. *Oltrepò Pinot Grigio*
Sciatt Fritters of buckwheat and white flour, bitto cheese and grappa. *Valtellina Sforzato*
Tortelli di zucca Pasta filled with pumpkin paste flavoured with Amaretto and nutmeg, served with butter and grated grana. *Lugana*
Vitello tonnato Veal fillet dressed with a tuna-flavoured cream sauce. *DOCG Franciacorta*

Restaurants

Recommended in or near wine zones:
Brescia-Franciacorta *Miramonti* at Caino; *Il Gambero* at Calvisano; *Il Priore* at Cazzago San Martino; *Miramonti l'Altro* at Concesio; *L'Albereta di Gualtiero* Marchesi at Erbusco; *Artigliere* at Gussago; *I Due* Roccoli and *Il Volto* at Iseo; *Osteria della Villetta* at Palazzolo sull'Oglio; *Due Colombe* at Rovato; *Ringo* at Travagliato.
Colli Morenici-Mantova *Dal Pescatore* at Canneto sull'Oglio; *Al Bersagliere* at Goito; *Trattoria dei Martini* at Mantova;

L'Ambasciata at Quistello.
Garda-Lugana *Cavallino* and *Esplanade* at Desenzano; *La Tortuga* at Gargnano del Garda; *Villa Fiordaliso* at Gardone; *Vecchia Lugana* at Lugana di Sirmione; *Capriccio* at Manerba del Garda.
Oltrepò Pavese *Vecchio Mulino* at Certosa di Pavia; *Al Pino* at Montescano; *Vecchia Pavia* at Pavia.
Valcalepio *Da Vittorio* and *Lio Pellegrini* at Bergamo; *Brughiera* at Villa d'Almè.
Valtellina *Al Cenacolo* at Chiavenna; *Sassella* at Grosio;

Osteria del Crotto at Madonna di Morbegno; *Sozzani* at Sondrio; *Lanterna Verde* at Villa di Chiavenna.

Trentino-Alto Adige *Trentino-Alto Adige*

The northernmost region of Italy, with its fragrant white wines and German-accented syllables, is sometimes compared with Alsace. They have vines in common – Riesling, Sylvaner, Pinot Blanc, Pinot Noir, Pinot Gris, and Muscat – and it is said that the Traminer variety, a superior clone of which became Gewürztraminer in Alsace, took its name from the Alto Adige village of Tramin. But analogies should not be overdrawn, for Trentino-Alto Adige has its own clear styles and a strong line in reds.

Trentino (the province of Trento or Trent) and Alto Adige (the more northerly province of Bolzano or Bozen, also known as the South Tyrol or Südtirol, bordering Austria) share a gorgeous region of Alps drained by the Adige River. The two provinces are, however, quite distinct with Alto Adige vaunting autonomous status and official Italian-German bilingualism, and there is little collaborative overlap among wine producers. Nevertheless, despite ethnic contrasts between Alto Adige's German-speaking citizens, who cling tenaciously to Austrian traditions, and the Italian-speaking majority the entire region is a model of

Wine Areas

1　Meranese di Collina
2　Valle Isareo
3　Valle Venosta
4　Valdadige
5　Santa Maddalena
6　Terlano
7　Colli di Bolzano
8　Teroldego
9　Sorni
10　Trento
11　Casteller

oenological efficiency with more than eighty per cent of the wine DOC and producers handling a multitude of grape varieties with aplomb.

Both Trentino and the Alto Adige produce notable amounts of the popular Pinot Grigio, Chardonnay, and Sauvignon, as well as Pinot Bianco and the sometimes (deliberately) understated Riesling and Müller-Thurgau. Gewürztraminer, Moscato, and Sylvaner can be enticingly perfumed and unexpectedly longlived. Trentino, which pioneered sparkling wine making by the classic method early in the century, has retained its leading position and these sparklers are now grouped under theTrento DOC. They are predominantly Chardonnay based and the extensive amounts of Chardonnay in Trentino's vineyards reflects the importance of this production.

Distinctive reds come from Alto Adige's indigenous Lagrein and Trentino's native Teroldego and Marzemino, which can be matched in class by Cabernet, Merlot, and, rarely, Pinot Nero. Some winemakers have even achieved a note of complexity with the pleasant but lightweight Schiava (Vernatsch).

The Tentino-Alto Adige paradox is that despite the leading role taken by its elegant, aromatic whites and the demand for them, the emphasis in output still remains on unexceptional reds, for which the region has long served as central Europe's bargain basement. Curiously, in South Tyrolean valleys so cramped for space that there should be no alternative to the quest for excellence, the dominant variety is the mundane Schiava. More positively, though, a large number of wine producers rate high quality over high yields and make the most of the cool Alpine slopes to extract refined reds and graceful whites that could rank with Europe's elite. Many of the best come from single vineyards, which even the dominant cooperative wineries now produce with exemplary style. Trentino-Alto Adige, with its towering Dolomites, glacier lakes, and Alpine forests is one of central Europe's favourite vacation spots. Millions of tourists a year cross the Brenner Pass from Austria or venture up from Milan, Venice, Verona, and Lake Garda to ski, climb, and relax amidst the beauty of Gothic and Romanesque villages nestled into green mountainsides. Wine is a major attraction. The Adige valley is traversed by wine roads in both provinces, leading to an imposing array of vineyards. Both provinces hold wine fairs that coincide in late April/early May: the Bozner Weinkost in Bolzano and the Mostra dei Vini Trentini in Trento. The South Tyrol's wines are displayed in the *Castel Mareccio/Maretsch* in Bolzano. Recommended shops are *Vinoteque Alois Lageder* at Bolzano, *Enoteca Zum Kuckuk* at Cermes, *Enoteca Johnson & Dipoli* at Egna/Neumarkt, and *Lunelli* at Trento.

Recent Vintages

2002 A difficult year in Trentino with poor weather making stringent selection essential but many fine wines nonetheless. Alto Adige escaped the rains and produced excellent wines.

2001 A very good year, though without reaching the excellence of 2000. Whites of good acidity and aroma, reds tending to elegance.

2000 Outstanding vintage with balanced, ripe, healthy grapes giving exceptional reds and excellent whites.

1999 Very good year in Alto Adige for white wines, while the reds in Trentino suffered rather as a result of rainy weather in the autumn. Good year for white wines in Trentino but rather bad for late varieties.

1998 Generally good year, though better for whites than late-harvested reds.

1997 Outstanding harvest for Cabernet, Merlot, Lagrein, Teroldego, also favourable for whites.

1996 Ample crop of generally good-quality whites and reds.

1995 Small crop, good to excellent for whites and reds, particularly Cabernet and Merlot.

1994 Though limited in size, quality was good to very good for whites and reds.

1993 Attractive whites, though sometimes lacking structure; mixed results with reds.

Notes on earlier vintages Earlier fine vintages: 90, 86, 85, 83, 82, 79, 76, 75, 74, 71, 70.

Wines

ALTO ADIGE/SUDTIROLER *DOC*

This blanket denomination covers all the classified wines of Alto Adige, except those of Caldaro (or Lago di Caldaro/Kalterersee) and Valdadige/Etschtaler, whose zones extend into Trentino. It embraces many wines from once independent DOCs that have been incorporated as sub-zones: Colli di Bolzano/Bozner Leiten, Meranese di Collina/Meraner Hugel, Santa Maddalena/St Magdalener, Terlano/Terlaner, and Valle Isarco/Eisacktaler, as well as the newer sub-zone of Val Venosta/Vinschgau. The comprehensive list includes reds, rosés, and whites, mostly dry but also sweet; and varietals, blends, and sparklers. Varietals must contain at least 95% of the grape named on the label.

Bianco *w dr s/sw DYA* Simple wines from at least two of Chardonnay, Pinot Bianco, and Pinot Grigio with, optionally more aromatic varieties. *Passito* (dried grape) versions also exist.

Cabernet *r dr* ☆☆→☆☆☆ *90 93 94 95 96 97 98 99 00 01 02* Cabernet Sauvignon and/or Cabernet Franc make appealing deep, ruby-coloured wines, whether light and fruity or ample and complex. The bigger wines can take from 4 to 10 years to mature as the early herbaceous traits soften. Cabernet Sauvignon alone is especially impressive, achieving some of northern Italy's highest standards of quality. Age: *riserva* 2 yrs.

Cabernet-Lagrein *r dr* ☆☆→☆☆☆ *95 96 97 98 99 00 01 02* The blend can give wines of distinction. Age: *riserva* 2 yrs.

Cabernet-Merlot *r dr* ☆☆→☆☆☆ *95 96 97 98 99 00 01 02* The blend of classic bordeaux varieties sometimes surpasses single varietals. Age: *riserva* 2 yrs.

Chardonnay *w dr (sp) (s/sw)* ☆☆→☆☆☆ *98 99 00 01 02* Some of Italy's best Chardonnay is made here, both in the popular fresh, young style, and with oak-aged complexity, some approaching burgundy standards with age. Sparkling versions may carry the name.

Lagrein Scuro/Dunkel *r w dr* ☆☆→☆☆☆ *90 93 94 95 96 97 98* Alto Adige's most distinctive native varietal can make a soft, easy beaujolais-style red or a powerful, dark, intricate wine for ageing up to a decade from certain vintages. Lagrein di Gries/Grieser Lagrein from the slopes of Gries near Bolzano is particularly prized.

Lagrein Rosato/Kretzer *p dr* ☆☆ *DYA* Sometimes delightful rosé from Lagrein. Cherry-pink, fragrant, and fruity, with balanced acidity.

Lagrein-Merlot *r dr* ☆☆→☆☆☆ *99 00 01 02* Effective blend bringing fleshy softness around a firm centre. Age: *riserva* 2 yrs.

Malvasia/Malvasier *r dr* ☆→☆☆ *DYA* Dark Malvasia makes a rare ruby-garnet wine, well scented, and generously mellow in youth.

Merlot *r dr* ☆☆→☆☆☆ *97 98 99 00 01 02* Deep ruby, usually soft, and finely scented with the flavour of herbs, whether drunk young or aged 3 to 6 years. Merlot from near Terlan and the slopes around Cortaccia can be first-rate. Age: *riserva* 2 yrs.

Merlot Rosato/Kretzer *p dr DYA* Varietal rosé can be pleasant.

Moscato Giallo/Goldenmuskateller *w (dr) sw ☆☆ DYA* Can be dry but more revered as a golden-yellow, aromatic, sweet but not cloying dessert wine, best young.

Moscato Rosa/Rosenmuskateller *r p s/sw ☆→☆☆☆ 97 98 99 00 01 02* This rare *amabile* can be as flowery and graceful as its pretty ruby-rose colour indicates. Young, it makes a charming sipping wine; with some age it gets smoother and more elegant but loses some of its exceptional fruity fragrance.

Müller-Thurgau or Riesling-Sylvaner *w dr ☆☆→☆☆☆ 00 01 02* Though the popular style is for attractively crisp wines to drink young, the variety can develop depth, fragrance, and tone with a little age.

Pinot Bianco/Weissburgunder *w dr (sp) ☆☆→☆☆☆ 99 00 01 02* Pinot Grigio and Chardonnay may win the popularity contests, but Pinot Bianco often shows more class, albeit somewhat understated. Convincing in *spumante* and young still wines, it can become even more impressive with age, retaining freshness for a decade or longer.

Pinot Grigio/Ruländer *w dr ☆→☆☆☆ 01 02* Though overtaxed due to demand, the variety can produce admirable wines here, with more backbone and lasting power than the flowery but fragile versions from other places. Usually pale in colour but some are lightly coppery.

Pinot Nero/Blauburgunder *r dr ☆→☆☆☆ 95 96 97 98 99 00 01 02* Rarely does the red from Pinot Nero completely fulfill expectations but producers are increasingly successful in producing mellow, fruity wines with a mid-ruby red colour and an aroma that develops a hint of mint after 2–3 years. Many are quite excellent. Good examples of this typical Blauburgunder are Laimburg.

Pinot Nero Rosato/Blauburgunder Kretzer *p dr (sp) ☆☆ DYA* Rosé; may be still or sparkling.

Pinot Nero Spumante *w dr sp ☆☆ DYA* Sparkling wine from Pinot Nero, vinified white.

Riesling Italico/Welschriesling *w dr ☆ DYA.*Unexceptional wine: little is made.

Riesling Renano/Rheinriesling *w dr ☆→☆☆☆ 00 01 02* The true Riesling is respected in Alto Adige in very dry, straw-green wines, fresh, fruity, and finely scented, which occasionally approach the nobility of Rieslings from Alsace and the Rhine.

Sauvignon *w dr ☆☆→☆☆☆ 00 01 02* Sauvignon Blanc is often classy, notably when from the sub-zone of Terlano. Usually light and dry, with delicate scents of herbs and gunflint, it can show depth and style with 3 to 5 years of age.

Schiava/Vernatsch *r dr ☆→☆☆☆ DYA* The popular family of vines makes light, almondy, garnet to cherry-hued wines to drink young and chilled.

Schiava Grigia/Grauvernatsch *r dr ☆→☆☆☆ 01 02* Schiava's promise lies in this superior sub-variety.

Spumante *w (p) dr sp ☆☆ 99 00 01 02* Sparkling wines from the Pinots and Chardonnay made by Charmat or *metodo classico*.

Sylvaner or Silvaner *w dr ☆→☆☆☆ 00 01 02* Though often light and simplistic, this variety can show style from high-altitude vineyards in wines that need 2 or 3 years or more to express their aromatic fruity qualities.

Traminer Aromatico/Gewürztraminer *w dr ☆☆→☆☆☆☆ 00 01 02* Usually delicately, rather than opulently, perfumed, lightly spicy, and with a fresh aroma. Best drunk young.

COLLI DI BOLZANO/BOZNER LEITEN

r dr ☆→☆☆ DYA Ordinary Schiava from the hills

around Bolzano, easygoing and
enjoyable when young.

MERANESE DI COLLINA/MERANER HUGEL

r dr ☆→☆☆ *DYA*

From Schiava grapes grown in the
hills surrounding the town of
Merano, this is light ruby red,
pleasantly fragrant, and easy
drinking, best when young and
chilled. That produced in the small
area of Contea may be called del
Bulgraviato/Burggräfler.

SANTA MADDALENA/ST MAGDALENER

r dr ☆→☆☆☆ *00 01 02*

Once considered the leading
wine of the region and still very
popular locally, it was overhyped
by Mussolini in 1941 as one of
the three great wines of Italy
(the others being Barolo and
Barbaresco). It is produced
from Schiava grapes grown on
hills that start just walking distance
from Bolzano. It is light red, with
the typical Schiava aroma of
almonds and violets. Dry, rounded,
often velvety with a pleasant, bitter
aftertaste, it reaches its peak after 1
to 2 years but can be kept for
longer. *Classico* comes from a small
heartland area around the village
of Santa Maddalena itself.

TERLANO/TERLANER

This Alto Adige sub-zone follows the
hills along the Adige, northwest and
southwest of Bolzano, comprises
eight different types of white wine.
Production is limited and is centred
around the towns of Terlano, Nalles,
and Andriano, where wines may be
referred to as *classico* (Klassisches
Ursprungsgebiet).

Terlano/Terlaner *w dr* ☆☆ *01 02*
Seductive, very drinkable wine,
made from Pinot Bianco and
Chardonnay with the optional
addition of other, aromatic, white
grape varieties. Pale yellow, fruity
with refreshing acidity.

Chardonnay *w dr* ☆☆→☆☆☆ *01 02*

Chardonnay shows its usual
class here.

Müller-Thurgau *w dr* ☆☆ *DYA* Small
production; lively, light, very
refreshing when young.

Pinot Bianco/Weissburgunder *w dr
(sp)* ☆☆→☆☆☆ Leading grape of
the region (with Chardonnay);
stands up proudly against its
fellow varieties.

Riesling Italico/Welschriesling *w dr*
☆→☆☆ *DYA* Good everyday wine,
sometimes with good style.

Riesling Renano/Rheinriesling *w dr*
☆☆ *DYA* Fruity, delicately fragrant
wine, straw-yellow-greenish and
exhibiting all the character of the
variety if in a light mould.

Sauvignon Blanc *w dr* ☆☆→☆☆☆☆
01 02 Only small amounts are
cultivated but results are good,
with its classic, *fumé* aroma and
fascinating fruity aftertaste.

Sylvaner or Silvaner *w dr* ☆☆ *DYA*
Does not achieve a high level here
but can be fragrant and ideal as an
everyday wine.

VALLE VENOSTA/VINSCHGAU

The high Val Venosta, stretching
west from the Adige River to the
Swiss border has only small
outcrops of vine growth but the
cool conditions produce steely
wines with fuity aromas. All the
wines come from one of nine
varietals, of which Riesling,
Gewürztraminer, and Pinot
Bianco are the most successful.

Chardonnay *w dr*

Kerner *w dr*

Müller-Thurgau *w dr*

Pinot Bianco/Weissburgunder *w dr*
☆☆→☆☆☆ *96 97 98 99 00 01 02*

Pinot Grigio/Rülander *w dr*

Pinot Nero/Blauburgunder *r dr* ☆☆
99 00 01 02

Riesling *w dr* ☆☆→☆☆☆☆ *98 99 00 01 02*

Schiava/Vernatsch *r dr*

Traminer Aromatico/Gewürztraminer
w dr ☆→☆☆☆ *99 00 01 02*

VALLE ISARCO/EISACKTALER

Sub-zone producing six varietal
whites and a generic red called

Klausner Leitacher, all grown at high altitude along the Isarco (Eisack) River northeast of Bolzano. The district of Bressanone (Brixen) may be cited on labels. This is Italy's most northerly DOC zone.

Klausner Leitacher *r dr* ☆☆ *DYA* This breezy red is usually based on Schiava (sometimes Portoghese, Lagrein, or Pinot Nero) and takes its name from the town of Chiusa (Klausen in German).

Müller-Thurgau *w dr* ☆☆→☆☆☆ *99 00 01 02* Smooth with a floral bouquet, good when drunk young, although many vintages develop a certain elegance when kept for 2 to 4 years and some wines are intensely aromatic.

Kerner *w dr* ☆☆ *01 02* Riesling/Schiava cross, making light, attractively scented whites.

Pinot Grigio/Ruländer *w dr* ☆☆ *01 02* Well-rounded wine with a delicate fragrance and a fresh taste.

Sylvaner or Silvaner *w dr* ☆☆→☆☆☆ *99 00 01 02* A very popular variety here, producing wines with more purity of style than anywhere else in Italy and as good as many from Franconia in Germany. Often enjoyed young and fresh, it can develop an opulent aroma and fullness if allowed to age.

Traminer Aromatico/Gewürztraminer *w dr* ☆☆ *99 00 01 02* Though similar in style to that of Termeno, here the wine develops a fresh aroma and a supple fragility when young.

Veltliner *w dr* ☆☆ *DYA* This wine (DOC only here is only produced in small amounts. It has a distinctive greenish shimmer and is light with a pleasantly fruity aroma and taste.

CABERNET

Cabernet Sauvignon and Franc are widely grown in the region, both for varietals and in blends with Merlot and other varieties. Much Cabernet in the past showed bitter, grassy traits. Now, improved techniques in cultivation and vinification, for instance in smaller

barrels, has resulted in wines which meet international standards.

CALDARO OR LAGO DI CALDARO/KALTERERSEE

DOC r dr ☆→☆☆☆ *00 01 02*
This is the Alto Adige's *Gemütlich* quaffing wine and is better known in German-speaking lands than in its native Italy. It is made in quantity (about 12 million litres a year) from Schiava sub-varieties Grossa, Gentile, and Grigia grown in an extensive area along the Adige valley as far south as Trento. Light garnet to almost pink, it has the noted Schiava grapey fragrance and unusually refreshing verve and fluidity with an almondy finish. It is best young – inside 2 or 3 years – and cool. Its name comes from the pretty lake southwest of Bolzano and wines produced around the lake may be called *classico* or, with 10.5% alcohol and some refinement, *classico superiore*. With 11% alcohol, it may be called *scelto* or *auslese*, suggesting it comes from late-harvested grapes (which it doesn't).

CASTELLER

DOC r p dr (s/sw) ☆→☆☆ *DYA*
Zesty everyday wine from Schiava, Merlot, and Lambrusco, with, optionally grown along the Adige from north of Trento south to the Veneto. Light ruby to bright pink, light, and dry or a touch *amabile* – drink inside two years. *Superiore* is a shade stronger.

CHARDONNAY

Chardonnay is highly fashionable in both Alto Adige and, especially, Trentino. Wines range from the popular light and fruity, to fairly full and mellow, to impressively rich, complex, oak-aged versions. Chardonnay also dominates the region's sparkling wines.

GEWÜRZTRAMINER OR TRAMINER AROMATICO

Named after the Alto Adige village of Termeno (Tramin), this variety makes perfumed whites, though it can be confused with the less noble Traminer.

INCROCIO MANZONI

A Riesling/Pinot Bianco cross sometimes used in Trentino in IGT varietals and blends.

KERNER

The vine, a cross of Riesling and Schiava, makes simple whites in the Alto Adige sub-zones Venosta and Valle d'Isarco.

LAGREIN

Admired variety of Bolzano used for red and rosé in various parts of the region – sometimes blended with Cabernet or Schiava.

LAMBRUSCO

Trentino's native and unique Lambrusco a Foglia Frastagliata figures in blends of Casteller and Valdadige Rosso DOC.

MALVASIA/MALVASIER

Dry red wine from dark Malvasia Nera is DOC under Alto Adige.

MARZEMINO

Native variety that thrives in the Vallagarina around Isera in Trentino for soft fruit-driven wines.

MERLOT

Seen in the region both as a varietal and blended with Cabernet.

MITTERBERG IGT

Non-DOC wines from the hills of Alto Adige will often come under this IGT.

MOSCATO/MUSKATELLER

Both Moscato Giallo (Goldenmuskateller) and Moscato Rosa (Rosenmuskateller) are highly regarded in Alto Adige and Trentino.

MÜLLER-THURGAU

Wines are lightly fragrant in Trentino, more penetrating on Alto Adige's higher sites.

NOSIOLA

This native variety is used for dry whites and as base of *vin santo* in Trentino.

PINOT BIANCO

Pinot Blanc, also known as Weissburgunder in Alto Adige, makes some of the region's finest and best ageing white wines. It also serves in blends with other Pinots and Chardonnay in sparkling wines.

PINOT GRIGIO

Pinot Gris, also known as Ruländer in Alto Adige, continues to enjoy unhindered popularity. Its white wines are often light and simple, but occasionally have notable class.

PINOT NERO

Pinot Noir, also known as Blauburgunder in Alto Adige gives reds that show impressive class at times. However, much can be anonymous. Also used in whites and rosés, especially sparkling.

RIESLING

Both Riesling Italico (Welschriesling) and the far superior Riesling Renano (Rheinriesling) are DOC under Alto Adige and Trentino.

SANTA MADDALENA/ST-MAGDALENER

See Alto Adige/Südtirol DOC.

SAUVIGNON BLANC

Sauvignon Blanc makes appealing varietal whites in both provinces, notably in the Alto Adige's Terlano area.

SCHIAVA/VERNATSCH

The dominant vine of Alto Adige, where it figures widely. It is also prominent in Trentino. The sub-variety Schiava Grigia (Grauvernatsch) produces wines with more stuffing than the usual light quaffers.

SORNI

See Trentino DOC.

SPUMANTE

Trentino and the Alto Adige are major producers of sparkling wines by both Charmat and *metodo classico*. The latter, based on Chardonnay (mainly) and Pinots, can rank along with Italy's finest. Alto Adige sparkling wines may come under the Alto Adige DOC. In Tentino they have their own DOC, Tento.

SYLVANER OR SILVANER

The chief varietal of Alto Adige's Valle Isarco.

TERLANO/TERLANER

See Alto Adige/Südtiroler DOC.

TEROLDEGO ROTALIANO

DOC r (p) dr ☆☆→☆☆☆☆ *95 96 97 98 99 00 01 02*
Native to the gravelly high plain of the Campo Rotaliano, where the Noce River joins the Adige between Mezzolombardo and San Michele all'Adige, this is one of the most distinctive reds of northern Italy. Though it is often impressive when youthful and richly fruity, the better wines need 6 or 7 years to reveal their full glory. Dark ruby to violet-red, full-bodied, robust, and slightly tannic, there are pleasantly bitter undertones and a splendid bouquet of flowers and berries. A vivacious *rosato* may also be found. *Superiore* and *riserva* must have at least 12% alcohol. Age: *riserva* 2 yrs.

TRAMINER

See Gewürztraminer.

TRENTINO *DOC*

The zone covers much of the vineyard territory of Trentino along the Adige, as well as the high Cembra area to its east and the more westerly Sarca valley north of Lake Garda. The DOC comprises mainly varietals, but there are also *bianco*, *rosato*, *rosso*, and *vin santo*, plus a sub-zone, Sorni, with white and red wines. Sweet, *vendemmia tardiva* (late-harvest) versions are permitted for each of the white varietals. These must be aged for at least 14 months.

Bianco *w dr* ☆☆→☆☆☆☆ *97 98 99 00 01 02* Based on Chardonnay and/or Pinot Bianco with, optional, small amounts of more aromatic white varieties some very fine wines of depth and style result, including a number fermetned in oak. Age: *riserva* 2 yrs.

Rosato or Kretzer *p dr* ☆→☆☆☆ *DYA* This is a light rosé from the likes of Schiava, Teroldego, and Lagrein.

Rosso *r dr* ☆→☆☆☆☆ *96 97 98 99 00 01 02* Numerous successful wines come from this blend of Cabernet Sauvignon and/or Franc with Merlot. Age: *riserva* 2 yrs.

Cabernet *r dr* ☆→☆☆ *96 97 98 99 00 01 02* These wines, from a Cabernet Sauvignon/Cabernet Franc blend can be distinctive and are now much better than those produced several years ago Age: *riserva* 2 yrs.

Cabernet Franc *r dr* ☆→☆☆ *97 98 99 00 01* Producers may specify this once dominant variety, but few do, preferring to label them simply as Cabernet. Age: *riserva* 2 yrs.

Cabernet Sauvignon *r dr* ☆☆→☆☆☆ *90 91 93 94 95 96 97 98 99 00 01 02* This shows more class than Cabernet Franc to which it is generally preferred. Age: *riserva* 2 yrs.

Chardonnay *w dr (sp)* ☆☆→☆☆☆☆ *97 98 99 00 01 02* Trentino's ruling white variety encompasses wines ranging from fresh and fruity to oaky and complex, sometimes with impressive depth of flavours. Age: *riserva* 2 yrs.

Lagrein Rosso *r dr* ☆☆ *97 98 99 00 01 02* At its best this can rival the Lagrein of Alto Adige. Age: *riserva* 2 yrs.

Lagrein Rosato *p dr* ☆☆ *DYA* An uncomplicated, tasty rosé.

Marzemino *r dr* ☆☆→☆☆☆ *99 00 01 02* This Trentino native can show beaujolais-like charm when young, though its full-bodied, grapey softness evolves towards a deeper, richer, almost aristocratic tone accented by an almondy bite after 2 to 3 years. The best wines traditionally came from Isera near Rovereto, though production covers much of the Vallagarina area. Age: *riserva* 2 yrs.

Merlot *r dr* ☆☆→☆☆☆ *97 98 99 00 01 02* New clones of Merlot have given considerable class and longevity to wines which were once also-rans. Age: *riserva* 2 yrs.

Moscato Giallo *w am s/sw sw* ☆☆ *DYA* The yellow Muscat makes lightly sweet to sweet wines usually at their fragrant best young; the richer *liquoroso* can take some age.

Moscato Rosa *p s/sw sw* ☆☆☆ *DYA* Flowery in fragrance and roseate in colour, this pink sweet wine rivals that of Alto Adige. The *liquoroso* can age a bit.

Müller-Thurgau *w dr* ☆☆→☆☆☆ *95 96 97 98* The potential of this variety is best realized on the province's highest vineyards notably in the Val di Cembra.

Nosiola *w dr* ☆☆→☆☆☆ *00 01 02* Distinguished native traditionally used for *vin santo*, it also makes an unusual, nutty, dry white with fruity aroma, smooth flavour, and an exhilaratingly bitter background.

Pinot Bianco *w dr* ☆☆→☆☆☆ *95 96 97 98 99 00 01 02* Pinot Bianco makes some of the province's classiest wines, refined, evenly balanced, and longlived. Yet Chardonnay remains the name that attracts. Age: *riserva* 2 yrs.

Pinot Grigio *w dr* ☆→☆☆☆ *DYA* This is rarely distinguished but often reliably sound.

Pinot Nero *r dr* ☆☆→☆☆☆ *97 98 99 00 01 02* Quality of the wines varies from decent to very good but continues to improve. Age: *riserva* 2 yrs.

Rebo *r dr* ☆☆ *00 01* This local cross of Marzemino and Merlot makes a softly vivacious red to drink young and fresh.

Riesling *w dr* ☆☆ *01 02* Riesling Renano, though rare here, can be tasty.

Riesling Italico *w dr* ☆ *DYA* Little evidence of worth.

Sauvignon Blanc *w dr* ☆→☆☆☆ *99 00 01 02* A choice few producers make Sauvignon Blanc that can stand among the finest of Italy.

Traminer Aromatico *w dr* ☆→☆☆☆ *99 00 01 02* Softly spicy wines where fruit often wins over perfume.

Vin Santo *am sw* ☆☆→☆☆☆ *90 91 93 94 95 96 97 98 99 00 01 02* This luscious golden to amber wine is made from Nosiola grapes grown in the Valle dei Laghi which undergo an extensive drying period, gaining a type of "noble rot". After ageing in small barrels this gives an exquisite bouquet and an intricate range of flavours although styles vary considerably from producer to producer. Age: 3 yrs.

TRENTO

DOC w p sp ☆☆→☆☆☆
Denomination for sparkling wines from Trentino made from any or all of Chardonnay, Pinto Bianco, Pinto Meunier, Pinto Nero. *Rosato* versions take their colour from the latter. The wines, almost invariably brut, made by the classical bottle-fermentation method, must age on their lees at least 15 months before being sold, 24 months for *millesimato* or vintage types and 36 months for *riserva*.

VALDADIGE/ETSCHTALER *DOC*

A strange DOC: blanketing much of Alto Adige and Trentino, and even further southward well into the Veneto, it would appear to be the home of the region's lower ranking wines. Yet it is often regarded highly locally, especially in Trentino, where most of the production is concentrated, so much so that a sub-zone, Terre dei Forti, has recently been created. This stretches over a long, narrow strip straddling the Adige in the southern Vallagarina, between Avio (in Trentino) and Rivoli (in Veneto). With two years of age

Terre dei Forti reds may
be *riserva*.

Bianco *w dr* ☆→☆☆ *01 02* Whites
based on any or all of Pinot Bianco,
Pinot Grigio, Müller-Thurgau,
and Chardonnay with, optionally,
Trebbiano, Nosiola, Sauvignon,
and/or Garganega.

Rosso *r dr* ☆→☆☆ *DYA* Schiava and/or
Lambrusco form the bulk (or the
entirety) of this blend, with any or
all of Merlot, Pinot Nero, Lagrein,
Teroldego, Cabernet Franc, and
Cabernet Sauvignon making up
the rest.

Rosato *p dr* ☆→☆☆ *DYA* Rosé with
the same choice of grapes as
the *rosso*.

Chardonnay *w dr* ☆→☆☆ *DYA*

Pinot Bianco *w dr (fr)* ☆→☆☆ *DYA*

Pinot Grigio *w dr* ☆→☆☆ *DYA*

Schiava *r dr* ☆→☆☆ *DYA*

Terre dei Forti Rosso Superiore *r dr*
Both Lambrusco and Merlot go
into this blend plus, optionally,
Cabernet Franc, Cabernet
Sauvignon, Lagrein, Teroldego.

Terre dei Forti Enantio *r dr* Enantio is
the local name for Trentino's
Lambrusco a Foglia Frastagliata.

Terre dei Forti Cabernet Franc *r dr*

**Terre dei Forti Cabernet
Sauvignon** *r dr*

Terre dei Forti Chardonnay *w dr*

Terre dei Forti Pinot Bianco *w dr*

Terre dei Forti Pinot Grigio *w dr*

Terre dei Forti Sauvignon *w dr*

VALLE ISARCO/EISACKTALER

See Alto Adige/Südtiroler DOC.

VIGNETI DELLE DOLOMITI

Most non-DOC Trentino wines
come under this IGT.

Producers

Producer lists are divided between
the Alto Adige and Trentino.

ALTO ADIGE

All Alto Adige producers are in the
province of Bolzano/Bozen. Town
names are given in Italian rather
than German. DOC zones and
wines are also in Italian (the German
names are given in the wine listings).
"AA" stands for Alto Adige. "K"
stands for *Kellereigenossenschaft*
(co-op cellar).

**Abbazia di Novacella/Stiftskellerei
Neustift**, Varna. Wines from
this landmark abbey set quality
standards in the Valle Isarco. Tautly
aromatic Sylvaner, Sauvignon, and
Gewürztraminer are matched by
fine Kerner, Pinot Grigio, Lagrein,
Pinot Nero, and Moscato Rosa.
The top wines are grouped in
the Praepositus line.

Brigl, Cornaiano. Good AA Caldaro,
Santa Maddalena, Sauvignon,
Lagrein Scuro.

Cantina Convento Muri Gries,
Bolzano. Situated above Bolzano
in Lagrein's heartland, this winery
naturally concentrates on AA

Lagrein Scuro (Abtei, Gries) and
rosato – to excellent effect.

Cantina H. Lun, Egna. Long-standing
winery making large numbers
of reliable AA varietals in three
lines, "basic", Sandbichler, and
the top Albertus.

**Cantina Produttori di Andriano/
K Andrian**, Andriano. Fine
range of organic AA varietals
led by Lagrein Scuro, Merlot,
Chardonnay, Gewürztraminer,
and Terlano Sauvignon.

**Cantina Produttori Bolzano/Kellerei
Bozen**, Bolzano. Formed from
the fusion of the Gries and Santa
Maddalena co-ops. Lagrein Scuro,
Moscato Ciallo, and Merlot top the
range from the former; Lagrein
Scuro (again), Sauvignon,
Cabernet, and, naturally, Santa
Maddalena from the latter.

Cantina Produttori Burggräfler,
Marlengo. Quality directed co-op
drawing from well-sited vineyards.

**Cantina Produttori Colterenzio/K
Schreckbichl**, Cornaiano. Leading
AA co-op with superb quality
throughout. Chardonnay (Cornell)
and Cabernet Sauvignon (Lafola)

stand over starry Pinot Bianco (Weisshaus), Gewürztraminer (Cornell), Lagrein (Cornell), Merlot (Cornell), Cabernet/Merlot (Cornelius), and more.

Cantina Produttori Cornaiano/K Girlan, Cornaiano. Reliably good AA varietals. Wines from selected vineyards carry the Premium label; top wines the select Art label.

Cantina Produttori Cortaccia/K Kurtatsch, Cortaccia. Excellent AA reds form Lagrein, Cabernet, Merlot; whites from Gewürztraminer, Sauvignon, all from well-sited vineyards.

Cantina Produttori di Merano/K Meran, Merano. Co-op with rapidly improving wines.

Cantina Produttori Nalles Niclara Magré/K Nals Entiklar Margreid, Nalles. AA Chardonnay, Pinot Grigio, Terlano Pinot Bianco lead the range from this impressive three-centre co-op.

Cantina Produttori San Michele Appiano/K St Michael Eppan, Appiano. Fabulous AA wines including superb Sauvignon, Lagrein, Gewürztraminer, Cabernet, Pinot Grigio, and Gewürztraminer *passito* (Comtess) all with the St Valentin label.

Cantina Produttori Terlano/K Terlan, Terlano. Long-admired selections of AA Terlano, led by Pinot Bianco, Sauvignon, Lagrein, and a long-aged Terlano blend.

Cantina Produttori Termeno/K Tramin, Termeno. Impressive AA wines led by fabulous Gewürztraminer (Nussbaumerhof).

Cantina Produttori Valle Isarco/K Eisacktaler, Chiusa. All Valle Isarco varietals are notable here.

Casòn Hirschprunn, Magrè. Alois Lageder's (*q.v.*) second estate for Mitterberg IGT blends Contest and Etelle (both based on Pinot Grigio, Chardonnay), and Casòn and Corolle (both based on Merlot and Cabernet).

Castello/Schloss Rametz, Merano. Historic estate makes numerous wines.

Castello/Schloss Schwanburg, Nalles. Good Terlano and varietals.

Peter Dipoli, Egna. Alto Adige's wine guru Dipoli makes just AA Sauvignon (Voglar) and Merlot–Cabernet Sauvignon (Yugum). Vineyards lie above Cortaccia.

Falkenstein, Naturno. Emerging Valle Venosta estate with good Pinot Bianco, Gewürztraminer, Riesling.

Franz Gojer Glögglhof, Bolzano. Excellent Santa Maddalena (Rondell) and AA Lagrein Scuro.

Graf Castel Sallegg Kuenburg, Caldaro. Softish Caldaro and AA varietals.

Graf Pfeil Weingut Kränzel, Cermes. Smart, reliable AA range produced near Merano.

R. Malojer Gummerhof, Bolzano. Red AA varietals lead here.

Franz Haas, Montagna. Consistently stylish, well-honed AA varietals led by Pinot Nero and Moscato Rosa.

Haderburg, Salorno. Hausmannhof and Stainhauser vineyards yield sound AA wines, especially the brut and pas dosé sparklers.

Hofstätter, Termeno. Renowned winery where Gewürztraminer and Pinot Nero lead an impeccable AA range.

Kettmeir, Caldaro. Reliable still and sparkling wines.

Köfererhof, Varna. Small, new Valle Isarco estate making waves with wines that are stylish and varietally intense throughout.

Kössler, Appiano. Good AA range led by notable *spumante classico* Praeclarus Brut and Noblesse.

Kuenhof, Bressanone. Fine, complex, long-ageing Valle Isarco whites.

Alois Lageder, Magrè. Large and influential house making archetypal AA wines in three lines: classic varietals, single-vineyard selections, and the flagship single-estate Pinto Nero, Chardonnay, and Cabernet Sauvignon.

Laimburg, Ora. Provincial agriculture school research centre makes sound AA varietals.

Manfred Nössing–Hoandlhof, Bressanone. Newish estate making refined AA Valle Isarco for ageing.

Karl Martini & Sohn, Cornaiano.
AA Lagrein Scuro, Caldaro.

Josephus Mayr, Cardano. AA Santa
Maddalena Lagrein and Cabernet
of notable class.

Thomas Mayr & Sohn, Bolzano.
Good AA Lagrein Scuro and
Santa Maddalena (Rumplerhof).

Georg Mumelter, Bolzano. AA Santa
Maddalena full of character.

Josef Niedermayr, Cornaiano. AA
Lagrein and IGT Aureus (*passito*
Chardonnay/Sauvignon) set the
pace here.

Ignaz Niedriest, Cornaiano.
Consistent class with AA
Sauvignon, Pinot Nero,
Riesling Renano, and Lagrein.

Prima & Nuova/Erste & Neue,
Caldaro. Admirable co-op
with good Caldaro and Puntay
AA selections.

Pfeifer Johannes, Bolzano. Rapidly
improving estate with fine AA
Lagrein Scuro in the lead.

Georg Ramoser, Bolzano. Good
Santa Maddalena, Merlot, and
Lagrein Scuro.

**Elena Walch-Castel Ringberg &
Kastelaz**, Termeno. Top
estate with impeccable AA
Gewürztraminer and exemplary
wines throughout including
intriguing newcomer AA
Bianco "Behind the Clouds".

Hans Rottensteiner, Bolzano. Fine
AA Lagrein Scuro, Santa
Maddalena (Premstallerhof);
intense, sweet Gewürztraminer.

Heinrich Rottensteiner, Bolzano.
Hand-crafted AA Santa Maddalena,
Lagrein Scuro.

Josef Sölva–Niklaserhof, Caldaro.
Small winery mostly successful
with AA Pinot Bianco, Sauvignon,
and other whites.

Stroblhof, Appiano. AA Pinot Bianco,
Gewürztraminer, and Pinot Nero
lead here.

Thurnhof, Bolzano. Good AA Moscato
Giallo, Lagrein Scuro, Cabernet,
and others.

Tiefenbrunner, Estate famed for
Feldmarschall, superbly pure-
toned, aromatic Müller-Thurgau

grown at 1,000 metres (3,280 feet)
high (and therefore IGT), also makes
excellent AA Gewürztraminer,
Moscato Rosa, Cabernet
Sauvignon, and Chardonnay
(all Linticlarus), and more.

Viticoltori Caldaro/K Kaltern, Caldaro.
Exemplary AA Caldaro Pfarrhof
and Campaner, Cabernet
Sauvignon both Pinot Nero and
passito Moscato Giallo.

Vivaldi, Meltina. Alto Adige's leading
sparkling wine producer: brut and
extra brut, blanc de blanc. The label
is Arunda in Aa, Vivaldi elsewhere.

Plattner-Tenuta Waldgries, Bolzano.
Classy AA Santa Maddalena
Classico, Lagrein Scuro,
Cabernet, Sauvignon, and
bianco passito (Peperum).

Clemens Waldthaler, Ora. Notable
Lagrein Scuro and Cabernet
from the Raut vineyards.

Baron Widmann, Cortaccia. Decent
range of AA varietals and blends.

Peter Zemmer-Kupelwieser, Cortina.
Two lines (Zemmer, Kupelwieser),
large number of AA varietals,
good throughout.

TRENTINO

All producers are in the province
of Trento. Unless otherwise
specified varietals come under
the Trentino DOC and IGTs under
Vigneti delle Dolomiti.

Abate Nero, Trento. Admired Trento
Brut, Extra Brut, and Brut Riserva.

Battistotti, Nomi. Admirable
Marzemino, both "standard" and
Verdini. Good Moscato Rosa.

Bolognani, Lavis. Good Nosiola,
Müller-Thurgau, Moscato Giallo.

La Cadalora, Ala. Decent varietals
from Vallagarina.

Cantina di Toblino, Sarche di
Calavino. Good *vino santo*.
Also Rebo, Nosiola, and others.

Cantina Rotaliana, Mezzolombardo.
Classy Teroldego Rotaliano
(Clesurae, Canevarie).

Castel Noarna, Nogaredo.
Impressive Cabernet (Romeo),
Nosiola, and Bianco di
Castelnuovo (4-grape blend).

Ca' Vit, Trento. Ca' Vit groups 13 co-ops that make and sell a major share of reasonably priced Trentino wines. Wines from individual vineyards, prefixed "Maso" are particularly interesting, along with Trento Brut (Graal), Lagrein Scuro, and Marzemino.

Cesarini Sforza, Trento. Specialists in DOC Trento and Charmat sparkling wines, owned by La Vis (*q.v.*).

Cesconi, Pressano di Lavis. Chardonnay, Pinot Grigio, Nosiola, Traminer, and Olivar (Chardonnay/ Pinot Bianco/Pinot Grigio) lead a range of weight and style.

Barone de Cles, Mezzolombardo. Distinctive Teroldego (Maso Scari).

Concilio Vini, Volano. Good value varietals, with Enantio (Lambrusco), and Mori Vecio red blend.

Conti Bossi Fedrigotti, Rovereto. Impressive Marzemino, Chardonnay, Pinot Grigio, Merlot, and red and white Fojaneghe blends.

Conti Martini, Mezzocorona. Refined, distinctive Teroldego Lagrein, Chardonnay, Pinot Bianco, and dry Moscato Giallo.

CS Isera, Isera. Notable Marzemino (Etichetta Verde).

CS di Nomi, Nomi. Good value wines.

Endrizzi, San Michele all'Adige. Rounded, fleshy Teroldego Rotaliano, Pinot Nero, Moscato Rosa, Nosiola Masetto red and white blends.

Equipe Trentina, Mezzolombardo. *Spumante* house admired for Trento Brut Equipe 5.

Giuseppe Fanti, Pressano di Lavis. Steadily improving wines led by Incrocio Manzono (IGT), Chardonnay, and Nosiola.

Ferrari, Trento. Leading sparkling wine house, with excellent Trento Classico, including outstanding Giulio Ferrari Riserva del Fondatore and brut, brut perlé, brut rosé, maximum brut.

Graziano Fontana, Faedo. Good Müller-Thurgau, Pinot Nero, and Lagrein.

Foradori, Mezzolombardo. Exemplary Teroldego Rotaliano (Morei,

Sgarzon, Cranato). Also refined, long-ageing Pinot Bianco and Pinot Bianco-based blend Myrto.

Fratelli Dorigati, Mezzocorona. Superb sparkler Trento Methius *Riserva*; stylish Teroldego Rotaliano (Diedri), plus good Rebo/Pinot Grigio. New Cabernet (Grener).

Fratelli Lunelli, Trento. Owners of Ferrari (*q.v.*) make impressive Chardonnay, Sauvignon, Pinot Nero, and Maso Le Viane (bordeaux-style blend).

Gaierhof, Roverè della Luna. Well-priced varietals led by Chardonnay and Müller-Thurgau.

Instituto Agrario Provinciale, San Michele all'Adige. Reliably good wines from school vineyards.

Letrari, Rovereto. Solid, reliable wines spanning a huge range, including Terra dei Forti Enantio.

Longariva, Rovereto. Fine Pinot Bianco (Pergole), Cabernet Sauvignon (Marognon), Chardonnay (Praistel), Merlot (Tovi), Pinot Grigio (Graminè).

Madonna della Vittoria, Arco. Steadily improving wines (notably Chardonnay, Pinot Grigio), and Trento Brut.

Marco Donati, Mezzocorona. Classy, individual Teroldego Rotaliano (Sangue del Drago, Bagolari) lead intriguing range.

Maso Bastie, Volano. New estate specializing in sweet and semi-sweet wines from dried grapes.

Maso Cantanghel, Civezzano. Exquisite Pinot Nero, Chardonnay (Vigna Piccola), Cabernet Sauvignon (Rosso di Pila), Merlot (Tajapreda), and Sauvignon (Solitaire).

Maso Furli, Lavis. Emerging estate with good Chardonnay, Sauvignon, Traminer Aromatico and bordeaux blend, Furli.

Maso Martis, Trento. Some still wines but mainly high-quality sparklers: Trento Brut, Brut Riserva, Brut Rosé.

Maso Poli, Pressano di Lavis. Classy Pinot Nero, Pinot Grigio, Chardonnay, and Trentino Sorni Bianco.

Maso Roveri, Avio. Enantio Terra dei Forti Riserva and others.

Le Meridiane, Trento. Sound range of varietals and Aresino IGT blends.

MezzaCorona, Mezzocorona. Large, reliable co-op Teroldego Rotaliano (Maioliche, Millesimato) and Trento Rotari Brut Riserva lead wide range of varietals.

Gino Pedrotti, Cavedine. Small family winery near Lake Garda specializing in *vino santo*.

Fratelli Pisoni, Sarche di Lasino. Vino Santo and Nosiola lead here.

Pojer & Sandri, Faedo. First class range of finely-toned wines: Müller-Thurgau, Chardonnay, Pinot Nero, Nosiola, Traminer Aromatico, IGT Bianco Fayè (Chardonnay/Pinot Bianco), Rosso Fayè (Cabernet/Merlot/Lagrein), and sweet Essenzia from a blend of botrytized late-harvested white grapes.

Francesco Poli, Santa Massenza di Vezzano. Unusual *vino santo*.

Giovanni Poli, Santa Massenza di Vezzano. Balanced *vino santo*.

Pravis, Lasino. Deep, modern-styled wines: Lagrein (Niergal), Nosiolo (Le Frate), Rebo (Rigotti), Cabernet (Fratagranda), Müller-Thurgau (St Thomà), Pinot Grigio (Polin), plus IGT Syrae (Syrah), and Stravino di Stravino (4-grape white blend).

Tenuta San Leonardo, Borghetto all'Adige. Just 4 grapes: Merlot, Cabernet Sauvignon, Cabernet Franc, Carmenère, and three wines: Merlot, Villa Gresh (mainly Merlot), and San Leonardo (bordeaux blend), all extremely powerful and longlived.

Alessandro Secchi, Ala. Good red varietals and bordeaux blend Corindone.

Armando Simoncelli, Admired range led by Marzemino Pinot Bianco, Lagein, and Rosso Navesel.

Enrico Spagnolli, Isera. Worthy range led by Marzemino, Pinot Nero, and Traminer Aromatico.

De Tarczal, Isera. Winning Marzemino d'Isera (Husar), admired Cabernet/ Merlot blend Pragiara, and more.

Vallarom, Avio. Noted viticultural expert Attilo Scienza and family make studied wines, including Cabernet Sauvignon, Pinot Nero, Chardonnay (Vigna Brioni), and white blend Vadum Caesaris.

Vallis Agri, Calliano. Convincing Marzemino (Vigna Fornas, Vigna dei Ziresi), Merlot, Pinot Grigio lead.

La Vis, Lavis. High ranking co-op with incisive varietal character across the board, especially with leading Ritratti range. Excellent Ritratti Bianco and Rosso, too.

Zeni, San Michele all'Adige. Fine, impressive Teroldego Rotaliano (I Plini), good Pinot Nero, Müller-Thurgau, Tento Brut, Pinot Bianco (Sorti), and more.

Wine & Food

The cooking of Trentino and the Alto Adige derives from distinct heritages, one Italo-Venetian, the other Austro-Tyrolean, but the intermingling of peoples drawing on shared resources along the Adige Valley has taken the sharp edges off the contrasts. Something akin to a regional style of cooking has emerged. True, the Italian-speaking population still relies more heavily on polenta, gnocchi, and pasta, the German-speaking on *wurst*, black bread, and soups.

But the fare found in *ristoranti* and *Gasthäuser* here has been enriched by the points in common. The *Knödel*, for example, has become *canederli* in Italian and savoured just as avidly. The same can be said for *sauerkraut* or *crauti*. Game, trout, *speck* (smoked pork flank), and Viennese-style pastries are further evidence of a unity of taste that makes the long hours spent at table in the warm, wood-panelled *Stuben* so enjoyable.

Wines to accompany each dish
are suggested below in italics.
Biroldi con crauti Blood
sausages with chestnuts, nutmeg,
and cinnamon, served with
sauerkraut. Marzemino
Blau Forelle Alpine trout boiled
with white wine and flavourings.
Pinot Bianco or *Veltliner*
Leberknödelsuppe Bread
dumplings flavoured with calf's liver
and herbs served in broth. *Caldaro*
Carne salata Beef marinated with
herbs and spices, served with
polenta and beans. *Teroldego,* young
Gemsenfleisch Chamois cooked
Tyrolean-style with red wine
vinegar and served with polenta.
Lagrein Dunkel

Gerstensuppe Barley soup
with bacon, onions, and, celery.
Meranese di Collina
Gröstl Beef, potatoes, and
onions, cooked together in
a mould. *Pinot Nero*
Krapfen Tirolese Fried pastry
with marmalade and powdered
sugar. *Moscato Rosa*
Säuresuppe Flavoursome
tripe soup traditionally eaten
mid-morning on market days.
Colli di Bolzano
Smacafa Buckwheat cake
with sausages, onion, lard,
and cheese. *Merlot*
Speck Smoked pork flank
sliced onto black bread.
Santa Maddalena

Restaurants

Recommended in the region:
Alto Adige *Zur Rose* at
Appiano/Eppan; *Vögele* at
Bolzano/Bozen; *L'Elefante* at
Bressanone/Brixen; *Marklhof* at
Cornaiano/Ghirlan; *Gasthaus Zur
Rose* at Cortaccia/Kurtatsch;
Enoteca Johnson & Dipoli at
Egna/Neumarkt; *Würstlhof* at
Laives/Leifers; *Flora and Sissi* at
Merano/Meran; *Pichler* at Rio di
Pusteria/Mühlbach; *Berghotel*

Zirmerhof at Redagno/Radein;
Rosa Alpina and *La Siriola* at San
Cassiano/St Kassian; *Steinbock* at
Villandro/Villanders; *Zum Löwen*
at Tesimo/Tisen.
Trentino *Il Cantuccio* at Cavalese;
Maso Cantanghel at Civezzano;
Al Sole at Mezzolombardo; *Malga
Panna* at Moena; *Mezzosoldo* at
Mortaso; *Al Borgo* at Rovereto;
Chiesa and *Le Due Spade* at
Trento; *Fior di Roccia* at Vezzano.

Veneto *Veneto*

Venice's region is a verdant land of vines that flourish in hills and plains
as northern Italy's most abundant source of wine. The region ranks third
nationally, after Puglia and Sicily, in volume of wine produced, but has no
rivals in DOC(G) output with about a quarter of Italy's total. Two-thirds of
that comes from the province of Verona, where the famous trio of Soave,
Valpolicella, and Bardolino are complemented by Bianco di Custoza,
Lugana, the extensive Garda, and the new Arcole.

The large Veronese producers, after decades of talking quality but selling
cheap-and-cheerful worldwide have now become more truly quality-
directed and the wines, most notably Soave and Valpolicella, show far more
distinct character. Indeed, after years of wrangling over the degree of
severity to impose, Soave Superiore has finally been upgraded to DOCG,
following close on the heels of Bardolino Superiore. Verona's flagship wine
is Amarone della Valpolicella, a strong, powerful red of uniquely dynamic
dimensions. But the revival is bringing new class to all the traditional
Veronese wines which, creditably, remain predominantly based on native

vines. Yet Verona by no means stands alone in a region whose range of wines is as remarkable as the array of vines they come from.

The central hills around Vicenza and Padova (Padua) boast an eclectic mix of native and foreign varieties in wines from the DOC zones of Gambellera, Lessini Durello, Breganze, Colli Berici, Colli Euganei, Merlara, and Bagnoli. The Prosecco grape, grown on the steep hills between Conegliano and Valdobbiadene makes lightly and fully sparkling wines that have become far and away Italy's favourite. There are also some lighly characterful still wines from DOC Colli di Conegliano in the same area. The province of Venezia extends northeast along the Adriatic across the DOC zones of Piave and Lison-Pramaggiore, bountiful sources of Merlot and Cabernet. The Pinots, Sauvignon Blanc, and increasingly Chardonnay thrive here too, alongside such native varieties as white Verduzzo and Tocai, and red Raboso.

The Veneto's twenty-five DOC(G)s include five that extend into adjacent regions: Lison-Pramaggiore (shared with Friuli-Venezia Giulia), Valdadige (Trentino-Alto Adige), Garda, Lugana, and San Martino della Battaglia (Lombardy). There are also a good ten IGT areas contained wholly or partly within the region.

Visitors who wander into Venice's hinterland in quest of wine food, will also find a heritage of art, architecture and history amid inspiring landscapes. Vinitaly, held each April in Verona, is the nation's premier wine fair. Wine roads lead through Verona's hills, as well as through Breganze, the Piave valley, and the splendid Trevigiani hills of the

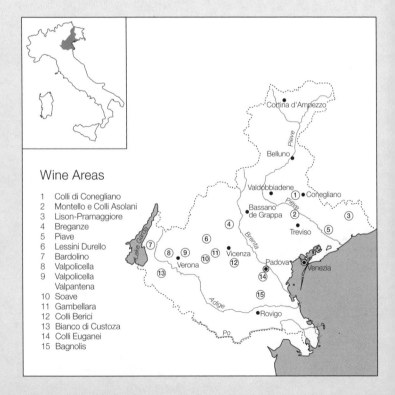

Wine Areas

1   Colli di Conegliano
2   Montello e Colli Asolani
3   Lison-Pramaggiore
4   Breganze
5   Piave
6   Lessini Durello
7   Bardolino
8   Valpolicella
9   Valpolicella
    Valpantena
10 Soave
11 Gambellara
12 Colli Berici
13 Bianco di Custoza
14 Colli Euganei
15 Bagnolis

Prosecco zone northwest of Treviso. A local habit that is easy to take to is calling at a bar for a small, reviving glass of wine, called an *ombra*, at any time of day. Impressive wine shops include *Bei Leo* and *La Caneva* at Jesolo, *Tastevin* at Mirano, *Enoteca Angelo Rasi* in Padua, *Enoteca Regionale Veneto* at Pramaggiore, *Mario Rossi* in Treviso, *Al Volto* at Venice, *Bottega del Vino,* and *Istituto Enologico Italiano* in Verona.

Recent Vintages

Most wines are designed to be drunk young in a region where whites account for more than seventy-five per cent of production. Certain Cabernets, Merlots, and other reds of the eastern Veneto age well. Verona's sweet Recioto della Valpolicella often improves with time, and its dry counterpart, Amarone, is one of the world's great wines for ageing. Some sturdy Valpolicella can age well, too, as can Custoza, Lugana, Soave Classico, and Recioto di Soave.

2002 A rainy late summer with hailstorms led to great variability. However, most producers picked the healthiest grapes and thereby gained fine quality.
2001 A good year throughout the region but without the quality peaks of 2000.
2000 Excellent vintage for white and red wines in the whole of the Veneto. Poor weather after the vintage compromised some Amarone.
1999 Showers in mid-September affected the quality of certain grape varieties (especially Pinot Grigio) while the reds are satisfactory to good.
1998 Large crop; mixed quality, harmed by hail and harvest rains.
1997 Reduced crop of excellent quality, superb year for Amarone.
1996 Abundant harvest, good to very good through the region.
1995 Fine year in general; grapes of exceptional concentration made what some are calling the vintage of the century for Amarone.
Notes on earlier vintages Earlier good vintages for Amarone: 90, 88, 86, 85, 83, 79, 76, 74, 71, 70, 67, 64.

Wines

AMARONE DELLA VALPOLICELLA
See Valpolicella DOC.

ARCOLE *DOC*
New zone for wines produced from silty, sandy soild in an area straddling Verona and Vicenza provinces.
Bianco *w dr (sp)* Garganega and others.
Rosso *r dr (fr)* Merlot and others. Also Novello.
Cabernet *r dr* Franc and/or Sauvignon and/or Carmenère. Age: *riserva* 2yrs
Cabernet Sauvignon *r dr* Age: *riserva* 2yrs
Chardonnay *w dr (fr)*
Garganega *w dr*
Merlot *r dr* Age: *riserva* 2yrs
Pinot Bianco *w dr*
Pinot Grigio *w dr*

BAGNOLI/BAGNOLI DI SOPRA
DOC
Wines from 15 provinces in the plains between Padova and Rovigo. Wines from the commune of Bagnolidi Sopra itself may be called *classico*.
Bianco *w dr* Chardonnay blended with Tocai Friulano, Sauvignon, and others.
Rosato *p dr* Mainly Raboso with Merlot.
Rosso *r dr* Red from Merlot, Cabernet, Raboso, and others. Age: *riserva* 2 yrs.
Cabernet *r dr* Cabernet Sauvignon and/or Franc and/or Carmenère. Age: *riserva* 2 yrs.
Friularo *r dr sw* Red from Raboso Piave. There is also a *vendemmia tardiva* (late-harvest) version. Age: *riserva* 2 yrs.

Merlot *r dr* Age: *riserva* 2 yrs.
Passito *r s/sw* Sweetish red based on Raboso. Age: 2 yrs.
Spumante *w p dr sp* Raboso with Chardonnay; vinified as white or pink sparkling wine.

BARDOLINO

DOC r p dr (sp) ☆→☆☆☆ *98 00 01 02*
Light red and rosé wines from Corvina, Rondinella, Molinara, and Negrara grown on southeast shores of Lake Garda, most noted in *classico* zone around town of Bardolino. Red Bardolino is grapey, dry, and fragrant, sometimes with a hint of prickle and light bitter undertone – to drink in 1 to 4 years. There is also a popular *novello* version. Bardolino Chiaretto, cherry-pink, is lighter, more fragile, for early drinking. It may also be *spumante*.

BARDOLINO SUPERIORE

DOCG r dr ☆☆→☆☆☆ *98 99 00 01 02*
From the same grapes as Bardolino DOC, with a lower maximum yield, higher minimum alcohol, and at least 1 year's ageing, producers' hopes are on this new classification to heighten Bardolino's image.

BIANCO DI CUSTOZA

DOC w dr (sp) ☆→☆☆ *00 001 02*
White wine of the class to match good Soave Lake Garda and overlapping part of Bardolino. From a blend based on Trebbiano Toscano, Garganega, and Tocai, it is classically pale and flowery, with clean, dry, softly fruity lines but crisp finish, although more structured, longer-lived versions are now emerging. A *spumante*, usually Charmat, is also seen.

BREGANZE *DOC*

The glacial moraine of this zone north of Vicenza is well suited to vines. *Superiore* versions have a slightly higher alcohol content.
Bianco *w dr* ☆→☆☆ *DYA* Based on the Tocai Friulano variety, this is a pale lemon-yellow wine, delicate in scent, smooth, and buoyantly good when young.
Rosso *r dr* ☆→☆☆☆ *99 00 01 02* Based on Merlot, this dominant Breganze wine is ruby-red in colour, grapey, and nicely rounded with a hint of tannin. Age: *riserva* 2 yrs.
Cabernet *r dr* ☆☆→☆☆☆ *97 98 99 00 01 02* From Cabernet Franc, Cabernet Sauvignon, and/or Carmenère, this is usually a good, sturdy red and can be excellent. Age: *riserva* 2 yrs.
Cabernet Sauvignon *r dr* ☆☆→☆☆☆☆ *95 96 97 98 00 01 02* Pure Cabernet Sauvignon can match the blended types. Age: *riserva* 2 yrs.
Chardonnay *w dr* ☆☆→☆☆☆ *98 00 01 02* Both light and floral and more forceful oaked versions are seen.
Marzemino *r dr* A welcome sighting of this variety outside of its native Trentino. Age: *riserva* 2 yrs.
Pinot Bianco *w dr* ☆☆→☆☆☆ *00 01 02* Light straw-green, fresh, and fruity, this can develop silky texture and flowery fragrance over 2 to 3 years.
Pinot Grigio *w dr* ☆→☆☆ *DYA* A hint of copper in its pale, straw colour, it is lithe and smooth.
Pinot Nero *r dr* ☆→☆☆ *98 99 00 01 02* Light ruby, fruity, and dry with light bitter undertone, it can be tasty. Age: *riserva* 2 yrs.
Sauvignon *w dr* ☆→☆☆☆ *00 01 02* Fresh and fruity with a flinty quality, can develop fragrance over 2 to 3 years.
Torcolato *am s/sw* ☆☆→☆☆☆☆ *95 96 97 98 99 00 01 02* From semi-dried Vespaiolo, this may be lightly or fully sweet. At its best it is opulent when young, developing a mellow warmth over 6 to 8 years, with a clear golden colour, flowery aroma, good balance, and a long, clean finish. Age: *riserva* 2 yrs.
Vespaiolo *w dr* ☆☆ *DYA* The local variety makes a bright straw-yellow, brisk, almost lemony white, with a hint of almond underneath.

CARTIZZE OR SUPERIORE DI CARTIZZE

See Prosecco di Conegliano-Valdobbiadene.

COLLI BERICI DOC

Hills adjacent to Vicenza were more noted for wine historically than today. The zone can give characterful wines yet they often lack style.

Cabernet *r dr* ☆→☆☆☆ 99 00 01 02 From Cabernet Franc and/or Cabernet Sauvignon, this bright ruby-garnet wine can reveal a rich herby bouquet. Age: *riserva* 3 yrs.

Chardonnay *w dr* ☆→☆☆ DYA The style is usually light and fruity.

Garganega *w dr* ☆→☆☆ DYA Pale yellow, subtly scented, the light, brisk, almondy traits of the zone's popular white can be attractive when young.

Merlot *r dr* ☆→☆☆☆ 98 99 00 01 02 Fruity, full-bodied, and soft, the better examples have enough stuff to show well for 4 to 5 years.

Pinot Bianco *w dr* ☆→☆☆ DYA Pale greenish-yellow and flowery, its dry, smooth flavour has a zesty bite.

Sauvignon *w dr* ☆→☆☆ DYA Pale with distinct varietal scent, refreshing, gun-flint qualities.

Tocai Italico *w dr* ☆ DYA Pale lemon-yellow, lightweight.

Tocai Rosso *r dr* ☆→☆☆☆ DYA This dark Tocai (a strain of Grenache) thrives here as a brilliant ruby-crimson wine, grapey with a hint of liquorice and a cleansing tannic bite, refreshing when young.

Spumante *w dr sp* ☆→☆☆ DYA At least 50% Garganega; can be refreshing.

COLLI DI CONEGLIANO DOC

The highly popular Prosecco is complemented, locally at least, by these still wines from a similar but slightly more extensive area around Conegliano, north of Treviso.

Bianco *w dr* ☆→☆☆ DYA From Incrocio Manzoni 6.0.13 (a Riesling/Pinot Bianco cross), Pinot Bianco and/or Chardonnay, and, optionally, a little Sauvignon and/or Riesling.

Rosso *r dr* ☆→☆☆☆ 99 00 01 02 Marzemino, Merlot, and Cabernet, this can show depth and style with 3 to 4 years of ageing. Age: 2 yrs.

Refrontolo Passito *r s/sw sw* ☆☆ 95 96 97 98 01 02 From the small sub-zone of Refrontolo, northwest of Conegliano, this curious but tasty sweet red from partly dried Marzemino grapes.

Torchiato di Fregona *w dr sw* ☆☆ 00 01 A sub-zone in the north of the area making sweet and dry *passito* wines from Prosecco and the obscure Verdiso and Boschera.

COLLI EUGANEI DOC

The dramatic hills rising from between the Brenta and Adige Rivers south of Padua have been noted for wine since Roman times. Now, after a postwar lull, interest has been revived once more.

Bianco *w dr (sp)* ☆→☆☆☆ DYA From Garganega, Prosecco, and others, this straw-yellow wine is fruity in scent with a dry, soft flavour, best young. Also bubbly.

Rosso *r dr* ☆→☆☆☆ 97 98 99 00 01 02 Based on Merlot with Cabernet, Barbera, and Raboso, this singular red has a fresh, grapey bouquet, sturdy structure, and mellow flavour that can improve for 3 to 6 years. A *novello* version may be seen. Age: *riserva* 2 yrs.

Cabernet *r dr* ☆→☆☆☆ 97 98 99 00 01 02 From Cabernet Sauvignon and/or Franc, this is tasty when young, taking on some style with age. Age: *riserva* 2 yrs.

Cabernet Franc *r dr* ☆→☆☆ 98 99 00 01 02 This is noted for a mellow, somewhat bittersweet taste of plums and herbs. Age: *riserva* 2 yrs.

Cabernet Sauvignon *r dr* ☆→☆☆☆ 97 98 99 00 01 02 This is often classier than Cabernet Franc. Age: *riserva* 2 yrs.

Chardonnay *w dr (sp)* ☆→☆☆ DYA Usually light and dry, although oaked versions have appeared here too, sometimes sparkling.

Fior d'Arancio *w am s/sw sw (sp)* ☆→☆☆ DYA From a strain of Moscato called Fior d'Arancio (orange blossom), this has enticing sweetness and sometimes a sparkle. The *passito* version is richer and smoother.

Merlot *r dr* ☆→☆☆☆ 98 99 00 01 02
Although much is grapey and soft, for drinking young, it can develop a full bouquet and rich, complex flavours. Age: *riserva* 2 yrs.

Moscato *w s/sw sw (sp)* ☆→☆☆
DYA From Moscato Bianco, this golden wine has an attractive aromatic sweetness, whether still or bubbly.

Pinello *w d (fz)* ☆→☆☆ *DYA* Pinella or Pinello, a local variety, makes a soft white, sometimes fizzy.

Pinot Bianco *w dr* ☆→☆☆☆ 98 99 00 01
Does well here as a white that can show real class.

Serprino *w dr fz* ☆→☆☆ *DYA* The local name for Prosecco, which some say originated here, applies to a soft but sprightly white, usually bubbly.

Tocai Italico *w dr* ☆→☆☆ *DYA* This zesty white is usually dry and fleetingly youthful.

GAMBELLARA
DOC w dr ☆→☆☆ *DYA*
This zone is, in effect, the eastward continuation of Soave into Vicenza province and its wine. Also made from Garganega with Trebbiano, is all too similar to its neighbour. Light straw-gold, somewhat fruity in scent, its dry, balanced softness has a hint of acidity on the finish. *Classico* applies to wines from the heartland commune of Gambellara.

Gambellara Recioto *w sw sp* ☆☆ *DYA*
From slightly raisined grapes, this golden dessert wine is intense in aroma and flavour, usually *frizzante* or *spumante*.

Gambellara Vin Santo *am sw* ☆→☆☆
A rarity from semi-dried grapes. After ageing in barrel it is amber, aromatic, sweet, and smooth. Age: 2 yrs.

GARDA
See Lombardy.

MONTI LESSINI OR LESSINI
DOC
Once restricted to wines from the local Durella variety, producers in the Lessini uplands in the provinces of Verona and Vicenza now have more flexibility under this DOC.

Bianco *w dr* From at least 50% Chardonnay with any or all of Pinot Bianco, Pinot Grigio, Pinot Nero, and Sauvignon.

Cabernet Franc *r dr* From at least 50% Merlot with any or all of Pinot Nero, Corvina, Cabernet, Carmenère. Age: *riserva* 3 yrs.

Durello *w dr (s/sw) (sw) sp* The rare Durella grape produces steely dry or, more usually, sparkling wine. Semi-sweet or sweet versions from dried grapes may sometimes be seen.

Spumante *w p dr sp* Whether white or rosé (Pinot Noir giving the colour), the character comes from Chardonnay.

LISON-PRAMAGGIORE *DOC*
Zone extending through the eastern Veneto's alluvial plains into Friuli.

Bianco *w dr* ☆☆ *DYA* Fresh white mainly from Tocai.

Cabernet *r dr* ☆→☆☆ 99 00 01 02
Cabernet Sauvignon and Cabernet Franc combine in warm, somewhat tannic reds. Age: *riserva* 2 yrs.

Cabernet Franc *r dr* ☆ 00 01 02 Style occasionally rises above the everday. Plain. Age: *riserva* 3 yrs.

Cabernet Sauvignon *r dr* ☆→☆☆ 99 00 01 02 Infrequently seen despite the cachet of the name. Age: *riserva* 2 yrs.

Chardonnay *w dr fr (sp)* ☆→☆☆ 00 01 02 As reliable here as everywhere else.

Malbech *r dr* 99 00 01 02 The Malbec variety is only occasionally seen.

Merlot *r dr (p)* ☆→☆☆ 99 00 01 02
Can have a grapey robustness when young, fleshing out over 2 to 4 years. Sometimes made as a rosé. Age: *riserva* 2 yrs.

Pinot Bianco *w dr (sp) (fr)* ☆→☆☆ *DYA* Light, fresh, and fruity.

Pinot Grigio *w dr (sp)* ☆→☆☆ *DYA* Soft, easy, and fruity.

Refosco dal Peduncolo Rosso *r dr*
☆→☆☆☆ 99 00 01 02 Performs
as well as in the plains of
neighbouring Friuli.

Riesling *w dr DYA* From
Riesling Renano.

Riesling Italico *w dr (sp) DYA*

Sauvignon *w dr* ☆☆ 00 01 02
Wines of style now emerging.

Tocai Italico or Tocai or Lison *w dr*
☆→☆☆ *DYA* Can be called *classico*
if grown around the town of
Lison. Can be fresh and clean
with character.

Verduzzo *w dr (fr) (sw)* ☆ *DYA* Usually
bone-dry with a bite, it can be
zesty in summer.

LUGANA

Partially situated in the Veneto.
See Lombardy.

MERLARA *DOC*

Wines from fertile soils straddling
the Verona/Padova provincial
border were often sold on until
the development of this DOC in
2000. The *Cantina Sociale* controls
most production.

Bianco *w dr (fr)* Predominantly from
Tocai Friulano.

Rosso *r dr* From Merlot with Cabernet
and/or Marzemino this juicy red is
sometimes *novello*.

Cabernet *r dr*

Cabernet Sauvignon *r dr*

Malvasia *w dr*

Merlot *r dr*

Tocai *w dr*

MONTELLO E COLLI ASOLANI
DOC

The zone covering two ranges
of hills across of the Piave from
Conegliano is noted for Palladian
villas as much as for wine. The
Prosecco here rivals, but rarely
matches, that from the more
famous zone across the river, but
Merlot and, increasingly, Cabernet
are bringing it regard, although
they are not often seen. Age:
superiore 2 yrs for all the reds.

Cabernet *r dr* ☆→☆☆

Cabernet Franc *r dr* ☆→☆☆

Cabernet Sauvignon *r dr* ☆→☆☆

Chardonnay *w dr (sp)* ☆→☆☆

Merlot *r dr* ☆→☆☆☆

Pinot Bianco *w dr (sp)* ☆→☆☆

Pinot Grigio *w dr* ☆→☆☆

Prosecco *w dr s/sw fz sp* ☆→☆☆

Rosso *r dr* ☆→☆☆ From Merlot
and Cabernet.

Oseleta Rare red grape now gradually
being revived.

PIAVE OR VINI DEL PIAVE *DOC*

Large zone on either side of the
Piave River, extending from the
edge of Treviso's hills through
the alluvial plains north of Venice.
Wines are rarely outstanding but
increasingly make for enjoyable,
rewarding drinking.

Cabernet *r dr* ☆→☆☆ 99 00 01
Cabernet Franc and/or Sauvignon
make a robust ruby to garnet wine
with bouquet and flavour gaining
style over 3 to 6 years. Age: *riserva*
2 yrs.

Cabernet Sauvignon *r dr* ☆→☆☆ 98 00
01 Supple wines of promise. Age:
riserva 2 yrs.

Chardonnay *w dr* ☆→☆☆ 00 01 Potential
is far more often being realized.

Merlot *r dr* ☆→☆☆ 00 01 02 Piave is a
major source of Merlot from plain
to delicious. Age: *riserva* 2 yrs.

Pinot Bianco *w dr* ☆☆ *DYA* Clean, fresh,
and attractive.

Pinot Grigio *w dr* ☆→☆☆ *DYA* Fair to
good, if light.

Pinot Nero *r dr* ☆ *DYA* Out of place here.

Raboso *r dr* ☆→☆☆☆ 99 00 01 02 Noted
for its warm, rich, tannic wines that
need time to mellow and develop
bouquet. Age: 3 yrs.

Tocai Italico *w dr* ☆→☆☆ *DYA* Pale and
delicate, this can develop some tone.

Verduzzo *w dr* ☆ *DYA* A pale-green
lightweight, it can be snappily
fresh when young.

PROSECCO DI CONEGLIANO-
VALDOBBIADENE

DOC w dr s/sw sw fz sp ☆→☆☆☆ *DYA*
The Prosecco grape variety, grown
on the steep hills north of the Piave

River, between Conegliano and Valdobbiadene, makes wines that range between dry, semi-dry, and sweet; and still, lightly sparkling, and fully sparkling. It is, though, probably at its finest and most seductive when it is refreshingly young and has just a hint of sweetness and just a tingle of sparkle. Yet ever more frequently, serious, dry, fully sparkling versions are emerging to fulfill increasing demand as it becomes Italy's favourite apéritif. It is pale white to light golden, with a hint of almond in its fruity scent and soft, round flavour. Labels may carrry the name of both or just one or other of the towns. There is also a small inner area near Valdobbiadene known as Cartizze or Superiore di Cartizze, which is reputed to produce wines with the greatest finesse. But this is not always the case, especially since they are often unbalanced by sweetness. **NB**: in common with all sparkling wines made in the European Union, brut means dry and extra brut bone dry, but extra dry means lightly sweet and dry fairly sweet.

RECIOTO

The name, possibly derived from from the ancient wine called Retico or from the dialect word *recia* for the "ear" of the grape bunches, is applied to wines from grapes dried on racks or mats after the harvest. The process, used mainly for sweet wines, may also be applied to dry, as for Amarone della Valpolicella.

RECIOTO DI SOAVE

DOCG w am sw ☆☆→☆☆☆☆ *95 96 97 98 00 01*
This prized dessert wine from semi-dried grapes comes from the same zone and the same varieties as for Soave. The wine is light-golden to amber and, after 2 to 3 years of ageing, moderately strong (14%), with an aroma of currants and, in particularly good years, of botrytis; supple, full-bodied, and

sweet. There is also an increasingly rare *spumante* version (best avoided). The *classico* zone is the same as for Soave.

SAN MARTINO DELLA BATTAGLIA

Only particularly in Veneto. *See* under Lombardy.

SOAVE

DOC w dr (sp) ☆→☆☆☆☆ *00 01 02*
Soave remains one of Italy's most popular whites: light, fresh, fruity, consistent, and affordable, and remains its third most voluminous classified wine after chianti and Asti. Much Soave, made from Garganega with up to 30% of Trebbiano di Soave (a characterful variety not related to the bland Trebbiano Toscano), and/or Chardonnay, and/or Pinot Bianco, comes from vineyards in the plains where personality is not easily achieved. But Soave Classico, from the hills between Soave and Montcforte d'Alpone, has far more to offer, sometimes with depth of character and ageing potential that may be described as noble. A *spumante* version is also made, mainly for local consumption. *See also* Recioto di Soave, Soave Superiore.

SOAVE SUPERIORE

DOCG w dr ☆☆→☆☆☆☆ *01 02*
The rehabilitation of Soave from attractive but forgettable to a wine of class that impresses has been taken one stage further with DOCG for *superiore* versions with lower yield (70 as against 100 hectolitres per hectare/2.47 acres) and higher alcohol (12% compared with 10.5%). There is also a *Riserva* category for wines with 2 years ageing, which mainly embraces oak-fermented Soave. Grape varieties and the *classico* zone are as for Soave DOC.

VALDADIGE

One part of this DOC is in the Veneto. *See* under Trentino-Alto Adige.

· VALPOLICELLA

DOC r dr ☆☆→☆☆☆☆ *97 98 99 00 01 02*

The DOC status covers the ordinary red wine, which is easy to drink, the more robust *superiore*, the powerful, dry Amarone, and the rare sweet Recioto, all deriving mainly from Corvina, Rondinella, and Molinara grapes grown in the last wave of Alpine foothills north of the Adige River's eastward trail through Verona province. Valpolicella's grape make-up mimics Bardolino but it is sturdier, deeper, and usually longer-lived, even in its lighter versions. Regular Valpolicella is an all-purpose wine of ruby to purple hue, solid to plump body, with a cherry-like aroma and flavour, and a light bitter finish. Usually, ordinary Valpolicella tastes best young, between 6 months and 3 years, and those from the best producers and with higher proportions of Corvina show traits that approach refinement. Some age well beyond, most notably those enriched by the process of *ripasso*, a refermentation with the pomace of Amarone, which gives greater weight and complexity. The full zone stretches east almost to Soave but the best wines come from the more westerly *classico* zone, northwest of Verona, notably around Gargagnano, Marano, Negrar, Fumane, and San Pietro in Cariano. Including Amarone and Recioto, Valpolicella is usually fourth behind Chianti, Asti, and Soave in DOC production. Age: *superiore* 1 yr.

AMARONE DELLA VALPOLICELLA

r dr ☆☆→☆☆☆☆ *83 85 88 90 95 97 98 01*

An important variant of Valpolicella coming from grapes, preferably Corvina, dried on racks for an average of 3 months after the harvest to concentrate flavours then fermented (almost) to dryness to give a powerful, strong wine that yet can achieve burgundy-like allure. It can age for 20 years or longer, gaining enormous finesse and complexity; however, many prefer it younger when its lively fruitiness is still intact. Age: 2 yrs.

RECIOTO DELLA VALPOLICELLA

r s/sw sw (sp) ☆☆→☆☆☆☆ *95 97 98 01*

The term applies to wines made from semi-dried grapes, as for Amarone, but those that are (semi-) sweet, not dry. The classic Recioto dessert wine is deep purple tending to garnet-red, with ample bouquet and structure. Rich, strong (minimum 14%), with a concentrated, semi-sweet flavour and a bitter aftertaste, it may be a little pulpy when young but becomes smoother with age. There is also an extremely rare *spumante* version.

VALPANTENA

Unfortunately this was declared a Valpolicella sub-zone although the wine's best grapes usually come from elsewhere. However it is rarely cited on labels.

VICENZA *DOC*

An umbrella DOC covering the wines of Vicenza province which do not come under its other DOCs (Gambellara, Breganze, Colli Berici, Monte Lessini, Arcole). Age: *riserva* 2 yrs (applies to all reds).

Bianco *w dr (fr) (sp) (sw)* From at least 50% Garganega. May be *passito*.

Rosso *r dr* From at least 50% Merlot. May be *Novello*.

Rosato *dr (sw) (fz)* From at least 50% Merlot.

Cabernet *r dr* From Cabernet Franc and/or Sauvignon, and/or Carmenère.

Cabernet Sauvignon *r dr*

Chardonnay *w dr (sp)*

Garganego *w dr (sp) (sw)* From Garganega.

Manzoni Bianco *w dr*

Merlot *r dr*

Moscato *w s/sw sw (sp)*

Pinot Bianco *w dr (sp)*
Pinot Grigio *w dr*
Pinot Nero *r dr*
Raboso *r dr*
Riesling *w dr* From Riesling Italico and/or Renano.

Sauvignon *w dr*
Wildbacher Native grape which gives punchy, structured wines with brambly fruitiness and a slightly rustic finish.

Producers

Provinces: Belluno (BL), Padova (PD), Rovigo (RO), Treviso (TV), Venezia (VE), Verona (VR), Vicenza (VI). "V" stands for Valdobbiadene; "C" stands for Conegliano.

Accordini Stefano, Pedemonte (VR). DOC full, firm, refined Valpolicella (Acinatico), Amarone (Il Fornetto), Recioto.

Adami, Colbertaldo di Vidor (TV). Excellent series of Prosecco di V.

Allegrini, Fumane (VR). Lively, youthful Valpolicella; impressive Amarone, and 100% Corvina IGT La Poja.

Andreola Orsola, Col San Martino (TV). Good Prosecco di V, including Cartizzc.

Anselmi, Monteforte d'Alpone (VR). Famed for skilled use of oak on the Soave grapes. Capitel Foscarini, Capitel Croce, Recioto I, Capitelli all excel.

Armani, Dolcè (VR). Red from unique Foja Tonda on vineyards close to river Adige, near Trentino border. Also Terre dei Forti varietals, Corvara (Corvina/Cabernet/Merlot), and more.

Baltieri, Mizzole (VR). Promising Valpolicella, Amarone, Recioto.

Bepin de Eto, San Pietro di Feletto (TV). Notable Colli di Bianco (Il Greccio) and Rosso (Croda Ronca). Also Prosecco di V, Passito Faé.

Bertani, Negrar (VR). Long-standing house noted for Valpolicella Classico and Valpantena (Secco-Bertani), Soave, Bardolino, and especially famous for its old, cask-aged Amarone. Also white IGT Le Lave (Garganega/Chardonnay), red IGT Ripasso Catullo (Corvina/Cabernet), and admired Villa Novare (Cabernet Sauvignon).

La Biancara, Gambellara (VI). Impeccable Gambellara (La Sassaia) and Recioto.

Bolla, Verona. The house known worldwide for Soave Classico DOC (also Castellaro, Vigneti di Froscà), also makes noted Valpolicella Classico (Jago), Amarone, IGT Creso, and Chardonnay.

Borin, Monselice (PD). Emerging Colli Euganei estate.

Bortolin, Valdobbiadene (TV). Impressive Prosecco di V Brut, Cartizze.

Bortolomiol, Valdobbiadene (TV). Reliable Prosecco di V.

Paolo Boscaini & Figli, Marano (VR). Good range of Valpolicella and Amarone (Ca' de Loi, Marano) and others.

Bosco del Merlo, Anone Veneto (VE). Promising Lison-Pramaggiore wines.

Brigaldara, San Floriano (VR). Exceptional Amarone, good Valpolicella, Recioto.

Luigi Brunelli, San Pietro in Cariano (VR). Montecchia di Crosara.

Tommaso Bussola, Negrar (VR). Superb Recioto, very good Valpolicella, Amarone.

Ca' La Bionda, Marano (VR). Rapidly improving Valpolicella, Amarone, Recioto.

Ca' Lustra, Faedo di Cinto (PD). Colli Euganei Pinot Bianco, Cabernet, Chardonnay, Merlot, and Moscato Fior d'Arancio of notable quality and reasonable price.

Ca' Rugate, (VR). Leading Amarone (Campo del Titari). Good Valpolicella, Recioto. Superb Soave (Bucciato) and others.

Canevel, Valdobbiadene (TV). Attractive range of Prosecco di V.

Cantina del Castello, Soave (VR). Leading Soave (Monte Pressoni, Monte Carniga). Also Recioto.

La Cappuccina, Monteforte d'Alpone (VR). Beautiful Soave (San Brizio, Fontégo), Arzimo Passito, Campo Buri (Cabernet).

Carpenè Malvolti, Conegliano (TV). Pioneers of sparkling wine in the Veneto continue with respected range of Proseccodi C; MC *spumante* Carpenè Malvolti Brut.

Michele Castellani, Valgatara di Marano (VR). Highly esteemed Recioto and Amarone from Casalin I Castei and Ca' del Pipa vineyards. Good Valpolicella. All *classico*.

Castello di Roncade, Roncade (TV). Convincing range of Piave varietals and IGT Villa Giustinian blend.

Cavalchina, Custoza (VR). Excellent Bianco di Custoza, Bardolino, and Garda Merlot, and Cabernet Sauvignon.

Domenico Cavazza, Montebello (VI). A leading light in Colli Berici with Cabernet, Merlot, Pinot Bianco, and in Gambellara, also with Recioto.

Coffele, Soave (VR). Promising Soave Classico Superiore, Recioto.

Col de Salici, Valdobbiadene (TV). Stylish Prosecco di V, notably the elegant extra dry.

Le Colture, Valdobbiadene (TV). High quality Prosecco di V Brut, dry (Cruner), Cartizze, and non-sparkling Masarè.

Col Vetoraz, Santo Stefano di Valdobbiadene (TV). Finely honed Prosecco di V. (brut, extra dry, dry, frizzante, Cartizze, still).

Conte Collalto, Susegana (TV). Good Prosecco di C Brut, Extra Dry, Colli di C Rosso and Bianco, Piave Cabernet, Chardonnay, as well as IGT Colli Trevigiani varietals including white Incrocio Manzoni 6.0.13, red Incrocio Manzoni 2.15, and rare red Wildbacher.

Conte Loredan-Gasparini, Volpago del Montello (TV). Historic Venegazzù estate makes Montello e Colli Asolani varietals *spumante* mc Loredan Gasparini Brut; red IGT Bordeaux-style blends: Venegazzù della Casa and Capo di Stato.

Corte Gardoni, Valeggio sul Mincio (VR). Stylish Bardolino (including Chiaretto), Custoza, and sweet Garganega-based Fenili.

Corte Ruglin, Valgatara di Marano (VR). Up-and-coming Valpolicella Classico estate.

Corte Sant'Alda, Mezzane di Sotto (VR). Excellent Valpolicella and Amarone (Mithas).

CS di Soave, Soave (VR). Enormous production of decent Soave and others.

CS della Valpantena, Quinto di Verona (VR). Prime source of wines from the Valpantena sub-zone of Valpolicella.

CS della Valpolicella, Negrar (VR). Quality conscious co-op selects Amarone, Recioto (Domini Veneti), Valpolicella Classico, and Soave by site.

Desiderio Bisol e Figli, Valdobbiadene (TV). Reliable range of fine Prosecco di V.

Fasoli, Colognola ai Colli (VR). Rapidly improving Soave and IGT Merlot from organic vineyards.

Fattori & Graney, Monteforte d'Alpone (VR). Impressive Soave Classico, Superiore, and Recioto (Motto Piane).

De Faveri, Vidor (TV). Range of Prosecco di V with personality.

Aleardo Ferrari, Gargagnago (VR). Valpolicella Classico, Amarone, and Recioto.

Il Filò delle Vigne, Baone (PD). Emerging Colli Euganei estate.

Foss Marai, Valdobbiadone (TV). Fine range of Prosecco di V.

Le Fraghe, Cavaion (VR). Fresh Bardolino, attractive Camporengo Garganega, Valdadige Quaiave (Cabernet-based blend). Valdadige and Pinot Grigio Valdadige.

Nino Franco, Valdobbiadene (TV). Distinctive range of Prosecco di V includes brut, dry, Cartizze, old-style *rustico*, and *tranquillo* (still).

Fratelli Degani, Valgatara di Marano (VR). Admired Amarone, Recioto, and Valpolicella Classico.

Giacomo Montresor, Verona (VR).
Large winery with broad range
of decent Verona DOCs and IGTs.

Gini, Monteforte d'Alpone (VR). Soave
Classico (La Froscà, Contrada
Salverenza), and Recioto (Col
Foscarin, Renobilis) of personality.

Giuseppe Campagnola, Valgatara di
Marano (VR). Large, re-invigorated
winery for major Verona DOCs
especially all Valpolicella types.

Gorgo, Sommacampagna (VR).
Lively Bardolino and Bianco
di Custoza (Ca' Nova).

Gregoletto, Premaor di Miane (TV).
Irresistibly refreshing Prosecco di C
Attractive Colle di C, IGT Merlot.

Gruppo Italiano Vini, Calmasino (VR).
GIV, which produces 65 million
bottles is Italy's largest wine group.

Guerrieri-Rizzardi, Bardolino (VR).
Highly refined Bardolino Classico
(Fontis Vinae Munus, Tacchetto),
plus IGTs Castello Guerrieri (red
and white), and white Biacco San
Pietro, Dogoli. Also holdings in
Soave, Valpolicella, and Valdadige
Terra dei Forti.

Inama, San Bonifacio (VR).
Highly renowned Soave
Classico (Vigneti di Foscarino,
Vigneto du Lot, Vin Soave).
Also remarkable IGT Sauvignon
Vulcaia including a rich Fumé
and a late-harvest Aprés. Fine
IGT Cabernet, Chardonnay, too.

La Cappuccina, Costalunga di
Monteforte (VR). Elegance and
style mark out both the range
of 4 Soaves and the IGTs
from Sauvignon and Cabernet.

Lamberti, Lazise (VR). Owned by
Gruppo Italiano Vini cellars.
Huge production of all the
major Verona DOC(G)s.

La Montecchia, Selvazzano Dentro
(PD). Reliably elegant wines from
Colli Euganei.

Le Bellerive-Angelo Ruggeri,
Santo Stefano di Valdobbiadene
(TV). Good Prosecco di V in the
sweeter styles.

Lorenzo Begali, San Pietro in Cariano
(VR). Acclaimed Recioto and
Amarone (Monte Ca' Bianca).

Luigino Dal Maso, Montebello
Vicentino (VI). Emerging wines
from Colli Berici and Gambellara.

Giuseppe Lonardi, Marano (VR). Fine
Valpolicella Rcioto and Amarone
Classico plus IGT Privilegia Rosso.

Maculan, Breganze (VI). High-powered
modernist wines have become
Breganze archetypes. Huge range
(17 wines) spans from stylish
Breganze Bianco (Breganze di
Breganze), to intense Cabernet
Fratta by way of sweet Torcolato,
and more.

Masi, Gargagnago (VR). Amarone
(Mazzano, Campolongo di Torbe)
and Recioto (Mezzanella). Oddities
extend to Osar (based on the rare
Oseleta) and two wines from
Argentia. See also Serègo Alighieri.

Masottina, San Fior (TV). Reliable
wines from Piave (especially),
Prosecco di C. and Colli di C.

Roberto Mazzi, Negrar (VR). Admired
Valpolicella Classico (Poiega),
Recioto (Le Calcarole), Amarone
(Punta di Villa).

Merotto, Col San Martino (TV). Reliable
Prosecco di V.

Molon Traverso, Salgareda (TV). Wines
of pizazz from Piave.

Tenuta Musella, San Martino Buon
Albergo (VR). Convincing
Valpolicella, Amarone, Recioto.

Natalino Mattiello, Longare (VI).
Rapidly emerging Colli
Berici estate.

Angelo Nicolis e Figli, San Pietro
in Cariano (VR). Classy, if
expensive, Amarone (Ambrosan),
Recioto, and Valpolicella (Seccal).

Novaia, Marano (VR). Satisfying
Valpolicella and Amarone.

Ottella, San Benedetto di Lugana (VR).
Admired Lugana leads red and
white IGT blends.

Fratelli Pasqua-Cecilia Beretta,
Verona (VR). The Pasqua winery
makes a full array of sound Verona
wines under the Pasqua label. Cecilia
Beretta is a brand name for a line of
estate wines, led by Valpolicella and
Amarone from Terre di Cariano, and
Rocco di Mizzole, and Soave Classico
Case Vecie.

Pieropan, Soave (VR). Leonildo Soave Classico of unusual style and integrity, especially the single vineyard (Calvarino, La Rocca) versions. Also exquisite Recioto (Le Colombare), IGT Passito della Rocca (4-grape blend), and Santa Lucia (late-harvest Garganega).

Piovene Porto Godi, Villaga (VI). Promising wines from the often overlooked Colli Berici.

Prà, Monteforte d'Alpone (VR). Impressive Soave Classico Superiore (Colle Sant'Antonio, Vigneto Monte Grande).

Quintarelli, Negrar (VR). Singularly rich and complex Valpolicella Classico, unforgettable Amarone (the *riserva* is to die for), and Recioto from Monte Ca' Paletta vineyards; plus super-concentrated IGT Alzero (Cabernet Franc) and *passito* Amabile del Cerè.

Le Ragose, Arbizzano di Negrar (VR). Refined Valpolicella Classico, Amarone, and Recioto; also fine Garda Cabernet.

Raimondo–Villa Monteleone, Gargagnago (VR). Fruited Amarone, Recioto, Valpolicella Classico, good *passito* from Garganega.

Roccolo Grasso, Mezzane di Sotto (VR). Fine quality through all Valpolicella types.

Romano Dal Forno, Illasi (VR). The inspired individualist Romano Dal Forno produces one of the most impressive, super-concentrated, richly fruited DOC Valpolicellas and a signature unique Amarone.

Ruggeri & C, Valdobbiadene (TV). Large quantities of high quality Prosecco di V led by Extra Dry Giustino B. Also still Prosecco (Le Bastie).

Le Salette, Fumane (VR). Top-quality Amarone (La Marega, Pergole Vecie), Recioto (Le Traversagne, Pegola Vecie), and Valpolicella Classico (Ca' Carnocchio).

San Rustico, Marano (VR). Approachable Valpolicella, Recioto, and Amarone Classico (Gaso).

Tenuta Sant'Antonio, Mezzane di Sotto (VR). Impressive Cabernet Sauvignon Capitello from semi-dried grapes complements esteemed Amarone (Campo dei Gigli).

Santa Margherita, Portogruaro (VE). House that shot Pinot Grigio to fame in 1960, then expanded production to a wide range of regional DOCs and IGTs from cellars in Veneto and Alto Adige. Also owns Cantine Torresella with similar range of economy wines, and two estates in Chianti Classico.

Santi, Illasi (VR). Owned by Gruppo Italiano Vini. Reliable range of Verona DOCs, most notably Amarone (Proemio), Soave Classico (Monteforte, Sanfederici).

Serafini e Vidotto, Nervesa della Battaglia (TV). Headline-grabbing IGT Rosso dell'Abazia (Cabernet/Merlot) reigns over acclaimed Phigaia After the Red (bordeaux blend), Bianco dell' Abazia (Chardonnay/Sauvignon), and Pinot Nero. Also Prosecco di Montello.

Serègo Alighieri, Gargagnago (VR). The historic estate of Pieralvise Serègo Alighieri (a descendant of Dante) makes notable Valpolicella, Amarone, and Recioto Classico, all marketed by Masi.

Fratelli Speri, Pedemonte (VR). Good Valpolicella, Amarone, and Recioto Classico from I Comunai, Monte Sant'Urbano, and La Roverina vineyards.

Suavia, Soave (VR). Impeccable Soave Classico Superiore (Le Rive, Monte Carbonare). Excellent Recioto (Acinatium).

Santa Sofia, Pedemonte (VR). Large winery with reliable Verona DOCs and IGTs.

Sorelle Bronca, Vidor (TV). Despite good Prosecco di V efforts centre on the lesser Colli di Cto good effect.

Tamellini, Soave. New, quality-conscious Soave estate.

Tanoré, Valdobbiadene (TV). Attractive Prosecco di V.

Fratelli Tedeschi, Pedemonte (VR). Valpolicella Classico Superiore (Capitel dei Nicalò), Amarone (Capitel Monte Olmi), and Recioto (Capitel Monte Fontana). Also acclaimed IGT Rosso della Fabriseria, and others.

Le Tende, Lazise (VR). Bardolino Classico, Bianco di Custoza, Garda Cabernets.

Tommasi, Pedemonte (VR). Large, good-quality producers of the major Verona DOCs. Also unusual Crearo della Conca d'Oro from Corvina, rare Oseleta, and Cabernet Franc.

Trabucchi, Illasi (VR). Traditional Amarone. Good Valpolicella (Cereolo, San Colombano), Recioto.

Massimino Venturini, San Floriano (VR). Amarone, Recioto, and Valpolicella Classico of personality.

Vignalta, Arqua Petrarca (PD). The leading light in Colli Euganei with consistency throughout the impressive range of varietals and blends.

Le Vigne di San Pietro, Sommacampagna (VR). Excellent Bardolino, Bianco di Custoza, and IGT Refolà (Cabernet Sauvignon).

Vigneto Duo Santi, Bassano del Grappa (VI). Finely tuned, characterful, and good value Breganze wines.

Villa Bellini, San Pietro in Cariano (VR). Beautifully elegant Valpolicella, Amarone, and Recioto.Berici (VI). The leading Colli Berici estate with small range of stylish wines led by Merlot and Pinot Bianco.

Villa Erbice, Mezzane di Sotto (VR). Re-emerging Valpolicella estate.

Villa Sceriman, Vò Euganeo (PD). Broad range from Colli Euganei.

Villa Spinosa, Negrar (VR). DOC Valpolicella, Amarone, and Recioto Classico.

Viviani, Negrar (VR). Highly admired Valpolicella, Amarone, and Recioto Classico.

Daniele Zamuner, Sona (VR). Excellent Garda sparklers plus numerous good Garda-area wines.

Martino Zanetti, Pieve di Soligo (TV). Case Bianche estate produces outstanding Prosecco di V, from Col Sandago estate come mainly Camoi (Bordeaux Blend, the rare, ripe Wildbacher.

Zardetto, Conegliano (TV). Delightful Prosecco di C. Brut, Extra Dry, Dry, Cartizze, and still that express all the joy of bubbly wine.

Fratelli Zeni, Bardolino (VR). Solid performance from Marogne and Vigne Alte lines of Bardolino, the Valpolicella family, Bianco di Custoza, and Lugana.

Zenato, San Benedetto di Lugana (VR). Classy range of Verona DOCs – impressive Amarone (Sergio Zenato) and Lugana from select vineyards.

Zonin, Gambellara (VI). Family wine empire makes wide range of Veneto DOC, IGT, and sparkling wines, specializing in estate bottlings from Gambellara (Il Giangio) and Valpolicella (Il Maso). The company also owns leading estates in Piedmont, Lombardy, Friuli, Tuscany, and Sicily, as well as in Virginia and California in the USA.

Wine & Food

Whether the setting is a smart *ristorante* on the Grand Canal or a country *trattoria* with a spit turning before an open fire in the *fogolar*, dining in the Veneto is a civilized pleasure. Few regions have such equilibrium in food sources – from fertile plains, lush hillsides, woods, lakes, streams, and the Adriatic – and few other cooks combine them with such easy artistry. Dishes can be lavish, ornate, exotic (the Venetians introduced spices to Italy), but the elements of the cooking are simple: rice, beans, polenta, sausages, salami, poultry, game, mushrooms, and mountain cheese. Venice is the showcase, but the food is every bit as delicious in Verona, Vicenza, Padua, Belluno, Rovigo, and most of all in Treviso, a sanctuary of Venetian gastronomy. Listed are but a few of the delights.

Wines to accompany each dish are suggested below in italics.

Asparagi in salsa Tender white asparagus of Bassano del Grappa with sauce of hard-boiled eggs chopped with vinegar and oil. *Breganze Bianco*

Bigoli con l'anara Thick, handmade spaghetti with duck ragout. *Piave Merlot*

Carpaccio Venetian invention of raw beef sliced thin and served with mayonnaise or other sauces. *Bardolino Chiaretto*

Fegato alla veneziana Calf's liver cooked with onions and wine. *Colli Euganei Merlot*

Granseola alla veneziana Spider crab with oil and lemon. *Prosecco di Valdobbiadene*

Pasta e fasioli Soups of pasta and beans are very popular

throughout the Veneto region. *Bardolino Classico*

Pastissada a caval Horse meat stewed with wine and served with gnocchi or polenta. *Valpolicella Classico*

Risi e bisi Rice and peas cooked together Venetian style. *Ferrata Sauvignon*

Risotto nero The rice is cooked with squid, blackened by its ink. *Soave Classico*

Sopa coada Thick soup – stew really – of pigeon meat, bread, wine, and vegetables. *Colli di Conegliano Rosso*

Torresani all peverada Spit-roasted pigeons with a sausage-liver-anchovy-herb sauce on a bed of polenta. *Colli Euganei Rosso*

Restaurants

Recommended in or near wine zones:
Padova: Colli Euganei/Bagnoli *La Montanella* at Arquà Petrarca; *Trattoria degli Amici* at Arquà Polesine; *La Torre* at Monselice; *Antica Trattoria* Ballotta at Torreglia.
Treviso/Venezia: Conegliano/Valdobbiadene-Montello Piave *Ca' Derton* at Asolo; *Al Caminetto* at Follina; *Da Paolo Zanatta* at Maserada; *Da Gigetto* at Miane; *Marchi* at Montebelluna; *La Panoramica* at Nervesa della Battaglia; *Doppio Fogher* at San Pietro di Feletto; *Gambrinus* at San Polo di Piave; *Da Lino* at Solighetto; *Capitello* at Tarzo; *Ca' Busatti* at Zero Branco.

Verona: Bardolino/Soave-Valpolicella/Custoza *Aurora* at Bardolino; *Gabbia d'Oro* at Isola della Scala; *Perbellini* at Isola Rizza; *Da Bepi* at Marano della Valpolicella; *Bacco d'Oro* at Mezzane di Sotto; *Dalla Rosa Alda* at San Giorgio di Valpolicella; *Groto di Corgnan* at Sant' Ambrogio di Valpolicella; *Scudo* at Soave; *Antica Locanda Mincio* at Valeggio sul Mincio; *Al Calmiere, Ostaria La Fontanina*, and *Il Desco* at Verona.
Vicenza: Breganze/Gambellara/Lessini Durello/Colli Berici *Casin del Gamba* at Altissimo; *Principe* at Arzignano; *Da Penacio* and *Trattoria da Zamboni* at Arcugnano; *La Peca* at Lonigo; *Da Piero* at Montecchio Precalcino; *Ca' Masieri* at Trissino.

Friuli-Venezia Giulia *Friuli-Venezia Giulia*

Friuli's hills are Italy's sanctuary of modern white wine. The climate of this northeastern corner of Italy is influenced by the mingling of cool Alpine air flowing down from the north and warm Adriatic air wafting inland from the south, creating propitious conditions for vine growth in Collio, Colli Orientali del Friuli (COF), and Carso, in the narrow band of hills that rise gently into the border with Slovenia. But nature's gifts aren't limited to the

Wine Areas

1   Friuli Grave
2   Colli Orientali del Fruili
3   Collio Goriziano
4   Friuli Annia
5   Carso

hills. The rising status of Isonzo, nestling under Collio on the plain, has helped further the reputaiton of Friuli's eastern frontier as one of Italy's prime wine territories.

The region emerged in the early 1970s with revelatory white wines that were acclaimed as "the Friuli style" but which were as nothing compared with the classy, distinctive wines of today. Pinot Grigio popularized the mode, but now Pinot Bianco, Chardonnay, Sauvignon Blanc, and local favourite Tocai Friulano often show greater character. Dessert wines – legendary Picolit and rejuvenated Verduzzo – also show unmistakably Friulian grace. Tocai is now gaining recognition abroad, but its name is under notice of prohibition by the EU because of potential confusion with Hungary's tokaji. Producers have to seek a pseudonym for their historic vine.

Today's Friuli style is represented by polished whites of pure, soft, yet fresh aromas, smooth textures, and alluring flavours, a fine-tuned balance that depends on picking perfectly ripe grapes processed by creative tacticians able to pay minute attention to detail. When it works – which it does ever more often – few whites anywhere are as exquisite as those of Friuli. Yet their refinement and poise are sometimes lost on palates attuned to bolder tastes. Hence some winemakers are now fermenting and ageing some or all of their wines in oak barrels, to give them the depth and complexity that critics often regard as essential in world-class whites.

Friuli's wine list is by no means confined to white, however. The region also makes a major share of Merlot and Cabernet, along with distinctive reds from the native Refosco, and such local curiosities as Schioppettino, Pignolo, and Tazzelenghe. Most of these reds have weight, firm structure, excellent fruit, and incisive character. Overall, though, Friuli produces much less wine than neighbouring Veneto and accounts for only twenty per cent of northern Italian wine exports. Prices tend to be high but demand still oustrips supply for the better wines and few other regions share the foresight, versatility, and grit of Friulian winemakers in their devotion to raising standards.

There are nine DOC(G) zones (plus a slice of Veneto's Lison-Pramaggiore) but all are sub-divided into numerous varietal versions with most varieties common to most of the denominations. Most comprise a red, white, and rosé blend too. Thankfully, most producers no longer aim to make all styles but only those best suiting their particular vineyards.The names of the five DOC zones on the broad Adriatic plains – the small Annia, Aquileia, Isonzo, and Latisana, and the large Grave – are preceded by the term Friuli to enhance the regional identity. There are also three IGTs: Alta Livenza, in the province of Pordenone, Venezia Giulia, for wines produced in the coastal area and Delle Venezie which spreads across the whole region as well as Veneto, and Trentino (but not Alto Adige).

The region is a crossroads of Germanic, Slavic, and Italianate cultures. There is a prominent Slovenian minority in the southeast around Gorizia and in the invigorating capital of Trieste, where the West meets Central Europe with great self-assurance. Despite its wines' renown, and lying an easy drive from Venice, Friuli is not yet overrun by wine buffs. *Casa del Vino* at Udine has a selection of the region's wines, as does the *Enoteca La Serenissima* at Gradisca d'Isonzo, Italy's first public wine library. Recommended wine shops are *Farmacia dei Sani* at Lignano Sabbiadoro and *Volpe Pasini* at Udine.

Recent Vintages

As a rule, Friulian dry whites are best at up to three years, though Pinot Bianco, Chardonnay, and Sauvignon Blanc often defy the rule. Reds are usually styled to age at least a few years, many longer.

2002 Sporadic rains in August and September caused difficulties, especially with Pinot Grigio and other early ripeners, except in Colli Orientali where reds were also affected.
2001 Another very good year across the board.
2000 Great year for both whites and, especially, reds.
1999 A very good year for both reds and whites.
1998 Great vintage of decent to very good wines.
1997 Good to excellent vintage, favourable to red wines for ageing.
1996 Ample harvest of mixed results, better for white wines than reds, which lack structure for long ageing.
1995 Small crop of medium to good wines; whites can lack aroma.
Notes on earlier vintages Earlier good vintages: 90, 94.

Wines

CABERNET

Qualified as DOC in all of Friuli's zones, the traditional Cabernet Franc is losing ground to Cabernet Sauvignon, increasingly in bigger, barrel-aged reds sometimes blended with Merlot or other local varieties. Note: the Cabernet Franc of northeastern Italy is probably in reality the rustic, primeval variety Carmenère.

CARSO *DOC*

The Carso plateau, whose chalky slopes extend along the Adriatic between Trieste and Gorizia and into Slovenia, has long been noted for red wines based on Terrano (a strain of Refosco), and whites from Malvasia but the DOC also reflects modern developments, covering the unique variety of Vitovska and other, more common, grapes.

Carso *r dr* ☆→☆☆ *DYA* Sharply flavoured, dark-ruby wine, with earthy goodness from minimum 70% Terrano.

Carso Terrano or Terrano del Carso *r dr* ☆→☆☆☆ *98 99 00 01* From a heartland sub-zone northeast of Trieste, this red from at least 85% Terrano can show inviting bouquet with a berry-like flavour that can take on hints of finesse with 3 to 6 years of ageing.

Cabernet Franc *r dr* ☆→☆☆☆ *99 00 01* When well made develops rich fruit and good weight.

Cabernet Sauvignon r dr ☆☆→☆☆☆ *97 99 00 01* Can produce warm, rounded wines of great style here.

Chardonnay *w dr* ☆→☆☆☆ *99 00 01 02* Ranges between light, crisp, and simple to full, rounded, and creamy.

Malvasia *w dr* ☆☆ *01* From Malvasia Istriana, the classic white of Carso is fragrant, softly dry, and enticingly drinkable.

Merlot *r dr 00 01 02* Rarely seen.

Pinot Grigio *w dr* ☆☆ *DYA* Can be good but not exceptional here.

Refosco del Peduncolo Rosso *r dr* ☆→☆☆☆ *99 00 01* Less well suited to the terrain than the Terrano strain.

Sauvignon *w dr* ☆→☆☆☆ *99 00 01* Full, rounded versions show well.

Traminer Aromatico *w dr* ☆☆ *DYA* Develops good varietal characteristics without excessive intensity.

Vitovska *w dr* ☆→☆☆☆ *98 99 00 01* This peculiar variety makes a deeply fruited wine of distinct character, with sufficient structure to last for 3 to 4 years.

CHARDONNAY

Chardonnay has star status in Friuli, where styles vary from light and fruity to rich and complex oak-fermented wines. It is covered by DOC in all zones.

COLLI ORIENTALI DEL FRIULI *DOC*

An elite zone that extends northeast from the Slovenian border by Corno di Rosazzo to Tarcento, Colli Orientali makes some of Friuli's finest whites and some highly impressive reds. Most are concentrated in the more southerly part, across the valleys south of Cividale, where conditions are barely distinguishable from the adjacent zone of Collio. The DOC covers 20 separate varietals and *bianco*, *rosato*, and *rosso* blends. All, even the rosé, may be *riserva* if aged for more than 2 years. There are also 2 sub-zones, Cialla in the east (where *riserva* demands 4 years) and Rosazzo in the south, each with their own, smallish, list of varietals and Cialla with a more restrictive content of the *bianco* and *rosso*. A further sub-zone, Ramandolo, is now DOCG in its own right (*q.v.*).

Bianco *w dr* ☆☆→☆☆☆ *99 00 01 02* This can be made from any of the zone's white wine varieties, except the aromatic Traminer Aromatico, in blends that are often impressive.

Rosato *p dr DYA* This can be made from any of the zone's red wine varieties, though is not seen very often.

Rosso *r dr* ☆☆→☆☆☆ *94 95 96 97 98 99 00 01* This can be made from any of the zone's red wine varieties although Cabernet is usually present. Blends can show class.

Cabernet *r dr* ☆☆→☆☆☆ *94 97 99 00 01* This may be Cabernet Franc, Cabernet Sauvignon, or both. Wines can be soft, round, and youthful and best in 2 to 3 years, though more often they show impressive structure and a capacity to age for anything up to a decade.

Cabernet Franc *r dr* ☆→☆☆ *99 00 01*
Usually wines of pronounced varietal character that start to show well at 2 to 3 years.

Cabernet Sauvignon *r dr* ☆☆→☆☆☆ *94 97 99 00 01* Innate class comes through in both young and aged versions.

Chardonnay *w dr* ☆☆→☆☆☆ *99 00 01 02* This ranges from the crisp, fruity type to the richer, oak-fermented versions of depth and style.

Malvasia Istriana *w dr* ☆☆ *DYA* Zippy white with a delicate aroma that sometimes reaches refinement.

Merlot *r dr* ☆☆→☆☆☆ *97 98 99 00* Versions are either supple, smooth, and soft, drinking from 2 to 3 years, or full and even aristocratic, gaining stature with age.

Picolit *w s/sw sw* ☆☆→☆☆☆ *94 95 96 97 98 99 00 01 02* This legendary variety reached peaks in vineyards here as long as two centuries ago. The wine must be made in limited quantities in vineyards with extremely low permitted yields. Types vary from pale golden and lightly sweet with an alluring, delicate perfume and a clean, fresh finish to a fully sweet barrique-tempered dessert wine with a deep, gold-amber hue. The area of Rocca Bernarda was historically important for Picolit.

Pignolo *r dr* ☆☆→☆☆☆ *94 97 98 99 00* The vine native to Colli Orientali has been revived in rare red wine of resilient individuality. Of a luminous, ruby-cherry colour, Pignolo has enticingly fresh aromas and vibrant flavours of ripe fruit and berries. The sub-zone of Rosazzo may be cited on labels of Pignolo from vineyards there. Dorigo and Walter Filiputti produce excellent wines from this grape variety.

Pinot Bianco *w dr* ☆☆→☆☆☆ *97 98 99 00 01 02* Pinot Bianco peaks in the eastern Friuli hills. It is enticingly fragrant, creamily fruity, with refinement and harmony, and the structure to improve over 2 to 5 years, or occasionally more.

Barrique-fermented versions also have class.

Pinot Grigio *w dr* ☆☆→☆☆☆ *00 01* Pinot Grigio, too, whether light, crisp, and fruity, more developed, and slightly nutty, or fermetned with the skins to give a fuller wine with a *ramato* (copper-toned) hue, is at its most convincing in eastern Friuli.

Pinot Nero *r dr* ☆→☆☆ *97 99 00 01* Red burgundy's grape hasn't yet acquired grandeur but is fleshy, smooth, and enjoyable.

Refosco dal Peduncolo Rosso *r dr* ☆☆→☆☆☆ *96 97 99 00 01* Wine from this native variety sometimes surpasses the better known varieties in class and ageing potential. Deep violet tending to garnet with age, its sturdiness, warm, full, lightly tannic flavour, and brambly fruit come into its own in 4 to 6 years.

Ribolla Gialla *w dr* ☆☆→☆☆☆ *97 98 99 00 01 02* Much underrated, particularly locally where it is often relegated to crisping up blends, this white can be zesty and sharp in flavour when young but supported by a buttery roundness as it develops. With careful oak ageing it can become broader and more dignified.

Riesling *w dr* ☆☆ *DYA* Few producers invest energy in extracting the character from this true, Renano, strain of Riesling, which tends to remain light and floral with a dry, fruity freshness.

Sauvignon Blanc *w dr* ☆☆→☆☆☆ *98 99 00* This is regularly among the most impressive whites of Friuli, even standing up to Sauvignon from France. Pale straw, with gold-green highlights, elegant fruit-acid balance, and a flowery, flinty nose, it is smooth and long, full of varietal character.

Schioppettino *r dr* ☆☆→☆☆☆ *97 98 99 00 01* This esoteric bright-ruby red comes from an indigenous variety, also called Ribolla Nera, which grows exclusively in these hills. It is followed by a cult which adores its power, singular breed, scent of fresh berries, and marked acidity that enhance its depth and length of flavours as it ages over 3 to 6 years or more.

Tazzelenghe *r dr* ☆☆☆→☆☆☆☆ *96 97 98 99 00 01 02* The name, dialect for *tazzalingua* (tongue-cutter), alludes to its tannic sharpness on the tongue, though this dark, ruby-violet wine has a way of becoming gratifyingly smooth with 3 to 6 years of age.

Tocai Friulano *w dr* ☆☆→☆☆☆ *99 00 01 02* Even everyday Tocai can be good in eastern Friuli but at times it excels with a pale, straw colour, a scent of wild flowers, and a dry but ample flavour, hinting pears, liquorice, herbs, and citrus fruit, with a velvety texture and length.

Traminer Aromatico *w dr* ☆→☆☆ *00 01 02* Gewürztraminer here is usually calm and softly aromatic.

Verduzzo Friulano *w dr s/sw or sw* ☆→☆☆☆ *98 99 00 02* The dry type is light in body and scent and refreshingly crisp. The *amabile* and *dolce* versions often have more immediate appeal.

Colli Orientali Cialla High-lying sub-zone to the east, making particularly refined, long-lived wines from white varietals Picolit, Ribolla Gialla, and Verduzzo; and red varietals Refosco and Schioppettino. Cialla Bianco and Cialla Rosso come from a blend of these white and red grapes respectively.

Colli Orientali Rosazzo Southern sub-zone perfectly situated to benefit equally from cool air-flows from the north and warm air from the south. Just three varietal wines, from Picolit, Ribolla Gialla, and red Pignolo, are permitted but Rosazzo Bianco and Rosazzo Rosso may come from any of the Colli Orientali grapes.

COLLIO GORIZIANO OR COLLIO *DOC*

Hills along the border of Slovenia, from Gorizia west to Cormons and north to Mernico (and including the isolated rise to the south at Farra d'Isonzo), are reputed to have some of Europe's most privileged microclimates for white wines, a privilege they share with parts of adjacent Colli Orientali. Collio's elite status was established by small-scale growers who were the first to prove that Italy could make world-class whites of real personality from native and foreign varieties, although some large wineries have also built fine reputations. The DOC list covers 16 distinct varietals plus white and red blends. Reds may be *riserva* with 3 years ageing. There is not a distinct viticultural break between Collio and Collio Orientali and the 2 zones have many features in common.

Bianco *w dr* ☆☆ *DYA* This can be made from any of the zone's white wine varieties, except the aromatic Traminer Aromatico and Müller-Thurgau, in blends that are frequently notably distinctive.

Rosso *r dr* ☆☆-→☆☆☆ *96 97 98 99 00 01 02* This Cabernet/Merlot blend often shows more complexity than wines from Cabernet alone.

Cabernet, Cabernet Franc, Cabernet Sauvignon, Chardonnay, Malvasia Istriana, Merlot *See* Colli Orientali del Friuli.

Müller-Thurgau *w dr* ☆☆ *DYA* Fresh and finely scented, enticing in its youth.

Picolit *w s/ws sw* ☆☆ *94 95 96 98 99 00 01 02* Though more at home in Colli Orientali, Picolit can develop a certain style here.

Pinot Bianco, Pinot Grigio, Pinot Nero, Ribolla Gialla *See* Colli Orientali del Friuli.

Riesling Italico *w* ☆→☆☆ *DYA* Good, lively, dry to off-dry white with fruity flavour and aroma, and a pale-gold colour.

Riesling Renano *w dr* ☆☆ *97 98* New as a DOC; Schiopetto has succeeded in producing wines with all the qualities of a true Riesling.

Sauvignon Blanc, Tocai Friulano, Traminer Aromatico *See* Colli Orientali del Friuli.

FRANCONIA OR BLAUFRANKISCH

An oddball that can be fascinating as a DOC red in Isonzo and Latisana. Known variously as Franconia, Limberger, Blaufränkisch, and Bleufrancs, the vine probably came from Croatia.

FRIULI ANNIA *DOC*

Lying in the plains between the ancient Roman city of Aquileia and Latisana, the climate and terrains are very similar to those of the Latisana zone. It became DOC in 1995 yet its wines are still rarely seen. Reds aged 2 years may be *riserva*.

Bianco *w dr* May come from any or all of the zone's white varieties except Traminer Aromatico.

Rosato *p dr (fz)* May come from any or all of the zone's red varieties.

Rosso *r dr* May come from any or all of the zone's red varieties.

Spumante *w dr sp* Based on Chardonnay and/or Pinot Bianco.

Cabernet Franc *r dr*
Cabernet Sauvignon *r dr*
Chardonnay *w dr (fz)*
Malvasia Istriana *w dr (fz)*
Merlot *r dr*
Pinot Bianco *w dr (fz)*
Pinot Grigio *w dr*
Refosco dal Peduncolo Rosso *r dr*
Sauvignon Blanc *w dr*
Tocai Friulano *w dr*
Traminer Aromatico *w dr*
Verduzzo Friulano *w dr s/sw (fz)*

FRIULI AQUILEIA *DOC*

Flat zone stretching from the Adriatic north past Aquileia to Palmanova and Trivignano. Red wines once prevailed in the sandy clay soil, though whites, often stylish, now match them. The DOC list includes 12 separate varietals and a rosé.

Cabernet *r dr* ☆☆ *98 99 00 01 02* Whether Cabernet Franc, Cabernet Sauvignon or both, wines tend to be bright ruby, round, fresh, and fragrant. Best 2 to 4 years.

Cabernet Franc *r dr 99 00 01 02* Lively, grassy reds. Best 2 to 4 years.

Cabernet Sauvignon *r dr* ☆☆ *98 99 00 01 02* Wines that can show considerable style.

Chardonnay *w dr (sp)* ☆☆ *00 01 02* A mix of youthful, fruity styles, also sparkling, and those with more pronounced varietal character.

Merlot *r dr* ☆☆ *99 00 01 02* The prevalent Aquileia varietal. Tasty, fruity, mid-weight, medium-ruby colour, to drink in 1 to 4 years.

Pinot Bianco *w dr* ☆☆ *00 01 02* Straw-yellow, soft, perfumed, and smooth; some varietal character.

Pinot Grigio *w dr* ☆☆ *DYA* Smooth, fruity, dry but flowery wines with a light golden-copper colour and sometimes personality.

Refosco dal Peduncolo Rosso *r dr* ☆☆→☆☆☆ *96 97 98 00 01 02* The most distinguished of Aquileia's reds. A deep, garnet-violet colour, fairly full body, and a pleasant fruity flavour with typically bitter undertone. To drink in 2 to 5 years, sometimes more.

Riesling Renano *w dr* ☆☆ *DYA* Small production of this light-golden, dry wine that sometimes does better than might be expected from these plains.

Rosato *p dr* ☆☆ *DYA* Based on Merlot with Cabernets and Refosco, this is light, cherry-hued, soft, and subtly grapey.

Sauvignon Blanc *w dr* ☆☆ *DYA* Bright, flinty whites can show personality in this coastal climate.

Tocai Friulano *w dr* ☆☆ *DYA* More delicate and drier than Tocai from the hills.

Traminer Aromatico *w dr* The mild climate brings fair weight to this varietal.

Verduzzo Friulano *w dr s/sw* ☆ *DYA* Light, lemony white.

FRIULI GRAVE *DOC*

Friuli's largest zone, the uplifted gravelly plains and low hills that cover almost the entire southern part of the region, except the hills of the extreme east and the alluvial coastlands, account for more than half of its DOC wine. Merlot is the major variety, but there's no shortage of Cabernets, Pinots, Tocai, or Chardonnay, which was DOC here before elsewhere in Italy. Most wines are for everyday, but more than a few come close to the gems of the hills in quality, if rarely in price. The 18 types include 14 varietals plus *bianco, rosato, rosso,* and *spumante.*

Bianco *w dr* ✩✩ DYA May come from any or all of the zone's non-aromatic white varieties.

Rosato *p dr (fz)* ✩✩ DYA Sometimes pleasant pink based on Cabernet but may come from any or all of the zone's red varieties.

Rosso *r dr* ✩✩ *99 00 01 02* Any or all of the zone's red varieties make a wine often to drink young, notably as *novello.*

Spumante *w dr sp* ✩✩ DYA From Chardonnay and Pinots, this can be attractive.

Cabernet *r dr* ✩✩→✩✩✩ *98 99 00 01 02* A blend of Franc and Sauvignon, made either to drink young, or to gain character with 5 years or more of ageing.

Cabernet Franc *r dr* ✩✩ *97 98 99 00 01 02* Often rounded wines with good varietal character.

Cabernet Sauvignon *r dr* ✩✩→✩✩✩ *96 97 98 99 00 01 02* Often preferred by producers to Cabernet Franc, especially for ageing.

Chardonnay *w dr (fz)* ✩✩ *99 00 01 02* As increasingly prominent here as everywhere else.

Merlot *r dr* ✩→✩✩✩ *99 00 01 02* Grave is a wellspring of affordable Merlot, much of it solid enough to improve over 3 to 5 years. Even the everyday stuff is often good – supple, fruity, and livley.

Pinot Bianco *w dr (fz)* ✩→✩✩✩ *99 00 01 02* Quality ranges from average to very good, with class and character.

Pinot Grigio *w dr* ✩→✩✩✩ DYA At its best, this concedes little to its neighbours in the hills.

Pinot Nero *r dr* ✩→✩✩ *99 00 01 02* The little produced tends to be rounded and balanced.

Refosco dal Penduncolo Rosso *r dr* ✩→✩✩✩ *97 98 99 00 01 02* Livley red that at times can rival the region's finest. Can age 4 to 7 years or more.

Riesling Renano *w dr* ✩→✩✩ DYA Not often seen.

Sauvignon Blanc *w dr* ✩→✩✩✩ *00 01 02* This seems well suited to Grave's gravelly soils; attractively scented and full of flavour.

Tocai Friulano *w dr* ✩→✩✩✩ *00 01 02* Tocai is plentiful in Grave; choice bottles rival the region's elite.

Traminer Aromatico *w dr* Rarely seen.

Verduzzo *w dr s/sw (fz)* ✩→✩✩ DYA Light golden-yellow with greenish tints, best young when its fruity freshness is offset by an almost salty dryness.

FRIULI ISONZO *DOC*

Zone nestling under the Collio hills on either side of the Isonzo River reaching southward to the coastal plain near Monfalcone. The flat terrain, iron-rich soils, and warm microclimate of the area appears to favour the Cabernet and Merlot varieties. But whites – in particular from Pinot Bianco and Grigio, Tocai, Sauvignon Blanc, and Chardonnay – also come close to Collio's finest. The DOC list covers 24 wine types: 20 varietals plus *bianco, rosato, rosso,* and *vendemmia tardiva.*

Bianco *w dr (fz)* ✩→✩✩ DYA Made from any of the zone's non-aromatic white varieties.

Rosato *p dr* ✩→✩✩ DYA Made from any of the zone's 7 red varieties.

Rosso *r dr (sp) (fr)* ✩→✩✩ *98 99 00 01 02* Can be made from any of the zone's 7 red varieties but usually containing Cabernet and Merlot.

Vendemmia Tardiva *w am s/sw sw* DYA Sweet wine from late-picked grapes from any or all of Tocai, Sauvignon, Verduzzo, Pinot Bianco, and Chardonnay.

Cabernet *r dr* ✩→✩✩✩ *97 98 99 00 01 02* A reliable blend of the 2 Cabernets, remarkably drinkable in 2 to 6 years.

Cabernet Franc *r dr* ✩✩ *99 00 01 02* The long-prevalent Cabernet

makes elegant reds that can
show buoyant character.

Cabernet Sauvignon *r dr* ☆☆→☆☆☆
97 98 99 00 01 02 Wines that show
real style with a bit of age.

Chardonnay *w dr* ☆☆→☆☆☆ *97 98 99
00 01 02* Chardonnay made with
devotion on the plains can rival
that of the hills.

Franconia *r dr* ☆☆ *99 00 01 02* Rare
variety, bright ruby and scented,
with hints of raspberry in its
dry flavour.

Malvasia *w dr* ☆→☆☆ *DYA* Mid-weight,
perfumed, and floral.

Merlot *r dr* ☆☆→☆☆☆ *97 98 99 00 01 02*
The dominant Isonzo wine, Merlot
shows consistent quality here.
Often brilliantly fresh in bouquet
and flavour, it can develop style
with 4 to 5 years of ageing.

Moscato Giallo *w s/sw (sp)* ☆→☆☆ *DYA*
Sweetish Muscat can be tasty .

Moscato Rosa *p sw (sp)* ☆→☆☆ *DYA*
Delicately aromatic sweet wine
of rose-petal colour.

Pinot Bianco *w dr (sp)* ☆☆→☆☆☆ *99 00
01 02* This can be light and fruity or
rich, complex, and ranking with the
elite of Friuli. Sometimes barrel-
fermented.

Pinot Grigio *w dr* ☆→☆☆☆ *01 02* Can be
pale, round, and tasty, or in certain
cases, full and elegant and ranking
with the best of Friuli. Sometimes
oak-fermented.

Pinot Nero *r dr* ☆→☆☆☆ *99 00 01 02*
Infrequently seen.

Refosco dal Peduncolo Rosso *r dr* ☆☆
97 98 99 00 01 02 The ever-enjoyable
Refosco does not disappoint here.

Riesling *w dr* ☆☆ *00 01 02* Riesling
Renano shows distinct class.
Pale, greenish-yellow and
fragrant, best young.

Riesling Italico *w dr DYA* Unproven.

Sauvignon Blanc *w dr* ☆☆→☆☆☆☆ *00
01 02* Often impressive, smooth,
finely scented, and full of flavour.

Schioppettino *r dr* Rarely seen.

Tocai Friulano *w dr* ☆→☆☆☆ *98 00
01 02* The popular white is usually
at least solid and good value, but
can rise to the level of Collio's
top echelon.

Traminer Aromatico *w dr q DYA* Styles
can be rich, fleshy, and perfumed.

Verduzzo Friulano *w dr s/sw* ☆ *DYA*
Crisp, tasty dry, or sweetish white.

FRIULI LATISANA *DOC*

This zone in the coastal plains
follows the Tagliamento River
from the Adriatic past the town
of Latisana. The list covers 13 types,
varietals. There is also a *rosato* and
spumante. Reds with 2 years ageing
may be *riserva*.

Rosato *p dr (fr)* ☆→☆☆ *DYA* Pink wine
from Merlot and other reds can
be refreshing in summer.

Spumante *w dr sp* Chardonnay and
Pinots combine in sparkling wine.

Cabernet *r dr* ☆→☆☆ *00 01 02* Cabernet
Sauvignon and Franc make soft,
light, scented wine to drink in 2
to 4 years.

Cabernet Franc *r dr* ☆→☆☆ *99 00 01 02*
The popular Cabernet is fruity
and tasty.

Cabernet Sauvignon *r dr* ☆→☆☆
98 99 00 01 02 Good, but does
better elsewhere.

Chardonnay *w dr (fz)* ☆→☆☆ *DYA*
Good, but does better elsewhere.

Franconia *r dr* Unproven.

Malvasia Istriana *w dr (fz) DYA* Fresh,
floral, and pleasant.

Merlot *r dr* ☆→☆☆ *00 01 02* Good
everyday wine, appreciable in
1 to 3 years.

Pinot Bianco *w dr (fz)* ☆→☆☆ *DYA*
Limited quantities, finely scented,
smooth, with varietal tone.

Pinot Grigio *w dr* ☆→☆☆ *DYA* The light
style prevails in limited quantities.

Pinot Nero *r dr (fr)* The grapes are
mostly used in sparkling wines.

Refosco dal Peduncolo Rosso *r dr*
☆→☆☆ *00 01 02* Although
overwhelmed in volume by
other reds, Refosco is more
robust and durable, and can
show distinctive style.

Riesling Renano *w dr* Rarely seen.

Sauvignon Blanc *w dr* ☆→☆☆ *DYA*
What little there is retains the
grape's character.

Tocai Friulano *w dr* ☆→☆☆ *DYA* The
favoured white is of good style.

Traminer Aromatico *w dr* Develops good perfume and varietal style.

Verduzzo *w dr* ☆ *DYA* Crisp, fresh, and attractive.

LISON-PRAMAGGIORE

Veneto DOC zone which extends into Friuli. *See* Veneto.

MALVASIA ISTRIANA

Malvasia from neighbouring Istria in Croatia makes crisp, lively, pleasantly scented whites in Friuli.

PICOLIT

Low-yielding grape that is difficult to cultivate but yields beautifully elegant, sweet wines, most notably in Colli Orientali.

PIGNOLO

Ancient indigenous red variety of Colli Orientali.

RAMANDOLO *DOC*

w s/sw sw ☆☆→☆☆☆☆ *99 00 01 02* Smoothly sweet, pale-golden dessert wine from Verduzzo Friulano grown around the village of Ramandolo, near Nimis, within the most northerly part of Colli Orientali

REFOSCO

Friuli's preferred native red vine. The dal Peduncolo Rosso strain does best in most of Friuli. The related Terrano del Carso thrives in Carso. There is also Refosco Nostrano.

RIBOLLA GIALLA

Underrated native vine makes lively whites in Colli Orientali and Collio that can impress.

RONCO

Ronco (also *ronc'*, *runk*, plural *ronchi*) is used in Friuli to denote favourably exposed hillside vineyards, often terraced. Terms may be part of the names of estates, individual vineyards or wines.

SCHIOPPETTINO

Also known as Ribolla Nera this native variety from Colli Orientali continues to gain ground.

TAZZELENGHE OR TACELENGHE

The name, dialect for *tazzalingua* (tongue-cutter), alludes to its tannic sharpness on the tongue, but this dark ruby-violet vdt can be gratifyingly smooth with 3 to 6 years of age from producers in Colli Orientali.

TERRANO DEL CARSO

See Carso DOC.

TOCAI FRIULANO

Friuli's prominent white varietry, a strain of the French Sauvignon Vert, is DOC in all zones but Carso. Producers are actively seeking an alternative name as Tocai will no longer be permitted in 2007 following a European court ruling that it caused confusion with the tokaji wine region of Hungary. Candidates include Tai Friulano and Sovràn.

VERDUZZO FRIULANO

This ancient vine is used for both dry and sweet whites, most notably that in Ramandolo DOCG.

Producers

Provinces: Gorizia (GO), Pordenone (PN), Trieste (TS), Udine (UD). COF stands for Colli Orientali (del Friuli).

Abbazia di Rosazzo, Manzano (UD). Abbey noted for wine since Middle Ages has vineyards and cellars under lease from the Diocese of Udine.

Angoris, Cormons (GO). Large and long-standing estate now with improving COF varietals and *bianco* (Chardonnay/Sauvignon).

Attems, Lucinico (GO). Fruit-led Collio, most notably Ribolla.

Aquila del Torre, Povoletto (UD). Steadily improving COF.

Bastianich, Premariacco, (UD). New COF estate already making headlines with gutsy Pinot Grigio, Tocai, Vespa Bianco (Sauvignon/Chardonnay/Picolit), and more.

Tenuta Beltrame, Bagnaria Arsa (UD). Consistently impressive Aquileia.

Borgo Conventi, Farra d'Isonzo (GO). Rapid change is afoot at this prime Isonzo estate following its purchase by Tuscany's Ruffino company.

Borgo del Tiglio, Brazzano di Cormons (GO).Outstanding Collio Tocai (Ronco della Chiesa), Chardonnay, *bianco*, and *rosso*.

Borgo Magredo, Tauriano (PN). Large Grave estate with admirable quality throughout, especially reds.

Borgo San Daniele, Cormons (GO). Just 4 Isonzo wines: stunning Tocai, superb Pinot Grigio, excellent IGT Arbis Bianco and Rosso blends.

Emiro Cav. Bortolusso, Carlino (UD). The leading estate in Annia. Notable Pinot Grigio, Sauvignon, Merlot, Malvasia.

Branko-Igor Erzetic, Cormons (GO). Emerging estate with individual, refined Collio whites.

Brojoli-Franco Clementin, Terzo d'Aquileia (UD). Up-and-coming Aquileia producer.

Livio e Claudio Buiatti, Buttrio (UD). Admired COF range.

Olivo Buiatti, Buttrio (UD). Boutique COF estate.

Buzzinelli, Cormons (GO). Collio both oaked (Ronc dal Luisline) and not.

Ca' Bolani, Cervignano del Friuli (UD). Zonin-owned Aquileia winery grouping wines from Ca' Vescovo and Molin di Ponte estates, too. Good Sauvignon, Refosco; blends lead stalwart range.

Ca' Ronesca, Dolegna del Collio (GO). Admired producer of Collio and COF (Sauvignon di Ipplis).

Cabert, Bertiolo (UD). Large co-op winery producing full spread of Grave and some COF, all of good quality and reasonable price.

Paolo Caccese, Pradis di Cormons (GO). Full spread of Collio including Müller-Thurgau.

Cantina Produttori di Cormons, Cormons (GO). Large quality-directed co-op with most memebers cultivating organically. Sound Collio, Aquileia, Isonzo, and unique *vino della pace* from more than 400 grape varieties grown on all 5 continents. The wine is white, the grapes both red and white. Bottles go to 90 world leaders.

Il Carpino, Sovenza (GO). Good Collio led by Merlot Rubrum.

Castelcosa, Cosa (PN). Individualistic wines known mainly abroad.

La Castellada, Oslavia (GO). Top-notch oak-fermented Collio, led by Bianco and Ribolla from one of the zone's best areas.

Castello di Spessa, Spessa di Capriva (GO). Historical estate revived with outstanding Collio Pinot Bianco and blended *rosso*.

Castelvecchio, Sagrado (GO). Wide range of Carso led by Cabernet Franc and Cabernet Sauvignon.

Collavini, Corno di Rosazzo (UD). Dependably good Collio and COF spanning many grapes and styles.

Colle Duga, Cormons (GO). Emerging Collio estate with fine Merlot, Tocai, and more.

Colmello di Grotta, Farra d'Isonzo (GO). Good Collio, Isonzo whites.

Conti D'Attimis Maniago, Buttrio (UD). Historical estate with large range of re-emerging COF.

Conti Formentini, San Floriano del Collio (GO). Noted Collio Merlot Tajut.

Damijan Podversic, Gorizia (GO). Rapidly emerging producer with excellent Collio vineyards.

Dario Coos, Ramandolo (UD). Fine Ramandolo and COF Picolit.

Dal Fari, Cividale (UD). Elegant COF, led by whites.

Marina Danieli, Buttrio (UD). COF Merlot, Cabernet Franc, Pinot Bianco, Tocai, and IGT red blend Faralta.

Girolamo Dorigo, Buttrio (UD). Fine COF in 2 ranges, "standard" and "gold". Pignolo, Chardonnay, Rosso Montsclapade receive most plaudity.

Do Ville, Rochi dei Legionari (GO). Rapidly improved Isonzo, mainly white.

Giovanni Dri, Ramandolo (UD). Leading producer Ramandolo also makes COF Picolit, Refosco Sauvignon, Cabernet; IGT Il Roncat Rosso (4-grape blend) and Monte dei Carpin (Schiopettino/Refosco).

Le Due Terre, Prepotto (UD). Boutique COF estate with prized Merlot, Pinot Nero, IFT Sacrisassi Rosso (Refosco/Schiopettino) and Bianco (Tocai/Sauvignon/Ribolla), plus Picolit-based Implicito. EnoFriulia, Capriva del Friuli (GO). Oak-free, good-value Collio.

Ermarcora, Premariacco (UD). Textbook COF wines.

Fantinel, Tauriano di Spilimbergo (UD). Large wine house has moved up-scale with vast vineyards in Grave, Collio, and COF producing premium wines.

Livio Felluga, Brazzano di Cormons (GO). Widely acclaimed COF from Rosazzo and other vineyards, led by Bianco Terre Alte (Tocai/Pinot Bianco/Sauvignon), Merlot-based Sossò, and Refosco.

Marco Felluga, Gradisca d'Isonzo (GO). Consistently appealing Collio wines including unique varietals Ovestein (white) and Marburg (red) from the Castello di Buttrio estate, alluring Bianco Molamatta (Pinot Bianco/Tocai/Ribolla), stylish varietals, and more.

Ferdinando e Aldo Polencic, Cormons (GO). Highly esteemed Collio whites, most notably Pinot Bianco.

Fiegl, Oslavia (GO). Two lines, "standard" and "Leopold" for attractive Collio, mostly white.

Walter Filiputti, Manzano (UD). Filiputti's winery is in the Abbazia di Rosazzo and produces a range of COF, including Pignolo, Pinot Grigio, Ribolla Gialla, Sauvignon Blanc, Picolit, and *bianco* (Poiesis,

Ronco degli Agostiniani, Ronco del Monastero), and a IGT red, Broili di Filip.

Foffani, Trivignano Udinese (UD). Emerging Aquileia estate.

Adriano Gigante, Corno di Rosazzo (UD). COF including Picolit.

Giovanni Donda, Aquileia (UD). Emerging Aquileia estate.

Gradnik, Plessiva di Cormons (GO). Collio led by Pinot Bianco.

Gradis'ciutta, San Floriano del Collio (GO). Refined range of COF.

Gravner, Oslavia (GO). Chardonnay, Sauvignon, stunning Ribolla Gialla, Bianco Breg (4 grapes). Also IGT Rosso Gravner (Merlot/Cabernet Franc) and Rujno (Merlot/Cabernet Sauvignon).

Il Roncal, Cividale del Friuli (UD). Steadily improving COF led by *bianco* (Ploe di Stelis), Schioppettino.

Isidoro Polencic, Cormons (GO). Reliably fine Collio whites, led by Pinot Grigio. IGT blend Oblin Blanc at same level.

Edi Kante, Duino Aurisina (TS). Carso leader with Terrano, Malvasia, Sauvignon, Chardonnay, and Vitovska.

Edi Keber, Zegla di Cormons (GO). Tocai, Merlot, *bianco*, and *rosso*.

Renato Keber, Zegla di Cormons (GO). Good Collio range.

Di Lenardo, Ontagnano di Gonars (UD). Modern, individual Grave and IGT blends, often wackily named (Father's Eyes, Pass the Cookies, Toh!, Woody).

Livon, Dolegnano (UD). Large range of Collio in three lines; *classica*, *cru*, and *grand cru*, this latter including leading Braide Alte white blend, Braide Mate Chardonnay Tiare Blu red blend, Tiare Mate (Merlot) and Picotis (Schioppettino). Also some COF; plus easy-going Grave from Villa Chiopris estate.

La Lozeta, San Giovanni al Natisone (UD). COF Tocai and others, and IGT Franconia.

Magnàs, Cormons (GO). Emerging estate for Isonzo whites.

Mangilli, Flumignano di Talmassons (UD). Grave, Collio, and COF.

Marega, San Floriano del Collio (GO). Good Collio range.

Masut da Rive, Mariano del Friuli (GO). notable array of Isonzo with good quality and price.

Mauro Drius, Cormons (GO). Stylish range of admired Collio, led by Pinot Bianco.

Davino Meroi, Buttrio (UD). Broad range of good quality COF.

Miani, Buttrio (UD). Remarkable COF Tocai, Merlot Bianco (Chardonnay/Pinot Grigio/ Riesling), and Rosso (Refosco/ Cabernet/Tazzelenghe), plus others.

Midolini, Manzano (UD). Good COF led by Refosco.

Davide Moschioni, Cividale del Friuli (UD). Admired COF, especially concentrated reds.

Mulino delle Tolle, Bagnaria Arsa (UD). Fine Aquileia, most notably Malvasia.

Lis Neris-Pecorari, San Lorenzo Isontino (GO). Impecccable range of Isonzo, including Chardonnay (Jurosa), Pinot Grigio (Gris), Sauvignon (Picòl), *rosso* (Lis Neris), and IGT *bianco* (Lis) Verduzzo *passito* (Tal Lùc).

Ornella Molon Traverso, Prepotto (UD). Huge COF range, led by the fine Vigna Traverso line.

Oscar Sturm, Cormons (GO). Emerging Collio wines showing refinement.

Petrucco, Buttrio (UD). Finely honed COF, especially whites.

Roberto Picech, Cormons (GO). Collio Bianco Jelka (Ribolla/ Tocai/Malvasia) and Pinot Bianco head the stylish range from this small estate.

Pierpaolo Pecorari, San Lorenzo Isontino (GO). Exemplary Isonzo, including Altis: selections of Pinot Grigio, Sauvignon, and reserve versions of Merlot, Sauvignon, Chardonnay, Pinot Grigio, and (especially) Refosco.

Petrussa, Prepotto (UD). Good COF Bianco, Rosso, Pinot Bianco, Sauvignon.

Pighin, Pavia di Udine (GO). Estates at Capriva for Collio and Risano for Grave. Reliable wines throughout.

Plozner, Barbeano di Spilimbergo (PN). Impressive, good-value range of Grave.

Podere dal Ger, Prata di Pordenone (PN). Good Lison-Pramaggiore wines.

Pradio, Bicinicco (UD). Steadily improving Grave wines.

Primosic, Oslavia (GO). Distinctive Collio, notably Ribolla Gialla Gmajne.

Princic, Pradis di Cormons (GO). Excellent Collio Tocai, Pinot Bianco, Malvasia.

Puiatti, Capriua del Friuli (GO). Textbook oak-free whites and decent reds from Collio and Isonzo.

Dario Raccaro, Cormons (GO). Fine Collio Bianco, Malvasia, Tocai, Merlot.

Stanislao Radikon, Oslavia (GO). Collio of power and individuality, most notably Merlot, Ribolla Gialla, and Bianco Oslavje.

Teresa Raiz, Povoletto (UD). Admired COF, led by Rosso (Decano), and Grave.

Rocca Bernarda, Ipplis di premariacco (UD). This historic property, owned by the Order of Malta, makes fine COF, especially Merlot (Centis) and top-notch Picolit.

Paolo Rodaro, Spessa di Cividale (UD). Fine COF, notably Sauvignon, Tocai, Refosco, and Pinot Bianco-based blend *ronc*.

Ronchi di Cialla, Cialla di Prepotto (UD). Highly classy and personalized COF Cialla: Cialla Bianco (Ribolla/ Verduzzo/Picolit), Refosco, Schioppettino, Verduzzo, Picolit.

Ronchi di Manzano, Manzano (UD). Concentrated COF led by Merlot (Ronc di Subule), but with fine quality throughout the large range.

Ronco dei Tassi, Cormons (GO). Just 5 wines: Collio Sauvignon, Tocai, Pinot Grigio, Bianco (Tocai/Malvasia/BP), *rosso* (Cjarandon) – all good.

Ronco del Gelso, Cormons (GO). Isonzo of enviable style and individuality, especially with Tocai, Sauvignon, Pinot Grigio, Merlot.

Ronco del Gnemiz, San Giovanni al Natisone (UD). Admired COF led by Chardonnay, Sauvignon Rosso (del Gnemiz).

Ronco delle Betulle, Manzano (UD). Fine COF Rosazzo, notably Ribolla Cialla, *rosso* (Narcisso), and IGT Franconia.

Roncùs, Capriva (GO). Emerging Collio estate noted for Pinot Bianco, Sauvignon, Tocai, and Roncùs Bianco (Pinot Bianco/Malvasia/Ribolla) from old vines.

Rosa Bosco, Rosazzo di Manzano (UD). Just COF Merlot (Boscorosso) and Sauvignon, both supreme.

Torre Rosazza, Poggiobello di Manzano (UD). Including admirable Pinot Nero, Merlot (L'Altromerlot), Refosco, and Pinot Bianco (Ronco delle Magnolie).

Rubini, Spessa di Cividale (UD). Good value COF.

Russiz Superiore, Capriva (GO). Model Collio estate, with supreme *bianco* (Russiz Disôre), *rosso* (Orzoni), Pinot Bianco, Tocai, Sauvignon leading fine range.

Mario Schiopetto, Spessa di Capriva (GO). Collio wines of immense stature with Collio, notably from Pinot Bianco, Sauvignon, and Tocai, plus new IGT blends, Mario Schiopetto Bianco (Chardonnay/Tocai), and Blumeri Rosso (Merlot/Cabernet Sauvignon/Refosco).

Roberto Scubla, Premariacco (UD). Distinctive COF led by late-harvest Verduzzo Bianco (Pomédes), Tocai (Graticcio), and Merlot.

Specogna, Corno di Rosazzo (UD). Good COF Merlot (Oltre) Pignolo, Sauvignon, Pinot Grigio.

Subida di Monte, Cormons (GO). White-orientated Collio.

Franco Toros, Cormons (GO). Dazzling, concentrated Collio whites led by Pinot Bianco. Also excellent Merlot.

Valle, Buttrio (UD). Vast range of reliable COF and Collio, led by Araldica, San Blas, and Collezione Gigi Valle selections.

Valpanera, Villa Vicentina (UD). Aquileia producer concentrating on Refosco, to good effect.

Redi Vazzoler, Mossa (GO).

Venica & Venica, Dolegna del Collio (GO). Impressive range of Collio, led by starry Sauvignon (Ronco delle Mele), Tocai (Ronco delle Cime), Pinot Bianco, Rivolla Gialla, and white blends (the Vignis, Prime Note).

La Viarte, Prepotto (UD). Respected COF, notably Pinot Bianco, Pinot Grigio, Tocai, Pignolo, Tazzelenghe, Bianco (Liende), and IGT Siùm (Picolit/Verduzzo).

Vie di Romans, Mariano del Friuli (GO). Masterful Isonzo whites with Sauvignon (Pière and Vieris), Chardonnay (Ciampagnis Vieris, Vie di Romans), Pinot Grigio (Dessimis), and Bianco (Flors di Uis) from Malvasia/Riesling/Chardonnay.

Vigna del Lauro, Cormons (GO). Good Collio Tocai, Sauvignon, Merlot, Bianco.

Vigne Fantin Noda'r, Premariacco (UD). Rapidly emerging COF estate.

Vigneti Le Monde, Prata di Pordenone (PN). Good value from Grave, especially Pinot Bianco, Pinot Nero, Sauvignon.

Vigneti Pittaro, Rivolto di Codroipo (UD). Admired Grave varietals; IGT red Agresto (Cabernet with local varieties), unusual sweet white Apicio, and sparklers.

Tenuta Villanova, Farra d'Isonzo (GO). Sound quality from Isonzo and Collio.

Villa Frattina, Prata di Pordenone (PN). Lison-Pramaggiore estate of worth.

Villa Russiz, Capriva (GO). Elegant Collio, led by refined, classy Sauvignon, and Chardonnay de La Tour, Merlot Graf de La Tour, Pinot Bianco, and Pinot Grigio.

Vincenti Orgnani, Pinzano al Tagliamento (PN). Distinctive Grave, local grape Uce Lut.

Vinnaioli Jermann, Villanova di Farra (GO). Although in the Collio zone, Silvio Jermann eschews the DOC in his impeccable varietals and blends such as Vinnae (Ribolla/ Riesling/Malvasia), Capo Martino in Ruttaris (Pinots/Tocai/Picolit/ Malvasia), and the singular Vintage Tunina, from late-harvested Sauvignon and Chardonnay with Ribolla, Malvasia, and a hint of Picolit, a wine that has long stood as one of Italy's whites of greatest stature.

Andrea Visintini, Corno di Rosazzo (UD). Reliable range of COF.

Vistorta, Sacile (PN). Just distinguished Merlot from this eminent Grave estate.

Viticoltori Friulani-La Delizia, Casarsa della Delizia (PN). This large, reliable co-op makes DOC of Friuli Grave and Aquileia; IGT and *spumanti*.

Volpe Pasini, Togliano di Torreano (UD). Admired COF under Zuc di Volpe label led by Pinot Bianco.

Le Vigne di Zamò, Rosazzo di Manzano (UD). Highly admired COF, most notably Merlot and Tocai (both *vigno cinquantanni*).

Zidarich, Duino Aurisina (TS). Impressive Carso Terrano, Vitovska, Malvasia from this small but eminent estate.

Zof, Corno di Rosazzo (UD). Steadily improving COF.

Zuani, San Floriano del Collio (GO). Just 2 wines, the unoaked Zuani Vigne, fresh and lively, and the oaked Zuani, both Collio Bianco, both from Tocai/Pinot Grigio/Chardonnay/ Sauvignon, both excellent.

Wine & Food

In Friuli, East meets West around the *fogolar* (cosy open hearth with a conical chimney). A melting pot of European cookery, Friuli-Venezia Giulia gives its own touch to *gulasch*, dumplings, cabbage and bean soups, and Viennese pastries. But the tangs of Slovenia, Croatia, Bohemia, Austria, and Hungary are merely a bonus added to Friuli's own tasty peasant heritage of pork, beans, mutton, sausages, soups, blood puddings, polenta, turnips, game, and cheese. Venezia Giulia, the coastal strip, gives fish to the menu with soups, chowders, and refined risottos with prawns, squid, or scallops that reflect the influence of Venice. From the hill town of San Daniele comes a *prosciutto* which some consider to be the most exquisite made.

Wines to accompany each dish are suggested below in italics.

Boreto alla graisana Fish chowder (turbot ideal) cooked with oil, vinegar and garlic; speciality of the port of Grado. *Malvasia Istriana*

Brovada Turnips marinated in fresh wine pressings, then cut into strips and cooked with *muset*, a pork sausage. *Refosco*

Capriolo in salmi Venison in rich wine sauce. *Cabernet/Schioppettino*

Frico Grated Montasio cheese, both fresh and aged, fried with onions in butter until crunchy. *Tocai*

Granzevola alla triestina Spider crab baked with breadcrumbs, garlic, and seasonings. *Sauvignon*

Gulasch Beef with tomato, onions, and paprika. *Terrano del Carso*

Jota Filling soup of pork, beans, cabbage, and cornmeal. *Carso*

Paparot Cream soup, includes spinach and cornflour. *Pinot Grigio*

Prosciutto di San Daniele Thin slices of air-cured ham. *Pinot Bianco*

Strucolo Friuli's answer to strudel, made with ricotta cheese, or apples, or other fruit. *Ramandolo*

Restaurants

Recommended in or near wine zones:

Aquileia-Latisana *Da Toni* at Gradiscutta di Varmo; *Alla Fortuna* at Grado; *Bella Venezia* at Latisana; *Bidin* at Lignano Sabbiadoro.

Carso *Carso da Bozo* at Monrupino; *Antica Trattoria* at Suban near Trieste.

Collio *Al Cacciatore della Subida, Felcaro,* and *Il Giardinetto* at Cormons; *Aquila d'Oro* and *Venica* at Dolegna; *Trattoria Blanch* at Mossa.

Colli Orientali *Le Officine* and *Trattoria al Parco* at Buttrio; *Frasca* at Cividale; *Campiello* at San Giovanni al Natisone.

Grave *La di Petrôs* at Colloredo di Monte Albano; *Trattoria agli Amici* at Godia di Udine; *Blasut* at Lavariano; *Da Toso* at Leonacco di Tricesimo; *Del Doge* in the Villa Marin at Passariano del Codroipo; *Pescatore* at Roveredo in Piano; *Al Cantinon* at San Daniele; *Trattoria La Primula* at San Quirino; *Al Grop* at Tavagnacco; *Boschetti* at Tricesimo.

Isonzo *Mulin Vecio* at Gradisca d'Isonzo; *Piave* at Mariano del Friuli; *Castellieri* at Monfalcone.

Emilia-Romagna *Emilia-Romagna*

Emilia and Romagna are northern Italy's cheerful oddities, making wines that have not much to do with those of their neighbours and little more to do with one another's. Emilia's gift to the world is red (or pink or even white) Lambrusco, whose bubbles buoy the masses while inspiring the disdain of wine snobs. Romagna keeps the Adriatic's sun-worshippers content with its white Albana, and proudly claims the virtues of its (non-Tuscan) Sangiovese. What the wines of Emilia and Romagna do have in common is that they are usually affordable, cheeringly drinkable, and, to native palates at least, provide an ideal complement to some of Italy's richest but most remarkable cooking.

Bologna is the axis of these abundantly fertile twin provinces, watered by the river Po to the north and Appenine streams ot the south. Emilia extends

Wine Areas

1 Colli Piacentini
2 Colli di Parma
3 Lambrusco Salamino di Santa Croce
4 Bosco Eliceo
5 Lambrusco di Sorbara
6 Reggiano
7 Lamabrusco Grasparossa di Castelvetro
8 Reno
9 Colli Bolognesi
10 Trebbiano di Romagna
11 Albana di Romagna
12 Sangiovese di Romagna
13 Cagnina di Romagna
14 Pagadebit di Romagna
15 Colli di Faenza
16 Colli di Imola
17 Colli di Rimini
18 Colli di Scandiano e di Canossa

westward through the the townships of Modena, Reggio, Parma, and
Piacenza where, adjacent to Lombardy's Oltrepò Pavese, its wine takes on
similar styles. It is otherwise noted mainly for lightish, bubbly, and often softly
sweet wines from both plains and hills – although the real Lambrusco admired
locally is dry – but more renowned for its Parma ham and Parmigiano
Reggiano cheese. Romagna stretches eastward from Bologna to the Adriatic,
across Ferrara and Faenza to Ravenna, Forli, Cesena, and Rimini. Here the
emphasis is on still wines led by the popular Albana, Trebbiano, and
Sangiovese but also taking in some local curiosities, especially close to the
coast, and some international stars, particularly in the Colli Bolognesi zone.

   Emilia-Romagna ranks second to the Veneto in volume of production in
northern Italy. Besides its twenty DOCs and single DOCG (Albana di
Romagna), there are a number of IGTs of which Emilia is the most extensive.
Wine tourism is well developed in the region, most notably in Romagna,
where the wine tavern, a local institution, has been revived at Bertinoro
(*Ca' de B*), Predappio Alto (*Ca' de Sanzves*), Ravenna (*Ca' de Vin*), and Rimini
(*Chsa de Vein*). In Emilia, the scenic Colli Bolognesi are a treasure trove of
little-known wines. In the Colli Piacentini, the *enoteca* at Castell'Arquato
displays wines of the zone. Lambrusco admirers can slake their thirst in the
lush plains around Modena and Reggio, specifically at the *enoteca* in the
castle at Levizzano Rangone near Castelvetro. The *Enoteca Regionale
Emilia-Romagna* is housed in the *Rocca Sforzesca* at Dozza in Romagna.

Recent Vintages

Lambrusco and most whites are for drinking young, but many reds age well.

2002 Summer rain meant quality was good only for carefully selected grapes.
2001 A very good year giving ripe, well-balanced wines.
2000 Excellent. Reds are concentrated, structured, and balanced.
Notes on ealier vintages Earlier good vintages include 99, 98, 95, 94, 93.

Wines

ALBANA DI ROMAGNA *DOCG*
It is regrettable that, for many
outside Italy, Albana is still
linked with the kerfuffle that
arose when it was, prematurely,
made Italy's first DOCG white
back in 1987. The wines from this
ancient Roman vine are now far
more often firm, elegant, and
inviting, whether dry or, less often,
sweet. The *passito* version (made
from semi-dried grapes with
botrytis, is still the best type, though,
and can be truly excellent. *See also*
Romagna Albana Spumante.

Secco *w dr* ☆→☆☆☆ *DYA* Dry
types often show restrained
style, with good fruit, intensity,
and softness.

Amabile, Dolce, Passito *w am s/sw sw*
☆☆→☆☆☆ *98 00 01* Albana's

characteristics are enhanced by
sweetness, with the *passito* version
especially convincing. Age: *passito*
6 mths.

BOSCO ELICEO *DOC*
The sandy seaside plains stretching
from the Po to Ravenna are home
to a grapey red from Fortana (or
Uva d'Oro), a rare, ancient variety
grown mostly in vineyards near the
once famous Bosco Eliceo woods.
The DOC also takes in other types.

Bianco *w dr (s/sw) fz* ☆ *DYA* Simple,
usually fizzy, white from at least
70% Trebbiano.

Fortana *r dr (fz) (s/sw)* ☆→☆☆ *DYA*
Curious Lambrusco-type red,
usually fizzy, and sharply acidic.
Traditionally consumed with eels
from the lagoon.

Merlot *r dr (fr)* ☆ DYA Lightweight of local interest only.

Sauvignon Blanc *w dr (fz) (s/sw)* ☆ DYA Zesty at best.

CAGNINA DI ROMAGNA

DOC r s/sw sw ☆→☆☆ DYA
The comeback of this softly sweet violet to purple wine is due to sprightly freshness and a mouth-cleansing tannic bite that are best within months of the harvest. Cagnina is the same variety as Friuli's Terrano or Refosco Nostrano, but it is more mellow in Romagna, and considered ideal with roasted chestnuts.

COLLI BOLOGNESI *DOC*

Picturesque hills south of Bologna, from Cabernet, Chardonnay, Pinot Bianco, and Sauvignon. Certain Colli Bolognesi wines made following stricter regulations may show the sub-zone Colline di Oliveto, Colline di Riosto, Colline Marconiane, Monte San Pietro, Serravalle, Terre di Montebudello, or Zola Predosa. Not all sub-zones apply to all varieties.

Bianco *w dr fz (s/sw)* ☆→☆☆ DYA Mostly from Albana, with Trebbiano, usually fizzy.

Barbera *r dr (fz) (s/sw)* ☆→☆☆ 97 98 99 00 01 02 Rich ruby-violet; brisk flavour (can be bubbly), mellowing over 2 to 5 years. Age: *riserva* 3 yrs.

Cabernet Sauvignon *r dr* ☆☆→☆☆☆ 94 95 97 98 99 00 01 02 Often the best red of the hills. Deep in colour with typical bouquet and flavour, its gentility comes across even when styled to drink young (1 to 5 years). Age: *riserva* 3 yrs.

Chardonnay *w dr (fz) (sp)* ☆→☆☆☆ 98 99 00 01 02 Styles vary from light and lively, to full-bodied with depth.

Merlot *r dr (s/sw)* ☆→☆☆☆ 97 98 99 00 01 02 Wines are usually dark-ruby, softly dry, smoothly fruity, and good for 2 to 6 years. From the Zola Predosa sub-zone, Merlot requires 2 years of ageing.

Pinot Bianco *w dr (fz)* ☆☆→☆☆☆ 99 00 01 02 Light green/straw, scented, and smooth. Can reach fine levels in good years.

Riesling Italico *w dr (fz) (s/sw)* ☆☆ DYA Delicately scented white of fruity, off-dry flavour that comes across best young and chilled.

Sauvignon Blanc *w dr (fz) (s/sw)* ☆☆→☆☆☆ 98 99 00 01 02 Often the best of the whites, crisp, dry, flinty, and scented, sometimes with Loire-like varietal tone.

COLLI BOLOGNESI CLASSICO PIGNOLETTO *DOC*

w dr ☆☆ Pignoletto wines from a more restricted area centred on Monte San Pietro with higher alcohol (12%), acidity, and extract may take this denomination which spotlights the dry, still style.

COLLI DI FAENZA *DOC*

Zone in Romagna's hills behind Faenza covering 5 types of wine, of which the Rosso and Sangiovese lead so far. Varietals must be 100%.

Bianco *w dr* Chardonnay (40–60%) with Pignoletto, Pinot Bianco, Sauvignon, and/or Trebbiano. Rarely seen.

Rosso *r dr* ☆☆→☆☆☆ 98 99 00 01 Sauvignon (40–60%) Cabernet with Ancellotta, Ciliegiolo, Merlot, and/or Sangiovese. Age: *riserva* 2 yrs.

Pinot Bianco *w dr* Rarely seen.

Sangiovese *r dr* ☆☆→☆☆☆ 98 99 00 01 Wines of good promise. Age: *riserva* 2 yrs.

Trebbiano *w dr* Rarely seen.

COLLI DI IMOLA *DOC*

Zone in Romagna's hills above Imola, taking in the towns of Dozza, Castel San Pietro Terme, and Borgo Tossignano. DOC applies to 8 types of wine, including 6 varietals.

Bianco *w dr (fz) (s/sw) (sw)* DYA May come from any approved non-aromatic white wine variety of Bologna province alone or in blends. *Superiore* has slightly higher alcohol. Usually light, unassuming.

Rosso *r dr (s/sw) (sw) 98 99 00* This may come from any approved non-aromatic red wine variety of Bologna province alone or in blends. Also *novello*. Wines can reveal unexpected class. Age: *riserva* 18 mths.

Barbera *r dr (fz)* Rarely produced.

Cabernet Sauvignon *r dr* ☆→☆☆☆☆ *99 00 01 02* This reliable variety shows promise here too. Age: *riserva* 18 mths.

Chardonnay *w dr (fz)* ☆→☆☆☆ *99 00 01 02* As reliable as ever here.

Pignoletto *w dr (fz)* Rarely produced.

Sangiovese *r dr 99 00 01 02* Characteristics, on paper, are similar to Sangiovese di Romagna; the differences depend on its producers. Age: *riserva* 18 mths.

Trebbiano *w dr (fz) DYA* Light and unassuming.

COLLI DI PARMA *DOC*

With the understandable desire to bring as much of their production as possible into the DOC net, as of 2002 Parma's erstwhile simple DOC structure of just 3 wines has been expanded to 14. Nevertheless, the area's gentle hills are still best noted for mellow, fragrant, bubbly Malvasia, considered the ideal match for the succulent, air-cured Prosciutto di Parma. *Riserva* versions of all styles (except Lambrusco and the *spumante*) are permitted after 18 months (whites) or 2 years (reds) ageing.

Rosso *r dr (fz)* ☆☆ *99 00 01 02* From Barbera with some Bonarda and Croatina, this bears a family resemblance to Piacenza's Gutturnio – dark ruby-violet, dry, bitter underneath, often with a prickle. Lamoretti makes an admirable version.

Barbera *w dr (fr)*

Bonarda *r dr (fr) (sw)*

Cabernet Franc *r dr*

Cabernet Sauvignon *w dr (fr)*

Chardonnay *w dr (fr) (sp)*

Lambrusco *r dr sw fr DYA* From Lambrusco Maestri.

Malvasia *w dr s/sw fz (sp)* ☆→☆☆ *DYA* From Malvasia di Candia with Moscato permitted at 15%, whether dry or *amabile*, the typical aroma of Malvasia is enhanced by a little fizz.

Merlot *r dr (fr)*

Pinot Bianco *w dr (fr) (sp)*

Pinot Grigio *w dr (fr)*

Pinot Nero *r dr*

Sauvignon *w dr (sp)* ☆→☆☆ *DYA* Dry, delicately flinty, this noble variety makes a white of refreshing simplicity here.

Spumante *w sp* From Pinot Bianco, Pinot Nero, and/or Chardonnay only.

COLLI DI RIMINI *DOC*

Zone in the hills above the beach resort of Rimini, producing 5 types of wine rarely seen outside the area.

Bianco *w dr DYA* Mainly from the Romagnan strain of Trebbiano, with the local Biancame and Mostosa.

Rosso *r dr* Mostly from Sangiovese, with Cabernet Sauvignon and optional others.

Biancame *w dr DYA* This local variety is good with fish but is unlikely to set hearts aflame.

Cabernet Sauvignon *r dr* Age: *riserva* 2 yrs.

Rébola *w dr s/sw s* Rébola is the local name for Pignoletto. *Passito* versions are attracting most interest but styles spread from sweet to dry.

COLLI DI SCANDIANO E DI CANOSSA *DOC*

Once simply Bianco di Scandiano the zone now takes in the hilly areas of Scandiano and Canossa, south of Reggio Emilia.

Bianco and Bianco Classico *w dr s/sw (sw) fz sp* ☆→☆☆ *DYA* Light white based on Sauvignon, known locally as Spergola. The *classico* comes from the historical heartland production zone, centred on Albinea. A *passito* version is also made.

Cabernet Sauvignon *r dr* ☆☆ *00 01 02* Age: *riserva* 2 yrs.

Chardonnay *w dr (sp)* ☆☆ *DYA*

Lambrusco Grasparossa *r dr fz (s/sw)*
(sw) ☆→☆☆☆ *DYA* Lambrusco here
can be among the finest of Emilia.

Lambrusco Montericco *r (p) dr fz (s/sw)*
(sw) ☆→☆☆☆ *DYA* Lambrusco here
can be among the finest of Emilia.

Malbo Gentile *r dr (fz) (s/sw) (sw) DYA*
Rare local variety may be used with
Croatina and/or Sgavetta in soft red
wine that may also be *novello*.

Malvasia *w dr s/sw fz (sw) (sp)* ☆→☆☆
DYA This is similar to the Malvasia
of Colli Piacentini and Parma.

Marzemino *r dr (s/sw) (sw) (fr)* Variety
from Trentino is rarely seen.

Pinot *w dr fz sp* Pinot Bianco and/
or Pinot Nero, used in still or
sparkling wine.

Sauvignon *w dr (s/sw) (sw) (fr)* ☆→☆☆
DYA Sweet *passito* made. Age:
passito 2 yrs.

COLLI PIACENTINI *DOC*
Large zone in the Apennine
foothills south of Piacenza,
adjacent to Lombardy's Oltrepò
Parese, to which some of its wines
are stylistically similar and covering
the valleys of the rivers Trebbia,
Nure, Arda, and Timone. Three
types within the DOC take their
names from one of these valleys.
There are also 8 varietals and the
pivotal Gutturnio, a lively Bonarda-
Barbera blend that (with Malvasia)
forms the backbone of the DOC.
Many of the styles are sometimes
off-dry (*abboccato*) and frequently
lightly bubbly (*frizzante*) – as
typified by the lively Malvasia.

Barbera *r dr (fz)* ☆☆ *00 01 02* Sturdy
reds, sometimes fizzy, usually
to drink inside 3 years.

Bonarda *r dr s/sw fz (sp)* ☆☆ *00 01 02*
Dark ruby, often lightly sweet
and fizzy, to drink in 2 to 3 years.

Cabernet Sauvignon *r dr* ☆☆→☆☆☆
96 97 98 00 01 Showing well here;
wines for moderate ageing.

Chardonnay *w dr (fr) (sp)* ☆☆ *01 02*

Gutturnio *r dr (fz)* ☆☆→☆☆☆ *99 00
01 02* Gutturnio, from Barbera and
Bonarda, usually dry and still, is
deep garnet to violet; generous
and smooth, with a fine bouquet.

Some are youthful drinking, others
age a good 3 to 4 years. Gutturnio
from Val Tidone, Val Nure, and
Val d'Arda may be called *classico*.
Age: *superiore* 1 yr, *riserva* 2 yrs.

Malvasia *w dr s/sw (sw) fz (sp)* ☆☆☆ *DYA*
The vivacious thirst-quencher of
these hills: aromatic, fizzy, off-dry.
Gains a touch of refinement in fully
sweet and *passito* versions.

Monterosso Val d'Arda *w dr fz (s/sw)
(sp)* ☆→☆☆ *DYA* From Malvasia
and Moscato, with Trebbiano and
Ortrugo, this delicate white is more
often *frizzante* than fully sparkling
and sometimes softly sweetish.

Novello *r dr* ☆→☆☆ *DYA* Barbera,
Croatina and Pinot Nero are
the base of this fruity red made
to be drunk immediately.

Ortrugo *w dr (fz) (sp)* ☆☆ *DYA* This fine
local grape variety makes zesty
whites of good flavour.

Pinot Grigio *w dr (fz) (sp)* ☆→☆☆ *DYA*
Increasingly popular, makes still
wines and *spumante*.

Pinot Nero *r dr* ☆☆ *01 02* Varietally
pure reds where elegance
penalizes solidity.

Pinot Spumante *w p dr (sp)* ☆→☆☆ *DYA*
Light, white, or pink sparklers
from Pinot Nero, with up to
15% Chardonnay.

Sauvignon *w dr s/sw (fz)* ☆→☆☆☆ *01 02*
Often light and lively style.

Trebbianino Val Trebbia *w dr fz (sp)*
☆→☆☆ *DYA* Delicate, spritzy white
from Ortrugo with Trebbiano,
Sauvignon, Malvasia, and Moscato
grown in the Trebbia Valley.

Val Nure *w dr (s/sw) fz (sp)* ☆→☆☆ *DYA*
From Malvasia with Ortrugo and/
or Trebbiano. Light and delicate.

Vin Santo *w am (dr) sw* Dry or sweet,
from a range of white varieties and
aged in small barrels. Vin Santo di
Vigoleno from a restricted zone and
sweet only is considered the model.
Age: 4 yrs, Vigoleno 5 yrs.

COLLI DELLA ROMAGNA
CENTRALE *DOC*
New and promising but so far
untested DOC for Cabernet
Sauvignon and Chardonnay

grown in a smallish, hilly zone above Cesena. Trebbiano and Sangiovese, produced with slightly more stringent criteria than for the blanket Di Romagna versions, are included as are *bianco* and *rosso* blends. All reds with two years ageing may be *riserva*.

Bianco *w dr* From Chardonnay with any or all of Bombino, Sauvignon, Trebbiano, Pinot Bianco.

Cabernet Sauvignon *r dr*

Chardonnay *w dr* From 100% of the grape. Age: *riserva* 2 yrs.

Rosso *r dr* From Cabernet Sauvignon with any or all of Sangiovese, Barbera, Merlot, Montepulciano.

Sangiovese *r dr* From 100% of the grape.

Trebbiano *w dr*

LAMBRUSCO

The vine in its various sub-varieties flourishes on Emilia's plains, especially around Modena and Reggio where its wines are DOC under 5 denominations. All DOC Lambrusco must be red (or pink) and naturally *frizzante*, usually by tank methods, though bottle-fermentation is sometimes seen. Classically it is dry, and is still the style of preference locally, although most of what is shipped abroad is sweet. White Lambrusco, not DOC, is regarded as a regrettable marketing phenomenon that has thankfully passed its day.

LAMBRUSCO DI SORBARA

DOC r p dr s/sw sw fz ☆→☆☆☆ DYA
Considered the classic, it is made from at least 60% of the Sorbara strain of Lambrusco. Pale-red with an aromatic fragrance of raspberry and a light fizz, it goes with rich Emilian dishes, especially pasta and pork. The *amabile* is rarely found and less interesting.

LAMBRUSCO GRASPAROSSA DI CASTELVETRO

DOC r p dr s/sw sw fz ☆→☆☆☆ DYA
Made from the Grasparossa strain of Lambrusco in a zone south of

Modena that includes Castelvetro. Often a little fuller in flavour than other types, the wine is ruby-violet and notably fragrant.

LAMBRUSCO SALAMINO DI SANTA CROCE

r p dr s/sw sw fz ☆→☆☆ DYA
Made from the Salamino strain in a zone north of Modena that includes the village of Santa Croce. Pale ruby to purple, rich, and lively, it's considered Modena's daily drink.

PAGADEBIT DI ROMAGNA

DOC w dr s/sw (fr) ☆→☆☆ DYA
Pagadebit menas "pays the debts" and this synonym of Bombino Bianco gives wines of gratifyingly soft fruit on an almondy background. Produced in southeast Romagna, south of Forlì, the small area of Bertinoro where it was restored from partial extinction has sub-zone status. Both dry and *amabile* versions are found.

REGGIANO *DOC*

This zone covers Lambrusco produced in the province of Reggio Emilia as well as a *rosso* from a Lambrusco blend.

Lambrusco *r p dr s/sw fz ☆→☆☆☆ DYA*
From a blend of sub-varieties, this is the most heavily produced Lambrusco (about 16 million litres a year) and the most exported. Though much is no more than light and refreshing, some shows unsurpassed colour, aroma, and flavour. Also *novello*.

Lambrusco Salamino *r p dr (s/sw) (sw) fz*
Wine from the Salamino strain is often dry.

Bianco Spumante *w dr sp ☆→☆☆ DYA*
Sparkling white (Lambrusco), from a number of sub-varieties, can be a refreshing alternative.

Rosso *r dr s/sw sw fr* Soft red based on Ancellotta and Lambrusco varieties. Also *novello*.

RENO *DOC*

Local DOC stretching across the Reno and Panaro valleys southwest of Bologna, dominated by the Montuni (or Montù) grape.

Bianco w dr s/sw sw fr DYA From Albana and Trebbiano with other varieties.

Montuni w dr s/sw sw f DYA Popular, usually fizzy, fresh white, the most common of this DOC's 3 variants.

Pignoletto w dr s/sw sw fr DYA

ROMAGNA ALBANA SPUMANTE

DOC w sw sp ☆→☆☆ DYA

A light, easy-going sweet sparkler from Albana grapes.

SANGIOVESE DI ROMAGNA

DOC r dr ☆→☆☆☆ 95 97 98 99 00 01 02

The wine closest to Romagna's heart is Sangiovese (Sanzves in dialect), a hearty red that goes well with many of the tasty meat and pasta dishes of the hill country. It is true that it rarely has the structure and complexity of Tuscan Sangiovese, but instead it has a more mellow character thanks to deeper acids and rounder tannins, admirably refined in the *superiore* version. A growing number of producers make Sangiovese of enviable depth and balance, but others are still unprepossessing, preventing a strong reputation outside the area. Sangiovese varies according to area in types described locally as *allegro*, *gentile*, *forte*, and *nobile* – the latter from the heart of the zone between the towns of Faenza and Cesena. Also *novello*. Age: *superiore* 5 mths, *riserva* 2 yrs.

TREBBIANO DI ROMAGNA

DOC w dr (fz) (sp) ☆→☆☆ DYA

Trebbiano (from a local clone of the family) is Romagna's everyday unassuming white. It is drunk copiously in fish restaurants along the Adriatic, where the sparkling (sometimes sweet) type also has fans. The few wines from the hills carry hints of flowers and fruit beyond the normal acidic nip. But that from the plains is more neutral.

Producers

Provinces: Bologna (BO), Ferrara (FE), Forlì-Cesena (FC), Modena (MO), Parma (PR), Piacenza (PC), Ravenna (RA), Reggio Emilia (RE), Rimini (RN). (Sangiovese refers to Sangiovese di Romagna unless stated otherwise.)

Francesco Bellei, Bomporto (MO), Exceptional bottle-fermented Lambrusco di Sorbara from organic grapes. Also good range of sparklers from Pinot Noir/Chardonnay.

La Berta, Brisighella (RA). Steadily improving estate with fine Sangiovese (Solana and Olmatello Riserva), good Colli di Faenza Rosso, and intruiging Almante from Alicante grapes.

Tenuta Bonzara, Monte San Pietro (BO). Classy Colli Bolognesi: Merlot and Cabernet (Rocca di Bonacciara), Sauvignon (Le Carrate), sweet Û Pâsa Passito from Sauvignon and delightful Pignoletto Frizzante.

Le Calbane, Meldola (FC). Good Sangiovese and unusual IGT Calbanesco from the vine of that name, a red of ample, berry-like bouquet and warm flavour with a bitterish hint.

Fratelli Caprari, Reggio Emilia. Reggiano Lambrusco, including 3 bottle-fermented *riservas*.

Carra, Langhirano (PR). Emerging Colli di Parma estate.

Casali, Pratissolo di Scandiano (RE). Colli di Scandiano e di Canossa Sauvignon (La Dogaia, Altobrolo), Malvasia (Acaia), and outstanding single-vineyard Lambrusco Reggiano (Bosco del Fracasso, Prà di Bosso), and bottle-fermented Roggio del Pradello.

Casetto dei Mandorli, Predappio Alta (FC). Sangiovese di Romagna

(Vigna del Generale), Tre Rocche, Vigne dei Mandorli), and Trebbiano.

Castelli del Duca, Piacenza. Promising new Colli Piacentini estate with well-typed, good-value wines.

Castelluccio, Modigliana (FC). Acclaimed IGT red Ronco delle Ginestre, Ronco dei Ciliegi and DOC Le More (all Sangiovese), and white IGT Lunaria and Ronco del Re (both Sauvignon). Sangiovese wines could rank with the cream of Tuscany; Ronco del Re is a singular white of luxuriant tone with unusual complexity, depth, and staying power.

Cavicchioli, San Prospero (MO). Remarkable Lambrusco di Sorbara (Vigna del Cristo dry) and Grasparossa de Castelvetro (Col Sassoso). Range of less special Lambrusco, too.

Celli, Bertinoro (FC). Full range of Romagna varietals led by admirable Albana Passito (Solara), and Sangiovese (Le Grillaie), also Sangiovese/Cabernet blend (Bron e Ruseval).

Umberto Cesari, Castel San Pietro Terme (BO). Large winery of high standing with Albana Colle del Re (both *secco* and *passito*), Sangiovese (Tauleto), IGT Malise (Pignoletto/Chardonnay), and Liano (Sangiovese/Cabernet) leading the field.

Chiarli 1860, Modena. Fine long-standing Lambrusco house, with more characterful wines under the Chiarli Cleto label.

Floriano Cinti, Sasso Marconi (BO). Good Colli BolOgnesi Pignoletto is now being joined by serious Cabernet Sauvignon, Merlot.

Civ & Civ, Modena. Huge co-op grouping. MaInly cheap and cheerful Lambrusco.

Conti, Faenza (RA). Albana special (Progetto 1, Progetto 2, Non Ti Scordar di Me), also making good reds.

Conte Otto Barattieri, *vin santo* and Il Faggio, from Brachetto Passito mark out this Colli Piacentini estate.

Contessa Matilde, Modena. Cellars make DOC Lambrusco for Premiovini of Lombardy.

Corte Manzini, Castelvetro di Modena (MO). Hand-crafted Lambrusco di Grasparossa stands out from its competitors.

CS Valtidone, Borgonovo (PC). Reliable Colli Piacentini range.

Fattoria Paradiso, Bertinoro (FC). Renowned estate with large range of individual, stylish wines, both from Romagna's Sangiovese, Albana, Barbarossa et al, and from international varieties. Mito (Cabernet/Merlot/Syrah) is currently gaining most plaudits.

Franco Ferrari, Soliera (MO). Good Lambrusco di Sorbara, Salamino di Santa Croce.

Stefano Ferucci, Castelbolognese (RA). Fine Albana Dolce and Passito, and Sangiovese Domus Caia (from late-harvested grapes).

Vittorio Graziano, Castelvetro (MO). Lambrusco Grasparossa full of character.

Istituto Professionale per l'Agricoltura e l'Ambiente, Faenza (RA). Wines from agricultural school concentrate on unusual varietals.

Lamoretti, Langhirano (PR). Colli di Parma includes Malvasia, Sauvignon, admired *rosso* (Vigna del Guasto, Vigna di Montefiore), and more.

Oreste Lini e Figli, Correggio (RE). Lambrusco including cherry-pink Labrusca.

Luretta, Gazzola (PC). Leading Colli Piacentini varietals.

Gaetano Lusenti, Ziano Piacentino (PC). Up-and-coming Colli Piacentini estate.

Giovanna Madonia, Bertinoro (FC). Good Sangiovese (Ombroso), Albana Passito (Remoto).

Maletti, Soliera (MO). Fine Lambrusco di Sorbara.

Enzo Manicardi, Castelvetro (MO). Lambrusco Grasparossa from hill vineyards.

Moro, Sant'Ilario d'Enza (RE). Unusual wines from low-yielding vines such as Vigna del Picchio (Lambrusco/

Ancellotta, picked late) and bottle-fermented Lambrusco.

Gradizzolo Ognibene, Monteveglio (BO). Unusually, Barbera from Colli Bolognesi.

La Palazza, Forlì (FC). Good Sangiovese di Romagna (Pruno, Notturno) beside highly admired IGT Cabernet Sauvignon (Magnificat), and Chardonnay (Il Tornese).

Poderi dal Nespoli, Civitella di Romagna (FC). Sangiovese (Prugneto, Santodeno), Albana; fine IGT Borgo dei Guidi (Sangiovese/Cabernet/Raboso) and Il Nespoli (late-picked Sangiovese).

Il Poggiarello, Travo (PC). Rapidly improving Colli Piacentini varietals.

Il Pratello, Modigliana (FC). Incisive Colli di Faenza wines from high-altitude, low-yield vines.

Riunite, Reggio Emilia. Major co-op group makes Lambrusco of various styles, mainly *amabile* and mostly exported, plus other Emilian wines.

Romagnoli, Vigolzone (PC). Colli Piacentini led by Gutturnio (Vigna del Gallo).

San Patrignano, Coriano (RN). Superb Sangiovese, bordeaux-blend Montepirolo, lead excellent range.

San Valentino, Rimini. Colli di Rimini newcomer of great promise.

Santarosa, Monte San Pietro (BO). Starry Colli Bolognesi wines led by excellent Merlot (Giòtondo), Cabernet (Giòcoliere).

Stefano Berti, Forlì (FC). Boutique winery with highly extolled Sangiovese (Calisto, Ravaldo).

La Stoppa, Ancarano di Rivergaro (PC). Fine Colli Piacentini Barbera, Gutturnio, and some outstanding Cabernet Sauvignon (Stoppa), along with Vigna del Volta (Malvasia Passito) and IGT red Macchiona (Barbera/Bonarda).

Terre Rosse, Zola Predosa (BO). Long-time leaders in Colli Bolognesi with Cabernet Sauvignon (Il Rosso di Enrico Vallania), Chardonnay (Cuvée Giovanni Vallania), Merlot, late-harvested Riesling (Malagò Elisabetta Vallania), and sweet Malvasia (Adriana Vallania).

Tizzano, Casalecchio di Reno (BO). Up-and-coming Colli Bolognesi estate.

La Tosa, Vigolzone (PC). Outstanding Colli Piacentini Gutturnio (Vignamorello), Cabernet Sauvignon (La Luna Selvatica), Malvasia (Sorriso di Cielo), Sauvignon (La Tosa).

Tre Monti, Imola (BO). Attractive Albana Passito and Dolce, Sangiovese (Thea), Colli di Imola of lustre with Cabernet (Turico), *bianco* (Salcerella), Boldo (Sangiovese/Cabernet), and, unusually, Barbera.

Treré, Faenza (RA). Smart Albana, and Sangiovese (Amarcord d'un Ross) lead convincing range of Romagna and Faenza DOCs.

Tenuta Uccellina, Russi (RA). Fine Sangiovese, Albana Dolce, and Passito, and oddity Burson from the very rare Longanesi.

Vallona, Castello di Serravalle (BO). Fine Colli Bolognesi Cabernet Sauvignon, Chardonnay, Sauvignon, Pignoletto, and Altr-Uve Passito (Pignoletto/Albana/Sauvignon).

Venturini Baldini, Roncolo di Quattro Castella (RE). Admirable Reggiano Lambrusco and more from organic grapes.

Vigneto Bagazzana, Zola Predosa (BO). Admired Colli Bolognesi, especially whites.

Zerbina, Marzeno di Faenza (RA). Leading Romagna estate with exemplary Albana Passito (Scaccomatto), and Dolce (Arrocco); impeccable Sangiovese; and superb Marzieno (Sangiovese/Cabernet/Merlot).

Wine & Food

Pasta alone would elevate Emilia-Romagna's cooking to the divine.

The making of tagliatelle, tortellini, tortelli, anolini,

cappelletti, passatelli and lasagne, to name a few, is a daily routine performed by the *sfogliatrice*, living testimony to the regional conviction that pasta must be fresh and made by hand. But pasta is just the entrée of a culinary heritage as religiously adhered to as any of France. Bologna "the fat", with its *mortadella* and *lasagne verdi* and a dozen other delights of its own, is the capital of regional gastronomy, but some provincial centres – especially Parma, Modena, Reggio, and Piacenza – can rival its battery of good things to eat. Foremost are Parmigiano Reggiano cheese (called Parmesan) and Prosciutto di Parma, but Modena weighs in heftily with its *zampone* (pig's feet sausage) and the true *Aceto Balsamico Tradizionale* (balsamic vinegar – too glorious to be considered vinegar – though imitations abound. There is so much more to Emilia-Romagna's cornucopia that this list could only whet the appetite.

Wines to accompany each dish are suggested below in italics.

Anatra alla romagnola
Duck cooked with bacon, wine, and seasonings in Romagna. *Sangiovese riserva*

Burlenghi Hot, fried pastry flavoured with lard, pork crackling, rosemary, garlic, grated cheese. *Lambrusco Grasparossa di Castelvetro*

Cappelletti in brodo Hat-shaped pasta with meat filling served in broth. *Albana secco*

Parmigiano Reggiano
This, the greatest of grating cheeses, is also eaten in chunks, sometimes topped with a drop of *Aceto Balsamico. Colli Piacentini Gutturnio*

Lasagne verdi al forno
Green lasagne cooked with layers of meat *ragù* and béchamel. *Lambrusco Reggiano*

Piadina Flat bread served with Pecorino cheese, ham, or Salami. *Reggiano Lambrusco*

Prosciutto di Parma con melone Parma ham with cantaloupe (or fresh figs). *Colli di Parma Malvasia*

Tortelli all'erbetta Large pasta envelopes filled with ricotta and *erbetta*, a chard-like green, served with melted butter and Parmesan. *Colli di Scandiano e di Canossa Sauvignon*

Zampone Pig's feet sausage from Modena, generally served with lentils or mashed potatoes. *Lambrusco Salamino di Santa Croce*

Restaurants

Recommended in or near wine zones:

Emilia *Picci* at Cavriago; *Villa Maria Luigia* at Collecchio; *Da Giovanni* at Cortina Vecchia; *Ostello Cantoniera* at Farini d'Olmo; *Cavallo Bianco* at Polesine Parmense; *Riva* at Ponte dell'Olio; *Osteria di Rubbiara* at Rubbiara; *Arnaldo-Clinica Gastronomica* at Rubiera; *Mamma Rosa* at San Polo d'Enza; *Formicone* at Savignano sul Panaro; *Da Amerigo* at Savigno;

Lancellotti at Soliera; *Il Caminetto da Papy* at Viano.

Romagna *Gigiolè*, *La Grotta* and *Strada Casale* at Brisighella; *Locanda Solarola* at Castelguelfo di Bologna; *La Frasca* at Castrocaro Terme; *La Buca* at Cesenatico; *Al Maneggio* at Forlimpopoli; *San Domenico* at Imola; *Locanda della Tamerice* at Ostellato; *Trattoria Marinelli da Vittorio* at Rimini; *Osteria del Povero Diavolo* at Torriana; *Locanda della Colonna* at Tossignano.

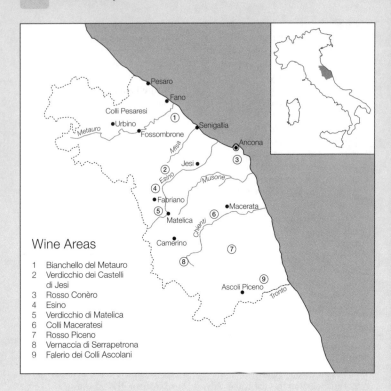

Wine Areas

1   Bianchello del Metauro
2   Verdicchio dei Castelli
    di Jesi
3   Rosso Conèro
4   Esino
5   Verdicchio di Matelica
6   Colli Maceratesi
7   Rosso Piceno
8   Vernaccia di Serrapetrona
9   Falerio dei Colli Ascolani

Marche *Marche*

Verdicchio put Marche on the wine map decades ago with its green, amphora-shaped bottle. But as the amphora gradually went out of style, Verdicchio grew well beyond its role as an astutely marketed, simple fish wine to become one of Italy's most multifaceted and dignified whites. Control of harvesting time and vinification method can produce a crisp, youthfully lively wine with a succulent heart or a deep, rich, buttery one that develops slowly and ages with aplomb – or various stages in-between. Oak can bring additional nuances, too, for those who wish to use it. Yet quality rises in the large Castelli di Jesi and small Matelica zones have generally outstripped price rises, so that Verdicchio remains a healthy cut above the general level of Italy's popular whites.

Verdicchio still firmly dominates the Marche's wine production. Neighbouring whites in this peaceful region between the Apennines and the Adriatic sea are for the most part light and insubstantial, the main exception being Bianchello del Metauro from its more northerly part. Reds are very much in second place, for quantity, but production is often quality led. Rosso Piceno, based on Sangiovese, can show class as one of the true bargains in aged red wines left in central Italy, although not a great deal leaves the region. Rosso Conero, based on Montepulciano grown on the outskirts of Ancona, can reach even greater heights, but here too its local admirers somehow manage much of it for themselves. And much as wine aficionados may search out the weird and wonderful Lacrima di Morro d'Alba or the curious sparkling red Vernaccia di Serrapetrona, (shortly to become DOCG) again they remain primarily local. Red or white, though, in general the Marche's wines retain the flavours of local varieties. DOCs number a manageable twelve, and the lone IGT is the region-wide Marche.

Most tourists come here to bask on Adriatic beaches, but those who wander into the interior will also find peaceful, relaxing scenery in the hills. Urbino is an art centre, Loreto a religious shrine, and Ascoli Piceno is one of many well-preserved medieval towns. The regional *Enoteca dei Vini Marchigiani* is located in the centre of Jesi. A tasteful choice of wines can be found at the *Enoteca Internazionale Bugari* at San Benedetto del Tronto.

Recent Vintages

Most white wines of the Marches are for drinking young, though Verdicchio from both Jesi and Matelica can develop impressively with 3 to 5 years of age, sometimes longer. Rosso Conero and Rosso Piceno may also sometimes be made to be drunk fairly young, but more frequently age well for a decade or more. Of the recent vintages, 2002 gave very good quality despite drastic yield reductions due to a rainy summer, 2001 was supreme (except in Ascoli Piceno province), and 2000, 1999, 1998; and 1997 all very succesful. Among older vintages, 1995 was very good and 1990 magnificent. Other good vintages to be remembered are 1988, 1987, 1985, 1983, and 1982.

Wines

BIANCHELLO DEL METAURO
DOC w dr ☆☆→☆☆☆ *DYA*
Biancame or Biancone grapes grown along the Metauro River make this popular white whose lemony zest appeals to summer crowds. But it need not always be taken lightly as some producers give it considerable style enabling it to become a sprightly alternative to Verdicchio.

COLLI MACERATESI *DOC*
The zone is large, stretching from the Adriatic inland past Macerata toward the Appennines, but little is made of this delicate white and newly delimited red.

Bianco *w dr (sw) (sp)* ☆→☆☆☆ *DYA*
Delicate white from 70% or more of the local Maceratino variety (also known as Ribona) and, optionally, up to 8 other varieties. There is a rare *passito* version, aged 2 yrs.

Ribona *w dr (sw) (sp)* ☆→☆☆☆ *DYA* An attempt to highlight the (unproved) qualities of the Ribona/Maceratino

variety unblended. Age: *passito* 2 yrs.

Rosso *r dr* From at least 50% Sangiovese and up to 7 others including Cabernet, Merlot, Lacrima, Montepulciano, and Vernaccia Nera. The higher proportion of Sangiovese and the choice of subsidiary varieties distinguish the wine from Rosso Piceno, whose zone it overlaps. A *novello* version exists. Age: *riserva* 2 yrs.

COLLI PESARESI *DOC*
The zone runs from Pesaro on the Adriatic west past Urbino to the Montefeltro range of the Appennines.

Bianco *w dr* ☆ *DYA* Based on Trebbiano Toscano, has little to offer.

Rosato *p dr DYA*
From 70% or more Sangiovese. Rarely seen.

Rosso *r dr* ☆→☆☆ *01 02* From 70% or more Sangiovese; little take-up of this variant from producers.

Sangiovese *r dr* ☆→☆☆ *00 01 02*

Somewhat variable but at its best has a lively berried fruitiness overlying a good, softish structure. Also *novello*. Age: *riserva* 2 yrs.

Trebbiano *w dr* ☆ *DYA*

From a restricted area west of Pesaro. Unexciting.

Biancame *w dr*

From the Biancame grape grown in a smallish area in the southern part of the region. So far unproved.

Focara *r dr* ☆→☆☆ *00 01 02*

Sub-zone. Red comes from at least 50% Pinot Nero, Cabernet Franc, Cabernet Sauvignon, and/or Merlot; the remainder can be all Sangiovese, but if there's none the four main grapes must account for at least 75%. There is also a varietal Pinot Nero version. Age: *riserva* 2 yrs.

Roncaglia *w dr* ☆→☆☆ *DYA*

Sub-zone. Rare white from Trebbiano Toscano with up to 15% Pinot Nero.

ESINO *DOC*

Ranging over hills along the course of the Esino River throughout the province of Ancona and part of Macerata, this denomination covers light and easy wines from the principal grapes of the region.

Bianco *w dr (fz)* ☆→☆☆ *DYA* Minimum 50% Verdicchio, this is zesty and often fizzy.

Rosso *r dr* ☆→☆☆ *DYA* Minimum 60% Sangiovese and/or Montepulciano, also *novello*.

FALERIO DEI COLLI ASCOLANI

DOC w dr ☆→☆☆ *DYA*

This white, from hills throughout Ascoli Piceno province, when made from the maximum of the traditional Passerina and Pecorino varieties (30% each), and the minimum (20%) of the dull Trebbiano, can show admirable style.

LACRIMA DI MORRO D'ALBA

DOC r dr (s/sw) (fz) ☆ *DYA*

From the curious Lacrima vine grown around Morro d'Alba on the edge of the Verdicchio di Jesi zone, this purple-crimson wine, with its slightly foxy, berry-like odour and ripe-fruit flavour has numerous devotees, although few, outside the small production area, venture to try it.

OFFIDA *DOC*

Promising, recently delimited zone in the south of the region, west of San Benedetto del Tronto.

Passerina *w dr (s/sw) (sw) (sp)* ☆→☆☆ *DYA 00 01 02* Potentially stylish wines from the Passerina grape. *Vino santo* version comes solely from the communes of Offida and Ripatransone. Age: *passito* 2 yrs, *vino santo*, 3 yrs.

Pecorino *w dr* ☆→☆☆☆ *DYA*

Floral wines with depth and style from the Pecorino grape.

Rosso *r dr*

Intriguing potential from a blend containing at least 50% Montepulciano and 30% Cabernet Sauvignon grown in a restricted part of the zone. Age: 2 yrs.

ROSSO CONERO

DOC r dr ☆☆→☆☆☆☆ *90 95 97 98 99 00 01 02*

Montepulciano's supremacy over Sangiovese along the Adriatic comes to the fore in this sometimes splendid red from Monte Conero and adjacent slopes south of Ancona. Known for vigour, it has a deep-ruby colour and a full, round flavour laced by noble tannins that allow it to keep for years from big vintages yet remain fine drinking after just a few years in lesser ones. It could well stand in the front ranks of Italian reds, if only there were more of it. Age: *riserva* 2 yrs.

ROSSO PICENO

DOC r dr ☆→☆☆☆ *95 97 98 99 00 01 02*

This rather variable red, based on 35–70% Sangiovese with Montepulciano at no more than 40%, comes from a vast zone covering much of the eastern

Marche between Ascoli Piceno and Senigallia. Ruby red to garnet, in 3 to 5 years it can become smooth and well composed, developing bouquet and flavour but only occasionally charm. *Superiore* covers a restricted area between Ascoli Piceno and the coast and many of the best bottles are concentrated here. Sangiovese dominates and a varietal Sangiovese version exists, but when Rosso Piceno shows class it is usually due to a telling dose of Montepulciano. May be *novello*. Age: *superiore* 1 yr.

VERDICCHIO DEI CASTELLI DI JESI

DOC w dr (s/sw) sp ☆☆→☆☆☆☆
97 98 99 00 01 02

Renowned Verdicchio comes from a large zone west of Ancona on hills drained by the Esino, Misa and Musone rivers and centred on the town of Jesi. The *classico* heartland takes in all but the northwest portion of this area. Verdicchio's fortune in its unique, amphora-shaped bottle, conceived by the Fazi-Battaglia winery, rapidly became its downfall and producers had their work cut out to develop a new, more quality-based image for the wine, despite the variety being one of Italy's most noble native whites. Now, Verdicchio's class shines through in more than a few (non-curvy) bottles and numerous wineries and estates make single vineyard versions or special *cuvées*, sometimes aged in barrels and often qualified as *riserva*. Indeed, some of them rank with the most sought-after whites of Italy. Producers have individual interpretations, though,

and the wines can range from light and crisp with faint greenish-yellow tones to full and richly textured with a golden hue, so that differences are often more apparent than their distinct familial traits. Sparkling Verdicchio too, is often impressive. Age: *riserva* 2 yrs, *passito* 1 yr.

VERDICCHIO DI MATELICA

DOC w dr (s/sw) (sw) (sp) ☆☆→☆☆☆☆
97 98 99 00 01 02

Vineyards of the second, and less well-known, Verdicchio zone lie near the towns of Matelica and Cerreto d'Esi on southwest-facing slopes. Some admirers who remember the past insist that the real Verdicchio – with depth of flavour and staying power from high acidity – came from Matelica. The wines from several producers seem to verify that claim although today top honours remain with Castelli di Jesi. Sometimes *spumante*, Verdicchio here may also be *passito* with 15% alcohol. Age: *riserva* 2 yrs, *passito* 1 yr.

VERNACCIA DI SERRAPETRONA

DOC r dr s/sw sw sp ☆→☆☆ *DYA*

Curious sparkling red wine based on dark Vernaccia grapes grown around Serrapetrona, west of Macerata (and unrelated to white varieties of the same name from Tuscany and Sardini). Deep garnet-purple, grapey, and fragrant with mouth-cleansing bitterness on the finish, it can be *secco*, *amabile*, or *dolce*. Upgrading to DOCG is due for confirmation shortly. Most have replaced the traditional special process of bottle-fermentation with modern tank methods.

Producers

Provinces: Ancona (AN), Ascoli Piceno (AP), Macerata (MC), Pesaro e Urbino (PS).

Belisario-CS di Matelica e Cerreto d'Esi, Matelica (MC). Admirable Verdicchio di Matelica including special bottlings of Vigneti del Cerro, Vigneti Belisano, and especially, Riserva Cambrugiano.

Boccadigabbia, Civitanova Marche (MC). Fine Rosso Piceno and a much praised IGT Cabernet

Sauvignon called Akronte, along with Merlot (Pix), Sangiovese (Saltapicchio), Chardonnay (Montalperti), Pinot Grigio (La Castelletta), white Mon' Anello, and more.

Brunori, Jesi (AN). Good San Nicolò and Le Gemme Verdicchio di Jesi Classico selections, Lacrima di Morro, Rosso Conero, Piceno.

Fratelli Bucci, Ostra Vetere (AN). Supreme, long-lived Verdicchio di Jesi Classico and Riserva Villa Bucci, possibly the zone's finest, and Rosso Piceno (Pongelli).

Le Caniette, Ripatransone (AP). Fine selection of rounded, powerful Rosso Piceno (Morellone, Nero di Vite). Also Offida Pecorino, *vino santo*, and more.

Casalfarneto, Serra de' Conti (AN). Classy Verdicchio di Jesi Classico (Cimaio, Fontevecchia, Gran Casale).

Bisci, Matelica (MC). Fine Verdicchio di Matelica (Vigneto Fogliano), red Villa Castiglioni (Sangiovese/Cabernet).

Cocci Grifoni, San Savino di Ripatransone (AP). Leading estate for Piceno Superiore (Il Grifone) and, now, Offida (Pecorino Colle Vecchio and others). Also a surprisingly classy Falerio (Vigneti San Basso).

Colonnara, Cupramontana (AN). Co-op makes reliably fine Verdicchio di Jesi Classico (Tufico, Cuprese), also in *spumante* mc version. Also Rosso Piceno.

Fattoria Coroncino, Staffolo (AN). Exquisite Verdicchio di Jesi Classico (Gaiospino, Il Coroncino).

Tenuta De Angelis, Castel de Lama (AP). High-ranking IGT Anghelos (Montepulciano/Sangiovese/Cabenet Sauvignon) leads confident range from Piceno Superiore, most notably red Etichetta Oro, and Offida.

Fattoria Dezi, Servigliano (AP). Fruit forward wines from biodynamic estate: Solo Sangiovese, Le Solagne (Verdicchio/Malvasia/Pecorino), Dezio (Montepulciano), and Rosso Piceno (Regina del Bosco).

Fattoria di Forano, Appignano (MC). Up-and-coming Colli Maceratesi estate with elegant wines. Rosso Piceno too.

Fazi-Battaglia, Castelplanio (AN). Long-time market leader now back in the limelight with Verdicchio di Jesi Classico Titulus still in amphora, plus selections Le Moie and San Sisto. Also Rosso Conero (Passo del Lupo).

Valentino Fiorini, Barchi (PS). Textbook Bianchello di Metauro (Tenuta Campioli).

Gioacchino Garofoli, Loreto (AN). Some of the most stylish and best-value wines of the Marche: Verdicchio di Jesi Classico (Macrina, Podium, Serra Fiorese) and *passito* (Le Brume), as well as *spumante* mc and Charmat, Rosso Conero (Piancarda, Grosso Agontano).

Fattoria Laila, Mondavio (PS). Emerging estate with good Verdicchio (Lailum) and Rosso Piceno.

Lanari, Ancona (AN). Refined yet intense Rosso Conero (Fibbio).

Conte Leopardi Dittajuti, Numana (AN). Impressive Rosso Conero (Vigneti del Coppo, Pigmento). Also IGT Sauvignon Blanc (Bianco del Coppo, Calcare), Casirano Rosso (Montepulciano/Cabernet/Syrah).

Malacari, Offagna (AN). Elegant, slow-ageing Rosso Conero (Grigiano).

Stefano Mancinelli, Morro d'Alba (AN). Leading producer of Lacrima di Morro (Santa Maria del Fiore, Sensazioni di Frutto, San Michele, Passito Re Sole). Also good Verdicchio di Jesi.

Mancini, Pesaro. IGT Pinot Nero (Impero Rosso, Impero Bianco, Selezione) add intrigue to Colli Pesaresi Roncaglia, Focara, and Sangiovese.

Marchetti, Ancona. Distinctive Rosso Conero (Villa Bonomi).

Marotti Campi, Morro d'Alba (AN). Fruit-rich Lacrima di Morro; stylish Verdicchio including *passito*.

Enzo Mecella, Fabriano (AN). Verdicchio di Matelica (Casa Fosca), Rosso Conero (Rubelliano); vdt red Braccano (Ciliegiolo/Merlot), all of character.

La Monacesca, Matelica (MC). Classy Verdicchio di Matelica (La Monacesca, Mirum). Also IGT Chardonnay (Ecclesia), *rosso* (Camerte).

Monte Schiavo, Maiolati Spontini (AN). Starry Rosso Conero, lively Verdicchio di Jesi Classico (Coste del Molino, Bando di San Settimio, Le Giuncare Riserva, Arché Passito, and late-harvested Pallio di San Floriano), IGT Esio Rosso (Montepulciano/Cabernet), Lacrima di Morro, and more.

Claudio Morelli, Fano (PS). Admirable Bianchello del Metauro (Borgo Torre, Le Terrazze) plus Colli Pesaresi Sangiovese and blended reds Suffragium, Magliano.

Alessandro Moroder, Ancona (AN). Leading producer of Rosso Conero led by classy selection Dorico.

Rio Maggio, Montegranaro (AP).Rosso Piceno, stylish Falerio dei Colli Ascolani (Telusiano). Also Artias line of international varieties.

Oasi degli Angeli, Cupra Marittima (AP). Just one wine, the famous, supremely impressive Kurni, from 100% Montepulciano.

Poderi San Savino, Ripatransone (AP). IGT Fedus (Sangiovese) and Ver Sacrum (Montepulciano) join Piceno Superiore and Offida Pecorino in a range with aplomb.

Saladino Pilastri, Spinetoli (AP). Piceno Superiore (Vigna Piediprato), good Falerio dei Colli Ascolani.

San Biagio, Matelica (MC). Verdicchio di Matelica.

San Giovanni, Offida (AP). Steadily improving range of Piceno Superiore; characterful Falerio.

Santa Barbara, Barbara (AN). Good range of styles of Verdicchio di Jesi Classico, Rosso Piceno, IGT *rosso*.

Santa Cassella, Potenza Picena (MC). Finely honed Rosso Piceno, Colli Maceratesi, and IGT Cabernet, Chardonnay.

Sartarelli, Poggio San Marcello (AN). Verdicchio di Jesi Classico of outstanding character in Tralivio and late-harvested Contrada Balciana.

Silvano Strologo, Camerano (AN). Highly admired Rosso Conero (Traino, Julius) of great class.

Spinsanti, Camerano (AN). Refined, tightly knit Rosso Conero (Adino, Camars), Sassòne (Montepulciano).

Le Terrazze, Numana (AN). Superb Rosso Conero (Sassi Neri, Visions of J), IGT Chaos (Montepulciano, Merlot, Syrah), refined pink *spumante* mc Donna Giulia (from Montepulciano), Le Cave (Chardonnay).

Terre Cortesi Moncaro, Montecarotto (AN). Good selections of Verdicchio di Jesi Classico, Rosso Conero.

Umani Ronchi, Osimo (AN). Exemplary range of Verdicchio di Jesi Classico (Casal di Serra, Villa Bianchi), and Rosso Conero (Cumaro, San Lorenzo), as well as Pelago (Cabernet/Merlot/Montepulciano), Le Busch (Chardonnay/Verdicchio), Maximo (botrytized Sauvignon), Bianchello del Metauro, and Montepulciano d'Abruzzo.

Vallerosa-Bonci, Cupramontana (AN). Reading Verdicchio di Jesi Classico in various styles, including mc brut and *passito*. Also good Rosso Piceno (Casa Nostra).

Ercole Velenosi, Ascoli Piceno. Producer on the rise with fine Rosso Piceno (Il Brecciarolo, Roggio del Filare), Falerio (Vigna Solaria), Velenosi Brut mc, relevatory IGT Ludi (Montepulciano/Cabernet/Merlot),and good Chardonnay (Rêve), and Sauvignon (Linaigre).

Vigneti Tavignano, Cingoli (MC). Emerging Verdicchio estate di Jesi.

Villa Ligi, Pergola (PS). Interesting dry red IGT called Vernaculum from Vernaccia.

Villa Pigna, Offida (AP). Impressive Piceno Superiore, Falerio dei Colli Ascolani, and others.

Fratelli Zaccagnini, Staffolo (AN). Beautifully refined, Verdicchio di Jesi Classico (Salmàgina).

Wine & Food

The food of the Marche, immediately likeable – like the wine or, for that matter, the people – never lets you down. Cooks draw from both land and sea and, without too much fuss, and put the best of both on the table, often together. Roast pig (*porchetta*) is cooked with wild fennel, rosemary, garlic, and pepper, as are duck, rabbit, and even shellfish. Both fowl and fish may be cooked in *potacchio*, (with tomato, rosemary, garlic, onion), and white wine.

Wines to accompany each dish are suggested below in italics.
Anatra in porchetta Duck cooked with wild fennel, garlic, ham, and salt pork. *Coniglio* (rabbit) may be done the same way. *Rosso Piceno Superiore*

Brodetto Among many fish soups of the name, Ancona's version is most famous, maybe because it includes at least 13 types of fish. *Verdicchio dei Castelli di Jesi Classico Riserva*
Faraona in potacchio Guinea-fowl cooked with onion, garlic, rosemary, and tomato in wine. *Rosso Conero*
Olive all'ascolana Hollowed giant green olives of Ascoli with a meat stuffing, fried in olive oil. *Falerio dei Colli Ascolani*
Stocco all'anconetana Salt cod cooked with an elaborate sauce that includes milk, tomatoes, carrots, garlic, rosemary. *Verdicchio dei Castelli di Jesi Classico,* young.
Vincisgrassi An elaborate lasagne that includes butter, cream, *prosciutto,* and black truffles. *Verdicchio di Matelica*

Restaurants

Recommended in or near wine zones:
North (Pesaro Urbino) *Symposium* at Cartoceto; *Da Nadia* at Fano; *Alceo* and *Da Teresa* at Pesaro; *La Rocca* at San Leo; *Cucco* at Urbania, *Vanda* at Urbino.
Center (Ancona, Jesi, Macerata, Matelica) *Passetto* at Ancona; *Dei Conti* at Cingoli; *Villa Amalia* at Falconara Marittima; *Hostaria Santa Lucia* at Jesi; *La Madonnina del Pescatore* at Marzocca di Senigallia; *Busche*

at Montecarotto; *Luma* at Montecosaro; *Palazzo Viviani* at Montegridolfo; *Costarella* and *Saraghino* at Numana; *Emilia, Fortino Napoleonico, Giacchetti* and *Il Laghetto* at Portonovo; *Torcoletto* at Porto Recanati; *Hotel Giardino* at San Lorenzo in Campo; *Riccardone's* and *Uliassi* at Senigallia.
South (Ascoli Piceno) *Osteria dell'Arancio* at Grottammare Alta; *Damiani e Rossi* at Porto San Giorgio; *Chichibio* at San Benedetto del Tronto.

Tuscany *Toscana*

Tuscans have evolved over a generation from downcast purveyors of flask chianti into the nation's prime movers of premium wine. The renaissance, as it's called, began in Florence when the influential house of Antinori revised a 600-year heritage with new styles in wines of international class. Others followed with wines that, rather than purely modern, might better be described as regenerated classics. The epicentre of this oenological revival was Chianti, the heart of Tuscany, but it spread into Montalcino and Montepulciano, and from there across the region

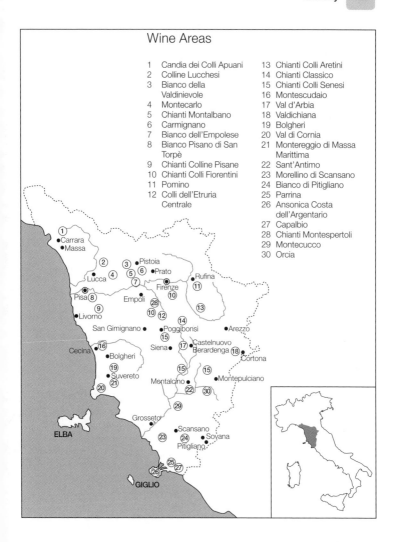

Wine Areas

1   Candia dei Colli Apuani
2   Colline Lucchesi
3   Bianco della
    Valdinievole
4   Montecarlo
5   Chianti Montalbano
6   Carmignano
7   Bianco dell'Empolese
8   Bianco Pisano di San
    Torpè
9   Chianti Colline Pisane
10 Chianti Colli Fiorentini
11 Pomino
12 Colli dell'Etruria
    Centrale

13 Chianti Colli Aretini
14 Chianti Classico
15 Chianti Colli Senesi
16 Montescudaio
17 Val d'Arbia
18 Valdichiana
19 Bolgheri
20 Val di Cornia
21 Montereggio di Massa
    Marittima
22 Sant'Antimo
23 Morellino di Scansano
24 Bianco di Pitigliano
25 Parrina
26 Ansonica Costa
    dell'Argentario
27 Capalbio
28 Chianti Montespertoli
29 Montecucco
30 Orcia

and the rest of Italy, attracting a lot of money and talent into the country along the way.

Chianti remains the nucleus of Tuscan viniculture, still the most voluminous of Italy's classified wines and the most prominent expression of the noble Sangiovese vine that dominates the region's reds. But its stage is shared with the majestic Brunello di Montalcino, the impressive Vino Nobile di Montepulciano, the rejuvenated of Vernaccia di San Gimignano, the classy Bolgheri, and, increasingly, Morellino di Scansano. This once "minor" wine, produced in the hills behind the coastlands of southern Tuscany, has seen unprecedented levels of interest in recent years as many of (mainly) Tuscany's leading producers have recognized its potential and scrambled to buy land in the zone. As the results of their investments begin to emerge Morellino's profile climbs ever higher. Chianti was also the original source of those controversial wines that became known as Super Tuscans. A rash of wines of unprecedented quality which blatantly scorned DOC restrictions caused such intense comment worldwide – and such acute embarrassment internally on a denomination system that could breed this rebellion – that eventually the entire DOC(G) regulations were overhauled. Now Tuscans are among the most DOC conscious of Italians and their denominations are regularly amended to expand their ambit and take improved production criteria into account. The Super Tuscans, whose names remain well known and highly admired, have therefore either been accommodated back into these revised DOC(G)s or have slipped naturally into an IGT, most commonly Colli della Toscana Centrale or the all-encompassing Toscana. Meanwhile many more IGT wines have been spawned, in innumerable shapes and styles, to the extent that it is practically *de rigeur* to produce at least one. As a corollary, the umbrella DOC Colli dell'Etruria Centrale, remains strangely under-utilized.

Modest yields on rugged contours bring volumes in Tuscany to eighth in rank among the twenty regions but third after the Veneto and Piedmont in production of classified wines. It boasts six of the nation's twenty-eight DOCGs, with Brunello, Carmignano, Chianti, Chianti Classico, Vernaccia di San Gimignano, and Vino Nobile, and a further thirty-four DOCs. The elevation of the entire, non-*classico*, chianti area to DOCG, a vast ring around the *classico* heartland producing very variable styles and qualities, has long been recognized as a clamorous error but one that no longer causes much heartache as ever fewer wines are released under the denomination.

Despite exciting Cabernet/Sangiovese blends, fine reds from Cabernet, Merlot, Syrah, and Pinot Noir, and equally fine whites from Chardonnay, Sauvignon, and the Pinots, it is Sangiovese that determines the intrinsic style and eminence of the region's output. Ever greater concentration on the variety and ever greater skills in drawing out and fine-tuning its supreme qualities are resulting in wines that grow in stature (and, sadly, price) year after year. Tuscany is less fortunate in its native whites but there have been some surprisingly impressive results from the uninspiring Trebbiano and Malvasia for those who dedicate enough effort to them and Vernaccia too, has much to offer the diligent winemaker.

Even non-wine-loving visitors who come to see Florence, Siena, Pisa, and San Gimignano will often tour the scenic vineyards that grace the hillsides, a rural civilization shaped over centuries into a landscape of extraordinary harmony and beauty. The most important wine route is the Chiantigiana, which winds its way through the heart of Tuscany between Florence and Siena (home of the *Enoteca Italiana* – the national wine library – in the Medici fortress). In Siena's province are the ancient hill-top villages of Montepulciano and Montalcino, which has an *enoteca* for Brunello in the town fortress. Recommended specialist wine shops are *Enoteca Lavuri* in Agliana (near Pistoia), *Fiaschetteria de' Redi* at Arezzo, *Castiglionese di Lenzi* at Castiglione della Pescaia, *Drogheria Franci* at Montalcino, *La Porta* at Monticchiello (near Montepulciano), *Wine Club* at Pescia, *Da Ghino* at Pienza, *Marcucci* at Pietrasanta, *Dante Alighieri* at Radda in Chianti, *I Terzi* and *San Domenico* at Siena, and *Puntodivino* at Viareggio. *Enoteca Gallo Nero* at Greve sells nearly all Chianti Classico. In Florence, the *Enoteca Pinchiorri* restaurant has an unrivalled collection of Italian and French wines.

Recent Vintages

Chianti Riserva, Vino Nobile, Carmignano, and many Super Tuscans approach primes around four to seven years, though some vintages favour ageing of a decade or more. Brunello often needs six to ten years to open up, and great vintages can last for decades.

2002 Despite much thinning of grapes, a rainy summer took its toll. Attractive wines of good drinkability but few long-livers and only small quantities of *crus*.
2001 Another hot, dry summer but a drop in temperature and some rain prior to harvest ensured impressivley fine, balanced wines. A hard frost in spring reduced quantities in some parts.
2000 Very hot, dry weather in August gave full, ripe wines of concentration, although some, in the hottest locations, may lack finesse.
1999 An average harvest in terms of quantity but very good quality.
1998 Bumper crop of mixed results due mainly to rain during the harvest; some good to very good red wines made nonetheless.
1997 Some rate this as the greatest vintage of the modern era for red wines throughout Tuscany, though quantities were painfully limited and prices have mounted.
1996 Rain took its toll – wines often lack substance and strength for long ageing, though good medium weight reds are available.
1995 Perfect weather in October turned doubts, after a damp summer, to delight in a small but memorable vintage for Brunello, Vino Nobile, and Chianti.
1994 Harvest rains did more harm in Chianti than points south, where Brunello and Vino Nobile ranged from good to excellent.
1993 Rain interrupted picking, but many estates made wines that were very good or better.
1992 Damp and cool weather made this, with few exceptions, a year to forget.
1991 Disappointing after the great 1990, yet certain Brunello, Vino Nobile, and Super Tuscans show class.
1990 Small crop considered the greatest of recent times for chianti and most other reds, with structure to last and harmony evident from the start.
Notes on earlier vintages Earlier fine vintages: 85, 83, 82, 79, 78, 77, 75, 71, 70, 64, 62, 58, 55, 47, 45.

Wines

ALEATICO

Ancient vine grown along the coast and on Elba makes soaringly rich red, softly sweet with bracing, bitter-cherry finish. Enjoying a modest revival in Tuscany.

ANSONICA COSTA DELL'ARGENTARIO

DOC w dr ☆→☆☆☆ *DYA*
Ansonica, the same variety as Sicily's Inzolia, thrives in the warm territory inland from the Argentario promontory and on the island of Giglio. Youthful florality rapidly develops into depth, power, and richness.

BIANCO DELLA VALDINIEVOLE

DOC w dr (s/sw) (sw) ☆ *DYA*
Simple white from Trebbiano in the Nievole valley.
Vin Santo A version (aged 3 yrs) also theoretically exists.

BIANCO DELL'EMPOLESE

DOC w dr (s/sw) (sw) ☆→☆☆ *DYA*
Unassuming white based on Trebbiano from the Empoli area. The *vin santo* version (aged 3 yrs) is rarely seen.

BIANCO DI PITIGLIANO

DOC w dr (sp) ☆☆ *DYA*
From Trebbiano with Greco,

Malvasia, and others grown around Pitigliano in southern Tuscany. It can bear a resemblance to Umbria's Orvieto. Generally reliable wines, ranging from light to fairly opulent. It may also be sparkling.

BIANCO PISANO DI SAN TORPE

DOC w dr (s/sw) (sw) ☆→☆☆ *DYA* Pisa's Trebbiano-based white can make pleasant sipping in summer. The (rare) *vin santo* is aged 3 yrs, or 4 for *riserva*.

BOLGHERI AND BOLGHERI SASSICAIA *DOC*

The Bolgheri area near the coast is famous for red wines based on Cabernet and Merlot, originally inspired by the runaway success of Sassicaia, which is now separately delimited in its own sub-zone. Other high-quality estates sprang up in its wake, some rapidly gaining legendary status too, most notably Ornellaia. The DOC also applies to white wines, rosé, and *vin santo*.

Bianco *w dr* ☆→☆☆ *DYA* Trebbiano and the more interesting Vermentino, and Sauvignon, may be used in varying proportions in whites that can show class.

Rosato *p dr* ☆☆ *DYA* Easy-drinking pink from varying proportions of Cabernet/Merlot/Sangiovese often shows style.

Rosso *r dr* ☆☆→☆☆☆☆ *94 95 96 97 98 99 00 01* Cabernet Sauvignon, Merlot, and Sangiovese in practically any proportions give ample scope to producers to interpret this classy denomination to their best advantage. Age: *superiore* 2 yrs.

Sassicaia *r dr* ☆☆☆→☆☆☆☆ *81 82 83 85 86 87 88 90 91 92 93 94 95 96 97 98 99 00 01* One of the first and certainly the most influential of modern Italian red wines aged in barriques. After the first bottles of 68 were released, Sassicaia triumphed in tastings, often being taken for a top bordeaux. Today, the average production is 100,000

bottles a year. Despite this, and its high price, the wine is rationed. Age: 2 yrs.

Sauvignon *w dr* ☆☆→☆☆☆ *98 99 00* Succulent, varietally pure wines of great style and finesse.

Vermentino *w dr* ☆→☆☆☆ *99 00 01* The variety is gaining prominence in coastal Tuscany, and makes admirable whites.

Vin Santo Occhio di Pernice *r-am s/sw sw* This sweet wine from semi-dried Sangiovese and Malvasia Nera grapes ages to a deep reddish-amber in small barrels. Age: 3yrs, *riserva* 4 yrs.

BRUNELLO DI MONTALCINO

DOCG r dr ☆☆☆→☆☆☆☆ *85 88 90 95 96 97 98 99 00 01* This majestic red from Sangiovese grown, in the community of Montalcino south of Siena, ranks as one of Italy's most prized and most expensive wines. Powerfully structured, it matures in cask and bottle into a warm, amply flavoured wine of deep ruby to brick-red colour and richly complex bouquet. Brunello is capable of austere grandeur with great age. But vineyards and production have expanded dramatically in the last 30 years and styles have become a little less uniform. Today, there are over 170 estates making about 5 million bottles of Brunello a year as well as 3 million bottles of Rosso di Montalcino (*q.v.*), from the same vineyards. A few are very large, others tiny. Brunello produced on the high, north-facing slopes in the north of the zone tends to be more racy and elegant than the opulent, rich wines from the warm south-facing vineyards. After endless soul-searching on the length of oak ageing, once 4 years and generally felt to be too long, this has now been reduced to a minimum of 2 years, within an overall ageing requirement (cask and bottle) of 5 years, 6 for the *riserva*.

CABERNET

Though known in Tuscany in the 18th century and used in blends with Sangiovese a century ago, Cabernet's modern success began with Sassicaia and spread rapidly with the advent of the Super Tuscans. It is also a component in classified reds of Bolgheri, Carmignano, and Pomino, and, optionally, even chianti. Cabernet Sauvignon is used alone in some wines but is more often blended with Sangiovese, Merlot or other varieties.

CANDIA DEI COLLI APUANI

DOC w dr (sw) (fr) ☆→☆☆ *DYA*
Softly dry, rustic white based on Vermentino grown at the foot of the Apuan Alps above Massa and Carrara in northwest Tuscany. A *vin santo* version theoretically exists.

CAPALBIO *DOC*

An area stretching a short way across southern Tuscany inland from Monte Argentario.

Bianco *w dr* ☆→☆☆ *DYA* Lightish white made predominantly from Trebbiano (minimum 50%). Small quantities of other grapes may add character.

Rosso *r dr* ☆→☆☆ *00 01* Decent red made mainly from Sangiovese (50% or more). Age: *riserva* 2 yrs.

Rosato *p dr* ☆→☆☆ *DYA* Easy-drinking, Sangiovese-based pink. Not often seen.

Cabernet Sauvignon *r dr* ☆→☆☆ *00 01* Another promising outing for Cabernet.

Sangiovese *r dr* ☆→☆☆ *00 01* Few examples so far of Tuscany's prime grape under this denomination.

Vermentino *w dr* ☆→☆☆ *DYA* Light, refreshing wines with a glint of style.

Vin Santo *w dr s/sw* ☆→☆☆ *DYA* Trebbiano-based dessert wine. Age: 2 yrs (in small casks).

CARMIGNANO

DOCG r dr ☆☆→☆☆☆☆ *85 88 90 92 95 97 98 99 00 01*

Recognized as one of Europe's first controlled wine zones by the Grand Duchy of Tuscany in 1716, Carmignano is noted for an aristocratic red that became DOCG in 1990. What set it apart from Tuscany's other Sangiovese-based wines was the inclusion of Cabernet, planted here in the 18th century. When young, the red has supple appeal, but with age from top vintages it acquires shadings of finesse reminiscent of Pauillacs. The classics come from the Contini-Bonacossi family estates of Villa di Capezzana and Villa di Trefiano, which make more than half the annual production. The zone lies west of Florence, within the Chianti Montalbano area, and also makes other wines covered under Carmignano DOC. Age: 2 yrs (1 in cask), *riserva* 3 yrs (2 in casks).

CARMIGNANO *DOC*

Applies to red and rosé wines and two types of *vin santo*.

Barco Reale di Carmignano *r dr* ☆→☆☆ *97 98 99 00 01* Light red from Sangiovese, Cabernet, and other varieties is named after the Medici hunting reserve that once covered this area. It provides a youthful taste of Carmignano at a lower price.

Rosato/Vin Ruspo *p dr* ☆☆ *DYA* A fresh, lively rosé with a floral, fruity aroma.

Vin Santo *am dr s/sw*

Vin Santo Occhio di Pernice *r-am sw* ☆☆→☆☆☆☆ *Vin santo*, from Trebbiano and Malvasia, is often dry here, though *amabile* versions are admirable. The red Occhio di Pernice, from Sangiovese and others is sweet. Age: 3 yrs, *riserva* 4 yrs.

CHIANTI *DOCG*

Italy's best-known wine is produced in a vast hilly ring around the heartland donomination of Chianti Classico (*q.v.*) and covering much of central Tuscany. The zone extends from north of Florence to well south of Siena, and from the first the coast rises inland to the Apennines. Together, Chianti and Chianti Classico produce about 90 million litres of wine a year, the largest amount of any of Italy's classified wines. Once generally derided for its grape blend, which contained a significant proportion of white Trebbiano and Malvasia grapes alongside the red Sangiovese and Canaiolo, and the wicker-covered flasks in which it was sold, it is now treated far more seriously. White grapes are now included in minimal quantities, if at all, Sangiovese is frequently used exclusively and the wicker fiasco is almost forgotten. Even so, a considerable proportion of the wine is still little more than attractive easy-drinking and elevating the whole district to DOCG is probably best described as an excess of optimism over realism. Indeed many producers make their best wines under other denominations which overlap the chianti zone and deliberately keep their chianti fresh and uncomplicated. The most impressive chianti, though, is deep, rich, well structured, with good ageing capacity, and some producers make both a *riserva* to age and lighter types to sell young. Others may use small quantities of Cabernet, Merlot, or Pinot Nero to give additional fruity roundness. But variability is the key. Chianti is split into 7 sub-zones, each with distinct terrains and microclimates, and its hundreds of producers express individual attitudes and styles and there is rarely any signal to the consumer of the wine's type, style, or value. Still, the district names, when they are used, can have significance, especially Rufina, whose quality level is often as high as that in Chianti Classico. Age: *riserva* 2 yrs.

Chianti Colli Aretini *r dr* ☆☆ *97 98 99 00 01* Soft, well-scented chianti from hills overlooking the Arno valley east of Chianti Classico. Most is of medium body to drink within 4 years, but a few examples are more concentrated and age longer.

Chianti Colli Fiorentini *r dr* ☆☆→☆☆☆ *90 95 96 97 98 99 00 01* Perennial source of the flask wines consumed in Florence, the hills south and east of the city, and along the Arno and Pesa valleys, also makes good estate-bottled chianti. Most is soft and round, for drinking young. The ruby-garnet *riserva*, later takes on amber-orange highlights and can be robust, austere, aristocratic, and complete in bouquet and flavour, to drink in 5 to 10 years.

Chianti Colli Senesi *r dr* ☆☆→☆☆☆ *90 95 96 97 98 99 00 01* This zone, the largest, is split into 3 sectors: one around Montalcino, one around Montepulciano, and the rest in an arc from San Gimignano running eastward south of the *classico* zone. Chianti here ranges from highly refined to innocuous. But most falls in between, often with youthful vitality for days when when Brunello or Vino Nobile seem too imposing.

Chianti Colline Pisane *r dr* ☆→☆☆☆ *97 98 99 00 01* From hills around Casciana Terme and San Miniato southeast of Pisa, this zone has a mild maritime climate and its chianti is generally regarded as the lightest, softest, and shortest-lived. But a few estates are championing fuller, more complex wines.

Chianti Montalbano *r dr* ☆→☆☆ *97 98 99 00 01* The Montalbano balcony southwest of Prato is more noted for Carmignano, but chianti can also be persuasive, usually in soft, fruity wines to drink in 1 to 5 years.

Chianti Montespertoli *r dr* ☆☆ *97 98 99 00 01* Part of the commune of Montespertoli, although lying within Colli Fiorentini is a distinct sub-zone in its own right.

Chianti Rufina *r dr* ☆☆→☆☆☆☆ *88 90 95 96 97 98 99 00 01* The smallest zone, in hills above the Sieve River, east of Florence, produces some of the most incisive, refined chianti anywhere. Rufina's vineyards lie at a relatively high altitude, which can be sensed in the rarefied bouquet and lingering elegance of its wines, once aged.

CHIANTI CLASSICO

DOCG r dr ☆☆→☆☆☆☆ *88 90 93 96 97 98 99 00 01*

The Classico is chianti's hearland, the historical area between Florence and Siena where the original Chianti League was formed in the 13th century, where Barone Bettino Ricasoli devised the formula for chianti production in the mid-1800s and where today, the "golden triangle" of Castellina, Radda, and Gaiole are considered the true chianti core. These three communes lie in the province of Siena although the *classico* is split between Florence's and Siena's territory. Long-term rivalry between the two has given rise to talk of a "Florentine style" and a "Sienese style" but a complex geological structure and microclimatic differences means that there is considerable variability from commune to commune and, often, estate to estate. Nevertheless, overall, *classico* wines are distinct from non-*classico* and quality tends to be consistently good. Regular Chianti Classico can be drunk from 2 to 7 years, although many of the leading *riservas* can rank with the best of Italy – and may improve for well beyond a decade from top vintages. The producer consortium, symbolized by the ancient Chianti League's *gallo nero* (black rooster), is highly active and has spearheaded moves to amend the DOCG to ensure a higher-quality base as well as pursuing programmes to improve wines, mainly through better vine material. Currently, Chianti Classico may come from 80–100% Sangiovese. The additional varieties (for those not using 100% Sangiovese) may include the traditional Canaiolo or Colorino, for instance, or the international

Cabernet or Merlot. Use of white grapes is restricted to 6% and this will disappear totally in 2006. Age: 1 yr, *riserva* 2 yrs.

COLLI DELL'ETRURIA CENTRALE *DOC*

A gap-filler for wines not covered by chianti and other denominations of Tuscany's central hills, here alluded to rather wistfully as Etruria, home of the Etruscans, giving producers fair but not exaggerated leeway on grape varieties.

Bianco *w dr* ☆→☆☆ *DYA* From at least 50% Trebbiano with options on Malvasia, Vernaccia, the Pinots, Chardonnay, Sauvignon, and, in small measure, others, this can be light and breezy with as little as 10% alcohol or more complex.

Rosato *p dr* ☆→☆☆ *DYA* Rosé, from at least 50% Sangiovese with options on Cabernet Sauvignon and Franc, Merlot, Pinot Nero, Canaiolo, and, in smaller measure, others.

Rosso *r dr* ☆→☆☆ *97 98 99 00 01* The same grape choices apply as for the *rosato*. Can be light and easy-going, made using the *governo* method, or of Super Tuscan stature. A *novello* version, with Canaiolo, Merlot, Gamay, and/or Ciliegiolo alongside the Sangiovese exists.

Vin Santo *am dr s/sw sw* This comes mainly from Malvasia and Trebbiano, designed to bring unclassified *vin santo* under DOC, if producers choose. Age: 3 yrs in barrels, *riserva* 4 yrs.

Vin Santo Occhio di Pernice *r-am sw* A red *vin santo* from at least 50% Sangiovese and other red varieties. Age: 3 yrs in cask, *riserva* 4 yrs.

COLLI DELLA TOSCANA CENTRALE

IGT used by many Chianti Classico producers to house their Super Tuscans.

COLLI DI LUNI

Part of this zone, centred in Liguria, extends into northwestern Tuscany. *See* under Liguria.

COLLINE LUCCHESI *DOC*

Lucca's plunging hills are rainier than much of central Tuscany and Sangiovese sometimes has difficulty in ripening fully. Hence the various alternatives under this denomination.

Bianco *w dr* ☆→☆☆☆ *99 00 01* With a Trebbiano base but plentiful options in Greco, Grechetto, Vermentino, Malvasia (up to 45%), and Chardonnay, and/or Sauvignon (up to 30%). The wines range from light and uncomplicated to rich, deep, and characterful.

Rosso *r dr* ☆→☆☆☆ *97 98 00 01* Based on Sangiovese with options on Canaiolo, and/or Ciliegiolo, and a small addition of Merlot. Whether soft and light or fuller and more powerful, good fruit usually marks out the style. Age: *riserva* 2 yrs.

Merlot *r dr* ☆☆→☆☆☆ *97 98 99 00 01* The variety promises well here. Age: *riserva* 2 yrs.

Sangiovese *r dr* ☆→☆☆☆ *97 98 00 01* This more classically styled wine does best on Lucca's more sheltered slopes. Age: *riserva* 2 yrs.

Sauvignon *w dr* ☆→☆☆☆ *00 01* Wines can be a little austere but have good varietal character.

Vermentino *w dr* ☆→☆☆ *DYA* Simple, attractive, fleshy wines.

Vin Santo *am dr s/sw DYA* From any approved local white varieties. Age: 3 yrs

Vin Santo Occhio di Pernice *r-am sw DYA* From any approved local red varieties. Age: 3 yrs

CORTONA *DOC*

Denomination so far best exploited by Montepulciano producers seeking diversification (or a DOC into which to slot their already existing non-Montepulciano wines). 11 varietals, without particular ageing requirements, 2 types of *vin santo* with very severe ageing requirements, and a rosé make this seem tailor-made for their needs.

Cabernet Sauvignon *r dr*
Chardonnay *w dr*
Gamay *r dr*
Grechetto *w dr*
Merlot *r dr*
Pinot Bianco *w dr*
Pinot Grigio *w dr*
Riesling Italico *w dr*
Rosato *p dr* From Sangiovese with Canaiolo.
Sangiovese *r dr*
Sauvignon *w dr*
Syrah *r dr*
Vin Santo *am s/sw sw* From Trebbiano, Grechetto,and/or Malvasia. Age: 3 yrs *riserva* 5 yrs.
Vin Santo Occhio di Pernice *sw* From Sangiovese and Malvasia Nera. Age: 8 yrs!

ELBA *DOC*

This romantic island is noted for having iron-rich soil which lends vigour to traditional wines, particularly Aleatico. But modern production consists mainly of lightweight wines aimed at the booming tourist trade.

Bianco *w dr (sp)* ☆→☆☆ *DYA* Mainly from Trebbiano (locally called Procanico) with Ansonica, and/or Vermentino, this is light straw-gold, delicately scented, dry but rather full-bodied, and soft, though the best have a crisp finish. A *spumante* is permitted.

Rosato *p dr* ☆→☆☆ *DYA* Based mainly on Sangiovese, this can be light and fleeting.

Rosso *r dr* ☆→☆☆ *95 96 97 98 99 00 01* Based mainly on Sangiovese, this is usually bright ruby and grapey, an all-purpose wine to drink young, though some examples show greater body, depth, and bouquet. Age: *riserva* 2 yrs.

Aleatico *r sw* ☆→☆☆☆ *95 96 97 98 99 00 01* This is a traditional vine that has been revived in recent years and gives sweet red wines of great character.

Ansonica *w (am) dr (sw)* ☆→☆☆☆ *DYA* This vine of maritime Tuscany either makes a dry white or a sweet *passito* from semi-dried grapes, both of interest.

Moscato *w sw* ☆→☆☆☆ *DYA* Sweet wine from semi-dried (*passito*) grapes.

Vin Santo *am dr s/sw*
  From Trebbiano and, optionally,
  Ansonica and/or Vermentino.
  Age: 3 yrs, *riserva* 4 yrs.
Vin Santo Occhio di Pernice *r-am*
  s/sw sw Mostly from Sangiovese.
  Age: 3 yrs.

GALESTRO
  w dr ☆☆ *DYA*
  Once popular white originally
  made to mop up surplus white
  grapes in Chianti vineyards. Based
  on Trebbiano, the wine may include
  Chardonnay, Pinots, Sauvignon,
  Riesling, and others up to 40%
  but is basically a light, dry, pale,
  modern wine, fresh and fruity, and
  made in volume with consistency.
  Because Trebbiano is no longer in
  excess in vineyards, Galestro has
  lost much of its original appeal
  for wine houses.

MONTECARLO *DOC*
  The pretty hill town east of Lucca
  has been noted for white wine of
  singular style. The appellation
  also covers a red and *vin santo*.
Bianco *w dr* ☆→☆☆ *DYA* Unique
  blend of Trebbiano with Sémillon,
  Pinots, Vermentino, Sauvignon,
  and Roussanne; varieties from
  dull to smooth and sumptuous.
Rosso *r dr* ☆→☆☆☆ *95 96 97 98 99 00*
  From Sangiovese with a little
  Canaiolo and optional Ciliegiolo,
  Colorino, Malvasia Nera, Syrah,
  and Cabernet this red can be
  impressive as often as it
  disappoints. Age: *riserva* 2 yrs.
Vin Santo *am dr s/sw*
Vin Santo Occhio di Pernice *r-am s/sw*
  From the same varieties as the
  bianco and *rosso* respectively.
  Age: 3 yrs, *riserva* 4 yrs.

MONTECUCCO *DOC*
  Zone in the province of Grosseto,
  just south of Montalcino, slowly
  being colonized by quality-
  conscious producers from
  Montalcino and elsewhere
  but so far to little effect.
Bianco *w dr DYA* Based on Trebbiano.

Rosso *r dr 99 00 01* Based on
  Sangiovese. Age: *riserva* 2 yrs.
Sangiovese *r dr 99 00 01* Age: 2 yrs.
Vermentino *w dr DYA*

MONTEREGIO DI MASSA MARITTIMA *DOC*
  The hills around Massa Marittima
  and neighbouring towns in the
  Maremma near Grosseto produce
  four types of wine and *vin santo*.
  Most are drunk locally.
Bianco *w dr* ☆→☆☆ *DYA* Made from
  Trebbiano with Ansonica, Malvasia,
  Vermentino, and other varieties,
  this is light and fresh.
Rosato *p dr* Mostly from Sangiovese,
  not much in evidence.
Rosso r dr ☆→☆☆☆ *97 98 99 00 01*
  Made mainly from Sangiovese.
  Numerous promising versions
  may be found. It may also be
  novello. Age: *riserva* 2 yrs.
Vermentino *w dr* ☆☆ *DYA* The variety
  has potential to yield class here.
Vin Santo *am d s/sw* Mostly from
  Trebbiano and Malvasia. Age:
  3 yrs, *riserva* 4 yrs.
Vin Santo Occhio di Pernice *r-am s/sw*
  From Sangiovese, Malvasia Nera,
  and others. Age: 3 yrs.

MONTESCUDAIO *DOC*
  The wines are produced along
  the Cecina valley, below Volterra.
  The white and red are greatly
  appreciated locally, but infrequently
  seen elsewhere. The jury is still out
  on the varietals, delimited more
  recently and not yet fully exploited
  by producers. All reds, aged 2 yrs,
  may be *riserva*.
Bianco *w dr* ☆→☆☆ *DYA* From at least
  50% Trebbiano and others, this is
  generally light and breezy.
Rosso *r dr* ☆→☆☆ *98 99 00 01* From at
  least 50% Sangiovese and others,
  can be attractive when aged a
  couple of years.
Cabernet *r dr* May be from Cabernet
  Franc or Cabernet Sauvignon.
Chardonnay *w dr*
Merlot *r dr*
Sangiovese *r dr*
Sauvignon *w dr*

Vermentino *w dr*
Vin Santo *am dr s/sw* From at least
50% Trebbiano. Age: 4 yrs.

MORELLINO DI SCANSANO

DOC r dr ☆☆→☆☆☆☆ *95 96 97 98 99
00 01*

Coming from around Scansano and
Montemerano, on the hills that rise
sharply a short way inland from
Grosseto, this is currently one of
Italy's most talked-about and closely
watched wines, with a rash of new
plantings by (mainly) leading central
Tuscan estates, which has also
produced a quality-enhancing
stimulus to longer-standing
producers. It is made predominantly
from a local clone of Sangiovese
known as Morellino. Sangiovese
develops a distinctive character
here in deep-ruby wines tending to
garnet, with a full bouquet and a dry,
warm, austere, fairly robust flavour,
and long finish in 4 to 5 years. Age:
riserva 2 yrs. A revision to the DOC
is in the pipeline.

MOSCADELLO DI MONTALCINO

DOC w am s/sw sw fz ☆→☆☆☆☆ *DYA*

This much-praised sweet wine is
more a reincarnation than a revival
of the one once made from the
Moscadelletto vine, renowned in
Montalcino in the Middle Ages.
Today's Moscadello, still or *frizzante*,
comes from the aromatic Moscato
Bianco, the base of Moscato d'Asti,
yet it rarely compares with the
Piedmontese prototype. There is
also a *vendemmia tardiva* version
that is richer and smoother. The
authentic Moscadelletto vine is
not officially approved, but tender
shoots can still be found. Age:
vendemmia tardiva 1 yr.

ORCIA

Much of the countryside along the
Orcia valley between Montalcino
and Montepulciano is not overly
suitable for vine-growing but that
which is has been incorporated into
this fairly recent DOC with a simple
split into 3 types of wine.

Bianco *w dr DYA* From Trebbiano (50%
or more) and others.
Rosso *r dr* From Sangiovese (60% or
more). A *novello* version exists.
Vin Santo *am dr s/sw* Mainly from
Trebbiano and Malvasia. Age: 3 yrs

PARRINA *DOC*

The first rises of the Maremma hills
behind Mount Argentario, around
an important agricultural property
called La Parrina, make a trio of
highly attractive, versatile wines
Bianco *w dr* ☆☆ *DYA* From Trebbiano
Ansonica and/or Chardonnay, this
is invariably crisp and refreshing.
Rosso *r dr* ☆☆→☆☆☆☆ *95 96 97 98 99
00 01* From Sangiovese
predominantly, this is buoyant
and stylish when young, while
the *riserva* is usually robust and
durable. Age: *riserva* 2 yrs.

POMINO *DOC*

The resurrection of this parcel
of history as DOC is a credit to
Marchesi de' Frescobaldi, whose
Tenuta di Pomino estate produces
some of Tuscany's most drinkable
modern wines from vineyards, at
up to 700 metres (2,297 feet).
Pomino was delimited in 1716 as an
area that covered much of what is
now Chianti Rufina, but today's
DOC is restricted to the commune
of the same name where vines from
France, planted in the last century,
figure in today's blends.
Frescobaldi owns much of the
land here but other small-scale
producers can be found.
Bianco *w dr* ☆☆→☆☆☆☆ *95 96 97 98 99
00 01* Pinot Bianco and Chardonnay
combine in a wine made in a fresh,
modern style, and a *riserva*,
exemplified by Frescobaldi's Il
Benefizio, which seems to have
been Tuscany's first barrel-
fermented modern white, and is
invariably one of its longest lived.
Rosso *r dr* ☆☆→☆☆☆☆ *95 96 97 98 99
00 01* Sangiovese is complemented
by Canaiolo, Cabernet Sauvignon,
and Merlot in a full-bodied red
that drinks well in 2 to 3 years but

attains real elegance after
5 or 6. Age: 1 yr, *riserva* 3 yrs.

Vin Santo and Vin Santo Rosso *am r*
s/sw sw ☆☆ The same varieties that
are used for the *bianco* and *rosso*
go into in these golden-amber or
rare garnet-red dessert wines.
Age: 3 yrs in barrels.

ROSSO DI MONTALCINO

DOC r dr ☆☆→☆☆☆ *95 96*
97 98 99 00 01
At the start of the 1980s the
producers in Montalcino had a
separate DOC for a second, more
youthful wine to sit alongside their
famous Brunello di Montalcino.
Rosso di Montalcino comes from
the same Sangiovese grapes as
Brunello but ages a mere 4 months,
providing a less imposing, less
expensive wine that nevertheless
expresses the essence of Brunello's
class. Most producers select which
grapes will become *rosso* and which
will become Brunello each year,
some allocate different vineyard
areas to the 2 wines.

ROSSO DI MONTEPULCIANO

DOC r dr ☆☆→☆☆☆ *97 98 99 00 01*
Growers in Montepulciano soon
took the lead from Rosso di
Montalcino (*q.v.*) to produce a
lighter red from the same grapes as
their Vino Noble to drink young.
Some are light and fruity, others
have the depth to benefit from a
few years' ageing.

SAN GIMIGNANO *DOC*

Although San Gimignano is famous
for its white Vernaccia many of its
producers also make one or more
reds. Some fit into the Chianti
Senesi DOCG, others come under
this denomination, which also
embraces rosé and *vin santo*.

Rosso *r dr* ☆→☆☆ *99 00 01* From at least
50% Sangiovese with a wide choice
of others. If 85% is used the grape
name may be shown on the label.
May be *novello*. Age: *riserva* 2 yrs.

Rosato *p dr* ☆☆ *DYA* Lively rosé based
on Sangiovese, with some Canaiolo

and, optionally, white Trebbiano,
Malvasia, and Vernaccia.

Vin Santo *am dr s/sw* Predominantly
Malvasia, with Trebbiano and
Vernaccia. Age: 3 yrs

Vin Santo Occhio di Pernice *r-am sw*
Predominantly or exclusively
from Sangiovese. Age: 3 yrs.

SANGIOVESE

Tuscany's dominant dark variety
is the main component of nearly all
its classified reds, though its many
sub-varieties impart different traits
to the wines. The historical name
Sangioveto is still used for a small-
berried type native to Chianti, while
Montalcino's Brunello and
Montepulciano's Prugnolo Gentile
are supposedly *grosso* (large). But
the situation is less clear than it
appears and clonal selection is still
taking place to determine which sub-
varieties are best suited. Sangiovese
was often blended with Canaiolo,
now Cabernet is its more frequent
partner. However, it can, and does,
stand alone remarkably well.

SANT'ANTIMO *DOC*

Producers in the Montalcino
area wanting to work with grape
varieties other than Sangiovese and
Moscato have this DOC at their
disposal, which takes its name from
the landmark abbey in the middle
of the zone. The list includes *bianco*
and *rosso* (from a liberal range of
white and red varieties respectivley),
and varietal Cabernet Sauvignon,
Chardonnay, Merlot, Pinot Grigio,
Pinot Nero, and Sauvignon. There
is also *vin santo*, both white and
the red Occhio di Pernice version,
which must be aged for 3 years,
riserva 4 years.

SASSICAIA

See Bolgheri DOC.

SOVANA *DOC r (p) dr*

A range of promising reds produced
in an area of southern Tuscany,
around Sovana and Pitigliano, better
known for its whites (*see* Bianco di

Pitigliano). The *rosso*, from at least 50% Sangiovese, is the most frequently seen although there is also varietal Aleatico, Cabernet Sauvignon, Merlot, and Sangiovese. These varietals, aged 30 months, may be *riserva*. A Sangiovese-based *rosato* may also be found.

VAL D'ARBIA

DOC w dr (s/sw) (sw) ☆→☆☆☆ DYA The ample Arbia River basin in Siena province lends its name to a dry white and *vin santo*, both from Trebbiano and Malvasia with a little Chardonnay, which vary from mundane to enthusing. Age: 3 yrs in barrel for *vin santo*. Well reputed wines from lands along the Comia stream which reaches the coast opposite Elba.

VAL DI CORNIA *DOC*

Well-reputed wines from lands along the Cornia stream which reaches the coast opposite Elba. Despite a goodly range of varietals, it is the *rosso* and *bianco* which inspire most interest. The small area around Suvereto forms a separate sub-zone. Age: *superiore* 16 mths, *riserva* 2 yrs.

Bianco *w dr ☆→☆☆ DYA* Trebbiano and Vermentino combine in a refreshing white that can be zesty.

Rosato *p dr ☆→☆☆ DYA* At least 50% Sangiovese with the remainder from Cabernet and/or Merlot make an enticing rosé.

Rosso *r dr ☆→☆☆☆ 97 98 99 00 01* An intriguing red, which has some similarities with those from nearby Bolgheri, made from the same grape proportions as the *rosato*. Age: *superiore* 18 mths, *riserva* 2 yrs.

Aleatico Passito *r s/sw DYA*

Ansonica *w dr (s/sw) DYA* A sweetish *passito* version (from semi-dried grapes) is also made.

Cabernet Sauvignon *r dr 99 00 01* Age: *superiore* 18 mths, *riserva* 2 yrs.

Ciliegiolo *r dr 99 00 01*

Merlot *r dr 99 00 01* Age: *superiore* 18 mths, *riserva* 2 yrs.

Sangiovese *r dr 99 00 01* Age: *superiore* 18 mths, *riserva* 2 yrs.

Vermentino *w dr DYA*

Suvereto *r dr ☆→☆☆☆ 00 01 02* From at least 50% Cabernet Sauvignon, Merlot making up the rest. The sub-zone also permits varietal versions from Cabernet Sauvignon, Merlot, and Sangiovese. Age: 26 mths.

VALDICHIANA *DOC*

Despite a few years having passed since the Bianco Vergine Valdichiana denomination was expanded to cover other wines, the Bianco Vergine (or simply Bianco) still dominates the scene along the tranquil Chiana valley between Arezzo and Chiusi. Potential for is stablemates remains high, though.

Bianco or Bianco Vergine *w dr (s/ws) (fz) (sp) ☆→☆☆ DYA* Made from Trebbiano but with up to 80% of Chardonnay, the Pinots, and/or Grechetto, this can be lightweight or have fragrance, fruit, and style.

Rosso and Rosato *dr s/sw* Based on Sangiovese with Cabernet/ Merlot/Syrah.

Chardonnay *w dr*

Grechetto *w dr*

Sangiovese *r dr*

Vin Santo *am s/sw sw* Based on Trebbiano and Malvasia. Age 3 yrs, *riserva* 4 yrs.

VERNACCIA DI SAN GIMIGNANO

DOCG w dr ☆→☆☆☆ 99 00 01 From the ancient Vernaccia vine grown around the medieval town of towers and tourist haunt San Gimignano, northwest of Siena, this is Tuscany's most famous white with a built-in market among its visitors. It claimed a bit of history in 1966, as the nation's first DOC. Since then it has evolved from tiredly traditional to monotonously modern and then following its upgrade to DOCG in 1992, onto characterful, elegant, and sometimes classy. Diversification has also crept in with many producers making several versions: "straight" (100% Vernaccia),

Vernaccia with Chardonnay (exploiting the 10% of "other" varieties permitted under DOCG) and *riserva* (often oak conditione). Age: *riserva* 16 mths.

VIN SANTO

Tuscany's traditional "holy" wine is made from grapes semi-dried, either on racks or by hanging from rafters They are then pressed and together with the *madre*, (a concentrated mother or starter left from the last batch) left to ferment and mature for at least 3 years. Sealed in small barrels called *caratelli* which are placed in a loft – or any site where they are exposed to summer heat and winter cold. Results can be hit and miss, although they are becoming less variable and good *vin santo* can last for years. Most comes from Malvasia and Trebbiano, though other grapes – including red varieties that make a type called Occhio di Pernice – may be used. It may be sweet, semi-sweet, or dry: the sweeter versions have the most fans, but in any event it should be clear golden amber (ruddy if Occhio di Pernice), aromatic, strong (14 to 17%), and velvety. At best it is one of Italy's great dessert wines. *vin santo* is DOC in many zones of Tuscany but rough and ready *vin santo* made by the old fingers-crossed method can still be found. There are also some industrial imitations often based on Sicilian Moscato.

VIN SANTO DEL CHIANTI

DOC am r-am dr s/sw sw ☆☆→☆☆☆☆
Trebbiano and/or Malvasia grown in the territory of Chianti DOCG, these wines may carry the names of its sub-zones. An Occhio di Pernice version from Sangiovese and other red varieties is also found. Age: 3 yrs, *riserva* 4 yrs.

VIN SANTO DEL CHIANTI CLASSICO

DOC am r-am dr s/sw sw ☆☆→☆☆☆☆
Vin santo from Trebbiano, Malvasia, and others grown in the territory of Chianti Classico. Also permitted is Occhio di Pernice from Sangiovese and other red varieties. Age: 3 yrs, *riserva* 4 yrs.

VIN SANTO DI MONTEPULCIANO

DOC am r-am s/sw sw ☆☆→☆☆☆☆
Montepulciano's *vin santo* may come from Grecchetto as well as Trebbiano and Malvasia, Sangiovese dominates the Occhio di Pernice. Age: 5 yrs, *riserva* 8 yrs.

VINO NOBILE DI MONTEPULCIANO

DOCG ☆☆→☆☆☆☆ *95 96 97 98 99 00 01*

The hill town of Montepulciano in southeast Tuscany is the home of this red with the resounding name and the legend of having been described as "king of all wines" by the poet Francesco Redi in the 17th century. But it took promotion to DOCG in the early 1980s and a new generation of winemakers for it to start living up to its name. Vino Nobile bears family resemblances to both Chianti Classico and Brunello, since its mainstay is called Prugnolo Gentile, a variant Sangiovese. But it stands in a class of its own, due to the special conditions of soil and climate on slopes facing the Chiana valley and the presence in the blend of Canaiolo, which softens Prugnolo's inherent vigour, and Mammolo, which lends a telling bouquet of violets. Normal Vino Nobile does not need as long as Brunello to reach its peak, usually 4 to 7 years, a little longer for the *riserva*. Some producers aim to exalt its elegance, others to try for all-out power. Production has increased gradually to about 3 million bottles a year, and the list wines deserving the "noble" tag becomes increasingly longer. Age: 2 yrs, *riserva* 3 yrs.

Producers

Provinces: Arezzo (AR), Firenze (FI), Grosseto (GR), Livorno (LI), Lucca (LU), Massa Carrara (MS), Pisa (PI), Pistoia (PT), Prato (PO), Siena (SI).

Acquabona, Portoferraio (LI). Elba DOC led by fine Aleatico.

Agricoltori Chianti Geografico, Gaiole (SI). Reliable Chianti Classico (Contessa di Radda, Montegiachi), IGT Pulleraia (Merlot), and others.

Agostina Pieri, Montalcino (SI). Good Brunello, *rosso*.

Aiola, Vagliagli (SI). Chianti Classico, IGT Logaiolo (Sangiovese/ Cabernet), Rosso del Senatore (Merlot/Cabernet/Sangiovese).

Altesino, Montalcino (SI). Modernist estate for Brunello (Montosoli), and *rosso*, IGT Palazzo Altesi (Sangiovese), Alte d'Altesi (Sangiovese/Cabernet/Merlot).

Antica Fattoria Niccolò Machiavelli, Sant'Andrea in Percussina (FI). Winery belonging to Gruppo Italiano Vini combined with old Conti Serristori estate to provide value Chianti Classico.

Ambrosini, Suvereto (LI). Classy Val di Cornia (Subertum, Rosso Tabarò, Bianco Tabarò), IGT Riflesso Antico (Montepulciano), Armonia (Vermentino)

Argiano, Montalcino (SI). Brunello dripping with class.

Artimino, Carmignano (PO). Fairly large production of confident Carmignano DOCG and DOC.

Avignonesi, Montepulciano (SI). Montepulciano Vino Nobile (Riserva Grandi Annate), *rosso*, and a string of refined Cortona and IGT varietals and blends. The *vin santo* and Occhio di Pernice is legendary (and almost unobtainable). Property covers 4 estates in Montepulciano, Valdichiana, and Cortona.

Badia a Morrona, Terricciola (PI). Impressive chianti, Colli Etruria Centrale, Bianco Pisano di San Torpé, and others.

Baggiolino, La Romola (FI). Chianti; IGT Poggio Brandi (Sangiovese/Ciliegiolo).

Banfi, Montalcino (SI). Huge American-owned estate, marketing a similarly huge range of wines under the Castello Banfi and Villa Banfi labels, including Brunello Rosso (Castello Banfi, Poggio alle Mura, Poggio all'oro Riserva), and *rosso*; Sant'Antimo. Excelsus (Cabernet Sauvignon/Merlot), Summus (Sangiovese/Cabernet Sauvignon/ Syrah), Cum Laude (same 3 grapes plus Merlot), varietals, and more. Also Chianti Classico.

Erik Banti, Scansano (GR). Distinctive Morellino.

Jacopo Banti, Campiglia Marittima (LI). Stylish range of Val di Cornia, led by Aleatico.

Baroncini, San Gimignano (SI). Sound range of Vernaccia, Chianti Colli Senesi, San Gimignano Rosso.

Basciano, Rufina (FI). Stylish Chianti Rufina; Erta e Corta (Sangiovese) Cabernet, I Pini (Syrah too).

Bindella, Montepulciano (SI). Sound Vino Nobile, *rosso* (Fossolupaio), and IGT Vallocaia (Prugnolo/Cabernet).

Biondi Santi, Montalcino (SI). Renowned Brunello. Austere wines from old vines destined for marathon ageing. Prices are astronomical for aged riserva, regular Brunello, and *rosso* still high

Le Bocce, Panzano (FI). Re-emerging Chianti Classico estate.

Boscarelli, Montepulciano (SI). Supreme Vino Nobile (rare Riserva del Nocio is stellar) and excellent IGT Boscarelli (Sangiovese/Merlot/ Cabernet).

La Braccesca, Montepulciano (SI). Antinori-owned estate with reliable Vino Nobile, *rosso* (Sabazio), and IGT Merlot.

La Brancaia, Radda (SI). IGT Brancaia Blu (Sangiovese/Merlot/Cabernet Sauvignon) steals the limelight over good Chianti Classico.

La Calonica, Montepulciano (SI). Greatly improved Vino Nobile, *rosso*, Cortona Rosso (Girifalco), IGT Signorelli (Merlot).

Le Calvane, Montespertoli (FI). Chianti Colli Fiorentini (Quercione, Il Trecion Riserva), IGT Borro del Boscone (Cabernet).

I Campetti, Roccastrada (GR). Promising Montereggio di Massa Marittima Bianco and Almabruna (Viognier).

Campogiovanni, Montalcino (SI). Impressive Brunello made by Chianti estate San Felice.

Canalicchio, Montalcino (SI). Brunello, *riserva*, *rosso*.

Canalicchio di Sopra, Montalcino (SI). Good Brunello, *riserva*, *rosso*, Sant'Antimo Bianco.

Canneto, Montepulciano (SI). Improving Vino Nobile.

Cantina Cooperativa del Morellino di Scansano, Scansano (GR). Commendable Morellino (Sicomoro, Roggiano, and others).

Capanna di Cencioni, Montalcino (SI). Brunello of personality.

Capannelle, Gaiole (SI). Well-structured Chianti Classico. 50:50 made with Sangiovese and Merlot from Avignonesi.

Tenuta Caparzo, Montalcino (SI). Admired estate with succulent Brunello (La Casa), *rosso* (La Caduta), Sant'Antimo Ca' del Pazzo (Sangiovese/Cabernet), Le Grance (Chardonnay/Sauvignon/Traminer), white Val d'Arbia Le Crete.

Capezzana, Carmignano (PO). Once supremely elegant Carmignano now with greater power and impact (Villa di Capezzana, Villa di Trefiano). Also DOC Barco Reale, rosé Vin Ruspo, *vin santo*, IGT Ghiaie della Furba (Cabernet/Merlot/Chardonnay).

"Fuso" Carmignani, Montecarlo (LU). Spirited Montecarlo Rosso (Sassonero), and Bianco (Stati d'Animo), IGT Syrah/Sangiovese blend called "For Duke" – Ellington, that is.

Podere Il Carnasciale, Mercatale Valdarno (AR). Extraordinary Caberlot from a vine that represents a cross of Cabernet and Merlot.

Carobbio, Panzano (FI). First-rate Chianti Classico, IGT Leone (Sangiovese), Pietraforte (Cabernet).

Carpineto, Dudda (FI). Reliable house for Chianti Classico and others.

Carpineta Fontalpino, Castelnuovo Berardenga (SI). Admired Chianti Colli Senesi, IGT Do Ut Des (Sangiovese/Cabernet Sauvignon/Merlot).

Casa alle Vacche, San Gimignano (SI). Improving range of Vernaccia, Chianti Colli Senesi, San Gimignano Rosso.

Casa Emma, Barberino Val d'Elsa (FI). Starry Chianti Classico, IGT Soloio (Merlot).

Casa Sola, Barberino Val d'Elsa (FI). Lively Chianti Classico.

Casaloste, Panzano (FI). Rapidly improving Chianti Classico.

Le Casalte, Montepulciano (SI). One of the most beautifully refined DOCG Nobile di Montepulciano, also good *rosso*.

Casanova di Neri, Montalcino (SI). Highly impressive Brunello (Tenuta Nuova, Cerretallo) *rosso*.

Case Basse, Montalcino (SI). Brunello of power and finesse, often equaled by IGT Intistieti (Sangiovese)

Casina di Cornia, Castellina (SI). Good Chianti Classico, IGT L'Amaranto (Cabernet).

Castagnoli, Castellina (SI). Admirable Chianti Classico; fine Syrah, Merlot.

Castel Ruggero, Antella (FI). Just fine Chianti Classico.

Castelgiocondo, Montalcino (SI). Extensive estate of Marchesi de' Frescobaldi makes impressive Brunello, *rosso* (Campo ai Sassi); sought-after IGT Lamaione (Merlot), Vergena (Sauvignon). A separate winery makes Luce – premium red from Frescobaldi's joint venture with California's Mondavi.

Castellare di Castellina, Castellina (SI). Remarkable Chianti Classico; also highly rated IGTs I Sodi di San Niccolò (Sangiovese/Malvasia Nera), and others.

Castelli del Grevepesa, Mercatale Val di Pesa (SI). Large co-op selects for output of large number of Chianti

Classico (Castelgreve, Lamole, Clemente VII, and more).

Castell'in Villa, Castelnuovo Berardenga (SI). Chianti Classico of noble lineage.

Castello dei Rampolla, Panzano (FI). Impeccable Chianti Classico, IGT Sammarco (Cabernet/Sangiovese), and La Vigna di Alceo (Cabernet Sauvignon/Petit Verdot).

Castello della Paneretta, Barberino Val d'Elsa (FI). Fine Chianti Classico (Torre a Destra Riserva), IGT Le Terrine (Sangiovese/Canaiolo), Quattrocentenario (Sangiovese).

Castello di Albola, Radda (SI). Zonin of the Veneto here produces refined Chianti Classico (Le Ellere); impressive IGT Acciaiolo (Sangiovese/Cabernet), Le Fagge (Chardonnay).

Castello di Ama, Gaiole (SI). Individual Chianti Classico of consistent class notably *crus* Bellavista and La Casuccia; exemplary IGT L'Apparita (Merlot), Il Chiuso (Pinot Nero), Al Poggio (Chardonnay).

Castello di Bossi, Castelnuovo Berardenga (SI). Revived estate makes Chianti Classico (*riserva* Berardo), Corbaia/Sangiovese/ Cabernet Sauvignon), Cirolamo (Merlot) of personality.

Castello di Brolio, Gaiole (SI). Afer a long lull, the winery at the castle where Bettino Ricasoli resurrected chianti in the 1800s has been restored to its former glory. There are 2 lines (Brolio and the premier Castello di Brolio) and concentration is on Chianti Classico 3 lines; fine IGT red Casalferro (Sangiovese), and white Torricella (Chardonnay), and *vin santo*.

Castello di Cacchiano, Gaiole (SI). Elegant Chianti Classico.

Castello di Camigliano, Montalcino (SI). Large estate being revived with Brunello, Rosso, Sant'Antimo.

Castello di Farnetella, Sinalunga (SI). Under same ownership as Felsina. Superb Chianti Colli Senesi; IGT Nero di Nubi (Pinot Nero), Rosa Rosae (Mosato Rosa), Lucilla (Sangiovese/ Cabernet Sauvignon), Sauvignon, and outstanding Poggio Granoni (Sangiovese/Cabernet/Merlot/Syrah).

Castello di Fonterutoli, Castellina (SI). Benchmark Chianti Classico (Castello di Fontemtoli). Classy IGT Siepi (Sangiovese/Merlot), and Morellino di Scansano (Belguardo) from estate in the Maremma.

Castello La Leccia, Castellina (SI). Promising Chianti Classico.

Castello di Meleto, Gaiole (SI). Decent range of Chianti Classico.

Castello di Monsanto, Barberino Val d'Elsa (FI). Rich, powerful Chianti Classico (Il Poggio); excellent IGT Fabrizio Bianchi (Sangiovese, Chardonnay), Nemo (Cabernet Sauvignon), Tinscvil (Sangiovese/ Cabernet/Merlot).

Castello di Poppiano, Montespertoli (FI). Admirable Chianti Colli Fiorentini, IGTs Syrah, Tricorno (Sangiovese/Cabernet Sauvignon/ Merlot), Tosco Forte (Sangiovese/ Syrah), and others. Also Morellino di Scansano, Vernaccia, *vin santo*.

Castello di Querceto, Greve (FI). Refined Chianti Classico; IGT Cignale (Cabernet/Merlot), La Corte (Sangiovese), Il Querciolaia (Sangiovese/Cabernet).

Castello di San Polo in Rosso, Gaiole (SI). Fine Chianti Classico; IGT Cetinaia, a delicious model of pure Sangioveto, and Rosa d'Erta lead the range.

Castello di Selvole, Castelnuovo Berardenga (SI). Multilayered Chianti Classico of good style; IGT Selvole (Sangiovese).

Castello di Verrazzano, Greve (FI). Highly rated Chianti Classico; IGT Sassello (Sangiovese), Bottiglia Particolare (Sangiovese/ Cabernet). And new Rosso Di Verrazzano, mixing red and white grapes, dubbed by the estate a "Mini Tuscan".

Castello di Vicchiomaggio, Greve (FI). Finely tuned, refined Chianti Classico (La Prima, Petri, San Jacopo), IGT Ripa delle More, Ripa delle Mandorle (both Sangiovese/Cabernet, different proportions, different ageing).

Castello di Volpaia, Radda in Chianti (SI). Supremely impressive Chianti Classico, especially Coltassala (once IGT). Also elegant IGT Balifico (Sangiovese/Cabernet); Bianco Val d'Arbia (Sauvignon/Chardonnay), *vin santo*.

Castello Romitorio, Montalcino (SI). Artist Sandro Chia makes restrained Brunello Rosso and Sant'Antimo, Romito di Romitorio (Sangiovese/Cabernet).

Castiglion del Bosco, Montalcino (SI). Revived Brunello, Rosso.

Luigi Cecchi & Figli, Castellina Scalo (SI). Large company with 5 estates, Castello di Montauto for Vernaccia, Val delle Rose with Morellino di Scansano, Tenuta Alzatura (Umbria), but best known are Villa Cerna for reliable Chianti Classico and Cecchi, with smarter Chianti Classico, (Messer Pietro di Teuzzo), Brunello, Vino Nobile, IGT Spargolo (Sangiovese), and much more.

Cennatoio, Panzano (FI). Classically styled Chianti Classico; IGT Etrusco (Sangiovese), Arcibaldo Merlot.

Centolani, Montalcino (SI). Two properties, Friggiali and Pietranera with good Brunello, *rosso*, IGTs of differing styles.

Vincenzo Cesani, San Gimignano (SI). Vernaccia (Sanice); highly admired IGT Luenzo (Sangiovese/Colorino).

Cerbaiona, Montalcino (SI). Grand DOCG Brunello, IGT Cerbaiona (Sangiovese).

Le Chiuse di Sotto, Montalcino (SI). Fine Brunello, *rosso*, IGT Amor Costante.

Ciacci Piccolomini d'Aragona, Montalcino (SI). Classy Brunello (Vigna di Pianrosso), *rosso* (Vigna della Fonte), Ateo (Sangiovese/Cabernet).

La Ciarlana, Montepulciano (SI). Rapidly emerging Vino Nobile.

Cima, Massa. Large range of admired wines from Candia di Colli Apuani zone, led by Vermentino.

Col d'Orcia, Montalcino (SI). Cinzano family estate makes splendid Brunello (Riserva Poggio al Vento), *rosso* (Banditella), Moscadello (Pascena); Sant'Antimo Pinot Grigio, and an impeccable range of IGT varietals and blends.

Colle ai Lecci, San Gusmé (SI). Chianti Classico (San Losma).

Collelungo, Castellina (SI). Concentrated Chianti Classico of personality.

Colle Santa Mustiola, Chiusi (SI). Just one wine, IGT Poggio ai Chiari, Sangiovese of finesse.

Colle Verde, Capannori (LU). Colline Lucchesi Rosso (Brania di Castello, Brania delle Ghiandaie, Matraia).

Il Colombaio di Cencio, Gaiole (SI). Chianti Classico (I Massi), IGT Il Futuro (Sangiovese/Cabernet Sauvignon/Merlot), both of stature.

Coltibuono, Gaiole (SI). Full, firm Chianti Classico in Badia a Coltibuono line, including notable old reserves and IGT Sangioveto Vin Santo and Coltibuono line, includes more fruit-forward Chianti Classico RS, Chianti Cetamura, white Trappoline, Cetamura.

Contucci, Montepulciano (SI). Solid Vino Nobile (Mulinvecchio, Pietra Rossa), DOC *rosso*, *vin santo*, and others.

Concadoro, Castellina (SI). Refined Chianti Classico (Vigna di Gaversa).

Le Corti Corsini, San Casciano (FI). Revived class in Chianti Classico (Don Tommaso).

Corzano e Paterno, San Casciano Val di Pesa (FI). Fine Chianti Colli Fiorentini (Terre di Corzano, I Tre Born), IGT Il Corzano (Sangiovese/Cabernet), Aglaia (Chardonnay). Also *vin santo*.

Costanti, Montalcino (SI). Elegant, intensive, classy Brunello, Rosso; IGT Vermiglio (Sangiovese), Argingo (Cabernet Sauvignon/Merlot).

Dei, Montepulciano (SI). Elegant Vino Nobile; IGT Sancta Catharina (Sangiovese/Cabernet/Syrah).

Dievole, Vagliagli (SI). Chianti Classico (Dieulele, Novecento); IGT Broccato (Sangiovese).

La Doccia, Greve (FI). Steady Chianti Classico.

Donatella Cinelli Colombini, Montalcino (SI). 2 estates, Fattoria del Casato in Montalcino and Il Colle in Trequando produce distinctive range led by unique Brunello Prime Donne whose style, all elegance and fruit-forward restraint, is guided by experts of 4 nationalities – all women. Newcomer Cenerentola, from Sangiovese and rare Foglia Tonda, aims to put DOC Orcia on the map.

Due Portine, Montalcino (SI). Good Brunello, *rosso* (Le Potazzine).

Casale Falchini, San Gimignano (SI). Leading producer of Vernaccia (Castel Selva, Riserva Vigna a Solatio); much admired IGT Campora (Cabernet Sauvignon), Paretaio (Sangiovese), plus *spumante* mc Falchini Brut and *vin santo*.

Fanetti-Tenuta Sant'Agnese, Montepulciano (SI). Vino Nobile (*riserva* Vigneto San Giuseppe), *rosso*, IGT Vin del Sasso (Cabernet), *vin santo*.

Fanti, Montalcino (SI). Much admired Brunello, *rosso*.

Le Farnete, Carmignano (PO). DOCG Carmignano from Le Farnete, chianti from Cantagallo, and Chianti Classico from Matroneo at Greve.

Fassati, Montepulciano (SI). Vino Nobile (Salarco, Pasiteo), *rosso* (Selcaia), Chianti (Le Gaggiole), and more from company owned by Fazi-Battaglia in the Marche.

Fattoria Ambra, Carmignano (FI). Respected DOCG Carmignano (Elzana, Vigna di Montefortini, Santa Cristina in Pilli, Vigne Alte), DOC Barca Reale.

Fattoria dei Barbi, Montalcino (SI). Well-rated Brunello (Vigna del Fiore), *rosso* (Sole dei Barbi); IGT Brusco dei Barbi and Bruscone dei Barbi (both from Sangiovese), and *vin santo*.

Fattoria del Buonamico, Montecarlo (LU). Montecarlo Bianco and Rosso, sometimes eclipsed by IGT Rosso di Cercatoja (Sangiovese, Canaiolo, Ciliegiolo), Il Fortino (Syrah), and Vasario (Pinot Bianco).

Fattoria Casabianca, Murlo (SI). Good Chianti Colli Senesi, IGT Tenuta Casabianca (Cabernet Sauvignon/Merlot)

Fattoria del Cerro, Montepulciano (SI). Fruit-forward Vino Nobile (Antica Chiusina), Rosso, Chianti Colli Senesi, Vin Santo. Good IGT Manero (Sangiovese), Poggio Colo (Merlot), Cerro Bianco (Chardonnay), Braviola (Trebbiano), and more.

Fattoria dell'Uccelliera, Fauglia (PI). Good Chianti Colline Pisane, fine IGT Castellaccio Bianco (Sauvignon/Pinot Bianco/Chardonnay), and *rosso* (Sangiovese/Cabernet Sauvignon/Syrah).

Fattoria di Felsina, Castelnuovo Berardenga (SI). Much admired estate produces exemplary Chianti Classico (Riserva Rancia), along with prized IGT Fontalloro (Sangiovese), Maestro Raro (Cabernet), I Sistri (Chardonnay), and *vin santo*.

Fattoria di Manzano, Cortona (AR). Originally known for Bianco Vergine Valdichiana but now acclaimed for IGT Le Terrazze (Sauvignon), Podere di Fontarca (Chardonnay/Viognier), Viognier, Podere Il Vescovo (Gamay), and, above all, Podere del Bosco (Syrah).

Fattoria Montecchio, Tavarnelle Val di Pesa (FI). Revived Chianti Classico estate.

Fattoria di Petroio, Castelnuovo Berardenga (SI). Excellent Chianti Classico and *riserva*.

Fattoria di Sammontana, Montelupo Fiorentino (FI). Good Chianti Colli Fiorentini.

Fattoria del Teso, Montecarlo (LU). Montecarlo Rosso, *bianco*, *vin santo*, IGT Anfidiamante (Sangiovese/Syrah/Merlot/Canaiolo), and the unusual white Stella del Teso (Rousanne/Vermentino/Sauvignon/Chardonnay).

Tenuta Il Corno, San Pancrazio (FI). Chianti Colli Fiorentini (San Camillo); IGT Colorino, Corno Rosso (Sangiovese/Colorino/Cabernet Sauvignon), Corno Bianco (Chardonnay); *vin santo*.

Fattoria Il Poggiolo, Carmignano (PO). Carmignano DOC, DOCG, *vin santo*.

Fattoria Le Pupille, Istia d'Ombrone (GR). Long-term Morellino di

Scansano leader (Poggio Valente) most notably with IGT. Saffredi (Cabernet/Merlot/Alicante), sweet white Solalto, Poggio Argentato (Gewürztraminer/Sauvignon).

Fattoria Montellori, Fucecchio (FI). Chianti (Vigne del Moro); IGT Dicatum (Sangiovese), Montellori Brut Spumante mc, and others.

Il Paradiso, San Gimignano (SI). Good Vernaccia (Biscondola); but more plaudits gained recently for Saxa Calida (Merlot/Cabernet), Paterno II (Sangiovese).

Fattoria Petrolo, Excellent IGT Torrione (Sangiovese) and Galatrona (Merlot).

Fattoria di Ambra, Ambra (AR). Chianti, (Vigna Bigattiera), IGT, Casamurli (Sangiovese/Malvasia Nera), Gavignano (Cabernet/Sangiovese).

Fattoria Castello Sonnino, Montespertoli (FI). Chianti (Castello di Montespertoli); IGT Cantinino (Sangiovese), Sanleone (Merlot/Sangiovese); *vin santo*.

Faltoria Vistarenni, *See* S.M. Tenimenti Pile e Lamole.

Ficomontanino, Chiusi (SI). Chianti Colli Senesi (Tutulus); IGT Lucumone (Cabernet), Porsenna (Sauvignon).

Le Filigare, San Donato in Poggio (FI). Notable Chianti Classico (Maria Vittoria, Lorenzo); IGT Podere Le Rocce (Cabernet/Sang.).

Le Fioraie, Castellina (SI). Stylish Chianti Classico.

La Fiorita, Montalcino (SI). Emerging Brunello estate.

Le Fonti, Panzano (FI). Reliable Chianti Classico; Fontissimo (Sangiovese/Cabernet).

Fontodi, Panzano (FI). Renowned estate with excellent Chianti Classico (Vigna del Sorbo); IGT Flaccianello della Pieve (Sangiovese), Case Via (Pinot Nero, Syrah), Meriggio (Pinot Bianco).

La Fortuna, Montalcino (SI). Sound Brunello, *rosso*.

Eredi Fuligni, Montalcino (SI). Excellent Brunello (Vigneti dei Cottimelli), Rosso (Ginestreto).

Grati Vetrice, Rufina (FI). Reliable Chianti Rufina and others.

La Gerla, Montalcino (SI). Admired Brunello, *rosso*; IGT Birba (Sangiovese).

I Giusti e Zanza, Fauglia (PI). Admired IGT Belcore (Sangiovese/Merlot), Dulcamara (Cabernet Sauvignon/Merlot).

Grattamacco, Castagneto Carducci (LI). Superb Bolgheri Rosso Superiore (Grattamacco), very good Bolgheri Bianco.

Greppone Mazzi, Montalcino (SI). Brunello estate owned by Ruffino.

Gualdo del Re, Suvereto (LI). Admirable Val di Cornia Rosso, Bianco Aleatico, Merlot, and Vermentino.

Guicciardini Strozzi-Fattoria di Cusona, San Gimignano (SI). Historical estate for Vernaccia (Perlato, San Biagio); also IGT Sòdole (Sangiovese), Selvascura (Merlot), and others.

Incontri, Suvereto (LI). Emerging Val di Cornia estate.

Isole e Olena, Barberino Val d'Elsa (FI). Fabulous, fruit-rich Chianti Classico, top IGT Cepparello (Sangiovese), remarkable Syrah, and rich, refined *vin santo* lead an impeccable range.

Ispoli, San Casciano Val di Pesa (FI). Organic Chianti Classico, IGT Ispolaia (Sangiovese/Cabernet Sauvignon/Merlot), Podere Ispoli (Sangiovese/Merlot).

La Lastra, Stylish range of Vernaccia; IGT Rovaio (Sangiovese/Merlot/ Cabernet Sauvignon).

Lambardi, Montalcino (SI). Very good traditional Brunello, *rosso*.

Lanciola, Pozzolatico (FI). Chianti Classico Classico (Le Masse di Greve); impressive IGT Terricci (Sangiovese/Cabernet).

Le Macchiole, Bolgheri (LI). Exceptional Bolgheri Rosso Superiore and Sauvignon (both Paleo), stunning Messorio (Merlot), and others.

La Madonnina, Greve (FI). Admirable Chianti Classico (La Palaia, Bello Stento).

La Marcellina, Panzano (FI). Emerging Chianti Classico estate.

La Massa, Panzano (FI). Highly rated Chianti Classico especially superb Giorgio Primo.

Le Masse di San Leolino, Panzano (FI). Good Chianti Classico made by Scot Norman Bain.

Il Lebbio, San Gimignano (SI). Admired for intriguing blended IGT reds.

Lisini, Montalcino (SI). Admired Brunello (Ugolaia), *rosso*.

Livernano, Radda (SI). Admired IGT Livernano (Merlot/Cabernet Sauvignon/Cabernet Franc/Sangiovese), Puro Sangue (Sangiovese), Anima (Chardonnay/Sauvignon/Traminer).

Lodola Nuova, Montepulciano (SI). Ruffino estate with good Vino Nobile, *rosso*.

Il Mandorlo, San Casciano Val di Pesa (FI). Up-and-coming Chianti Classico.

Mantellassi, Magliano in Toscana (GR). Attractive Morellino di Scansano (San Giuseppe, Le Sentinelle); IGT Querciolaia (Sangiovese/Alicante).

Marchesato degli Aleramici, Montalcino (SI). Emerging Brunello, Sant'Antimo estate.

Marchesi L. & P. Antinori, Firenze (FI). Lynchpin of The Tuscan scene, Antinori led the Tuscan renaissance in 1970s, first with Tignanello (Sangiovese/Cabernet), then Solaia (Cabernet/Sangiovese) from their Santa Cristina estate in Chianti. Now the tone of a comprehensive range is set by Chianti Classico (Tenute Marchese Antinori, Villa Antinori, Badia a Passignano, Pèppoli), IGT Santa Cristina (Sangiovese/Merlot), Villa Antinori Bianco (Trebbiano/Malvasia/Chardonnay), Marchese Antinori Extra Brut and Millesimato (mc), *vin santo*, and sweeter Aleatico, from Southern Tuscany. There are also estates in Bolgheri (Guado al Tasso), Montalcino (Pian delle Vigne), and Montepulciano (La Braccesca).

Marchesi de' Frescobaldi, Firenze (FI). The illustrious Florentine family, active in wine since 1300, has numerous extensive estates and a range of exemplary wines typified by Chianti Rufina (Nipozzano, Montesodi), Pomino Rosso, Bianco (including Il Benefizio); IGT Mormoreto (Cabernet). A joint venture with Robert Mondavi of California has resulted in the illustrious Luce, from Sangiovese and Merlot grapes grown.

Marchesi Pancrazi-Fattoria Bagnolo, Montemurlo (PO). Renowned for outstanding Pinot Nero.

Marchesi Torrigiani, Barberino Val d'Elsa (FI). Emerging estate with IGT Guidaccio (Sangiovese/Cabernet Sauvignon/Merlot), Sangiovese-based Torre di Ciardo.

Il Marroneto, Montalcino (SI). Good, sound Brunello.

Massanera, San Casciano Val di Pesa (FI). Chianti Classico and range of IGTs.

Massa Vecchia, Massa Marittima (GR). Individual wines from Monteregio di Massa Marittima zone, DOC and IGT, mainly based on varietals Vermentino (Ariento), Sauvignon (Patrizia Bartolini), Alicante (Terziere), Aleatico (Il Matto delle Giuncaie), Cabernet Sauvignon (La Fonte di Pietrarsa).

Mastrojanni, Montalcino (SI). Brunello (Schiena d'Asino), and *rosso* of winning style.

Meleta, Roccatederighi (GR). Fine IGT Bianco della Rocca (Chardonnay), Rosso della Rocca (Cabernet/Merlot), Pietrello (Sangiovese), and more.

Melini, Poggibonsi (SI). Gruppo Italiano Vini winery with esteemed Chianti Classico most notably La Selvanella and Vernaccia (Le Grillaie).

Fattoria di Montechiari, Montecarlo (LU). Emerging estate with fine IGT Montechiari Rosso (Sangiovese), Chardonnay, Cabernet, and Pinot Nero.

Montenidoli, San Gimignano (SI). Highly individual Vernaccia in 3 styles (*tradizionale, fiore, carato*); also pink Canniuolo, red Sono Montenidoli (Sangiovese/Malvasia Nera), Chianti Colli Senesi.

Montepeloso, Suvereto (LI). Admired Val di Cornia, IGT Nardo (Sangiovese/Cabernet), Gabbro (Cabernet Sauvignon).

Montevertine, Radda (SI). High-class wine mixing refinement with power remains strictly IGT (though qualifying for DOC): Le Pergole Torte (Sangiovese) leads. Il Sodaccio, Monte Vertine and Pian del Ciampolo (all Canaiolo/Sangiovese), tasty Montevertine Bianco and "M" (both Trebbiano/Malvasia).

Montiverdi, Gaiole (SI). Classy range of Chianti Classico (Cipressone, Ventesimo, Maisano); IGT Le Borranine (Cabernet).

Monte Oliveto, San Gimignano (SI). Good Vernaccia from estate owned by giant Zonin of the Veneto.

Moris Farms, Massa Marittima (GR). Admired wines: Morellino di Scansano, Montereggio di Massa Marittima. IGT Avvoltore (Sangiovese/Cabernet).

Mormoraia, San Gimignano (SI). Reliable Vernaccia; IGT Ostrea Grigia (Vernaccia/Chardonnay), Neiteia (Sangiovese/Cabernet Sauvignon).

Le Murelle, Lucca (LU). Estate making mainly Chardonnay, Sauvignon.

Fattoria Nittardi, Castellina (SI). Reliably impressive Chianti Classico (Nittardi, Casanuova di Nittardi.

Nottola, Montepulciano (SI). Vino Nobile (Vigna del Fattore).

Nozzole, Greve (SI). Ruffino-owned estate, Chianti Classico (La Forra); IGT Il Pareto (Cabernet), Le Bruniche (Chardonnay).

Ornellaia, Bolgheri (LI). Lodovico Antinori built this estate into a major force before selling to Mondavi. Bolgheri Superiore Ornellaia, Bolgheri Le Serre Nuove, Le Volle (Sangiovese/Cabernet Sauvignon/ Merlot), and especially Masseto (Merlot) practically define the zone.

Siro Pacenti, Montalcino (SI). Impeccable Brunello, and *rosso*.

Pacina, Castelnuovo Bernardenga (SI). Beautifully honed Chianti Colli Senesi, IGT Malena (Sangiovese/Syrah)

Palagetto, San Gimignano (SI). Improved style in Vernaccia, Chianti Colli Senesi, IGT Sottobosco (Sangiovese/Cabernet/Merlot), l'Niccolo (Vermentino/Chardonnay).

Il Palagio, Colle Val d'Elsa (SI). Estate owned by the large Zonin company. Good Chianti Colli Senesi and

Vernaccia (La Gentilesca) eclipsed by Chardonnay and Sauvignon IGTs Il Palagio.

Il Palazzone, Montalcino (SI). Impressive Brunello, *rosso*.

Panizzi, San Gimignano (SI). Leading producer of slow-ageing Vernaccia, including oaked *riserva*. Also Ceraso (Sangiovese/Canaiolo), Chianti Colli Senesi.

Panzanello, Panzano (FI). Rapidly improving Chianti Classico, IGT Il Manuzio (Sangiovese).

La Parrina, Orbetello (GR). In effect, the sole producers of Parrina DOC. Elegant white, excellent Ansonica; stylish red, notably Muraccio, refined *riserva*. Also IGT Radaia (Merlot).

Pasolini dall'Onda, Barberino Val d'Elsa (FI). Chianti (Montoli, Drove), Chianti Classico (Badia a Sicelle), Novello, *vin santo*, and red and white IGTs. Partner estate in Romagna.

Badia a Passignano, Tavarnelle Val di Pesa (FI). Chianti Classico made by Antinori.

Paterno, Montepulciano (SI). Rapidly improving Vino Nobile.

Petreto, Bagno a Ripoli (FI). Chianti Colli Fiorentini; IGT Bocciolè (Sangiovese), Pourriture Noble (Sauvignon/Semillon).

Piaggia, Poggio a Caiano (PO). Highly esteemed Carmignano DOCG, IGT Il Sasso (Sangiovese/Cabernet Sauvignon/Merlot).

Piancornello, Montalcino (SI). Highly admired Brunello, *rosso*.

Pietrafitta, San Gimignano (SI). Historic estate makes enjoyable range of Vernaccia, Chianti Colli Senesi, San Gimignano, *vin santo*.

Pietraserena, San Gimignano (SI). Vernaccia (Vigna del Sole), Chianti Colli Senesi, IGT Ser Gervasio (Merlot).

Pieve Santa Restituta, Montalcino (SI). Angelo Gaja of Piedmont produces much-praised Brunello (Rennina, Sugarille), IGT Promis (Sangiovese/Cabernet).

S.M. Tenimenti Pile e Lamole, Greve (FI). Santa Margherita group of Veneto makes arrange of Chianti Classico from the now-linked estate of Vistarenni and Lamole. Also IGT Codirosso (Sangiovese) Lamoro) Cabernet Sauvignon/Sangiovese).

Podere Aia della Macina, Scansano (GR). Emerging Morellino di Scansano estate.

Podere Capaccia, Radda (SI). Fine Chianti Classico; even better IGT Querciagrande (Sangiovese).

Podere Il Palazzino, Gaiole(SI). renowned Chianti Classico (Grosso Sanese La Pieve, Argenina).

Podere Salicutti, Montalcino (SI). Greatly esteemed Brunello, *rosso*, IGT Dopoteatro (Cabernet/Sangiovese/Canaiolo)

La Poderina, Montalcino (SI). Admired Brunello (Poggio Banale), *rosso*, Moscadello.

Poggerino, Radda (SI). Gem of an estate, with splendid Chianti Classico (Riserva Bugialla), IGT Prmamateria (Sagiovese/Merlot).

Poggio al Sole, Tavarnelle Val di Pesa (FI). Highly-respected Chianti Classico (Casasilia), Seraselva (Syrah).

Poggio Antico, Montalcino (SI). Among the most elegant of the normal one is fuller); *rosso*.

Poggio Argentaria, Grosseto. Rich, powerful Morellino di Scansano (Capa Tosta, Bella Marsilia) making waves.

Poggio Bonelli, Castelnuovo Berardenga (SI). Good Chianti Classico; IGT Tramonto dell'Oca (Sangiovese).

Poggio di Sotto, Montalcino (SI). Carefully honed, refined Brunello, *rosso*.

Poggio Gagliardo, Montescudaio (PI). DOC Montescudaio led by Malemacchie Rosso.

Poggio Salvi, Montalcino (SI). Biondi Santi-owned estate makes Brunello and *rosso* with impressive IGT Lavischio (Merlot), and under Jacopo Biondi Santi name, Sassoalloro (Sangiovese), Schidione (Cabernet/Sangiovese/Merlot), Rivolo (Sauvignon).

Poggio Salvi, Sovicille (SI). Promising

Chianti Colli Senesi, IGT Campo del Bosco (Sangiovese), Refola (Sauvignon).

Poggio San Polo, Montalcino (SI). Re-emerging Brunello, *rosso*, IGT Mezzopane (Sangiovese/Cabernet Sauvignon), and others.

Podere Poggio Scalette, Greve (FI). Outstanding IGT Il Carbonaione (Sangiovese).

Il Poggiolino, Sambuca Val di Pesa (FI). Fine Chianti Classico; vdt Le Balze (Sangiovese).

Il Poggiolo, Montalcino (SI). DOCG Several selections of Brunello (Terra Rossa, Beato, Five Stars, Sassello). Also *rosso*, Sant'Antimo.

Il Poggione, Montalcino (SI). A pillar of Montalcino; Brunello and *rosso* of immense stature, even in "off-years". Moscadello in true traditional style.

Poggiopiano, San Casciano Val di Pesa (FI). Superb Chianti Classico, IGT

Poliziano, Montepulciano (SI). Concentrated, powerful Vino Nobile (Vigna Asinone), solid *rosso*; IGT Le Stanze (Cabernet/Merlot). Rosso di Sera (Sangiovese/Colorino).

Pratesi, Carmignano (PO). Emerging estate with concentrated Carmignano, IGT Locorosso (Sangiovese/Merlot)

Pruneto, Radda (SI). Decent Chianti Classico.

La Querce, Impruneta (FI). Revived Chianti Colli Fiorentini.

Querceto di Castellina, Castellina (SI). Up-and-coming producer of Chianti Classico, IGT Podalirio.

Quercia al Poggio, Barberino Val d'Elsa (FI). Sound Chianti Classico, IGT Le Cataste (Sangiovese/Cabernet Sauvignon/Cabernet Franc).

Querciabella, Greve (FI). Endless plaudits go to leading Chianti Classico; plus excellent IGTs Batàr (Chardonnay/Pinot Bianco), Camartina (Sangiovese/Cabernet), and new Palafreno (Merlot/Sangiovese). Also have land in the Maremma.

La Rampa di Fugnano, San Gimignano (SI). Refined Vernaccia (Privato, Alata); Chianti Colli Senesi, IGT Bombereto (Sangiovese), Gisèle

(Merlot), Vi Ogni E' (Viognier!),
vin santo.

Rascioni e Cecconello, Fonteblanda
(GR). Promising IGT, Poggio
Capitana (Sangiovese), Poggio
Ciliegio (Ciliegiolo).

Redi, Montepulciano (SI). Good value,
sound Vino Nobile (Briareo), *rosso*.

La Regola, Ripabella (PI). Improving
Montescudaio Rosso, Bianco.

Riecine, Gaiole (SI). Superb Chianti
Classico; excellent IGT La Gioia
(Sangiovese), Sebastiano (*passito*
from Malvasia/Trebbiano). Briton
John Dunkley passed ownership
to Sean O'Callaghan in the 1990s.

Riseccoli, Greve (FI). Admired
Chianti Classico, IGT Saeculum
(Sangiovese/Cabernet/Merlot),
vin santo.

Roberto Bellini, Montalcino (SI). Ex-
owner of Pieve di Santa Restituta
(sold to Piedmont's Angelo Gaja)
now reaffirming his fine reputation
for Brunello at his new estate. IGTs
from Merlot and Cabernet
Sauvignon, too.

Rocca della Macìe, Castellina (SI).
Much improved Chianti Classico
(Fizzano, Sant'Alfonso); admired IGT
Roccato (Sangiovese/Cabernet), and
Ser Gioveto (Sangiovese) lead large
range, including Morellino di
Scansano.

Rocca di Castagnoli, Gaiole (SI). Large
estate with vineyards at Castagnoli
and La Capraia at Castellina makes
good Chianti Classico (Poggio a'
Frati, Capraia); IGT Buriano
(Cabernet), Stielle (Sangiovese/
Cabernet). Le Pratole (Merlot),
Molino delle Balze (Chardonnay).

Rocca di Montegrossi, Monti (SI).
Much improved Chianti Classico
(San Marcellino), fine *vin santo*; IGT
Geremia (Sangiovese).

Rodano, Castellina (SI). Opulent Chianti
Classico (Viacosta); IGT Monna
Claudia (Sangiovese/Colorino).

Romeo, Montepulciano (SI). Vino Nobile,
Rosso, *vin santo*.

Tenimenti Ruffino, Pontassieve (FI).
Venerable firm with estates in all
Tuscany's major areas makes huge
range including Chianti Classico

(Aziano, Riserva Ducale Oro),
chianti. Romitorio di Santedame
(Colorino/Merlot), Nero al
Tondo (Pinot Nero), Libaio
(Chardonnay/Pinot Grigio).

Russo, Suvereto (LI). Val di Cornia
producer making waves.

La Sala, San Casciano Val di Pesa (FI).
Reliably good Chianti Classico,
IGT Campo all'Albero (Sangiovese/
Cabernet).

Salcheto, Montepulciano (SI). Rapidly
rising Vino Nobile estate.

Salvioni-La Cerbaiola, Montalcino
(SI). Small amounts of often
wonderful Brunello.

San Fabiano Calcinaia, Poggibonsi
(SI). Outstanding Chianti Classico
Riserva Cellole, fine IGT Cerviolo
Rosso (Sangiovese/Cabernet/
Merlot), and Bianco (Chardonnay).

San Felice, Castelnuovo Berardenga
(SI). Model estate with ever-
improving Chianti Classico
(Civettino, Il Grigio, and
outstanding Riserva Poggio
Rosso); IGT Vigorello, (Sangiovese/
Cabernet). Also an estate in
Montalcino (Campogiovanni).

San Giusto, Piombino (LI). Impressive
Val di Cornia Bianco, IGT
Rosso degli Appiani
(Sangiovese/Montepulciano).

San Giusto a Rentennano, Gaiole (SI).
Big, long-lived DOCG Chianti
Classico, fine IGT Percarlo
(Sangiovese), La Ricolma (Merlot),
and divine *vin santo*.

San Leonino, Castellina (SI). Decent
Chianti Classico (Monsenese).

San Luciano, Monte San Savino (AR).
Well-rated Valdichiana estate
concentrating on red blends
based on Sangiovese and
Montepulciano and whites
based on Chardonnay.

San Luigi, Piombino (LI). Val di Cornia
Bianco, IGT Fidenzio (Cabernet
Sauvignon/Cabernet Franc)

Santa Lucia, Grosseto (GR). Improving
Morellino di Scansano, Capalbio
Bianco, *rosso*.

San Vincenti, Gaiole (SI). Very fine
Chianti Classico Riserva, IGT
Stignano (Sangiovese/Merlot).

San Vito in Fior di Selva, Montelupo Fiorentino (FI). Wholesome Chianti Colli Fiorentini.

Sant'Andrea, Panzano (FI). Promising Chianti Classico (Panzanello).

Santa Vittoria, Foiano della Chiana (AR). Impressive range of Valdichiana including *vin santo*.

Santedame, Castellina (SI). Ruffino estate for Chianti Classico and IGTs.

Enrico Santini, Castagneto Carducci (LI). Rapidly emerging Bolgheri producer.

Sapereta, Porto Azzurro (LI). Eminent Elba Rosso, *bianco*, Aleatico, Moscato.

Chigi Saracini, Castelnuovo Berardenga (SI). Chianti Colli Senesi, IGT Poggiassai.

Serraiola, Monterotondo Marittimo (GR). Good Monteregio di Massa Marittima Rosso, *bianco*, Vermentino, IGT Campo Montecristo (Sangiovese/Merlot).

Livio Sassetti-Pertimali, Montalcino (SI). Superb Brunello, *rosso*.

Sassotondo, Sorano (GR). Impressive Bianco di Pitigliano, Sovana, IGT San Lorenzo (Ciliegiolo), Sassotondo (Ciliegiolo/Alicante/Sangiovese).

Michele Satta, Castagneto Carducci (LI). Inspired grower makes admired Bolgheri Rosso (Piastraia), IGT Costa di Giulia (Vermentino), Vigna a Cavaliere (Sangiovese), Giovin Re (Viognier).

Savignola Paolina, Greve (FI). Chianti Classico, IGT Granaio (Sangiovese).

Scurtarola, Massa (MS). Rare Candia dei Colli Apuani.

Sellari-Franceschini, Scansano (GR). Morellino di Scansano (Morello), curious IGT white Biondello dei Gaggioli (Procanico/Malvasia/Ansonica).

Selvapiana, Rufina (FI). Chianti Rufina (Riserva Bucerchiale) of great refinement and lasting style, Pomino Rosso, fine *vin santo*, IGT Fornace (Cabernet/Merlot/Sangiovese).

Solaria – Cencioni, Montalcino (SI). Approachable, well-structured Brunello, IGT Solarianne (Cabernet Sauvignon).

Solatione, Mercatale Val di Pesa (FI). Chianti Classico, *vin santo*.

Sorbaiano, Montecatini Val di Cecina (PI). Stylish Montescudaio Rosso (delle Miniere), *bianco* (Lucestraia), *vin santo*, IGT Pian del Conte (Sangiovese).

La Stellata, Manciano (GR). Bianco di Pitigliano (Lunaia); IGT Lunaia Rosso (Sangiovese/Ciliegiolo/Montepulciano).

Talenti, Montalcino (SI). First-rate Brunello, *rosso*, IGT Talenti Rosso (Sangiovese/Syrah) on small estate.

Tenimenti Luigi D'Alessandro, Cortona (AR). Syrah specialists (Cortona Il Bosco, Vescovo II) from high-density vineyards. Also Cortona Bianco Fontarca (Chardonnay/Viognier), *vin santo*.

Tenuta di, Montalcino (SI). Brunello and *rosso* (Vigna di Capraia).

Tenuta Belvedere, Bolgheri (LI). Antinori estate for Bolgheri Rosso Superiore (Guado al Tasso), *rosato* (Scalabrone), Vermentino.

Tenuta Il Borro, Loro Ciuffenna (AR). Estate owned by Ferragamo family making IGT Il Borro (Merlot/Cabernet Sauvignon/Syrah).

Tenuta di Bossi, Pontassieve (FI). Good Chianti Rufina, *vin santo*, IGT Mazzaferrata (Cabernet/Sangiovese).

Tenuta Carlina – La Togata, Montalcino (SI). Newly eminent Brunello, *rosso*, IGT Azzurreta (Sangiovese).

Tenuta di Ghizzano, Peccioli (PI). Chianti Colline Pisane has been abandoned here in favour of prized IGT Veneroso (Sangiovese/Cabernet) and Nambrot (Merlot/Cabernet).

Tenuta Guado al Tasso, Bolgheri (LI). Antinori-owned estate, producing eminent Bolgheri Rosso Superiore (Guado al Tasso), *rosato* (Scalabrone), Vermentino.

Tenuta di Sesta, Montalcino (SI). Improving Brunello, *rosso*.

Tenuta Farneta, Sinalunga (SI). Chianti Colli Senesi plus IGTs Bongoverno (the best regarded), Bentivoglio (both Sangiovese), Bonagrazia (Chardonnay).

Tenuta La Chiusa, Portoferraio, Elba (LI). Admired Elba, *bianco*, *rosso*, *rosato*, Ansonica, and, especially, Aleatico.

Tenuta Roccaccia, Pitigliano (GR). Bianco di Pitigliano, Sovana Rosso, and IGTs led by intriguing Poggio Cavalluccio (Ciliegiolo).

Tenuta San Guido, Bolgheri (LI). Home of the famous, long-lived Bolgheri Sassicaia.

Tenuta Sette Ponti, Terranuova Bracciolini (AR). New estate gaining attention for IGT Crognolo (Sangiovese), Oreno (Cabernet Sauvignon/Merlot), Grisoglia (Malvasia/Trebbiano *passito*).

Terre del Sillabo, Lucca. Concentration on Colline Lucchesi and IGT whites from Chardonnay, Sauvignon.

Tenute Silvio Nardi, Montalcino (SI). Rapidly improving Brunello (Manachiara), and *rosso*.

Tenuta Trerose, Montepulciano (SI). Fine Vino Nobile (La Villa, Simposio); IGT Busillis (Viognier)

Tenuta Valdipiatta, Montepulciano (SI). Greatly admired Vino Nobile, *rosso*; IGTs Trincerone (Merlot/Canaiolo), Trefonti (Cabernet Sauvignon/ Sangiovese/Canoilo).

Tenuta di Valgiano, Lucca (LU). Easily Colline Lucchesi's leading estate. Beautifully refined, ever-improving wines: Giallo dei Muri (Vermentino/ Trebbiano/Malvasia/Chardonnay), Palistorti (Sangiovese/Merlot/Syrah), Scasso dei Cesari (Sangiovese), Tenuta di Valgiano (Sangiovese/ Syrah/Merlot).

Terrabianca, Radda (SI). Fully oaked Chianti Classico (Vigna della Croce); IGT Campaccio (Sangiovese/ Cabernet), Ceppate (Cabernet Sauvignon/Merlot), Piano del Cipresso (Sangiovese), and more.

Castello del Terriccio, Castellina Marittima (LI). Successful IGTs Lupicaia (Cabernet/Merlot); Tassinaia (Cabernet/Merlot/ Sangiovese), Rondinaia (Chardonnay), and Con Vento (Sauvignon).

Teruzzi & Puthod-Ponte a Rondolino, San Gimignano (SI). High-tech methods make fine Vernaccia, Vigna Rondolino includes Chardonnay, the regular is without, Terre di Tufi is oak-kissed; white IGT Carmen (Sangiovese vinified off its skins), red Peperino (Sangiovese).

Tiezzi, Montalcino (SI). Brunello, Rosso, Sant'Antimo.

Torraccia di Presura, Greve (FI). Chianti Classico (Il Tarocco); IGT Lucciolaio (Sangiovese/Cabernet Sauvignon).

La Torre, Montalcino (SI). Improving Brunello, Rosso.

Torre a Decima, Molino del Piano (FI). Chianti Colli Fiorentini.

Le Trame, San Gusmè (SI). Chianti Classico of substance and tone.

Travignoli, Pelago (FI). DOCG Chianti Rufina; and several IGTs.

Trinoro, Sarteano (SI). Andrea Franchetti with fine red Bordeaux blends at his estate in the Orcia valley: Palazzi (Merlot-led) and Tenuta di Trinoro (Cabernet-led).

Tua Rita, Suvereto (LI). Very good Val di Cornia, remarkable IGT Redigraffi (Merlot), Giusto di Notri (Cabernet/Merlot), Perlato del Bosco Rosso (Sangiovese), and blended whites Lodano, Perlato del Bosco Bianco.

Uccelliera, Montalcino (SI). Stylish Brunello, Rosso, IGT Rapace (Sangiovese/Cabernet/Merlot).

Fratelli Vagnoni, San Gimignano (SI). Vernaccia (I Mocali), Chianti Colli Senesi.

Valdicava, Montalcino (SI). Impressive Brunello (Madonna del Piano), Rosso.

Val di Suga, Montalcino (SI). Impressive Brunello (Vigna del Lago, Spuntali), Rosso.

Valtellina, Gaiole (SI). Admired Chianti Classico; IGT Convivio (Sangiovese/Cabernet).

Varramista, Montopoli Val d'Arno (PI). IGT Frasca (Sangiovese/Merlot/ Syrah) now joins the impeccable Syrah-based Varramista.

Vecchie Terre di Montefili, Greve (FI). Fine Chianti Classico; acclaimed IGT Anfiteatro (Sangiovese), Bruno di Rocca (Sangiovese/Cabernet), and Vigna Regis (Chardonnay/ Sauvignon/Traminer).

Vignamaggio, Greve (FI). The estate where Mona Lisa was born, has renewed class in Chianti Classico (Monna Lisa Riserva); IGT Wine Obsession (Merlot/Cabernet Sauvignon/Syrah), Vignamaggio (Cabernet Franc).

Vignavecchia, Radda (SI). Resurgent estate with Chianti Classico; IGT Canvalle (Sangiovese/Cabernet), Raddese (Sangiovese), Titanum (Chardonnay).

Vignole, Panzano (FI). Good Chianti Classico, IGT Vignole (Merlot/Cabernet Sauvignon).

Villa Arceno, San Gusmè (SI). Kendall Jackson of California makes Chianti Classico but does better with varieties Cabernet Sauvignon, Syrah, Merlot at this vast estate.

Villa Cafaggio, Panzano (FI). Inspiring Chianti Classico (Riserva Solatio Basilica); splendid IGT Cortaccio (Cabernet), San Martino (Sangiovese).

Villa Cilnia, Pieve al Bagnoro (AR). Sound Chianti Colli Aretini; Vocato (Sangiovese/Cabernet), Cign'Oro (Sangiovese/Cabernet/Merlot).

Villa La Selva, Montebenichi (AR). Good chianti; *vin santo*, IGT Selva Maggio (Cabernet Sauvignon), Felciaia (Sangiovese) head long list.

Villa Le Prata, Montalcino (SI). Tiny estate; fine Brunello, *rosso*, IGT Le Prata (Merlot/Cabernet).

Villa Pillo, Gambassi Terme (FI). American John Dyson has planted mainly French varieties here on the fringes of Chianti and makes impressive IGT Merlot, Cabernet, and, especially, Syrah.

Villa Sant'Anna, Abbadia di Montepulciano (SI). Reliably fine Vino Nobile Rosso, Chianti Colli Senesi; IGT Vigna Il Vallone (Sangiovese/Cabernet), *vin santo*.

Viticcio, Greve (FI). Exemplary Chianti Classico (Beatrice); IGT Monile (Cabernet), Prunaio (Sangiovese).

Wandanna, Montecarlo (LU). Admirable Montecarlo Bianco and Rosso (Terre dei Cascinieri), IGT Virente (Cabernet Sauvignon/Cabernet Franc/Merlot/ Syrah), and more.

Wine & Food

Tuscan food is a triumph of nature; simplified country cooking, it lacks imagination, but expresses an almost mystical symbiosis between a people and their land. The elaborations exported to France by the Medici are long gone and mostly forgotten. Also vanishing, sadly, are the inspired dishes that used to take cheerful Tuscan mammas all morning to create. But the basics are still there: country bread baked in wood-fired ovens and the emerald-green *extra-vergine* olive oil that combines so well in *bruschetta* and *pane unto*; exquisite vegetables and greens that make a minestrone easy (Tuscans have always been more resourceful with soups than pasta); the rosemary, garlic, onion, sage, basil, bay leaves, and tarragon that heighten flavour; and, of course, the bean, so adored that when

detractors couldn't think of anything worse they called Tuscans *mangiafagioli* (bean eaters). Meat, simply grilled or roasted, is essential in the diet: chicken, pork, duck, and Florence's legendary *bistecca alla fiorentina* (hefty slab of Chianina beef). Boar and game birds are also prized in this most wooded Italian region. Some of Italy's tastiest Pecorino cheese comes from sheep grazed in the stark hills of Siena.

Wines to accompany each dish are suggested below in italic.

Arista Pork loin roasted with rosemary and garlic. *Vino Nobile di Montepulciano*

Bistecca alla fiorentina Thick steak charred on the outside, pink inside, served with white beans. *Chianti Classico*

Cacciucco alla livornese Piquant fish soup with garlic toast. *Val di Cornia Rosso*

Crostini di fegatini Breadcrusts with chicken-liver paté. *Chianti Colli Fiorentini*

Gramugia Ancient soup from Lucca, with onions, artichokes, fava beans, asparagus, and bacon. *Montecarlo Bianco*

Panzanella Stale bread soaked with water and crumbled with chopped tomatoes, onions, basil, oil, and vinegar in a sort of salad. *Vernaccia di San Gimignano*

Pappardelle alla lepre Wide ribbon noodles with rich hare sauce. *Chianti Rufina*

Ribollita Hearty soup with beans, black cabbage, and other vegetables, thickened with bread. *Chianti Colli Senesi*

Tordi allo spiedo Spit-roasted wood thrush. *Brunello di Montalcino*

Restaurants

Recommended in or near wine zones:

Bolgheri-Val di Cornia-Elba *Chiasso* at Capoliveri (Elba); *Da Ugo* at Castagneto Carducci; *Scacciapensieri* at Cecina; *Capo Nord* at Marciana Marina (Elba); *La Pineta* at Marina di Bibbona; *Gambero Rosso* at San Vincenzo.

Chianti Classico *L'Albergaccio di Castellina* at Castellina; *Da Antonio* at Castelnuovo Berardenga, *La Tenda Rossa* at Cerbaia; *Badia a Coltibuono* and *Osteria del Brolio* at Gaiole; *Vecchia Osteria* at Ponte a Bozzone.

Colli Aretini-Cortona-Val di Chiana *Vicolo del Contento* at Castelfranco di Sopra; *Il Falconiere* at Cortona; *Osteria di Rendola* at Mercatale Valdarno; *Il Canto del Maggio* at Terranuova Bracciolini.

Colli Fiorentini-Carmignano-Empoli *Da Delfina* at Artimino; *Cantina di Toia* at Bacchereto; *I Cavallacci* at Impruneta; *Sanesi* at Lastra a Signa; *Il Focolare*

at Montespertoli.

Colli Senesi-Montalcino-Montepulciano-San Gimignano *La Solita Zuppa* at Chiusi; *Antica Trattoria* and *Arnolfo* at Colle di Val d'Elsa; *Taverna dei Barbi* at Montalcino; *La Chiusa* at Montefollonico; *La Grotta* at Montepulciano; *Il Pozzo* at Monteriggioni; *Antica Trattoria Botteganuova* and *Osteria Le Logge* at Siena; *Locanda dell'Amorosa* at Sinalunga.

Colline Pisani *Mocajo* at Guardistallo; *Quattro Gigli* at Montopoli Val d'Arno.

Lucca-Montecarlo-Massa-Carrara *Enoteca Nebraska* at Camaiore; *Venanzio* at Colonnata; *Lorenzo* at Forte dei Marmi; *Nanni Barbero* a Moriano; *Romano* at Viareggio.

Maremma-Scansano *Bracali* at Massa Marittima; *Caino* at Montemerano; *Vecchio Castello* at Roccalbegna.

Umbria *Umbria*

The breadth of Umbrian wine styles is not as widely appreciated as it might be. Indeed, it is more usually considered a one-wine region: at one time, the only wine that stood out was Orvieto, from the hill town where the Etruscans mastered oenological techniques two millennia before its golden sweet wines inspired Renaissance artists. Then, the sole name attracting interest was the Lungarotti family's Torgiano. Time moved on and Torgiano was deemed *passé* and replaced by Montefalco as the single area worthy of consideration. Now attention has turned full scale to Colli del Trasimeno. Yet Umbria embraces all these and more. After a lapse, Orvieto has bounced back as one of Italy's most exported whites. Torgiano Rosso Riserva has claimed DOCG status, as has Montefalco Sagrantino, one of Italy's most potent and persuasive reds. And Colli del Trasimeno, although the current centre of attention, is surrounded by several other areas where assiduous winemakers are turning out a treasure trove of wines.

There are still oddities and examples of hit-and-miss peasant winemaking. But these are now outweighed by proficient, consistent styles that range from simple to inspired. Most of its eleven DOCs are towards the west of this land-locked hilly region, often straddling its river valleys (Colli Altotiberini, Orvieto, Rosso Orvietano, Colli Amerini) or its lakes (Colli del Trasimeno, Lago di Corbara) There are a further six IGTs but the region-wide Umbria is the most commonly used. A fair array of vines grow in the reigon. Central Italy's standard Sangiovese, Canaiolo, Trebbiano, and Malvasia naturally take centre stage but there is also the ancient and highly esteemed Grechetto and a full complement of international varieties, with emphasis on Chardonnay, Cabernet, and Merlot.

Discovering Umbria's wines can be as rewarding as exploring its ancient hill-top towns. Midway between Rome and Florence, the region mixes art and history with the bucolic attractions of a countryside noted as "the green heart

Wine Areas

1	Colli Altotiberini	5	Montefalco
2	Colli del Trasimeno	6	Colli Martani
3	Colli Perugini	7	Orvieto
4	Torgiano	8	Colli Amerini

of Italy". Oenophiles should not miss the Museo del Vino at Torgiano, a model of the genre, or the Enoteca Provinciale at Perugia. Well-stocked shops include the Enoteca Vino Vino at Terni and La Loggia and Vino Vino at Orvieto.

Recent Vintages

Umbria has a favourable climate for both reds and whites. 2001, 2000, 1999, 1997, and 1995 were superb, 1998, 1996, 1994, and 1993 good to very good, 2002, 1992, and 1991 fair; 1990 and 1988 outstanding, and 1985 first-rate, especially for reds. Earlier vintages of note are mentioned with entries of wines for ageing.

Wines

ASSISI *DOC*

Generally light wines grown in vineyards around the town and for the most part appreciated by visitors.

Bianco *w dr* ☆→☆☆ *DYA* Based on Trebbiano with Grechetto, this is light and easy.

Rosato *p dr* ☆→☆☆ *DYA* Sangiovese with Merlot yield an attractive rosé.

Rosso *r dr* ☆→☆☆ *99 00 01* Mainly Sangiovese with Merlot make a round, refreshing red. A *novello* is also permitted.

Grechetto *w dr* ☆→☆☆ *DYA* The native variety makes white of a certain tone.

COLLI ALTOTIBERINI *DOC*

Scenic zone stretching high along the upper reaches of the Tiber, from Perugia north past Città di Castello, but wines seen infrequently outside of the area.

Bianco *w dr* ☆ *DYA* Based mainly on Trebbiano with Malvasia, this is light, refreshing, and innocuous.

Rosato *p dr* ☆→☆☆ *DYA* Sangiovese with Merlot gives what can be an attractively bright, fragrant, fruity rosé.

Rosso *r dr* ☆→☆☆ *97 98 99 00 01* The same varieties make a fairly robust red that can hint at rusticity.

COLLI AMERINI *DOC*

Large zone mainly east of the Tiber around Amelia and Narni, extending along the Nera River to above Terni. The wines have gained esteem for sound quality at reasonable prices.

Bianco *w dr* ☆→☆☆ *DYA* Based on Trebbiano with Grechetto, Garganega, Verdello, and/or Malvasia, making a refreshing white of character.

Malvasia *w dr* ☆→☆☆ *DYA* Malvasia Toscana can be round and smooth.

Merlot *r dr* ☆→☆☆ *99 00 01* Firm, ripe wines can age a few years. Age: *riserva* 2 yrs.

Rosato *p dr* ☆→☆☆ *DYA* Sangiovese, with options among Canaiolo, Montepulciano, Ciliegiolo, Barbera, and Merlot, makes a pleasant rosé.

Rosso *r dr* ☆→☆☆ *98 99 00 01 02* The same varieties as *rosato* make a robust red of varying style that can become smooth with a few years of age. A *novello* is also permitted.

COLLI DEL TRASIMENO *DOC*

Large zone surrounding Lake Trasimeno makes wide range of wines that range from simply tasty to inspiring, although there has not been much take-up of the varietal options so far. Age: reds *riserva* 2 yrs.

Bianco *w dr (fr)* ☆→☆☆ *DYA* Grechetto, Chardonnay, Pinot Bianco, and/or Pinot Grigio above a Trebbiano base gives ample scope for wines of interest.

Bianco Scelto *w dr* ☆→☆☆ *DYA* In this "selected" white the Trebbiano is eliminated and any or all of 7 white varieties (including Grechetto, Vermentino, Chardonnay, Sauvignon) can be employed to yield wines of more or less personality and typicity.

Rosso *r dr (fr)* ☆→☆☆ *99 00 01*
  Ciliegiolo, Gamay, Merlot,
  and/or Cabernet add interest
  to a Sangiovese base in this up-
  and-coming type. May be *novello*.

Rosso Scelto *r dr* ☆→☆☆ *99 00 01*
  Gamay, Merlot, Cabernet Sauvignon,
  and/or Pinot Nero take leading place
  over a little Sangiovese in this
  "selected" red which is, as yet,
  not often seen.

Rosato *p dr* →☆☆ *DYA*
  Promising rosé from the same
  grapes as the *rosso*.

Cabernet Sauvignon *r dr*

Gamay *r dr*

Grechetto *w dr*

Merlot *r dr*

Spumante Classico *w dr sp DYA*
  Mc sparkler from Grechetto,
  Chardonnay, and/or the Pinots

Vin Santo *am d s/sw sw*
  From Trebbiano with Grechetto,
  Chardonnay, Pinot Bianco, and/or
  Pinot Grigio. Age: 18 mths

COLLI MARTANI *DOC*
  Large zone embracing Umbria's
  central hills between Todi and
  Foligno, and overlapping the
  Montefalco zone to the east,
  covering 3 local varietals.

Grechetto *w dr (s/sw)* ☆→☆☆☆ *99 00
  01 02* The star of the trio, this can
  make whites of distinctive character
  for drinking young, though some
  have the substance for ageing
  beyond 2 to 3 years. Grechetto
  di Todi comes from a sub-zone
  comprising the historical area
  around the town and may be
  abbocato as wel as dry.

Sangiovese *r dr* ☆→☆☆ *98 99 00 01*
  Some tasty reds from the grape
  have been made in the area, but
  bottles are not often seen. Age:
  1 yr, *riserva* 2 yrs.

Trebbiano *r dr* ☆ *DYA* Light and zesty.

COLLI PERUGINI *DOC*
  Promising wines from hills
  following the west bank of the
  Tiber from Perugia southwards
  almost to Todi. As well as the
  varietals within the DOC the

area is also home to some
intriguing local varieties.

Bianco *w dr* ☆→☆☆ *DYA*
  From at least 50% Trebbiano with
  a loose rein on the rest, this varies
  from anonymous to zestily fruity.

Rosso *r dr* ☆→☆☆ *97 98 99 00 01*
  With Sangiovese running from 50%
  to 100% and few limits on the other
  varieties used, this red can be stylish
  and elegant, full and chunky, – or
  disappointing. May be *novello*.

Rosato *p dr* ☆ *DYA*
  From the same range of grapes
  as the *rosso*. Rarely seen.

Spumante *w dr sp DYA*
  Tank or bottle-fermented sparkler
  from Grechetto, Chardonnay,
  and/or the Pinots.

Vin Santo *am dr s/sw sw*
  From Trebbiano and others.

Cabernet Sauvignon *r dr*

Chardonnay *w dr*

Grechetto *w dr*

Merlot *r dr*

Pinot Grigio *w dr*

Sanglovese *r dr*

Trebbiano *w dr*

GRECHETTO
  Ancient variety that expresses
  plentiful character when used as
  a pure varietal in central Umbria.
  It also figures in blends, most
  notably Orvieto, and is often used
  for *vin santo*.

LAGO DI CORBARA
  DOC r dr ☆☆→☆☆☆ *98 99 00 01*
  Small area above the lake of
  Corbara for deep, punchy, fruit-
  forward reds, mostly from
  Sangiovese, Cabernet Sauvignon,
  Merlot, and Pinot Nero. There are
  varietal versions from the latter
  three but the main wine comes
  from any or all of the 4, with a
  further 9 varieties that may
  be used in small part.

MONTEFALCO *DOC*
  This zone in the hills west of Foligno
  is named for the town of Montefalco
  at the centre of a vineyard area that
  takes in Bevagna and Gualdo

Cattaneo. The wine has considerable renown, thanks mainly to the noted versions made from Sagrantino, which have a separate DOCG. The DOC covers white and red blends that range from the everyday to wines of real class (and often good value).

Bianco *w dr* ☆☆→☆☆☆☆ *00 01 02* Based on Grechetto with Trebbiano and others, this can be pale, light, and easy or, in rare aged versions, fairly deep and complex in flavour, with colour tending toward golden.

Rosso *r dr* ☆→☆☆☆☆ *98 99 00 01 02* Based on Sangiovese with a good dash of powerfully flavoured Sagrantino gives often well-rounded, full-bodied, and, in certain cases, memorable red wines. Age: *riserva* 30 mths.

MONTEFALCO SAGRANTINO
DOCG

When this mysterious red was promoted to DOCG in 1992, it was a cult wine. It is still a cult wine, but the cult has grown and today, with production approaching 500,000 bottles a year, Sagrantino is coveted by connoisseurs and visitors to the uplands of central Umbria. The Sagrantino vine is grown only around Montefalco, though it's uncertain whether it's indigenous or if it arrived centuries ago with Franciscan monks or Saracen invaders. The name comes from *sagra* (Italian for festival or feast), because the wine was by tradition rich and sweet and reserved for celebrations. But the emphasis is now on dry versions, whose deep colour, voluptuous body, and sometimes staggering strength recall Verona's Amarone. Indeed from certain vintages the wine may be rated among the most distinguished reds of Italy. But techniques are evolving and Sagrantino's admirers may have some surprises in store.

Sagrantino di Montefalco *r dr*
☆☆→☆☆☆☆ *88 90 93 94 95 96 97 98 99 00 01* The dry version of this wine has gained a major share of critical acclaim, although styles vary as producers have different ideas on wood ageing (large casks or small barriques) and how best to tame the wines' rather harsh natural tannins. When at its best, it has a deep ruby-garnet colour, a lavish bouquet of spices, and berries and sumptuous flavours of ripe plums and blackberries with a hint of liquorice on the tongue. Age 30 mths.

Sagrantino di Montefalco Passito
r s/sw sw ☆☆→☆☆☆☆ *88 90 93 94 95 96 97 98 99 00 01* Sagrantino made from semi-dried or *passito* grapes into a red of soaring richness (min 14.5% alcohol) with a light tannic bite, which becomes smoother and more complex with age. Age: 30 mths.

ORVIETO

DOC w dr (s/sw) (sw) ☆☆→☆☆☆☆ *99 00 01 02*

Umbria's renowned white comes from Trebbiano, Verdello, Grechetto, and other white grapes grown in a large zone around the striking hill town of Orvieto and, extending north along the Paglia and south along the Tiber where it spills over into Lazio. Historically golden and softly sweet, most Orvieto is now pale, dry, and polished. Some is rather uninspiring but far more is crisp and good drinking, while some shows enviable fruit and harmony. The best wines, while good young, gain style with 2 to 3 years of age. Sweet Orvieto has made a comeback and the three types: *abboccato*, *amabile*, or *dolce* give increasing sweetness levels. In some years noble rot attacks the grapes (one of the few areas of Italy where it does) leading to a highly impressive *Botrytis cinerea*, with rich bouquet, mouth-filling flavours enhanced by some wood ageing, and velvety texture. However, whether dry or sweet, from the 20 million bottles produced a year, most good Orvieto comes from the *classico* heartland around the town itself.

PROCANICO

The chief grape of Orvieto is also called Trebbiano and therefore often confused with the similar but distinct, and inferior, Trebbiano Toscano.

ROSSO ORVIETANO OR ORVIETANO ROSSO

DOC r dr ☆→☆☆☆ *99 00 01*
Covering the same area as Orvieto (excluding the outcrop in Lazio), this DOC gives full compass to Orvieto producers wishing to express their skills in red wine production too. Any or all of Aleatico, Cabernet Franc, Cabernet Sauvignon, Canaiolo, Ciliegiolo, Merlot, Montepulciano, Pinot Nero, and Sangiovese may be used and, if used singly, the variety may appear on the label. As the proclivity of the area for red wines becomes ever more evident, use of this denomination is likely to increase significantly.

TORGIANO *DOC*

This small zone, streching southeast across the Tiber River from Perugia, is noted red and white wines of style. Production is dominated by Lungarotti, whose name and trademarks are better known around the world than the denomination they spawned.

Bianco *w dr* ☆☆→☆☆☆ *00 01 02* From Trebbiano and Grechetto, this pale, flowery white has attractive fruit-acid balance when young, may be aged in barrels, developing finesse over 3 to 4 years as is Lungarotti's Torre di Giano Il Pino.

Rosato *p dr* ☆☆ *DYA* From same grapes as the *rosso*, this can be refreshing.

Rosso *r dr* ☆☆→☆☆☆ *97 98 99 00 01* From Sangiovese with Canaiolo and, optionally, others, this is ruby red, round, and softly persuasive in 2 to 5 years.

Age: 1 yr. The *riserva* version is DOCG (*see* below).

Cabernet Sauvignon *r dr* ☆☆→☆☆☆ *95 96 97 98 99 00 01* The variety was pioneered in Umbria by Lungarotti and can show style. Age: 1 yr.

Chardonnay *w dr* ☆☆ *97 98 99 00 01* Can be fresh and fruity or, with oak ageing, richer.

Pinot Grigio *w dr* ☆☆ *DYA* Round and fruity, usually best young.

Pinot Nero *r dr* ☆☆ *98 99 00 01* Pleasant but rarely shows class. Age: 1 yr.

Riesling Italico *w dr* ☆ *DYA* Light and zesty.

Spumante *w dr sp* ☆☆ *DYA* Attractive sparkling wine from Chardonnay and Pinot Nero.

TORGIANO ROSSO RISERVA

DOCG r dr ☆☆→☆☆☆ *95 96 97 98 99 00 01*
This *reserva*, from Sangiovese with Canaiolo and, optionally, Montepulciano, Ciliegiolo, and Trebbiano Toscano, was once considered one of central Italy's most distinguished and slow-maturing reds, inspiring comparisons with leading wines from the Haut-Médoc and stimulating Lungarotti, its leading producer, to put it forward for DOCG. But overall quality standards, and consumer expectations, have rocketed in the last 10 to 15 years and new high-level wines have emerged. In addition, Lungarotti went through a period of stasis from which it has only recently emerged. As a result the wine now rarely excites as it once did. Age: 3 yrs.

VIN SANTO

Made nearly everywhere in Umbria, from Grechetto, Malvasia, Trebbiano, and other grapes semi-dried (in the past often hanging from rafters near a fireplace to pick up a smoky aroma) and aged in small, sealed barrels. Golden to amber, aromatic, and fairly strong, at best it is velvety and softly sweet.

Producers

Provinces: Perugia (PG), Terni (TR).
NB: Sangrantino implies Montefalco
Sagrantino.

Antonelli, Montefalco (PG).
Sagrantino of impeccable style;
very good Montefalco Rosso;
Colli Martani Grechetto.

Arquata-Fratelli Adanti, Bevagna (PG).
Despite ups and downs Adanti is
now back with mighty but mellow
Sagrantino, both dry and sweet, and
Montefalco Rosso and Bianco, Colli
Martani Grechetto and IGT Rosso
d'Arquata (Cabernet Sauvignon/
Barbera/Merlot).

Barberani-Vallesanta, Baschi
(TR). Admired Orvieto Classico
(Castagnolo), *amabile* (Pulicchio);
dolce Calcaia "Muffa Nobile");
Lago di Corbara Foresco and
Villa Monteicell (bothSangiovese/
Cabernet Sauvignon/Merlot),
IGT Grechetto and Moscao Passito
(both Villa Monticelli).

Eredi Benincasa, Bevagna (PG). Up-
and-coming estate for Montefalco
Rosso, Colli Martani Grechetto, and
especially IGT Vigna La Fornace
(Barbera/Merlot/Sagrantino).

Bigi, Orvieto (TR). Winery in Gruppo
Italiano Vini selects for notable
Orvieto Classico (Torricella) and
amabile (Orzalume); IGT Marrano
(Chardonnay/Grechetto), Umbria
Grechetto, Umbria Sangiovese.
Also wines from Lazio.

Candeto, Orvieto (TR). Large and
reliable co-op with Orvieto Classico
selections and excellent IGT
Umbria Arciato (Merlot/Cabernet
Sauvignon/Sangiovese), Nero della
Greca (Sangiovese/Merlot), Pinot
Nero, and more.

Arnaldo Caprai-Val di Maggio,
Montefalco (PG). Prestigious
Sagrantino (25 Anni, Colle Piano);
Montefalco Rosso and Colli
Martani Grechetto (Grecante
Villa Belvedere) of high quality
and international style.

La Carraia, Orvieto (TR). Supremely fine
Orvieto Classico (Poggio Calvelli);

IGT red Fobiano (Merlot/Cabernet),
Tizzonero (Cabernet/Merlot).

Cantina Colli Amerini, Fornole di
Amelia (TR). Model co-op provides
outstanding value in Colli Amerini
Rosso (Carbio, Terre Arnolfe), Bianco
Malvasia (La Corte) and Chardonnay.
Also Orvieto Classico; IGT Umbria,
Grechetto, Sangiovese, Aleatico.

Cantina Monrubio, Castel Viscardo
(TR). Proficient co-op with
Orvieto Classico selections, IGT
Palaia (Merlot/Pinot/Cabernet),
Nociano (Cabernet), good-value
Monrubio (Sangiovese/Ciliegiolo/
Montepulciano/Merlot), and others.

Le Crete, Giove (TR). Colli Amerini
Pietranera (Sangiovese/Merlot/
Barbera) and Malvasia (Cima del
Giglio), both rapidly gaining renown.

Casole, Otricoli (TR). Opulent IGT
Casole Rosso (Sangiovese/Cabernet)
and tasty Bianco (Malvasia/
Chardonnay/Sauvignon).

Castello di Antignano – Brogal Vini,
Perugia. Two estates, one in
Torgiano, one in Montefalco;
both ranges sound.

Castello delle Regine, Amelia (TR).
New estate exploding onto the
scene with 4 exciting reds, 2 from
Sangiovese (including oak-aged
Podernovo), a Merlot and Princeps
(Cabernet Sauvignon/Merlot/
Sangiovese), plus white Bianco
delle Regine (Sauvignon/Riesling
Renano/Pinot Grigio/Chardonnay).

Castello della Sala, Ficulle (TR).
Antinori's Umbrian estate makes
estimable Orvieto Classico DOC
(Campogrande) and an array of
IGT Umbria, led by the supremely
refined Cervaro della Sala, an
oak-fermented Chardonnay with
Grechetto and one of Italy's most
distinguished whites. The others,
all impressive, are sweet Muffato
della Sala (Sauvignon/Grechetto/
Gewürztraminer/Riesling with
"noble rot"), Conte della Vipera
(Sauvignon), and Pinot Nero
(Vigneto Consola). Chardonnay
and Sauvignon della Sala

are admirable and well-priced varietals.

Colpetrone, Gualdo Cattaneo (PG). Excellent Sagrantino of depth and finesse, much in demand. Very good *passito*, Montefalco Rosso.

Conti Fiumi-Petrangeli, Orvieto (TR). Organic Orvieto Classico.

Decugnano dei Barbi, Orvieto (TR). Fine Orvieto Classico ("IL" and sweet Pourriture Noble); acclaimed red IGT Umbria "IL", and new Pinot Nero; Lago di Corbara (Sangiovese/Montepulciano/Canaiolo), brut mc (Chardonnay/Verdello/Procanico) – all of convincing quality and allure).

Duca della Corgna, Castiglione del Lago (PG). Stylish Colli del Trasimeno Rosso (Corniolo, Baccio del Rosso), Bianco (Baccio del Bianco), Gamay, Grechetto.

Fanini, Castiglione del Lago (PG). Colli del Trasimeno Rosso (Morello del Lago and Bianco (Albello del Lago); and IGT varietals Merlot, Sangiovese (Vigna la Pieve), and Chardonnay (Robbiano) all of growing stature.

Fattoria Le Poggette, Montecastrilli (TR). Emerging estate with Colli Amerini Rosso and IGT varietals from Montepulciano, Canaiolo, and, especially, Grechetto. Of impressive dimensions.

Lamborghini La Fiorita, Panicale (PG). Estate founded by car magnate Ferruccio Lamborghini and revived by his daughter Patrizia makes starry IGT Campoleone (Merlot/Sangiovese) and admirable Trescone (Sangiovese/Ciliegiolo/Merlot).

Goretti, Perugia. Confident range of Colli Perugini: highly admired Rosso (L'Arrignatore), Bianco (Torre del Pino), Chardonnay, Grechetto. Also well-made IGT Umbria red, white, and rosé; new Sagrantino and Montefalco Rosso (both Le Mure Saracene).

Lungarotti, Torgiano (PG). After a disappointing period the well-known Lungarotti sisters are back on form with an extensive range of Torgiano, white, red, rosé, and sparkling, passing from light'n'easy through to weighty and complex,

and a supporting range of IGTs, *vin santo*, too. The trademark Rubesco applies to Torgiano Rosso and Rosso Riserva.

La Palazzola, Stroncone (TR). IGT Merlot and Rubino (Cabernet Sauvignon/Merlot, head a finely tuned array spanning Riesling, Moscato, Pinot Nero; dry, sweet, sparkling.

Palazzone, Orvieto (TR). Classy Orvieto Classico (Campo del Guardiano, Terre Vineate); and Muffa Nobile (Sauvignon), L'Ultima Spiaggia (Viognier). High standard in rest of range, too.

Pieve del Vescovo, Corciano (PG). Admired Colli del Trasimeno.

Poggio Bertaio, Castiglione del Lago (PG). Small estate with admired IGT Cimbolo (Sangiovese), Crovello (Merlot/Cabernet).

Rio Grande, Penna in Teverina (TR). Emerging IGT Casa Pastore (Cabernet Sauvignon/Merlot), Colle delle Montecchie (Chardonnay), Poggio Muralto (Merlot/Sangiovese/Cabernet Sauvignon).

Rocca di Fabbri, Montefalco (PG). Admired Montefalco Rosso, Sagrantino, and *passito*; classy IGT Faroaldo (Sagrantino/Cabernet Sauvignon), Pinot Nero, Grechetto; Colli Martani Sangiovese.

Scacciadiavoli, Montefalco (PG). Classy Sagrantino, *passito*, Montefalco Rosso.

Fratelli Sportoletti, Spello (PG). Admirable estate with leading Assisi, Rosso, Bianco, and Grechetto; IGT Fedelia Rosso (Merlot/Cabernet Sauvignon/Cabernet Franc), and *bianco* (Grechetto/Chardonnay).

Tenuta Alzatura, Montefalco (PG). New estate owned by Tuscany's Cecchi family with impressive Sagrantino (Uno di Uno).

Tenuta di Salviano, Civitella del Lago (TR). Emerging estate for Orvieto Classico and Lago di Corbara Rosso.

Tenuta Le Velette, Orvieto (TR). Much-admired Orvieto Classico. Rosso Orvietano and IGT Calaco (Sangiovese/Cabernet Sauvignon), Gaudio (Merlot).

Terre del Carpine, Magione (PG). Admired co-op for Colli del Trasimeno Rosso.
Terre de' Trinci, Foligno (PG). Emerging Sagrantino, Montefalco Rosso, IGT Cajo (Sagrantino/Merlot/Cabernet).
Vaglie, Baschi (TR). Emerging estate for Orvieto Classico (Matricale); IGT Momenti (Sangiovese/Merlot), Masseo (Sangiovese/Merlot/ Cabernet Sauvignon), Rosso Vaglie (Montepulciano/Sangiovese/ Canaiolo/Ciliegiolo).
VICOR, Castel Viscardo (TR). Respected co-op makes Orvieto Classico DOC (Roio, Salceto, Le Terrazze).

Wine & Food

Umbrians may relate as humbly as Franciscans how they eat only what their good earth provides. Granted, menus are spare, repetitive and orthodox – in other words, highly selective. Here seasonal produce is prepared in streamlined ways by country people without much time to spend in the kitchen – something like nouvelle cuisine, except that it has scarcely changed since the Middle Ages. Oil is so good that it's called Umbria's "liquid gold", though it's never used so sparingly. There are thick soups and exquisite pastas, including the always reliable homemade tagliatelle strewn across oval platters and mixed with ragout which often contains chicken livers. Meat and game are *di rigore* in this landlocked region: prized Perugina beef, farm poultry, wood pigeon, and lamb. Pork is so artfully prepared in the town of Norcia that pork-butcher shops throughout Italy are known as *norcinerie*. Among things that grow, a special place is reserved for cardoons, the artichoke-like thistles known here as *gobbi*. But the most delicious irony of this region's "modest" cuisine is the truffle – whether black or white, it is so prolific that Umbria has become the nation's (if not the world's) leading supplier.

Wines to accompany each dish are suggested below in italic.
Anguille alle brace Grilled eels from the Tiber or Lake Trasimeno. *Colli del Trasimeno Rosso*
Cicerchiata Carnival cake with honey, almonds, and candied fruit. *Montefalco Sagrantino Passito*
Gobbi alla perugina Fried cardoons with meat ragout. *Torgiano Rosso*
Mazzafegati Piquant pork-liver sausages, served around Christmas. *Montefalco Rosso*
Minestra di farro Soup of a grain called *farro* cooked with tomatoes, onions, in broth of a *prosciutto* bone. *Colli Altotiberini Rosato*
Palombacci alla ghiotta Spit-roasted wood pigeons with *ghiotta*, an intricate sauce of wine, vinegar, ham, livers, and herbs. *Montefalco Sagrantino*
Porchetta alla perugina Whole young pig roasted in a wood oven with wild fennel, rosemary, and garlic. *Torgiano Cabernet Sauvignon*
Spaghetti alla norcina Sauce of sausages with onions in cream may be topped with grated cheese or white truffles. *Orvieto Classico*
Stringozzi Short noodles dressed with garlic, oil, and sometimes tomatoes. *Torgiano Bianco*
Torcolo Sponge cake to be dipped in *vin santo*. *Vin santo*

Restaurants

Recommended in or near wine zones:
Colli Alto Tiberini-Colli Perugini-Colli del Trasimeno

Torgiano *Postale di Marco e Barbara* at Città di Castello; *Da Sauro* at Isola Maggiore; *Aladino* at Perugia; *Le Tre Vaselle* at Torgiano.

Montefalco-Spello-Assisi *Buca di San Francesco* and *Il Frantoio* at Assisi; *Da Nina* at Bevagna; *Villa Roncalli* at Foligno; *Villa Pambuffetti* at Montefalco; *La Cantina* at Spello; *La Taverna del Pescatore* at Trevi.

Orvieto *Vissani* at Civitella del Lago; *Antica Trattoria dell'Orso* and *I Sette Consoli* at Orvieto; *Locanda Casole* at Otricoli; *Taverna di Porta Nova* at Stroncone; *Oste della Mal'Ora* at Terni.

Lazio *Lazio*

Lazio's wines are, for the main part, Rome's wines, the once fragile whites of golden hue that made their precarious journey down from the Castelli Romani to cheer its populace, and the now far more stable wines that whizz down from that same green-clad ring of spent volcanoes to keep its tourists well refreshed. The Castelli harbour seven of Lazio's twenty-six DOC zones and lie within view of eight others but their star player is Frascati, one of Italy's most famous (or possibly infamous) whites and one of its most quaffed. Est! Est!! Est!!! di Montefiascone is Lazio's other resounding name but this white comes from vineyards surrounding the crater lake of Bolsena, in the north of the region, well distant from Rome. Another well-known name, Orvieto, although primarily situated in Umbria, extends into Lazio, too. Yet, despite the renowned names, most wines from this prolific region had been stuck with a somewhat everyday image, mostly because all the traditional whites – and ninety per cent of DOC output is white – come from the often unexciting Malvasia or Trebbiano or, most often, combinations of the two.

In the old days, the lush green vineyards of the Castelli Romani produced soft, fleshy, wines whose full flavours flowed winningly with the pungently spicy fare of *la cucina romana*. But those wines were so unstable that they often failed to survive the short trip into Rome. Modern winemaking has rendered pale, balanced, pure whites that can be shipped with confidence anywhere. But their proliferation on world markets – most notably Germany, Britain, and the USA – is based on competitive pricing and the ever-increasing number of producers who use studied methods to bring out the unmistakable personality that the grapes, select clones of Malvasia in particular, can express when yields are controlled, have found it difficult to gain a foothold. The world's wine judges have been slow in recognizing the excitement Lazio's whites can offer.

Perversely many of Lazio's most esteemed wines are red. As usual, there are several IGTs to embrace those that are not covered by DOC but the region-wide Lazio is easily the most commonly used.

The prime wine trip from Rome is a circuit of the Castelli Romani, taking in Frascati, Marino, Colli Albani, Colli Lanuvini, Montecompatri Colonna, and Velletri. An extended trip includes Zagarolo and the three DOC zones producing wine from the red Cesanese. Among shops with good choices of regional and national wines are the *Enoteca-Wine Bar Trimani, Bottigliera Tram Tram, Cavour, Piero Costantini, Al Parlamento, Arte del Bere, Fratelli Roffi Isabelli,* and *Semidivino,* all in Rome; and the *Enoteca Frascati* at Frascati.

Recent Vintages

For red wines and the few whites that may be kept more than a couple of years, recommended vintages appear with each entry.

Wines

ALEATICO DI GRADOLI

DOC r sw ☆☆ *98 99 00 01 02*
Little of this fragrant dessert
wine from the hills west of
Lake Bolsena is made. The
basic version from the ancient
Aleatico variety, is violet-red,
softly sweet, and aromatic,
best in early years with fruit,
especially cantaloupe. The fortified
liquoroso at 15% or more is for
after dinner, like port. Age:
liquoroso riserva 3 yrs.

APRILIA *DOC*

Three varieties grown in plains
around Aprilia south of Rome
have virtually disappeared
from commerce.

Merlot *r dr* ☆→☆☆ *00 01 02* Soft,
balanced, tasty with 1 to 3 years
of age, this is the best of the Aprilia
trio – when found.
Sangiovese *p dr* ☆ *DYA* Pale red or
dark pink, this rates little interest.
Trebbiano *w dr* ☆ *DYA* This neutral
white has little to offer.

ATINA

DOC r dr ☆→☆☆☆ *99 00 01 02*
Inland area in the south of the
region dedicated to red wines.
The basic Rosso comes from at
least 50% Cabernet Sauvignon
with Syrah, Merlot, and Cabernet
Franc. There is also a varietal
Cabernet (from Sauvignon and/
or Franc) Age: *riserva* 2 yrs.

Wine Areas

1 Colli Etruschi Viterbesi
2 Vignanello
3 Frascati
4 Genazzano
5 Castelli Romani
6 Colli Albani
7 Colli Lanuvini
8 Circeo
9 Colli della Sabina
10 Atina
11 Orvieto

BIANCO CAPENA

DOC w dr (s/sw) (fz) ☆→☆☆ *DYA*
From Malvasia and Trebbiano
grown around Capena and
Morlupo, north of Rome, the
superiore (of 12%) can equal
Castelli Romani whites.

CASTELLI ROMANI *DOC*

Straightforward wines from a
number of grape varieties grown
on the volcanic soil of the hills
southeast of Rome may carry this
well-known denomination.

Bianco *w dr (s/sw) (fz)* ☆→☆☆ *DYA*
From a variety of sub-varieties
of Trebbiano and Malvasia. Can
be tasty.

Rosato *p dr (s/sw) (fz)* ☆ *DYA*
Innumerable red and white
varieties can go into this
nondescript rosé.

Rosso *r dr (fz)* ☆→☆☆ *DYA* Red
that can also be *novello* from
Cesanese, Merlot, Montepulciano,
Sangiovese, and/or Nero Buono.

CERVETERI *DOC*

Large zone, extending from the
edge of Rome northwest past
the ancient towns of Cerveteri
and Civitavecchia, whose more
than decent wines are mainly
consumed locally.

Bianco *w dr (s/sw) (fz)* ☆☆ *DYA* From
Trebbiano with Malvasia, whether
dry or *abboccato*, this is mellow
with hints of class.

Rosato *p dr (fr)* ☆☆→☆ *DYA* This rosé
is made from the same grapes as
the *rosso*.

Rosso *r dr (s/sw)* ☆→☆☆☆ *98 99 00 01 02*
From Sangiovese and
Montepulciano with, optionally,
Cesanese and other varieties, this
can be tasty for 4 or 5 years or
more. May be novello. The *amabile*
version is best ignored.

CESANESE DEL PIGLIO OR PIGLIO

DOC r dr (s/sw) (sw) (fz) (sp) ☆→☆☆☆
99 00 01 02
Good, sound red from the superior
Cesanese Affile or the common-or-
garden Cesanese Comune grapes
grown in the Prenestina hills
southeast of Rome around the
villages of Piglio, Anagni, and
Paliano. There is a confusing range
of types – *secco, amabile, dolce,
frizzante*, and *spumante* – but the
dry versions are most convincing:
garnet-red, well-scented, tannic, and
warm, and good in 2 to 6 years. The
sweet and semi-sweet versions also
have their followers.

CESANESE DI AFFILE OR AFFILE

DOC r dr (s/sw) (sw) (fz) (sp)
In the past, some considered this to
be the best Cesanese, but production
has dwindled to nothing. Despite the
name both Affile and Comune sub-
varieties of Cesanese are permitted.

CESANESE DI OLEVANO ROMANO OR OLEVANO ROMANO

DOC r dr (s/sw) (sw) (fz) (sp)
Grown around Olevano Romano,
this Cesanese – if you manage to find
any – is virtually indistinguishable
from that of its neighbours.

CIRCEO *DOC*

Zone surrounding Sabaudia,
Terracina, and the Circeo
peninsula and covers 5 types
of wines for youthful drinking
but which rarely shine.

Bianco *w dr (s/sw) (fz)* Based on
Trebbiano Toscano with Malvasia
di Candia.

Rosato *p dr (s/sw) (fz)* Based on Merlot.

Rosso *r dr (s/sw) (fz)* Based on Merlot,
may be *novello*.

Sangiovese *r p dr (s/sw) (fz)* This may
be red or rosé.

Trebbiano *w dr*

COLLI ALBANI

DOC w dr (s/sw) (sw) (sp) ☆→☆☆ *DYA*
White from various Trebbiano sub-
varieties with Malvasia del Lazio and
Malvasia di Candia grown in the
Alban hills around Lago Albano and
Castel Gandolfo near Frasti. Soft,
straw-yellow, it is most often dry.

COLLI DELLA SABINA *DOC*

A large territory straddling the Tiber south of Rieti, centred on the Sabine hills. Certain hillsides have potential, but most production is handled by a co-operative.

Bianco *w dr (fz) sp* ☆→☆☆ *DYA* The main strains of Trebbiano and Malvasia make light, sometimes bubbly, wines of fresh fruit flavours.

Rosato *p dr (fz)* ☆→☆☆ *DYA* Sangiovese and Montepulciano in pink wine.

Rosso *dr (fr) (sp)* ☆→☆☆ *DYA* Sangiovese with Montepulciano can yield good reds. May be *novello*.

COLLI ETRUSCHI VITERBESI *DOC*

Denomination covers an extensive range of wines from a large area around Viterbo.

Bianco *w dr (s/sw) (fz)* Based on Malvasia/Trebbiano.

Rosato *p dr (s/sw) (fz)* Based on Montepulciano/Sangiovese.

Rosso *r dr (s/sw) (fz)* Based on Montepulciano/Sangiovese. May be *novello*.

Canaiolo *r s/sw* Based on Canaiolo Nero, this is red and *amabile*.

Grechetto *w dr (fz)* Based on Greco Bianco, locally called Grechetto. May be *novello*.

Greghetto *r dr* Based on Grechetto Rosso, locally known as Greghetto.

Merlot *r dr* Dry red.

Moscatello *w s/sw sw (fz)* Moscato Bianco can make an *amabile* white or richer *passito* from semi-dried grapes. May be *novello*.

Procanico *w dr (fz)* Procanico here refers to Trebbiano Toscano, not the Superior/Umbrian Trebbiano.

Rossetto *w dr (s/sw)* The local name for Trebbiano Giallo is Rossetto due to the ruddy tint of the grape skins, but its wines are white.

Sangiovese *p dr (s/sw) (fz)* This, unusually, is rosé.

Violone *r dr* Red from Montepulciano, whose local name is Violone.

COLLI LANUVINI

DOC w dr (s/sw) ☆☆ *DYA* Though not well known, this can be among the fuller of the whites from Rome's Castelli Romani hills. From Malvasia sub-varieties di Candra and Puntinata, and up to three types of Trebbiano grown around the town of Genzano, it is soft, usually dry, fresh, and fragrant.

CORI *DOC*

Zone around the town of Cori southeast of the Alban Hills makes 2 little-noted wines.

Bianco *w dr* ☆→☆☆ *DYA* The base is standard Malvasia with Trebbiano but when the optional indigenous variety Bellore is included (up to 30%) this can gain presence and character.

Rosso *r dr* ☆→☆☆ *99 00 01 02* The combination of Montepulciano, Cesanese, and local Nero Buono di Cori can produce fascinating results – if you can find them.

EST! EST!! EST!!! DI MONTEFIASCONE

DOC w dr (s/sw) (sw) ☆→☆☆☆ *01 02* The wine was once as ludicrous as the name, a hangover from a 12th century tale about a tippling bishop's servant whose graffiti – Est! on tavern walls – gave Montefiascone's wines a reputation. But, this white from Trebbiano Toscano with Malvasia Bianco and Trebbiano Giallo grown beside Lake Bolsena has taken on a new lease of life and is dry, lightly fruity, almondy, and often smoother than most other Lazio whites.

FRASCATI

DOC w dr (s/sw) (sw) (sp) ☆→☆☆☆ Frascati's pre-eminence among Roman wines was built initially on the proximity of the hill town that gave its name to the city, and then on its ample vineyards that roll north over the gentle slopes of the Campagna Romana. Nearly 20 million litres a year, about half of the Castelli Romani's DOC wine, originate in the zone, whose cooler, damper conditions in fine, dark soil account for generally superior

quality to its stable mates. In the
not-so-distant past, much Frascati
was a softly off-dry *abboccato*;
though the really prized old-time
version was the refined sweet
cannellino, especially when the
drying grapes took on nuances
of *Botrytis cinerea* (noble rot).
There has been a recent revival of
cannellino although, today, most
Frascati is dry and clear with a
straightforward character that can
be attributed to Trebbiano Toscano.
It is the choice of supplementary
grapes that marks out the better
Frascatis. Malvasia di Candia
gives a gentle harmony while the
superior Malvasia del Lazio gives
greater attack, weight, and fruit.
Greco is another option. Some
spumante is made and the range
of types also includes a *novello*.
Superiore must have 11.5% alcohol.

GENAZZANO *DOC*

Red and white wines from a
small zone around the town of
Genazzano in the Prenistini hills
east of Rome.

Bianco *w dr* From Malvasia di Candia
with local varieties Bellone and/
or Bombino, and optional others,
also *novello*.

Rosso *r dr* Mostly from Sangiovese
with some Cesanese, also *novello*.

MARINO

DOC w dr (s/sw) (sp) ☆→☆☆ DYA
The Marino zone lies adjacent to
Frascati in the Castelli Romani,
between the hill town of Marino
and low slopes around Rome's
Via Appia Antica. It has a nostalgic
following among some Romans
who remember it as being softer
and broader than Frascati, although
now it is often little more than a
fresh, balanced, modern white.
As ever, much depends on the
grape blend. The soft Malvasia di
Candia may reach 60% – or be
absent. The characterful Malvasia
di Lazio peaks at 45%. The rest is
usually Trebbiano, of various sub-
varieties. Marino may also be

abboccato or *amabile. Spumante*
is rare. *Superiore* must have
11.5% alcohol.

MONTECOMPATRI COLONNA

DOC w dr (s/sw) (fr) ☆→☆☆ DYA
Frascati's northerly next-door
neighbour in the Castelli Romani
comes from various sub-varieties
of Malvasia and Trebbiano. The
labels may carry the name of either
town or the full denomination.

NETTUNO *DOC*

Small area on the coast around
Nettuno and Anzio highlighting
the local Bellone variety, locally
called Cacchione.

Bianco *w dr (fr)* From Bellone with
Trebbiano Toscano.

Rosato *p dr (fr)* From Sangiovese
and Trebbiano Toscano.

Rosso *r dr* Based on Merlot and
Sangiovese. Also *novello*.

Cacchione or **Bellone** *w dr*

ORVIETO

Part of the DOC zone centred in
Umbria (*see* page 149) extends
south into Lazio.

TARQUINIA *DOC*

Large area, surrounding Tarquinia,
the Etruscan town northwest of
Rome, and stretching along the
coast from the mouth of the Tiber
north to the Tuscan border and
inland lake Bracciano.

Bianco *w dr (s/sw) (fz)* White from
Trebbiano and Malvasia.

Rosato *p dr* Pink wine from the same
grapes as *rosso*.

Rosso *r dr (s/sw)* Red wine from
Sangiovese, Montepulciano, and,
optionally, Cesanese; also *novello*.

VELLETRI *DOC*

The zone around Velletri at the
southern edge of the Alban Hills
makes the usual styles of Castelli
Romani white and the only
registered red of Rome's hills.

Bianco *w dr (s/sw) (sw) (sp)* ☆→☆☆ DYA
From sub-varieties of Trebbiano
and Malvasia, with, optionally, local

varieties Bellore and Bonvino, this is usually dry and sometimes more scented than its neighbours.

Rosso *r dr (s/sw)* ☆→☆☆ *00 01 02* From Montepulciano and Sangiovese sometimes with a little Cesanese, fresh and fruity when young, though the *riserva* can age. *Amabile* is rare. Age: *riserva* 2 yrs.

VIGNANELLO *DOC*

Hilly zone around the town of Vignanello between Mount Cimino and the Tiber valley north of Rome.

Bianco *w dr DYA* The usual blend of Trebbiano/Malvasia sub-varieties.

Rosato *p dr DYA* Pink wine from Sangiovese/Ciliegiolo.

Rosso *r dr* ☆☆ *98 99 00 01* Red from Sangiovese/Ciliegiolo may be *novello* or *riserva*. Age: *riserva* 2 yrs.

Greco *w dr (sp)* A local strain of Greco is the base of this unusual white.

ZAGAROLO

DOC w dr s/sw DYA ☆→☆☆

Once admired locally, the Malvasia/Trebbiano white of Zagarolo is rarely produced commercially.

Producers

Provinces: Frosinone (FR), Latina (LT), Rieti (RI), Roma (RM), Viterbo (VT).

Cantina Cerveteri, Cerveteri (RM). Co-op achieves notable style with Cerveteri Rosso and Bianco in Fontana Monella and, especially, Vigna Grande lines.

Cantina Colacicchi, Anagni (FR). The estate where in the 1960s Luigi Colacicchi created Torre Ercolana – an acclaimed red from Cabernet Sauvignon, Merlot, and Cesanese – is now run by the Rome wine merchant family, Trimani, who have restored the wine to its former grandeur. They have also revived Romagnano Bianco, from local clones of Trebbiano and Malvasia, and Romagnano Rosso, from the same varieties as Torre Ercolana, and introduced the lively red Schiaffo (meaning slap) (Cabernet/Merlot).

Cantine San Tommaso, Genzano (RM). Reliable source of good vlaue Colli Lanuvini, Castelli Romani DOC.

Casale della Ioria, Acuto (FR). Emerging estate with admired, elegant Cesanese del Piglio.

Casale Marchese, Frascati (RM). Individual Frascati, IGT Cortesia (Bombino/Trebbiano/Malvasia), Vigna del Cavaliere (Cabernet Sauvignon/Cabernet Franc/ Merlot/Montepulciano).

Casale del Giglio, Borgo Montello (LT). Varietal IGT Chardonnay, Sauvignon, Cabernet Sauvignon, Merlot, Petit Verdot, and Shiraz (Syrah), and blends Madreselva (Merlot/Cabernet), Mater Matuta (Syrah/Petit Verdot), Antinoo (Chardonnay/Viognier), Satrico (Trebbiano/Chardonnay), and Aphrodisium (various nobly rotted grapes) grown on Latina's plains have all achieved impressive class.

Castel de Paolis, Grottaferrata (RM). A breath of fresh air in the Castelli wines from acclaimed Frascati (Vigna Adriana, Campo Vecchio) and *cannellino*, IGT Selve Vecchie (Sauvignon/Chardonnay), Quattro Mori (Syrah/Merlot/Cabernet/Petit Verdot), Campo Vecchio Rosso (Syrah/Cesanese/Montepulciano/ Sangiovese), and sweet Muffa Nobile (Sauvignon/Sémillon), and Rosathea (Moscato Rosa).

Colle di Catone, Monteporzio Catone (RM). Individualist estate with fine Frascati ("bottiglia satinata") and remarkable, long-ageing Colle Gaio; elegant IGT Malvasia del Lazio (Villa Ari).

Colle di Maggio, Velletri (RM). IGT blends Velitrae Bianco and Rosso typify proficient range topped by Villa Tulino (white from Chardonnay, red from Syrah/Merlot/Cabernet Sauvignon/Petit Verdot).

Consorzio Produttori Vini di Velletri (Co Pro Vi), Campoverde di Aprilia (LT) Reliable Velletri Bianco Superiore (Villa Ginnetti), Rosso Riserva (Torreto), and others.

Conte Zandotti, Roma (RM). Reliably fine Frascati Superiore and *cannellino*, IGT Malvasia del Lazio Rumon, La Petrosa (Sangovese/Cabernet) from highly regarded name.

CS Cesanese del Piglio, Piglio (FR). Good Cesanese del Pigilio selections white (Etichetta Oro), red (Etichetta Rossa).

CS di Gradoli, Gradoli (VT). One of the few sources of rare Aleatico di Gradoli.

Falesco, Montefiascone (VT). Renowned oenologists Renzo and Riccardo Cotarella make excellent Est! Est!! Est!!! (Poggio dei Gelsi, Falesco), both dry and *vendemmia tardiva*; IGT Grechetto, Vitiano (Cabernet/Merlot/Sangiovese) Marciliano (Cabernet Sauvignon/Cabernet Franc), Pomele (Aleatico), but above all the acclaimed Montiano (Merlot).

Fontana Candida, Frascati (RM). Large winery owned by Gruppo Italiano Vini, producing Frascati of consistent class, peaking in the single-vineyard Santa Teresa, and supported by Malvasia del Lazio.

Gotto d'Oro, Marino (RM). Huge production of decent Frascati and Marino.

Iucci, Sant'Elia Fiumerapido (FR). IGT La Creta Bianco, Merlot, and the curious but convincing Sammichele (Syrah/Cabernet Franc) are gaining notice.

Mazziotti, Bolsena (VT). Fine Est! Est!! Est!!!, notably oaked (Canuleio), IGT Volgente (Merlot/Sangiovese/Montepulciano

Sergio Mottura, Civitella d'Agliano (VT). Organic estate with Orvieto outclassed by Grechetto (Latour a Civitella, Poggio della Costa), Magone (Pinot Nero/Montepulciano), Nenfro (Merlot).

Giovanni Palombo, Atina (FR). Estate for good Atina and range of international style IGTs, mainly red.

Paola Di Mauro-Colle Picchioni, Frattocchie di Marino (RM). Marino (Etichetta Verde, Selezione Oro) that is miles above the rest and wonderfully refined; IGT Le Vignole Bianco (Malvasia/Trebbiano/Sauvignon), Colle Picchioni (Merlot/Sangiovese/Cabernet), topped by the acclaimed Vigna del Vassallo (Merlot/Cabernet Sauvignon/Cabernet Franc).

Paolo d'Amico, Castiglione in Tevere (VT). Chardonnay rules here, oaked Falesia, and fresh Calanchi di Vaiano.

Pietra Pinta - Colle San Lorenzo, Cori (LT). Admired IGT Colle Amato (Cabernet Sauvignon/Syrah), Chardonnay, Merlot, and others.

Terre del Cesanese, Piglio (FR). Leading Cesanese del Piglio.

Trappolini, Castiglione in Tevere (VT). Important northern Lazio producer with impressive range led by IGT Paterno (Sangiovese), Chardonnay, Idea (Aleatico), Brecceto (Grechetto). Also good Est! Est!! Est!!!

Christine Vaselli, Castiglione in Teverina (VT). Supreme Rosso Orvietano (Torre Sant'Andrea), IGT Le Poggere (Cabernet Sauvignon/Merlot).

Villa Pallavicini, Colonna (RM). Good Frascati (Selezione Verde, Il Pigno) and large range of IGTs.

Villa Simone, Monteporzio Catone (RM). Top-notch Frascati (Vigneto Filonardi, Vigna dei Preti, Villa Simone), Cannellino, and new IGT red, Ferro e Seta (Sangiovese/Cesanese).

Wine & Food

Contemporary Roman cooking is a monument to miscellany, the foundations of which – the recipes of the ancient Romans and the *bourgeoisie* of ensuing epochs – have all but crumbled away. What remains has been patched together by the poor and propped up by what could be borrowed or stolen from other places. Yet, for all the salt cod, salt pork, tripe, brains, entrails, feet, tails, mussels, anchovies, beans, chickpeas, and salty Pecorino Romano, Rome lays one of the most pungently tasty and vividly coloured tables of Italy. A rare extravagance is *abbacchio,* irresistibly tender baby lamb. But what really enriches the Roman diet are the vegetables that arrive fresh daily from the region's gardens. Some dishes of Rome (and Lazio) don't seem to go with wine. The Roman answer is to quaff carafe whites from the Castelli Romani – sometimes mercifully diluted with some effervescent mineral water.

Wines to accompany each dish are suggested below in italic.

Abbacchio alla cacciatora Baby lamb cooked with rosemary, garlic, anchovies, and vinegar. *Torre Ercolana*

Bucatini alla matriciana Long, narrow pasta tubes with a sauce of *guanciale* (salt pork from the pig's jowl), red peppers (sometimes

tomatoes), and grated Pecorino. *Velletri Rosso*

Carciofi alla giudia Tender artichokes flattened flower-like and deep-fried, a speciality of Rome's Jewish quarter. *Carciofi alla romana* are sautéed in oil, garlic, and mint. *Water*

Coda alla vaccinara Oxtail stewed with onion, tomatoes, lots of celery, and wine. *Colle Picchioni*

Cozze alla marinara Mussels cooked in their juice with parsley, garlic, and tomato. *Marino*

Fettuccine al burro Feather-light egg noodles with lashings of butter, cream, and Parmesan. *Frascati Superiore*

Saltimbocca alla romana Veal filets with *prosciutto* and sage sautéed in butter. *elletri Rosso*

Spaghetti alla carbonara The hot pasta is plunged into a mix of *guanciale*, grated Parmesan and Pecorino, hot peppers, and raw eggs, which curdle and adhere to the strands. *Colli Lanuvini*

Restaurants

Recommended in or near wine zones:

Aprilia-Circeo *Pierino* at Anzio; *Il Focarile* at Aprilia.

Castelli Romani-Colli Albani *Antico Ristorante Pagnanelli* at Castel Gandolfo; *Cacciani* at Frascati; *La Briciola* at Grottaferrata; *Benito* al Bosco at Velletri.

Ciociaria-Prenestina-Frosinone *Le Colline Ciociare* at Acuto; *La*

Torre at Fiuggi; *Ratafià* at Isola dei Liri; *Antonello Colonna* at Labico.

Colli Etruschi Viterbese-Montefiascone-Colli della Sabina *L'Altra Bottiglia* at Civitacastellana; *Oca Giuliva* at Fiano Romano; *Pecora Nera* at Rieti; *L'Acqua delle Donne* at Trevignano Romano; *Ristorante-Enoteca La Torre* at Viterbo.

Abruzzo *Abruzzo*

Whereas growers in most of Italy's regions have scrambled to register ever more DOCs for their wines, Abruzzo, until not long ago, retained aloof, with an almost oversimplified structure. There were just two denominations, the mono-varietal Montepulciano d'Abruzzo for reds and Trebbiano d'Abruzzo for whites. Both covered practically all but the highest, least tractable lands in this beautiful, Adriatic region which stretches from the heights of the

Wine Areas

1 Controguerra
2 Colline Teramane
3 Montepulciano d'Abruzzo
4 Trebbiano d'Abruzzo

Appennines through tumbling foothills down to the coast. But then producers in the northerly province of Teramo, whose wines are more stylish than the heavier ones further south (most notably in Chieti province) sought recognition of their superiority and in the mid-1990s Colline Termane emerged as a Montepulciano d'Abruzzo sub-zone. This was swiftly followed by a new DOC, the small zone of Controguerra, with wines reflecting the more innovative scene in the region's far north, where it borders Marche. Now Montepulciano d'Abruzzo Colline Teramane has emerged with DOCG status in its own right. The Montepulciano variety (not to be confused with Tuscany's Vino Nobile di Montepulciano) is persuasive in the way it combines robust power with suppleness. Even its cherry-pink version, called Cerasuolo, can be impressive. Trebbiano d'Abruzzo refers to the rather classy local sub-variety of Trebbiano, more often called Bombino, as well as the denomination. Yet the DOC, somewhat perversely, also allows for the usually innocuous Trebbiano Toscano – and it is this that dominates white production. Overall, significant amounts of wine are produced: Abruzzo has Italy's fifth largest output at around 3 million hectolitres. The refinement of Teramo and the power of Chieti are balanced by wines from the intervening province of Pescara and counterpoised by the elegance of those from upland Aquila, where Cerasuolo is prevalent. Indeed, if you pick your spot carefully, you can find conditions suited to nearly every type of wine.

Wine tourism has not been explicitly developed in the region, but the coastal hills between Teramo and Chieti have numerous wineries and country inns where local wines can be tasted. At Chieti, the *Enoteca Templi Romani* provides a rigorous choice of wines from both Abruzzo and other regions.

Recent Vintages

Montepulciano improves with age, usually after three to six years, sometimes much more. Trebbiano is generally for drinking young although some, from certain producers, may be aged, in some cases for five years or more. Among recent vintages 2001, 2000, 1999, 1998, and 1997 were the most successful. 1996 was often disappointing, but 2002, 1995, 1994, and 1993 had good things to offer; 1992 and 1991 were better for whites than for reds; 1990 and 1988 were generally superb for reds. Earlier good vintages for reds were 87, 85, 83, 82, 79, 78, 77.

Wines

CONTROGUERRA *DOC*

Small zone covering in the communities of Controguerra, Torano Nuovo, Ancarano, Corropoli, and Colonello in the northern province of Teramo for a broad range of wines escaping the Montepulciano–Trebbiano straitjacket.

Bianco *w dr (fz)* Trebbiano Toscano with Passerina, and, optionally, small amounts of others.

Rosso *r dr* Red from Montepulciano with Merlot and/or Cabernet Sauvignon and, optionally, small amounts of others; also *novello*. Age: *riserva* 2 yrs.

Cabernet *r dr*
Chardonnay *w dr*
Ciliegiolo *r dr*
Malvasia *w dr*
Merlot *r dr*
Moscato Amabile *w s/sw*
Passerina *w dr*
Pinot Nero *r dr*
Riesling *w dr*

Passito Bianco *w (dr) s/sw sw* From semi-dried Trebbiano Toscano Passerina and Malvasia. Age: 1 yr, *annoso* 3 yrs

Passito Rosso *r (dr) s/sw sw* From semi-dried Montepulciano and others. Age: 1 yr, *annoso* 3 yrs.

Spumante *w sp* Trebbiano, Chardonnay, Verdicchio, and Pecorino may be used.

MONTEPULCIANO D'ABRUZZO

DOC r dr ☆☆→☆☆☆☆ *88 90 91 92 93 94 95 97 98 99 00 01 02*

From Montepulciano with up to 15% of other varieties grown over much of the region, this tends to be bold in its youth but is can be majestic and capable of long ageing. Deep ruby, in colour with robust structure and ample tannins softened by a supple roundness rare in central Italian reds. The best generally comes from the area around Teramo (*see* below). Age: *riserva* 2 yrs.

Cerasuolo *p dr* ☆☆ *DYA* Bracing and full, this can be a rosé of real character able to stand up to hearty pastas and soups. The raciest come from the valleys of L'Aquila province.

MONTEPULCIANO D'ABRUZZO COLLINE TERAMINE

DOCG r dr ☆☆→☆☆☆☆ *01 02*

The comparatively cool, sharply defined hill country of Teramo province produces some of Abruzzo's best Montepulciano and its superiority has been recognized by this DOCG which requires 90% minimum, any remainder being made up with Sangiovese, to make a firm, structured yet well fruited wine of at least 12% alcohol. Age: 2 yrs, at least 1 in wood; *riserva* 3 yrs.

TREBBIANO D'ABRUZZO

DOC w dr ☆→☆☆☆ *DYA*

From Bombino (known locally as Trebbiano d'Abruzzo) or (most often) Trebbiano Toscano, this can be a lacklustre white wine which can slip down. Then there are those that head towards far more: colour, body, rich aromas, concentration, length of flavour, and capacity to age.

Producers

Provinces: L'Aquila (AQ), Chieti (CH), Pescara (PE), Teramo (TE).

Agriverde, Ortona (CH). Improving Montepulciano (Plateo, Riseis, Natum); IGT Chardonnay.

Barone Cornacchia, Torano Nuovo (TE). Classy Montepulciano (Le Coste, Poggio Varano).

Cantina Tollo, Tollo (CH). Exemplary co-op provides outstanding value in Montepulciano (Aldiano, Cagiòlo, Colle Secco), Cerasuolo (Colle Cavalieri, Rocca Ventosa, Valle dell'Oro), and Trebbiano. Also good IGT Cagiòlo Bianco (Chardonnay).

Cantina Zaccagnini, Bolognano (PE). Reliably fine Montepulciano (Abbazia San Clemente) and Cerasuolo (Myosotis) plus large spread of IGTs.

Casal Thaulero, Roseto degli Abruzzi (TE). Quality-conscious co-op makes reliably good ranges of Montepulciano (Orsetto Oro), Cerasuolo, and Trebbiano.

Cataldi Madonna, Ofena (AQ). Elegant Montepulciano (Toni) and Cerasulo (Piè delle Vigne); good IGT Malandrino (Montepulciano/Cabernet) and white Pecorino.

Faraone, Giulianova (TE). Admired, Montepulciano, Cerasuolo, Trebbiano.

Farnese, Ortona (CH). Huge winery with good Montepulciano and esteemed Edizione Cinque Autoctoni from 5 varieties coming from old vines in 2 distinct areas.

Fattoria La Valentina, Spoltore (PE). High ranking Montepulciano (Spelt, Binomio, Bellovedere). Good Cerasuolo, Trebbiano.

Franco Pasetti, Francavilla al Mare (CH). Emerging estate with admirable Montepulciano (Pasetti, Testarossa), IGT Testarossa Bianco (Trebbiano/Pecorino/Chardonnay), Pecorino.

Lorenzo Filomusi Guelfi, Tocco di Casauria (PE). Impressive Montepulciano and Cerasuolo.

Dino Illuminati, Controguerra (TE) Notable Montepulciano (Riparossa, Zanna, Pieluni), Cerasuolo (Campirosa), Controguerra red (Lumen), white (Daniele, Ciafré, Cenalba, Costalupo), *passito* (Nicò), and more.

Lepore, Colonella (TE). Individual Colline Teramane, Montepulciano DOC (Luigi Lepore), Contoguerra Passerina.

Marramiero, Rosciano (PE). Impressive Montepulciano (Inferi, Dama), good Cerasuolo, and Trebbiano.

Masciarelli, San Martino sulla Marrucina (CH). Montepulciano Villa Gemma edges the DOC to new heights; Marina Cvetic is almost as starry; fine Cerasuolo (Villa Gemma), Trebbiano, and IGT Chardonnay (both Marina Cvetic) round out a supreme range.

Camillo Montori, Controguerra (TE). Incisive Colline Teramane (Fonte Cupa); Cerasuolo and Trebbiano (Fonte Cupa); Controguerra Leneo d'Oro (Trebbiano/Chardonnay/Passerina), Leneo Moro (Montepulciano/ Merlot/Cabernet Sauvignon).

Bruno Nicodemi, Notaresco (TE). Consistently good Montepulciano, Cerasuolo, and Trebbiano (all Bacco, Colli Venia).

Orlandi Contucci Ponno, Roseto degli Abruzzi (TE). Estate focused on IGTs Cabernet (Colle Funaro), Sauvignon (Ghiaiolo), and Liburnio (Cabernet/Merlot/Malbec) yet characterful Montepulaicano, too.

Sarchese Dora, Ortona (CH). Emerging estate for Montepulciano, Trebbiano, Chardonnay.

Valentini, Loreto Aprutino (PE). Wonderful Cerasuolo; quite remarkable, voluptuous Montepulciano that ages superbly; and the only Trebbiano anywhere to merit the eptithet "great".

Wine & Food

The people of Abruzzo like strongly flavoured food and lots of it. Though the Adriatic is full of fish, even coastal dwellers look to the land for sustenance. Abruzzo favoured meats are lamb and mutton. Ewe's milk is the source of Pecorino cheese. Pork is popular, too. The seasoning is often hot. The local dish is *maccheroni alla chitarra*.

Wines to accompany each dish are suggested below in italic.
Brodetto pescarese The Pescara version of Adriatic fish soup, cooked with green peppers. *Trebbiano*

Maccheroni alla chitarra Pasta noodles cut into sticks on a stringed instrument (the "guitar"), with meat ragout or tomato sauce *Cerasuolo* (tomato), *Montepulciano* (ragout)
'Ndocca 'ndocca Stew of pig's innards, ribs, feet, and head with peppers, rosemary, and vinegar, Teramo speciality. *Montepulciano*
Scrippelle 'nfuss (or **'mbusse**) Pancake-like fritters or crêpes served in broth. *Cerasuolo*
Virtù or **le sette virtù** Legendary soup of Teramo that once took seven days to put together. Today the "seven virtues" soup is less romantic but still good. *Cerasuolo*

Restaurants

Recommended in or near wine zones:
L'Angolo d'Abruzzo at Carsoli (AQ); *Beccaceci* at Giulianova Lido; *Villa Maiella* at Guardiagrele;

La Bilancia near Loreto Aprutino; *Leon d'Oro* at Martinsicuro; *Taverna de li Caldora* at Pacentro; *L'Angolino da Filippo* at San Vito Chietino; *Duomo* at Teramo.

Molise *Molise*

Molise, long an appendix of Abruzzo, is still sometimes regarded as an afterthought. References to the region's wines date back to Roman times, though little of special regard seems to have emerged from its vineyards since.

Through the ages, the hill people kept their rustic wines to themselves. The advent of DOCs Biferno and Pentro added official status in the 1980s, a step up from total obscurity. But wines from Pentro are notable by their absence and there are just two producers of note in Biferno. Additionally, a newer DOC, called Molise, now covers all of Biferno's DOC territory and the heartland of Pentro's, prompting thoughts that the future might be to ditch these two and give the region's winemakers a new start under a single denomination whose name will resonate – with Italians at least. For there is an undeniably high potential for wines from the sunny hillsides between the Apennines and the Adriatic, even though, so far, it has been ill expoited and wines that aren't consumed locally are as often as not directed towards the blending vats of neighbouring Abruzzo or Puglia.

Maybe the most inviting thing about Molise is that few people go there, possibly because few people know where it is. It has a narrow strip of Adriatic coast (at Termoli) and extensive uplands to explore, and offers rustically tasty wine and food at bargain prices in the local *trattorie*.

Recent Vintages

Recommended vintages are given with individual wines.

Wines

BIFERNO *DOC*

This zone covers the sun-drenched hills between the regional captial Campobasso and the coast. Few have exploited its promise.

Bianco *w dr* ☆→☆☆ *DYA* The minor proportions of Bombino and Malvasia to be used should be enough to overturn the blandness of the base Trebbiano Toscano for any diligent winemaker.

Rosato *p dr* →☆☆ *DYA* From Montepulciano with Trebbiano and Aglianico, this can be nicely fresh.

Rosso *r dr* ☆→☆☆ *99 00 01 02* From the same grapes as *rosato* (but better without the Trebbiano), this can be highly drinkable young, promising as *riserva*. Age: *riserva* 3 yrs.

MOLISE OR DEL MOLISE

DOC r w (fr) (sp) (s/sw) (sw)
Zone covering most of the region's more promising viticultural areas, spanning most of Campobasso province and the central hills of Isernia province, for white and red blends and varietal wines from Aglianico, Cabernet Sauvignon, Chardonnay, Falanghina, Greco Bianco, Montepulciano, Moscato Bianco, Pinot Bianco, Sangiovese, Sauvignon, Trebbiano, and Tintilia (the local name for Bovale). Any of these may be *riserva* (age: 2 yrs), sparkling, *frizzante*, *passito*, or *novello*. **NB:** Protests from Abruzzo resulted in "Montepulciano del Molise" being removed from permitted terminology; "Molise Montepulciano" is the only option for this grape.

PENTRO DI ISERNIA OR PENTRO *DOC*

Hills along the Verrino and Volturno valleys of Isernia province have potential for 3 types of wine, but less than 3 hectares, have been registered for DOC and production remains resolutely zero so quality remains hypothetical.

Bianco *w dr* From Trebbiano Toscano with Bombino Bianco.

Rosato *p dr* From Montepulciano and Sangiovese.

Rosso *r dr* Grapes are as for *rosato*.

Producers

Provinces: Campobasso (CB), Isernia (IS).

Borgo di Colloredo, Campomarino (CB). Emerging estate with emphasis on Biferno, white, and rosé, and varietals from Montepulciano, Aglianico, Falanghina, Trebbiano, and Sangiovese.

Masseria Di Majo Norante, Campomarino (CB). Despite this estate having been established in hot, sandy plains once considered unsuitable for vines, studied techniques have resulted in wines that are rarely matched for class even in more prodigious neighbouring terrains. There is Biferno, including a fine Rosso Ramitello, but the emphasis is on varietals from Aglianico, Sangiovese, Falanghina, Greco, and sweet Moscato Reale called Apianae (some Molise DOC, some IGT). There is also Molise, Biblos (Falanghina/Greco), Don Luigi (Montepulciano/ Tintilia), and Ramitello Bianco (Falanghina/Fiano).

Cantina Cooperativa Valbiferno, Guglionesi (CB). Biferno DOC.

Wine & Food

Molise doesn't have a *cucina* all its own, but instead shares recipes with Abruzzo, while picking up an occasional idea from Puglia, Campania, or Lazio. The cooking is rustic and authentically good. Lamb and kid are stalwarts in the hill country, where Pecorino cheese is eaten in chunks or grated over pasta, and pork is preserved as prosciutto and salame. Mountain streams provide freshwater trout and crayfish. And along the coast, simply prepared fish from the Adriatic is widely consumed.

Wines to accompany each dish are suggested below in italic.

Calcioni di ricotta Circular pasta shells containing ricotta and provolone cheese, *prosciutto*, and eggs, and then deep-fried in oil. *Biferno Rosato*

Gamberi d'acqua dolce ai ferri Freshwater crayfish grilled over coals. *Ramitello Bianco*

Mazzarelle d'agnello Lamb's lung and intestines wrapped in beet greens and cooked in oil and white wine. *Ramitello Rosso*

Tacconi Quadrangular pasta often served with meat sauce. *Biferno Rosso*

Zuppa di ortiche Soup of nettle sprouts, tomato, bacon, and onion. *Greco*

Restaurants

Recommended in or near wine zones: *Vecchia Trattoria Tonino* at

Campobasso; *Ribo* at Guglionese; *Z'Bass* at Termoli.

Puglia *Puglia*

Puglia's fortunes have changed more dramatically in the past decade than anywhere else in Italy. The once ignominious title of "Europe's wine cellar", earned for prodigious exports of blending wines, now has a more positive ring. Producers have learned to harness the fruit and vigour of their wines while eliminating their erstwhile rough edges and taming their tendency to develop prodigious amounts of alcohol. That, plus the comparatively low costs of production here have made Puglia a prime source of the mouthfilling, moreish wines of remarkably good value, reds in particular, that European markets crave. This is particularly so in the southernmost Salento peninsula, the sun-drenched "heel" of Italy where the Negroamaro, Malvasia Nera, and Primitivo varieties dominate. Negroamaro is the powerhouse but bush-trained Primitivo (the variety that became Zinfandel in California) thrives on the hot plains to produce a rich, strong wine of great character. Central and northern Puglia, north of a line drawn across the region from the port of Taranto, on the Ionian Sea, to Brindisi, on the Adriatic, are more the domain of red Uva di Troia, Montepulciano, and Bombino Nero. Rosés here show style rarely equalled elsewhere. Made by the *lacrima* (teardrop) system using only about half the juice of uncrushed grapes, they are delicately dry, and may be pale roseate in colour – comparable to what Americans call "blush" – or more deeply pink.

The climate is warm and dry along the coast, becoming cooler in the interior and reds may even have the delicately perfumed qualities of northerly wines. And, naturally, international varieties, white Chardonnay and Sauvignon in particular, have made inroads.

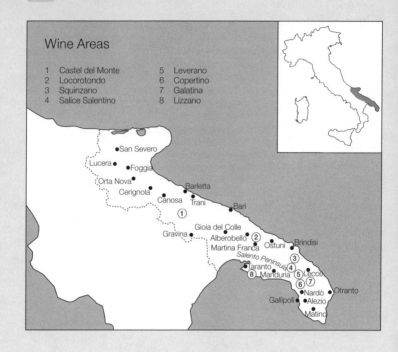

Wine Areas

1	Castel del Monte	5	Leverano
2	Locorotondo	6	Copertino
3	Squinzano	7	Galatina
4	Salice Salentino	8	Lizzano

●San Severo
Lucera ● ●Foggia
Orta Nova●
Cerignola● Barletta
Canosa Trani
●Bari
①
Gioia del Colle
Gravina ● Alberobello ②
Martina Franca Ostuni ●Brindisi
Salento Peninsula ③
⑧ Taranto ④ ⑤ Lecce
Manduria ⑥⑦
Nardò ●Otranto
Gallipoli● ●Alezio
Matino

All this is amply catered for by DOCs; there are twenty-five, although most of those in the Salento have similar criteria and are distinguished only by the geographical area they cover. Wines falling outside these criteria will come under one of six IGTs, of which Puglia and Salento are the most prevalent.

As Italy's perennial gateway to Greece, Puglia has remnants of Hellas, plus reminders of innumerable other peoples. The octagonal Swabian structure that gave Castel del Monte its name is well worth a visit, as is the Salento Peninsula with its ancient Greek cities of Lecce, now a marvel of baroque, and Gallipoli. Select Puglian wines are on display at the *Enoteca Vinarius De Pasquale* at Bari and the *Enoteca Internazionale and Regno di Bacco-Vinarius* both at Lecce.

Recent Vintages

Many Apulian reds are noted for their longevity, as are certain rosés of Salento, although, as a rule, the region's pink and white wines should be drunk when young. The hot Salento Peninsula tends to have more consistent harvests than do more temperate hilly zones. Recommended vintages are shown with each entry.

Wines

ALEATICO DI PUGLIA

DOC r sw ☆–→☆☆☆ *99 00 01 02*
Smooth, warm, crimson
dessert wine from Aleatico
grapes that are grown throughout

Puglia, though mostly in Bari
and Brindisi provinces, in 2
types: *dolce naturale* (15%)
and the fortified *liquoroso*
(18.5%). Age: *riserva* 3 yrs.

ALEZIO

DOC r p dr ☆☆→★☆☆☆ *97 98 99 00 01 02* Red and rosé from Negroamaro with Malvasia Nera, and/or Sangiovese, and/or Montepulciano grown in a small area around Alezio to the east of Gallipoli. The *rosso* is ample in colour and body, warm and well suited to ageing. The *rosato* is coral pink, fragrant, and attractively flavoured. Age: *rosso riserva* 2 yrs.

BRINDISI

DOC r p dr ☆→☆☆☆☆ *95 96 97 98 99 00 01 02*
Rosso and *rosato* from minimum 70% Negroamaro, grown inland from the port of Brindisi. Rosé can be pleasant; powerful red can be smooth and elegant with up to 8 years, occasionally more. Age: *rosso riserva* 2 yrs.

CACC'E MMITTE DI LUCERA

DOC r dr ☆ *DYA*
From the rolling plains of Capitanata around Lucera in the north, the name, in dialect, means "take out and put in" and, most believe, refers to pouring wine straight from the cask, drinking it down, and refilling your glass. Others maintain it came from the old practice of adding grapes to wine fermenting in vat and drawing off the surplus to drink. In any event youth is the main attribute of this simple red from Uva di Troia and other varieties, white as well as red.

CASTEL DEL MONTE *DOC*

This upland zone, of rocky, arid inclines where only certain pockets of land have enough topsoil to support vines, gives rise to some of the region's best and best-known wines. The name comes from Emperor Friedrich II von Hohenstaufen's octagonal castle, a local landmark. Rivera dominated production for years but now has keen competition.

Bianco *w dr (fr)* ☆→☆☆ *DYA* From Bombino Bianco, Pampanuto, and/or Chardonnay, and sometimes others, this is usually pleasantly light and fresh.

Rosato *p dr (fr)* ☆☆ *DYA* From Bombino Nero, Aglianico, and/or Uva di Troia, and one of Italy's prettiest and most enjoyed pinks.

Rosso *r dr* ☆☆→☆☆☆ *97 98 00 01 02* A wine of deep colour and opulent tone, from Uva di Troia, Aglianico, and/or Montepulciano. The *riserva* can age splendidly. May be *novello*. Age: *riserva* 2 yrs.

Aglianico *r (p) (fr)* ☆→☆☆ *98 99 00 01 02* The ancient variety does well here but better as red than rosé. Age: *riserva* 2 yrs.

Bombino Bianco *w dr (fr)* ☆→☆☆ *DYA*
Bombino Nero *r dr* ☆→☆☆☆ *99 00 01 02*
Cabernet *r dr* ☆→☆☆ *99 00 01* From Cabernet Sauvignon and/or Franc. Age: *riserva* 2 yrs.

Chardonnay *w dr (fr)* ☆☆ *DYA*
Pinot Bianco *w dr (fr)* ☆→☆☆☆ *DYA*
Pinot Nero *r dr* ☆→☆☆ *00 01 02*
Sauvignon *w dr (fr)* ☆→☆☆☆ *DYA*
Uva di Troia *r dr* ☆☆ *99 00 01 92* Age: *riserva* 2 yrs

COPERTINO

DOC r p dr ☆☆→☆☆☆☆ *97 98 99 00 01 02*
Red and rosé primarily from Negroamaro, grown around the township of Copertino. The *rosso* can be one of Salento's tastiest reds, especially when *riserva*. Deep ruby, smooth, rich in aroma and flavour, it has a nicely bitter undertone and improves with 4 to 10 years. The *rosato* is salmon pink and finely scented. Age: *rosso riserva* 2 yrs.

GALATINA *DOC*

A small inland area, south of Lecce, around the artisan village of Galatina on the Salento Peninsula.

Bianco *w dr (fz)* ☆→☆☆ *DYA* From Chardonnay and others, this can be tasty.

Rosato *p dr (fz)* ☆→☆☆ *DYA* From Negroamaro and others, this is pleasant.

Rosso *r dr* ☆→☆☆ *97 98 99 00 01 02*
From Negroamaro and others, this
compares with other reds of
Salento. Also *novello*. Age: *riserva*
2 yrs.

Chardonnay *w dr* ☆☆ *DYA*

Negroamaro *r (p) dr* ☆→☆☆ *97 98 99 00
01 02*

GIOIA DEL COLLE *DOC*

Infrequently seen wines from
extensive area around Gioia del
Colle, south of Bari. The Primitivo
is the most successful.

Bianco *w dr* Based on
Trebbiano Toscano.

Rosato *p dr* From Primitivo with
Montepulciano, Negroamaro,
and/or Sangiovese, and a little
Malvasia Nera.

Rosso *r dr* From the same grapes
as the *rosato*.

Aleatico *r sw* Not unlike Aleatico di
Puglia, whether naturally sweet
(15%) or fortified (18.5%). Age:
riserva 2 yrs.

Primitivo *r dr (s/sw)* ☆☆→☆☆☆ *97 98 99
00 01 02* The best-known wine
of the zone, this is big and strong,
sometimes *amabile*. Sometimes
called Primitivo di Gioia. Age:
riserva 2 yrs.

GRAVINA

DOC w dr (s/sw) (sp) ☆→☆☆ *DYA*
Pleasant white from Malvasia, Greco
di Tufo, and Bianco d'Alessano
grown around Gravina near the
border of Basilicata. The *amabile*
version is insignificant.

LEVERANO *DOC*

Small area between Copertino
and Salice Salentino with wines
of character.

Bianco *w dr (s/sw) (sw)* ☆→☆☆ *DYA*
From Malvasia Bianca, Bombino
Bianco, and others, this can be
softly drinkable or, as vendemmia
tardiva or *passito*, rich and sweet.

Rosato *p dr* ☆→☆☆ *DYA* Based on
Negroamaro with Malvasia
Nera, Montepulciano, and/or
Sangiovese can be attractively
rounded when young.

Rosso *r dr* ☆→☆☆☆ *99 00 01 02* From
the same grapes as the *rosato*, this is
enjoyable with a few years of age but
can also be *novello*. Age *riserva* 2 yrs.

Malvasia Bianca *w dr* ☆→☆☆ *DYA* Soft
and gentle.

Negroamaro *p r dr* The rosé version is
best young, the red rounds out with
a few years age.

LIZZANO *DOC*

Coastal zone just south of Taranto
but wines infrequently seen.

Bianco *w dr (fr) (sp)* From Trebbiano
with Chardonnay, and/or Pinot
Bianco, and optional others.

Rosato *p dr (fr) (sp)* From Negroamaro
with options on several others,
this rosé can be pleasant.

Rosso *r dr (fz)* From the same grapes
as *rosato*. May be *novello*. Age:
superiore 1 yr.

Malvasia Nera *r dr* The varietal is
rarely seen.

Negroamaro *r p dr* This may be red or
rosé. Age: *superiore* 1 yr. Unusually,
the term *giovane* may be found on
the *rosso* and *rosato* if bottled
young.

LOCOROTONDO

DOC w dr (sp) ☆→☆☆ *DYA*
From the little-seen Verdeca with
Bianco d'Alessano grown around the
whitewashed town of Locorotondo.
This can be one of Puglia's tastier
whites. Pale straw-green in colour,
subtly fruity, and briskly satisfying
with seafood. But unfotunately some
versions are insipid. A *spumante* is
sometimes seen.

MARTINA FRANCA OR
MARTINA

DOC w dr (sp) ☆→☆☆ *DYA*
Adjacent to Locorotondo and
almost identical to it in grapes
and personality. The zone extends
along the Itria valley to Alberobello,
capital of the conical trulli dwellings.
A *spumante* is permitted.

MATINO

DOC r p dr ☆ *98 99 00 01 02*
Southernmost DOC of Salento, both

rosso and *rosato* are based on Negroamaro. Salento style, but rarely seen.

MOSCATO DI TRANI
DOC w sw ☆☆→☆☆☆ *97 98 99 00 01 02* Rare, rich, golden dessert wine made from Moscato Bianco grapes grown right across central Puglia. Luscious and velvety, it rates as one of the better southern Italian Moscatos, in two versions: *dolce naturale* (12%) and *liquoroso* (16%). Age: *liquoroso* 1 yr.

NARDO
DOC r p dr ☆→☆☆☆*98 99 00 01 02* Typical red and rosé from Negroamaro with Malvasia Nera, grown around Nardò between the Ionian coast and the Salice Salentino/Copertino Salento heartland. The red, robust and warm with a grapey aroma, is best in 3 to 6 years. Age: *rosso riserva* 2 yrs.

ORTA NOVA
DOC r p dr ☆ *DYA* Rare red and rosé based on Sangiovese grown at Orta Nova south of Foggia.

OSTUNI *DOC*
The lands around the ancient town of Ostuni, north of Brindisi make 2 distinct wines, rarely seen outside the area.

Bianco *w dr* ☆ *DYA* Straw-yellow, delicate wine for seafood, from the obscure Impigno and Francaville grapes.

Ottavianello *r dr* ☆ *DYA* Light ruby, almost rosé, this subtle wine from the rarely seen Ottavianello grape adapts to a range of foods. Drink within 2 to 3 years.

PRIMITIVO
The name of this variety suggests "early ripening" in Italian, not "primitive". Its origins are uncertain, but there is little dissension that it is the same variety as Zinfandel, which apparently arrived in the USA from central Europe. Indeed, several Puglian producers have taken to labelling their Primitivo as Zinfandel. The white is strong, often sweet, and DOC around Manduria and Gioia del Colle.

PRIMITIVO DI MANDURIA
DOC r dr s/sw sw ☆→☆☆☆ *93 94 96 97 98 99 00 01 02* Puglia's archetypal blending wine was once only occasionally tamed into a gentle giant which, whether opulently dry or rather sweet, bore only a vague family resemblance to Zinfandel. But Puglian winemakers have now learned to coax class from this rich, punchy early ripening variety that dominates vineyards around the towns of Manduria and Sava. Whether *secco, amabile,* or *dolce* they are usually most alluring after a year or 2 when they still have a deep-violet hue and are bursting with fruit. But some examples age well too. The fortified *liquoroso* types of 17.5–18% alcohol, in particular, can take on some smoothness and complexity with hints of orange in colour after 4 to 5 years. Age: *liquoroso* 2 yrs.

ROSSO BARLETTA
DOC r dr ☆→☆☆ *99 00 01 02* Made from Uva di Troia with, sometimes, some Sangiovese and/or Montepulciano grown around the port of Barletta, this ruby-garnet wine can be refreshing young, though it can develop something resembling style within 3 to 4 years. Age: *invecchiato* 2 yrs (1 in wood).

ROSSO CANOSA
DOC r dr ☆→☆☆ *99 00 01 02* Red wine of significant structure based mainly on Uva di Troia grown around Canosa in north-central Puglia. Fresh and fruity when young, it develops finesse after several years' ageing. It may also be called Canusium after the town's Latin name. Age: *riserva* 2 yrs.

ROSSO DI CERIGNOLA
DOC r dr

In theory, one of north Puglia's better reds, it is based on Uva di Troia and Negroamaro grown around Cerignola, but none has been made for a while. Age: *riserva* 2 yrs.

SALENTO *IGT*

The long peninsula that forms the heel of the Italian boot makes one of Puglia's most utilized IGTs with 12 varietal whites an 7 varietal reds permitted as well as red and white blends and a rosé from Negroamaro. Despite the plethora of DOCs some of Apulia's finest wines still come under this IGT. However, as a major vineyard area with a well-known name and relative uniformity of wine types, it is legitimate to ask why Salento wasn't unified as a single DOC taking in the numerous similar classified areas as sub-zones.

SALICE SALENTINO *DOC*

The best-known of Salento's denominations covers 5 types of wine including the traditional *rosso* and *rosato* grown in the centre of the peninsular around the town of Salice Salentino.

Bianco *w dr* ☆→☆☆ *00 01 02* Based on Chardonnay, this can show a certain class.

Rosato *p dr (sp)* ☆→☆☆ *01 02* Negroamaro with Malvasia Nera can show depth; sometimes aged a little, as in Leone De Castris's legendary Five Roses.

Rosso *r dr* ☆→☆☆☆ *88 90 93 94 95 96 97 98 99 00 01* From the same grapes as the *rosato*, this can be rich and velvety, with bitter undertones and impressive durability; it stands out among Salento wines. May be *novello*. Age: *riserva* 2 yrs.

Aleatico *r sw* ☆→☆☆ *98 99 01 02* Sweet red from Aleatico can show some grace with age, though it can be more impressive as *liquoroso* at 16%. Age: *riserva* 2 yrs.

Pinot Bianco *w dr (sp)* ☆→☆☆ *DYA* The variety shows promise here, also as *spumante*.

SAN SEVERO *DOC*

Puglia most prolific DOC zone surrounds the town of San Severo, on the Capitanata plains of the north. The 3 types, dominated in volume by the white, are usually at least good drinking and good value if not more.

Bianco *w dr (sp)* ☆→☆☆ *DYA* From Bombino Bianco and Trebbiano Toscano, this is usually light and easy; also produces bubbly.

Rosato *p dr* ☆→☆☆ *DYA* From Montepulciano with Sangiovese, this rosé can be round and fruity in its youth.

Rosso *r dr* ☆→☆☆ *98 99 00 01* From the same grapes as *rosato*, this ranges from light and mellow to fairly firm, good in 1 to 4 years.

SQUINZANO
DOC r p dr ☆→☆☆ *98 99 00 01 02*

Sound wines from Negroamaro with Malvasia Nera and/or Sangiovese grown around the Salento town of Squinzano, north of Lecce. The *rosso* needs a couple of years to develop robust goodness, the *riserva* about 5 years. The *rosato* is bright coral pink, fresh, and tasty. Age: *rosso riserva* 2 yrs.

Producers

Provinces: Bari (BA), Brindisi (BR), Foggia (FG), Lecce (LE), Taranto (TA).

Accademia dei Racemi, Manduria (TA). Grouping of small, quality-directed estates working mainly with indigenous varietals, for mutual support and technical assistance. Includes Pervini (*q.v.*), Felline (*q.v.*), Masseria Pepe, Sinfarosa, Casale Bevagna. Particularly effective with Primitivo di Manduria.

Agricole Vallone, Lecce. Fine Brindisi (Vigna Flaminio) and Salice Salentino Rosso. Notable rich IGT Graticciaia (semi-dried Negroamaro) and 2 variations on Sauvignon, Corte Valesio, and dessert wine Passo delle Viscarde.

Albano Carrisi, Cellini San Marco (BR). Admired range of Salento, mostly reds.

Antica Masseria del Sigillo, Guagnano (LE). Good Salice Salentino, Salento Primitivo, and red Terre del Guiscardo (Primitivo/Merlot/ Cabernet Sauvignon).

Calatrasi Puglia, Campi Salentina (LE). The Sicilian Calatrasi company's venture into Puglia has produced an enviable range of varietals, Aglianico, Chardonnay, Negroamaro, Primitivo, Sangiovese under the Allora line, and the single-estate Morella (Sangiovese/Negroamaro).

Michele Calò & Figli, Tuglie (LE). Admired Alezio Rosso and, especially, *rosato*; Salento Bianco, and Rosso (Vigna Spano), Primitivo.

Francesco Candido, San Donaci (BR). Stylish Salice Salentino red, white, and fine, rare Aleatico; esteemed Cappello di Prete (Negroamaro), Duca d'Aragona (Negroamaro/ Montepulciano), and Immensum (Negroamaro/Cabernet Sauvignon), white Casina Cucci (Chardonnay) and Vigna Vinera (Sauvignon), and sweet Paule Calle (Chardonnay/Malvasia).

Cantele, Lecce (LE). Well-honed range of Salice Salentino, Salento Rosso, Bianco, Primitivo, Chardonnay, and Amativo (Primitovo/Negroamaro).

Cantina Cooperativa Botromagno, Gravina di Puglia (BA). Range led by admirable Gravina; IGT Primitivo Pier delle Vigne (Aglianico/Montepulciano), white Gravisano (Malvasia).

Cantine Due Palme, Cellino San Marco (BR). Go-ahead co-op with very good Squinzano, Salice Salentino, Salento red, and Primitivo.

Castel di Salve, Tricase (LE). Emerging estate with Priante (Negroamaro/ Montepulciano), Lama del Tenente (Primitivo, Montalcino, Malvasia), Il Volo di Alessandro (Sangiovese), Armecolo (Negroamaro/Malvasia), and other Salento IGTs.

Leone De Castris, Salice Salentino (LE). Huge family house distinguished by Salice Salentino Rosso (Donna Lisa Riserva, Majana); Salento Bianco (case alte, Messapia), and Primitivo. Also red IGT Messere Andrea (Negropamaro/Cabernet Sauvignon) and Legendary Five Roses, one of Italy's first bottled rosés.

Conte Spagnoletti Zeuli, Andria (BA). Emerging Castel del Monte estate led by Riserva Terranera.

Conti Zecca, Leverano (LE). Large family estate makes ranges of Leverano (led by red *riserva* Terra Saraceno line), Salice Salentino (*riserva* Cantalupi), Salento (Primitivo, high-rated Nero, Donna Marzia line).

Niccolò Coppola, Alezio (LE). Alezio from San Nicolà Li Cuti vineyards.

Cosimo Taurino, Guagnano (LE). Acclaimed, long-living, late-harvested Brindisi Patriglione; excellent Salento Notarpanaro; good Salice Salentino, white I Siern, nad others.

CS di Copertino, Copertino (LE). Huge cellars make textbook Copertino; good Salento Bianco Roasato.

CS Cooperativa Locorotondo, Locorotondo (BA). Huge range but what counts is Locorotondo, including select Talinajo, and *spumante* mc.

Felline, Mandura (TA). Rich, powerful trend-setting Primitivo di Manduria also prized IGT Vigna del Feudo (Primitivo/Malvasia Nera/Oltavianello), Salento Rosso Albarello (Primitivo/Negroamaro).

Marco Maci, Cellino San Marco (BR). Large winery with huge range led by IGT Sire (Negroamaro), Bella

Mojgan (Negroamaro/Malvasia), Dragonero (Merlot/Negroamaro).

Masseria Monaci, Copertino (LE). Excellent IGT Le Braci (Negroamaro) leads stylish Copertino (Eloquenzia); Salento Primitivo (I Censi) and Rosso (Simposia).

Fratelli Nugnes, Trani (BA). Good, if rustic, Moscato di Trani.

Pervini, Manduria (TA). Leading Primitivo di Manduria (Archidamo, Primo Amore). Also good range of Salento and IGT Moscato.

Rivera, Andria (BA). Long-time leading winery with range of Castel del Monte Rosso (Rupicolo, Puer Apuliae), *rosso riserva* (legendary Il Falcone), *rosato* (Rosé di Rivera), *bianco* (Fedora), and varietals from the Terre al Monte estate: Aglianico, Chardonnay, Pinot Bianco, and Sauvignon; also Moscato di Trani (Piani di Tufara).

Rosa del Golfo, Alezio (LE). The late Mino Calò was known as Italy's Prince of Rosa, as creator of the acclaimed pink del Golfo, bright cherry-pink with a flowery scent and dry, harmonious, exquisite flavour. His family continues with that and other IGT Salento: Primitivo; red Quarantale, Portulano, Scaliere; white Bolina.

Santa Lucia, Corato (BA). Reliable Castel del Monte.

Soloperto, Manduria (TA). Excellent range of traditional-style Primitivo di Manduria.

D'Alfonso del Sordo, San Severo (FG). Highly reputed northerly estate with fine San Severo and IGT varietals from Bombino Bianco, Uva di Troia, Merlot, and Cabernet Sauvignon.

Tenute Rubino, Brindisi. Superb Salento white, red (both Marmorelle), and Primitivo. Good Brindisi Rosso (Jaddico).

Tormaresca, San Pietro Vernotico (BR). The wines emerging from Tuscan giant Antonori's investment in Puglia show the expected class and refinement. Masseria Maime (Negroamaro), Castel del Monte Rosso (Bocca di Lupo), and Chardonnay (Pietrabianca), Tormaresca Rosso (Aglianico/Merlot/Cabernet Sauvignon), and Chardonnay are all impeccable.

Torre Quarto, Cerignola (FG). Revived long-standing estate with Uva di Troia-based reds, Primitivo, and others.

Torrevento, Corato (BA). Large, improving winery for Castel del Monte and others.

Valle dell'Asso, Galatina (LE). Simple but attractive range of Galatina.

Vigne & Vini, Leporano (TA). Emerging Primitivo di Manduria of style.

Vinicola Miali, Martina Franca (TA). Produces reliable Castel del Monte.

Vinicola Savese, Sava (TA). Good Primitivo di Manduria especially Tradizione del Nonno.

Wine & Food

Balance seems built into the Puglian diet, probably because the region, if not perennially rich, has certainly never lacked for nutritive elements. The northern plains provide grain for pasta and bread; the plateaux lamb, sausages, and cheese; the Adriatic and Ionian seas plentiful fish. Everywhere there are vegetables, herbs, fruit, olive oil (Puglia produces more than any other region), and wine. Some dishes date to the Greeks, though other historical influences can be tasted as well. Vegetarians could thrive here on the abundance of fresh produce. Meat, mainly lamb, is used sparingly, but the Mediterranean provides a gamut of seafood.

Wines to accompany each dish are suggested below in italic.

Agnello al cartoccio Lamb chops baked in paper with green olives and *lampasciuoli,* a wild, bitter-tasting bulb similar to onion. *Castel del Monte Rosso*
Burrata Soft, buttery cheese from the town of Andria. *Rosso Barletta*
Cavatieddi con la ruca Conch-shaped pasta served with *ruca* (rue), tomato sauce, and grated Pecorino. *Salento Rosato*
Cozze alla leccese Mussels cooked with oil, lemon, and parsley, one of dozens of ways of preparing this favourite shellfish. *Martina Franca*
Frisedde Hard rolls softened with water and served with fresh tomato, oregano, and olive oil. *Five Roses*
Gniumerieddi Lamb innards flavoured with Pecorino, lard,

lemon, and parsley, rolled, skewered, and cooked over coals. *Primitivo di Manduria*
'Ncapriata Dried fava beans boiled, peeled, and mashed with chicory, pimento, onion, tomato, and lots of olive oil. *Rosa del Golfo*
Orecchiette con cime di rapa Small, ear-shaped pasta served with boiled turnip greens and chilli. *Brindisi Rosato*
Ostriche alla tarantina Fresh oysters cooked with oil, parsley, and breadcrumbs. *Locorotondo*
Tiella Versatile baked layer concoction, always containing potatoes, usually rice, and vegetables, with meat, cheese or seafood, originally a Spanish dish. *Castel del Monte Rosato*

Restaurants

Recommended in or near wine zones:
North *Antica Cucina* at Barletta; *Il Ventaglio* at Foggia.
Centre *Il Poeta Contadino* at Alberobello; *Del Corso* at Altamura; *Jardin* at Castellana Grotte; *Il Fagiano* at Fasano; *Van*

Westerhout at Mola di Bari; *Bufi* at Molfetta; *Il Melograno* at Monopoli; *Torrente Antico* at Trani. *Vecchia Canosa* at Canosa.
South *Già Sotto l'Arco* at Carovigno; *Al Fornello-Da Ricci* at Ceglie Messapico; *Marechiaro* at Gallipoli; *Cucina Casareccia* at Lecce.

Campania *Campania*

The ancients knew that vines thrived as nowhere else in the volcanic soil of Campania. The Greeks introduced vines now known as Aglianico, Falanghina, and Greco; the Romans celebrated the wines of Falernum and the Campi Flegrei, Vesuvius, and Avellino. Wines of the Kingdom of Naples were raved about by chroniclers from the Renaissance to the Risorgimento. But in modern times viticulture had declined in a region that not only produced much less wine than its generous natural conditions permit but, worse, had been lagging behind the rest of Italy in terms of quality.

Then, suddenly, in a span of a few years, Campania has come bounding back with a new generation of winemakers who have grasped that it is pointless to expound on their unparalleled viticultural heritage without investing in the techniques and expertise that will bring wines stylish enough to reflect positively on the wisdom of the ancients. No longer is production of the premium wines of Campania confined to the single winery, Mastroberardino (now, in any event, split into two). Falernian has re-emerged with great class as Falerno, Vesuvius has regained respectability, and ancient lustre has been restored to the wines of Avellino with its trio of Taurasi, Fiano di Avellino, and Greco di Tufo all elevated to DOCG, the former the first wine of the south to be so distinguished. Wines from the Campi Flegrei, the Amalfi coast, the Sorrento Peninsula, the islands of Capri and Ischia, and even the more remote southern Cilento uplands are steadily rebuilding fine reputations, happily often based on traditional local varieties, to match the natural beauty of their terrains. All these areas are DOC, the region boasts nineteen in all and a further eight IGTs, of which Irpinia, the ancient name for the Avellino area, is most prevalent.

Visiting wine-lovers, who should enjoy Ischia in the off-season, might also be intrigued by the vineyards around Avellino and Benevento. Wine shops include the Enoteca Partenopea at Fuorigrotta near Naples and *Enoteca La Botte* at Caserta.

Recent Vintages

Among Campania's wines, Taurasi is the best known for longevity, though reds from Solopaca, Taburna, and Falerno del Massico also age well, as do white Fiano d'Avellino and Greco di Tufo. Recommended vintages for ageing are listed with each entry.

Wines

AGLIANICO DEL TABURNO
DOC r (p) dr ☆☆→☆☆☆ *95 96 97 98 99 00 01 02*
The Aglianico variety that grows across the slopes of Taburno near Benevento is made into admirable red and pink wines by a growing number of producers. (*See also* Taburno.) Age: 2 yrs, *riserva* 3 yrs.

AVERSA
DOC w dr (sp) ☆→☆☆☆ *DYA*
From the local Asprinio or Asprino grapes grown on high trellises around Aversa, north of Naples, this fragile, spritzy, lemon-yellow wine was traditionally served over the counter as a Neapolitan thirst-quencher. A recent comeback has revived production.

CAMPI FLEGREI *DOC*
This zone extends west from Naples across the gulf on volcanic soils in the communes of Pozzuoli, Bacoli, Quarto, and Marano and out onto the island of Procida. Its wines were renowned in antiquity and, after a long period of obscurity, are now enjoying a revival.

Bianco *w dr* ☆→☆☆ *DYA* From Falanghina with Biancolella and/or Coda di Volpe, this can be smooth, crisp, and tasty.

Rosso *r dr* ☆→☆☆ *99 00 01 02* From Piedirosso with Aglianico and/or Sciascinoso, and optionally others, this is pleasantly rounded and full; also *novello*.

Falanghina *w dr (sp)* ☆☆ *00 01 02* Can be full, crisp, and smooth.

Piedirosso or Per'e Palummo *r dr (s/sw) (sw)* ☆☆ *98 99 00 01 02* Typical red grape of the Gulf of Naples gives a ripe, rounded, dry red after 2 or 3 years but shows less promise as *dolce* or *passito* from semi-dried grapes. Age: *riserva* 2 yrs.

CAPRI *DOC*
The fabled isle's rocky soils can produce wines of class. But most are made to refresh its waves of tourists and rarely hit peaks.

Bianco *w dr* ☆→☆☆ *DYA* From the characterful Falanghina and Greco, this forms the bulk of Capri's output.

Rosso *r dr* ☆→☆☆ *99 00 01 02* From Piedirosso.

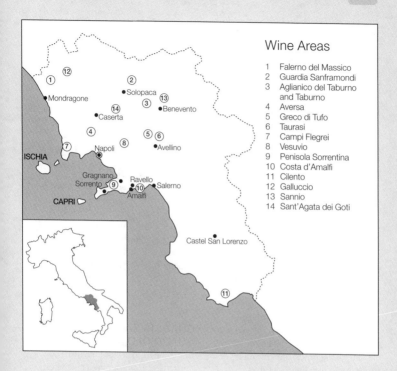

Wine Areas

1 Falerno del Massico
2 Guardia Sanframondi
3 Aglianico del Taburno and Taburno
4 Aversa
5 Greco di Tufo
6 Taurasi
7 Campi Flegrei
8 Vesuvio
9 Penisola Sorrentina
10 Costa d'Amalfi
11 Cilento
12 Galluccio
13 Sannio
14 Sant'Agata dei Goti

CASTEL SAN LORENZO *DOC*

Small zone in rugged hills around the town in southern Campania makes 5 types of wine rarely seen outside the area.

Bianco *w dr ☆ DYA* From the uninspiring Trebbiano and Malvasia.

Rosato *p dr ☆ DYA* From Barbera with Sangiovese.

Rosso *r dr ☆ 00 01 02* From Barbera with Sangiovese.

Barbera *r dr ☆→☆☆ 99 00 01 02* The variety makes hearty reds here. Age: *riserva* 2yrs.

Moscato *w sw sp ☆ DYA* Moscato Bianco makes still or sparkling wines that may be called *lambiccato* in sweetest version.

CILENTO *DOC*

The Cilento, the large hilly area along Campania's southern coast, was long considered the region's backwater, although of great potential. Now, at last, some highly interesting wines are starting to emerge. An area to watch.

Bianco *w dr ☆→☆☆ DYA* From Fiano with Trebbiano and/or Greco Bianco, and Malvasia.

Rosato *p dr ☆ DYA* Mainly from Sangiovese, Aglianico, and Primitivo, and/or Piedirosso: an intriguing formula.

Rosso *r dr ☆☆ 99 00 01 02* From Aglianico, with Barbera and Piedirosso, and/or Primitivo.

Aglianico *r dr ☆☆ 97 98 99 00 01 02* Most promising of the 4 types; of individual style. Age: 1 yr.

COSTA D'AMALFI *DOC*

This must be one of the world's most beautiful vineyard areas following the Amalfi coast past Furore, Ravello, and Tramonti, whose names may be mentioned as sub-zones. Its terraced vineyards are to steep to permit high yields, but what there is, is often thoroughly enjoyable, especially when sipped with a view.

Bianco *w dr* ☆→☆☆ *DYA* Falanghina and Biancolella make a fresh wine of some character.

Rosato *p dr* ☆→☆☆ *DYA* Piedirosso with Sciascinoso and/or Aglianico is burnished pink, clean, and easy.

Rosso *r dr* ☆→☆☆☆ *98 99 00* From the same grapes as *rosato*, this can be round and balanced, and capable of gaining style with age. Age: *riserva* 2 yrs from Furore, Ravello, or Tramonti.

FALERNO DEL MASSICO *DOC*

The zone is in Campania's northwest, where the ancient Roman *grand cru* of Falernian originated – extending from the Tyrrhenian coast at Mondragone onto the slopes of the Massico massif which can yield excellent quality. The red and white are from varieties known in Roman times, but Primitivo is a modern afterthought.

Bianco *w dr* ☆☆→☆☆☆ *00 01 02* From Falanghina alone, this is lightly floral with a firm backbone.

Rosso *r dr* ☆☆→☆☆☆ *93 94 95 96 97 98 99 00 01 02* From Aglianico with Piedirosso and, optionally, a bit of Primitivo, and/or Barbera, this can show class. Full in body and colour, its rich bouquet and flavour broaden with 4 to 6 years or more. Age: 1 yr, *riserva* 2 yrs.

Primitivo *r dr* ☆→☆☆ *97 98 99 00 01 02* Big wines, though lacking finesse. Age: 1 yr, *riserva* or *vecchio* 2 yrs.

FIANO DI AVELLINO

DOCG w dr ☆☆→☆☆☆ *00 01 02* Fiano is at its most enticing grown in hills around Avellino. Hints of pear and spices in its delicate aroma lead to toasted hazelnuts in its lingering flavour. The wine can sometimes age well for 3 to 6 years or more, gaining depth and complexity, though most producers aim for fresher, fruitier wines for earlier consumption. Labels may mention the Roman

name "Apianum" – in reference to its attraction to *api* (bees).

GALLUCCIO *DOC*

The town of Galluccio gives its name to wines so far rarely seen, though styles are not dissimilar from neighbouring Falerno del Massico. The *bianco* is based on Falanghina and the *rosso* and *rosato* on Aglianico. Age: red 1yr, *riserva* 2 yrs.

GRECO DI TUFO

DOCG w dr (sp) ☆→☆☆☆ *00 01 02* Greco, when produced in central Campania, north of Avellino, can give clear sensations of fruit and a crisp flavour that hints of toasted almonds. It is usually most impressive inside 2 to 3 years as a refreshing accompaniment to fish. On rare occasions, a *spumante* version may be seen locally.

GUARDIA SANFRAMONDI OR GUARDIOLO *DOC*

Wine from around the town of Guardia Sanframondi northwest of Benevento is appreciated locally.

Bianco *w dr* ☆→☆☆ *DYA* Malvasia with Falanghina makes soft, round white.

Rosato *p dr* ☆→☆☆ *DYA* Sangiovese is the base.

Rosso *r dr* ☆→☆☆ *99 00 01 02* Sangiovese makes a hearty red. May be *novello*. Age: *riserva 2 yrs.*

Aglianico *r dr* ☆→☆☆ *99 00 01 02* Full, firm red. Age: *riserva* 2 yrs.

Falanghina *w dr* ☆→☆☆ *DYA* This is promising.

Spumante *w dr sp* Falanghina is also the base of this purely local sparkling wine.

ISCHIA *DOC*

Unlike Capri, the wines of Ischia often rise above mere tourist hydration, although the steep, volcanic hills make cultivation a task requiring great dedication.

Bianco *w dr (sp)* ☆→☆☆ *DYA* From Forastera and Biancolella, this is a zesty, zippy white while the *superiore* has the strength and structure to stand up to substantial fish.

Rosso *r dr* ✩→✩✩ 99 00 01 02 From Guarnaccia and Piedirosso, this is soothingly tasty when young, sometimes gaining style after 2 to 4 years.

Biancolella *w dr* ✩✩→✩✩✩ 00 01 02 The variety is found almost exclusively on Ischia where it makes some of Campania's most promising whites. A pale, golden colour, it has a delicate fragrance but a fairly full flavour with character – usually drunk young, but sometimes aged for 2 to 3 years.

Forastera *w dr* ✩→✩✩ DYA Shows less class than Biancolella; but can be tasty.

Piedirosso or Per'e Palummo *r dr (sp) (sw)* ✩✩→✩✩✩ 00 01 02 Tasty red; rich, with berried fruit. Sweet *passito* versions less convincing.

LACRYMA CHRISTI
See Vesuvio DOC.

PENISOLA SORRENTINA *DOC*
The Sorrentine Peninsula hasn't much space for vineyards on its gorgeous plunging slopes overlooking the gulf of Naples but prominence is given to the historically important areas for viticulture, around Gragnano and Lettere, which are sub-zones, as is Sorrento.

Bianco *w dr* ✩ DYA Light white, from Falanghina, Biancolella, and Greco.

Rosso *r dr (fz)* ✩ DYA Light red, usually fizzy, from Piedirosso, Sciascinoso and Aglianico, may be called Rosso Sorrento when following rules of *bianco*.

Gragnano *r dr fz* ✩→✩✩ DYA The village of Gragnano was long noted for a rustically fizzy red that was popular in Naples and environs. Vineyards dwindled, but there are signs of a revival. Grapes are as for *rosso*.

Lettere *r dr fz* ✩→✩✩ DYA This village, set higher than Gragnano, made a fizzy red sometimes showing a bit more style than its neighbour's and is set to do so again.

Sorrento *w r dr fz* ✩→✩✩ DYA Lands towards the hip of the peninsula, east and west of Sorrento, form this sub-zone for non-fizzy red and white. A range of wines from the Sannio hills, around Benevento, which reflect sometimes peculiar winemaking styles. Most are simple and bubbly, and may be sweet (*passito*), but varietals can reach admirable levels.

Bianco *w dr fz (s/sw)* ✩ DYA Inconsequential, from Trebbiano.

Rosato *p dr (fz) (s/sw)* Pink based on Sangiovese.

Rosso *r dr (fz) (s/sw)* ✩→✩✩ 00 01 02 The Sangiovese grape makes tart but tasty red wines, also as *frizzante* and *novello*.

Spumante *w p dr (s/sw) sp* Aglianico, Greco, and Falanghina make base; by classic method.

Aglianico *r dr (sp) (s/sw)* ✩→✩✩ 00 01 02 This can be dignified.

Barbera *r dr (sp) (sw)* ✩ 00 01 02 Hearty red for everyday drinking.

Coda di Volpe *w dr (sp) (sw)* ✩ DYA Light and easy, bubbly or sweet.

Falanghina *w dr (sp) (sw)* ✩→✩✩✩ 01 02 The dry version can show class.

Fiano *w dr (sp)* ✩→✩✩ 01 02 Not particularly distinguished.

Greco *w dr (sp) (sw)* ✩→✩✩ 01 02 This can do well.

Moscato *w dr (sp) (sw)* ✩→✩✩ DYA Makes dry white, sometimes bubbly, appreciated locally.

Piedirosso *r dr (sp)* ✩→✩✩ 00 01 02 This firm red promises well.

Sciascinoso *r dr (sp) (sw)* The variety from Vesuvius is rare here.

SANT'AGATA DEI GOTI *DOC*
Wines from this area southeast of Caserta can evince a measure of prestige.

Bianco *w dr* ✩→✩✩ DYA Falanghina and Greco give a base of style.

Rosato *p dr* ✩ DYA Aglianico and Piedirosso make promising rosé.

Rosso *r dr* ✩→✩✩ 99 00 01 02 The same varieties as *rosato* combine in the red. Also *novello*.

Aglianico *r dr* ✩→✩✩✩ 95 96 97 98 99 00 01 02 Promising variety can show class. Age: 2 yrs, *riserva* 3 yrs.

Falanghina *w dr (sw)* ☆→☆☆ *DYA*
   Promising white. Also *passito*.
Greco *w dr* ☆→☆☆ *DYA* Tasty, though
   without the class of Greco di Tufo.
Piedirosso *r dr* ☆→☆☆ *95 96 97 98 99 00*
   01 Promising. Age: *riserva* 2 yrs.

SOLOPACA *DOC*
   The zone lies along the fertile
   Calore Valley west of Benevento.
   Though Trebbiano and Sangiovese
   shape the blends, some wines show
   enough style to have gained notice
   beyond Campania.
Bianco *w dr* ☆→☆☆ *DYA* From
   Trebbiano with Malvasia,
   Falanghina, and/or Coda de Volpe,
   can be smooth, round white.
Rosato *p dr* ☆ *DYA* Rosé from
   same varieties as *rosso*.
Rosso *r dr* ☆→☆☆☆ *98 99 00 01 02*
   Sangiovese with Aglianico and,
   optionally, Piedirosso, Sciascinoso,
   and others can show class and
   durability. Age: *superiore* 1 yr.
Aglianico *r dr* ☆→☆☆ *98 99 00* This
   shows promise. Age: 1 yr.
Falanghina *w dr* ☆→☆☆ *99 00 01 02*
   Starting to show style.
Spumante *w dr sp* Falanghina is the
   base of this sparkling wine.

TABURNO *DOC*
   Although Aglianico del Taburno
   remains a separate DOC, all the
   other styles made in this zone west
   of Beneveneto are grouped under
   the Taburno denomination.
Bianco *w dr* ☆ Trebbiano with
   Falanghina.
Rosso *r dr* ☆→☆☆ *00 01 02*
   Sangiovese with Aglianico;
   light red, sometimes tasty, also
   as *novello*.
Coda di Volpe *w dr* ☆→☆☆ *DYA* Can
   show singular character.
Falanghina *w dr* ☆→☆☆ *DYA* Wine
   made in greatest quantity and
   showing greatest promise in
   the zone.
Greco *w dr* ☆→☆☆ *DYA* Promising.
Piedirosso *r dr* Promising.
Spumante *w dr sp* Coda di Volpe and/or
   Falanghina make sparkling;
   consumed locally.

TAURASI
   DOCG r dr ☆☆→☆☆☆☆ *88 90 91 93*
   94 95 96 97 98 99 00
   The south's first DOCG wine comes
   from Aglianico grown in hills
   northeast of Avellino, centred in the
   village of Taurasi. Campania's most
   admired red is noted for long ageing
   due to the ample structure and
   tannins from late-ripening grapes.
   Youthful ruby turns mahogany
   with age as it develops remarkable
   depth of bouquet and flavour.
   Mastroberadino's 1968 Riserva is
   legendary, though some other
   versions are made for more
   immediate appeal. Other red
   varieties may be included at up to
   15%, but leading producers stick
   to pure Aglianico and age the wine
   in large casks before bottling it.
   Age: 3 yrs (1 in wood), *riserva* 4 yrs
   (1.5 in wood).

VESUVIO *DOC*
   Vines reached heights in the
   volcanic soil of Vesuvius even
   before cinders and dust buried
   Pompeii. But the fortunes of
   Vesuvio's wines have since been
   as capricious as the volcano's
   eruptions. Some, known as
   Lacryma Christi (Christ's Tear),
   became widely imitated, but
   usually as a loosely interpreted
   joke. Now the house has been put
   back in order. Vesuvio applies to
   basic white, rosé, and red, while
   Lacryma Christi del Vesuvio
   applies to superior versions of
   each, including sparkling types
   and a fortified version (*liquoroso*).
Bianco *w dr (sw) (sp)* ☆→☆☆ *DYA*
   From Verdeca and Coda di Volpe
   with Falanghina and Greco, this is
   usually a straightforward wine,
   though the Lacryma Christi
   version can be balanced and
   smooth. Lacryma Christi may
   also be *spumante* or *liquoroso*
   (fortified), although this latter
   type is rarely seen nowadays.
Rosato *p dr (sp)* ☆ *DYA* Piedirosso,
   Sciascinoso, and others,
   usually simple.

Rosso *w dr (sp)* ☆→✶☆☆ *99 00 01 02*
  Same grapes as *rosato*, this
  can be pleasantly tasty or fairly
  supple and round as Lacryma
  Christi, which may be *spumante*
  (not recommended).

Producers

Provinces: Avellino (AV), Benevento
  (BN), Caserta (CE), Napoli (NA),
  Salerno (SA).

D'Ambra Vini d'Ischia, Forio d'Ischia
  (NA). Inspiring wines, led by
  Ischia, Biancolella (Tenuta
  Frassitelli), *rosso* (Riserva Mario
  d'Ambra), and the weird Kyme
  from varieties from Greek Khalkis.

Antica Masseria Venditti, Castelvenere
  (BN). Organic estate with finely
  crafted ranges of Sannio and
  Solopaca, containing little-known
  local varieties such as Olivella,
  Crieco, and Ceretto, and local
  clones of the more common ones.

Antonio Caggiano, Taurasi (AV).
  Excellent Taurasi (Macchia dei
  Goti), good Fiano di Avellino, and
  Aglianico and Greco/Fiano blends
  from IGT Irpina.

Cantina del Taburno, Foglianise (BN).
  Go-ahead co-op with fine
  Aglianico del Taburno, Taburno
  Coda di Volpe, Falanghina, Greco,
  and acclaimed IGT Beneventano
  Bue Apis and Delius (both
  Aglianico).

Cantine Caputo, Carinaro (CE). Huge
  winery producing most of
  Campania's DOCs.

De Conciliis, Prignano Cilento
  (SA). Finely honed, stylish IGT
  reds Naima, Donnaluna (both
  Aglianico), and white Donnaluna,
  Traccia (both Fiano).

Benito Ferrara, Tufo (AV). Finely
  crafted Greco di Tufo (Cicogna).

Feudi di San Gregorio, Sorbo
  Serpico (AV). Dynamic estate
  with exceptional Taurasi,
  Pianodi Montevergine Selve di
  Luoti, and DOC Fiano di Avellino
  (Pietracalda), and Greco di Tufo
  (Cutizzi) and IGTs Campanaro
  (Fiano), Serpico (Aglianico), and
  Patrimo (Merlot). Styles tend to
  be international though.

Fontannavecchia, Torrecuso (BN).
  Notable Aglianico del Taburno
  (Vigna Cataratte) and *rosato*,
  Taburno Falanghina, IGT Orazio
  (Aglianico/Cabernet).

De Lucia, Guardia Sanframondi (BN).
  Leading estate in Sannio,
  especially for Sannio Aglianico,
  Falanghina.

Di Meo, Salza Irpina (AV). Large estate
  with sound Taurasi, Greco di Tufo,
  Fiano di Avellino, Sannio
  Falanghina, and IGT Coda di Volpe.

Galardi, Sessa Aurunca (CE). Just one
  wine, Terre di Lavoro (Aglianico/
  Piedirosso), but with almost
  cult status.

Gran Furor, Furore (SA). Leader in
  DOC Costa d'Amalfi with fine
  bianco and *rosso* from sub-zones
  Furore and Ravello, including
  white Furore Fior d'Uva from the
  local Fenile and Cinestra varieties.

Grotta del Sole, Quarto (NA). Large
  but well-made range led by
  Penisola Sorrentina Gragnano and
  Lettere. Also Campi Flegrei
  varietals, Ibis Quarto di Sole
  (Piedirosso/Aglianico), Quarto di
  Luna (Falanghina/Capretonne), and
  the irrepressible Aspriniodi Aversa.

Luigi Maffini, Castellabate (SA).
  Rising star in the Cilento area.
  IGT Cenito (Aglianico/Piedirosso),
  Kléos (Aglianico/Piedirosso/
  Sangiovese), and Kràtos (Fiano)
  are all of great style.

Mastroberardino, Atripalda (AV). Carlo
  and Pietro make Campania classics
  Taurasi (Radici), Fiano d'Avellino
  (Radici, More Maiorum), Greco di
  Tufo (Novaserra), plus Vesuvio
  Lacryma Christi Irpina Naturalis
  Historia (Aglianico/Piedirosso),
  and more.

Michele Moio, Mondragone (CE).
  Reputation gained with that
  oddity, Falerno del Massico
  Primitivo.

Mollettieri, Montemarano (AV). Impressive Taurasi (Vigna Cinque Querce) and Irpina Aglianico.

Montevetrano, San Cipriano Picentino (SA). Just one wine, the acclaimed IGT Montevetrano (Cabernet/Merlot/Aglianico) from this estate .

Mustilli, Sant'Agata dei Goti (BN). Admirable Sant'Agata dei Goti, *rosso* (Conte Artus), Falanghina, Greco (Fontanella, Primicerio), Aglianico (Cesco di Nece), Piedirosso.

Ocone, Ponte (BN). Respected organic estate with Aglianico del Taburno (Diomede), Taburno Piedirosso, Falanghina, Greco, and Coda di Volpe; *crus* Pezza la Corte (Aglianico) and Vigne del Monaco (Falanghina), and Calidonio (Piedirosso/Aglianico).

Pietratorcia, Forio d'Ischia (NA). Excellent wines of distinct personality: Bianco Superiore (Chignole, Cuotto); *rosso* (Ianno Piro), and others.

La Rivolta, Beneveneto. Rising star with Aglianico del Taburno, Taburno Falanghina, Coda del Volpe, and Piedirosso; white IGT (Falanghina/Fiano/Greco).

Giovanni Struzziero, Venticano (AV). Fine Greco di Tufa (Villa Giulia, Vigna delle Brecce), Fiano di Avellino and Taurasi (Campoceraso) are better known abroad than in Italy.

Telaro, Galluccio (CE). Prime movers in little-known Galluccio zone with good Aglianico, Fiano, Greco, and others (far better than their overdesigned web site).

Terredora, Montefusco (AV). Walter Mastroberardino's estate produces stylish Taurasi (Campore, Fatica Contadina), Fiano di Avellino (Campore, Terre di Dora), Greco di Tufo (Loggia della Serra, Terre degli Angeli), and a good range of IGTs from Aglianico, Falanghina, Coda di Volpe, and others (including a Fiano *passito*).

Vadiaperti, Montefredane (AV). Variable but interesting Fiano di Avellino, Greco di Tufo.

Vestini Campagnano, Caiazzo (CE). Emergent high-quality estate working with the almost extinct red and white Pallagrello and red Casavecchia varieties – to great effect.

Villa Matilde, Cellole (CE). Classy, refined Falerno del Massico Bianco (Vigna Caracci) and impeccable *rosso* (Vigna Camarato), Cecubo (Abbuoto/Piedirosso), delightful *rosato* (Terre Cerase), and more from this leading estate.

Villa Raiano, Serino (AV). New, promising Avellino estate.

Vinicola del Sannio, Castelvenere (BN). Sound Sannio varietals.

Wine & Food

It is hard to imagine that Naples was once a gastronomic capital – under the Romans and again under various monarchs between the late Middle Ages and Italy's unification. Nowadays culinary improvisations perfume the alleyways of Naples: pizza baking in wood-fired ovens; onions, garlic, and herbs stewing with tomatoes for *pommarola* sauce; pastries frying in hot oil; steaming espresso; and fresh fish. That many of Campania's specialities can be eaten standing up should not detract from their inherent worth.

Wines to accompany each dish are suggested below in italic.

Capretto in agrodolce Sweet-sour kid, a speciality of Irpinia. Lamb is also prepared this way. *Taurasi*

Cianfotta Peppers, onions, tomatoes, aubergines, and courgettes stewed in oil and eaten cold. *Costa d'Amalfi Rosato*

Mozzarella in carozza Mozzarella sandwiches coated with batter and deep-fried in olive oil. *Greco di Tufo*

'Mpepata di cozze Mussels served in their shells with lemon, parsley, and pepper. *Ischia Bianco*

Parmigiana di melanzane
Local classic: aubergine baked
with tomato sauce, mozzarella,
and Parmigiano cheese. *Fiano
di Avellino*
Pizza napoletana Marinara:
tomatoes, oregano, and fresh basil;
Margherita: mozzarella and grated
Pecorino. *Asprinio di Aversa*
Spaghetti alla puttanesca
"Strumpet's spaghetti", dressed
with tomato, pepper, capers, olives,
and anchovies, a speciality of
Ischia. *Ischia Biancolella*

Restaurants

Recommended in or near
wine zones:
**Amalfi-Sorrento-Sorrento-
Vesuvio** *La Caravella* and *Da
Gemma* at Amalfi; *La Capannina*
at Capri; *Quattro Passi* and *Taverna
del Capitano* at Marina del
Cantone; *Il Principe* at Pompeii;
Don Alfonso 1890 at Sant'Agata sui
Due Golfi; *Zi'ntonio* at Sorrento.

Avellino-Benevento *Antica
Trattoria Martella* at Avellino;
Minicuccio and *Oasis* at Vallesacarda.
Aversa-Falerno del Massico
Stalla-Caveja at Pietravairano; *Ninfeo*
at Santa Maria Capua Vetere.
Campi Flegrei-Ischia *La
Misenetta* at Bacoli; *Il Focolare*
at Casamicciola (Ischia); *Melograno*
at Forio d'Ischia.

Basilicata *Basilicata*

Basilicata lacks nearly every attribute that could bring it some sorely needed
attention. It has no major monuments to its Greek and Roman past – only two
meagre strips of seacoast – pleasant but hardly spectacular upland scenery,
and scarcely a restaurant of renown. That the region until very recently had
only one DOC, Aglianico del Vulture, and two IGTs, Basilicata and Grottino
di Roccanova, would seem to fit the pattern of deprivation. But Aglianico del
Vulture is one thing about Basilicata that is not innately underprivileged. Had
the fates been a little kinder, it might be universally recognized for what it is –
one of Italy's finest red wines.

Aglianico was brought to Basilicata in the sixth or seventh century BC
by the Greeks, who account for its name, a corruption of Hellenico. The few
other varieties of note include Malvasia and Moscato, also grown around
Monte Vulture, usually for sweet wine.

Basilicata is hardly a tourist paradise, but the ancient city of Matera has
antique charm, and wine-lovers seeking out-of-the-way places will find them
on Monte Vulture near the Naples-Bari *autostrada*.

Recent Vintages

Aglianico del Vulture has had fine recent harvests, notably 2001, 2000, 1999,1998,
1997, 1996, 1994, and 1993, following the excellent harvests of 1990, 1988, and
1985. Some good wines were also made in 2002, 1995, 1992, 1991, 1987, and 1986.
Earlier notable vintages for Aglianico were 82, 81, 79, 77, 75, and 73.

Wines

AGLIANICO DEL VULTURE
DOC r dr (sp) ☆☆→★☆☆☆ *88 90 93 94*
97 98 99 00 01 02
From Aglianico grapes grown
on the eastern slopes of Monte
Vulture and hills to the southeast
past Venosa and Genzano. Though
it may be sold after a year as a dry,

or occasionally an off-dry, wine or even as *spumante*, it is the aged Aglianico that stands in the front rank of southern Italian wines. Its colour is deep ruby to garnet, taking on orange reflections with age in barrel and bottle; its bouquet heightens as it becomes richly smooth with an unusual firmness and depth of flavours. The better grapes come from volcanic soil high up around Rionero and Barile where microclimates are similar to those in northern regions, and where *riservas* can approach ✩✩✩✩ levels. Age: 1 yr, *vecchio* 3 yrs (2 in wood), *riserva* 5 yrs (2 in wood).

ASPRINIO

Curiously acidic little white from Asprinio or Asprino grapes grown around the town of Ruoti. Most is sent with haste to Naples.

MALVASIA

White Malvasia is a speciality of the Val Bradano, though it seems to have more aroma and flavour in the *amabile* sparkling wines of the Vulture area.

MOSCATO

Sweet, usually bubbly Moscato is a speciality of Vulture, where some producers make sparkling wines with aroma as pronounced as in Asti Spumante, though with less finesse.

TERRE DELL'ALTA VAL D'AGRI
DOC

It took until summer 2003 for Basilicata to gain its second DOC, for red and rosé wines produced across a small part of the Agri valley in the south of the region, in the communities of Viggiano, Grumento Nova, and Moliterno. The *rosso* comes from at least 50% Merlot with Cabernet Sauvignon and, optionally, others. The *rosato* is similar except that some Malvasia, at least 10%, must be included.

Producers

Provinces: Matera (MT), Potenza (PZ).

D'Angelo, Rionero in Vulture (PZ). Benchmark estate for Aglianico DOC, including fine Vigna Caselle, though IGT Canneto, aged in small, oak barrels to take on added shadings of bouquet and flavour, wins most plaudits. Also an admirable IGT white from Chardonnay, Pinot Bianco, and Incrocio Manzoni, from the Vigna dei Pini estate.

Agricola Eubea-Famiglia Sasso, Admirable Aglianico (Brigante, Il Viola) and IGT Seduzione (Malvasia/Moscato/Aglianico).

Basilisco, Rionero in Vulture (PZ). Just one DOC Aglianico, highly admired.

Basilium, Acerenza (PZ). Reliably good range of Aglianico styles.

Cantina del Notaio, Rionero in Vulture (PZ). Fine range of DOC Aglianico led by acclaimed La Firma.

Cantina di Venosa, Venosa (PZ). Four types of Aglianico DOC, a red and a rosé IGT, dry and sweet Moscato, and dry Malvasia, all of good style, from this relaible co-op.

Carbone, Melfi (PZ). Decent Aglianico DOC; vdt Montelapis (Chardonnay).

Consorzio Viticoltori Associati del Vulture, Barile (PZ). Group of co-ops makes good Aglianico (Carpe Diem, Vetusto) and sparkling Moscato.

Armando Martino, Rionero in Vulture (PZ). Reliable Aglianico in numerous styes.

Di Palma, Rionero in Vulture (PZ). Highly promising Aglianico newcomer.

Paternoster, Barile (PZ). Superb DOC Aglianico (Rotondo, Synthesi, Don Anselmo) leads the way in Vulture. Also IGT Clivus (Moscato), Bianco di Cirte (Fiano).

Progetto DiVino, Matera. Makes unusual but stylish Aglianico/Merlot blend San Biagio.
Tenuta del Portale, Barile (PZ). Emerging Aglianico estate.
Tenuta Le Querce, Barile (PZ).

Impressive range of DOC Aglianico led by Vigna della Corona.
Terre degli Svevi, Venosa (PZ). Gruppo Italiano Vini-owned estate with excellent DOC Aglianico (Re Manfredi).

Wine & Food

The cooking of Basilicata may be as spare as the landscape, but it has a warmth that comes directly from the summer sun. Appetites are satisfied with ample servings of beans, pasta, soups, potatoes, and bread. Vegetables play a key role in stews cooked with olive oil and plenty of herbs and spices. Pimento (known as *diavolicchio*) goes into a sauce called *piccante*, fiery enough to live up to its name and more. In the old days, meat was used thriftily in, for example, preserved pork products: *soppressata, coppa,* or the piquant *luganighe* sausages.

Wines to accompany each dish are suggested below in italic.

Cazmarr Stew of lamb's innards, prosciutto, cheese, and wine. *Aglianico del Vulture* (young)
Ciammotta Peppers, potatoes, aubergine, tomato, and garlic – first fried, then stewed. *Malvasia secco*
Lasagne e fagioli Lasagne and beans laced with pepper and garlic. *Aglianico spumante*
Minuich Handmade pasta rolled into cylinders around a slim metal stick, sometimes served with cabbage greens. *Vigna dei Pini*
Pignata Lamb marinated with vegetables, hot peppers, cheese, and wine in a sealed earthenware pot (*la pignata*) and left to simmer on the hearth for hours. *Aglianico del Vulture Riserva*

Restaurants

Recommended in the region: *Venusio* at Matera;

Vaddone at Melfi; *La Pergola* at Rionero.

Calabria *Calabria*

Once a garden of the Greeks, who favoured its wines over others of Enotria, Calabria too often neglects its antique vinicultural splendour. Still, there are ever more signs of progress in this ruggedly handsome land. The family winery of Librandi excels in Cirò, while building production in a way that gives other winemakers a model to follow. Prominent on a smaller scale are Fattoria San Francesco with Cirò, Odoardi with Savuto, and Scavigna DOC and Cantine Lento in Lamezia DOC.

Calabrian athletes returning in triumph from an early Olympiad were hailed with Krimisa, if not the "world's oldest wine", probably among the earliest in Europe. Krimisa was made where Cirò is made today, on the Ionian coast. Cirò is the paragon of Calabrian wines, the only well-known name among the twelve DOCs. Its red and rosé derive from Gaglioppo, as do most Calabrian reds, but the others, if flavourful, rarely show the breed of the classic Cirò. White Cirò comes from the Greco variety, a lively relic whose sub-varieties are capable of making both bright, modern dry whites and luxuriant, old-style dessert wines. Calabria's red production is

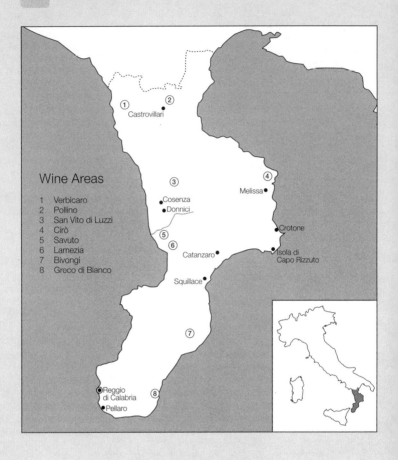

Wine Areas

1 Verbicaro
2 Pollino
3 San Vito di Luzzi
4 Cirò
5 Savuto
6 Lamezia
7 Bivongi
8 Greco di Bianco

dominated by Gaglioppo, a variety that shines with careful handling – but otherwise can be lacklustre. There are thirteen IGTs, including the region-wide Calabria.

The toe of the Italian boot is largely mountainous and its tourist attractions are mostly natural. The Sila Massif (Italy's "Little Switzerland") dominates the north around Cosenza and Catanzaro (the region's capital). The Aspromonte range dominates the south, overlooking Reggio Calabria and, across the straits, Sicily's Mount Etna. Remnants of the Greeks are evident along the coasts, the most scenic of which is the Calabrian Riviera between Reggio and Gioia Tauro. Wine tourism hasn't been developed, though there are innumerable inviting beaches and charming ancient towns nestled into the arid hills. A deft choice of wines from Calabria and other regions may be found at the *Enoteca Marino* at Crotone.

Recent Vintages

Among Calabrian reds Cirò and Savuto are best suited to ageing. Vintages from 1993 to 1998 were rated as very good to excellent, as was 1990, with 1992 and 1991 not far behind.

Wines

BIVONGI *DOC*

Small area sloping down towards the Ionian coast from the heights of Mount Consolino. Most consumption remains local.

Bianco *w dr* ☆→☆☆ *DYA* The broad range Greco Bianco, Montonico, and/or the local Guardavalle alongside Ansonica, and/or Malvasia Bianca allows for whites of variable style.

Rosato *p dr* ☆→☆☆ *DYA* From Gaglioppo, Greco Nero, Sicily's Nero d'Avola, and others, this is fairly substantial.

Rosso *r dr* ☆→☆☆ *99 00 01 02* Based on the same grapes as the *rosato*, can be *novello* or, aged 2 yrs, *riserva*.

CERASUOLO DI SCILLA

Cherry-pink IGT wine (Scilla is the legendary Scylla at the top of the Straits of Messina), is made from various grapes including Alicante.

CIRO *DOC*

Slopes along the Ionian coast around the hill village of Cirò and the beach town of Cirò Marina form the *classico* heartland of a zone of ancient renown for red wine and more modern regard for rosé and white. Calabria's best-known and most esteemed wine.

Bianco *w dr* ☆→☆☆ *DYA* The worthy Greco Bianco variety, gives wines of subtle floral aromas and ripe-fruit flavours that can be persuasive.

Rosato *p dr* ☆→☆☆ *DYA* From Gaglioppo, this can show a bright colour and fresh flavour, best drunk young.

Rosso *r dr* ☆→☆☆ *97 98 99 00 01 02* Once intense and long-lived at best but often disappointing, this now has better balance and flavour in general, as vineyard and cellar techniques have been updated.

DONNICI *DOC*

From hills just south of Cosenza, where much of it remains.

Bianco *w dr* ☆→☆☆ *DYA* Based on Montonico.

Rosato *p dr* ☆→☆☆ *DYA* From Gaglioppo with Greco Nero and others, this can be lively.

Rosso *r dr* ☆→☆☆ *99 00 01 02* Gaglioppo and Greco Nero give a bracing red when young, develops grace with age. Also *novello*. Age: *riserva* 2 yrs.

GRECO DI BIANCO

DOC w am sw ☆☆→☆☆☆ *93 94 95 96 97 98 99 00 01 02* The seaside town of Bianco, almost on the toe tip of Calabria, lends its name to this entrancing, but all too rare, honey-hued dessert wine, made from partially dried Greco grapes, whose hints of citrus fruits and herbs on the nose and palate, natural strength, richness of flavour, and tongue-caressing softness are unparalleled. The old name of Greco di Gerace is occasionally still seen.

LAMEZIA *DOC*

Area covering the plains and low hills overlooking the Gulf of Sant'Eufemia around Lamezia Terme and Nicastro with wines that can be good if not exceptional.

Bianco *w dr* ☆→☆☆ *DYA* Malvasia, Greco, Trebbiano, and others amy be found in this variable white.

Rosato *p dr* ☆→☆ *DYA* The same grapes as *rosso* in this rosé.

Rosso *r dr* ☆→☆☆ *96 97 98 99 00 01 02* Sicily's Nerello joins Greco Nero and Gaglioppo in this red which can approach ☆☆☆ in the *riserva* version. Also *novello*.

Greco *w dr* ☆→☆☆ *DYA* Can be fleshy, attractive wines with some style.

MAGLIOCCO

Although often referred to as a synonym of Gaglioppo, this unknown red variety was discovered on the Librandi estate in Cirò and found to make wines of style and fruity vigour unparalleled in the region. Now being taken up by neighbouring estates too.

MANTONICO

Local white variety also called Montonico that produces wines ranging from crisply dry to lusciously sweet or even sherry-like, with a lightly bitter almond undertone and citrus-like aromas. Montonico Nero is a synonym of Gaglioppo.

MELISSA *DOC*

Some maintain that Melissa, named after the village north of Crotone, is derived from a Greek term for sweetness whereas adjacent Cirò comes from a word meaning sharpness or bitterness. There is, however, no such divergence between the wines of Melissa and its more famous neighbour. Until recently completely overlooked by Cirò, Melissa is now the focus of renewed interest.

Bianco *w dr* ☆→☆☆ *DYA* Greco-based whites that shadow Cirò.

Rosso *r dr* ☆→☆☆ *00 01 02* Gaglioppo-based Cirò lookalikes. Age: *superiore* 2 yrs.

POLLINO

DOC r dr ☆→☆☆

Rarely seen red from Gaglioppo with Greco Nero and others grown along the southern flank of the Pollino range in inland northern Calabria. A cheery if powerful, firm wine that varies in colour from pale ruby to cherry. Age: *superiore* 2 yrs.

SAN VITO DI LUZZI *DOC*

Tiny area around the village of Luzzi, northeast of Cosenza, with limited production of wines that can rival Calabria's better-known names.

Bianco *w dr* ☆→☆☆ *DYA* Pleasant white from Malvasia Bianca and Greco.

Rosato *p dr* ☆→☆☆ *DYA* Based on Gaglioppo.

Rosso *r dr* ☆→☆☆ *00 01 02* Enjoyable Gaglioppo-based red.

SANT'ANNA DI ISOLA CAPO RIZZUTO

DOC r p dr ☆ *DYA*

Practically non-existent red and rosé from Gaglioppo and numerous others grown near the coast south of Crotone.

SAVUTO

DOC r dr ☆→☆☆☆ *95 96 97 98 99 00 01 02*

From Gaglioppo with Greco Nero, Nerello, and others, grown on steep slopes along the Savuto Valley southwest of Cosenza, probably the best of Calabria's mountain reds, though styles vary from the ruby and robust *superiore* to a lightweight, cherry-hued version. Sparse production is currently centred in the valley's warmer reaches. Age: *superiore* 2 yrs.

SCAVIGNA *DOC*

This small zone near the coast, abutting Savuto has much of its potential and is rapidly developing a reputation for stylish wines.

Bianco *w dr* ☆☆ *DYA* The (optional) Chardonnay in the blend with Trebbiano, Greco, and Malvasia helps this white stand out from the crowd in the region.

Rosato *p dr* ☆→☆☆ *DYA* Attractive rosé from Gaglioppo with Nerello.

Rosso *r dr* ☆→☆☆☆ *97 98 99 00 01 02* In the right hands this blend of Gaglioppo and Nerello with, significantly, Aglianico, can produce reds of remarkable class.

VERBICARO *DOC*

This sizeable area on the western side of north Calabria is much less noted today than in the past.

Bianco *w dr* ☆→☆☆ *DYA* From Greco with, optionally, Malvasia Bianca, Guarnaccia Bianca, and others.

Rosato *p dr* ☆→☆☆ *DYA* Average pink from Gaglioppo and Greco.

Rosso *r dr* ☆→☆☆ *98 99 00 01 02* Unproven red from Gaglioppo, Greco, and others. Age: *riserva* 3 yrs.

Producers

Provinces: Catanzaro (CZ), Cosenza (CS), Crotone (KR), Reggio di Calabria (RC).

Cantine Lento, Lamezia Terme (CZ). Fine range of Lamezia brings new lustre to this DOC, most notably *rosso riserva* and Tenuta Romeo, white Greco. Also admired IGT Federico II (Cabernet Sauvignon).

Caparra & Siciliani, Cirò Marina (KR). Respected producers of Cirò, notably white Cunale, red *classico* (Volvito). Also Lamezia.

Dattilo, Strongoli (KR). Modern-directed estate concentrating on international varieties.

Enotria, Cirò Marina (KR). Large reliable co-op makes Cirò.

Fattoria San Francesco, Cirò (KR). Admired Cirò Classico (Donna Madda, Ronco dei Quattro Venti), *rosato* and *bianco*, sweet IGT *passito* Brisi (Greco), and modern-leaning Pernicolo (Greco/Chardonnay), Marlà (Gaglioppo/Merlot).

Vincenzo Ippolito, Cirò Marina (KR). Revived range of Cirò.

Librandi, Cirò Marina (KR). One of the most dynamic wineries of Italy's south. The range of Cirò, topped by red Riserva Duca San Felice is impeccable, as is IGT Magno Megonio (Magliocco). Lands at Stringoli produce the award-winning Gravello (Gaglioppo/ Cabernet), light white Critone, pink Terre Lontane, and the sweet *passito* Le Passule. New vineyards in Melissa make red and white of great promise.

Luigi Vivacqua, Luzzi (CS). Rising star of San Vito di Luzzi.

Malena, Cirò Marina (KR). Emerging Cirò estate.

Odoardi, Nocera Tirinese (CZ). Eye-opening Savuto (Vigna Mortilla) and Scavigna especially red Vigna Garrone, and white Pian della Corte. Also IGT Valeo, a sweet Moscato of character.

Serracavallo, Cosenza. Admired wines from blends of indigenous and international grapes under Valle del Crati IGT.

Statti, Lamezia Terme (CZ). Good Lamezia, IGT *passito* Nósside, and IGT indigenous/ international blends.

Vintripodi, Reggio Calabria. Once known for the sweet Mantonico di Bianco, reds from Nerello with Alicante, and whites from Grecanico with Ansonica now dominate production here.

Wine & Food

Calabrians, behind their mountain barriers, have always lived in isolation. Their cooking, although drawing on standard southern Italian ingredients, expresses this independence. Pork is so important that the pig has been called Calabria's "sacred cow". The great country tradition (which survives in home kitchens, if rarely in restaurants) relies on soups, pastas, and vast arrays of vegetables. When not in season, peppers, courgettes, artichokes, aubergines, and mushrooms are preserved in olive oil, of which the region is a major producer.

Besides the usual range of shellfish, Tyrrhenian waters provide swordfish and tuna. Calabrians adore sweets, often based on citrus and other fruit, candied or dried, such as chocolate-covered figs.

Wines to accompany each dish are suggested below in italic.
Alalonga in agrodolce Tender small tuna caught in Calabrian waters cooked sweet-sour. *Cirò Bianco*
Cicirata Christmas pastry flavoured with honey or cooked grape juice and lemon. *Greco di Bianco*

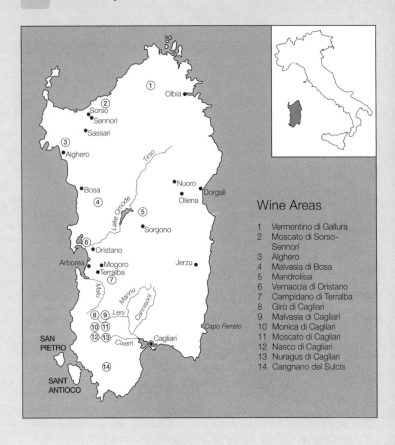

Wine Areas

1 Vermentino di Gallura
2 Moscato di Sorso-Sennori
3 Alghero
4 Malvasia di Bosa
5 Mandrolisai
6 Vernaccia di Oristano
7 Campidano di Terralba
8 Girò di Cagliari
9 Malvasia di Cagliari
10 Monica di Cagliari
11 Moscato di Cagliari
12 Nasco di Cagliari
13 Nuragus di Cagliari
14 Carignano del Sulcis

Mursiellu alla catanzarese
Rich stew of various cuts of pork, tomatoes, and peppers. *Savuto*
Mustica Newborn anchovies with oil and lemon. *Citrone*
Pesce spada Swordfish, a speciality of Bagnara on the Calabrian Riviera, with peppers, lemon, garlic, capers, and herbs. *Cerasuolo di Scilla*
Pitta chicculiata Calabrian pizza – a sort of pie filled with tuna, tomato, anchovies, black olives, and capers. *Cirò Rosato*
Sagne chine Festive lasagne baked with as many ingredients as possible, usually pork, peas, artichokes, and mushrooms. *Pollino*

Restaurants

Recommended in or near wine zones:
Cirò-Melissa-Isola Capo Rizzuto
L'Aquila d'Oro at Cirò; *Casa di Rosa* and *Sosta* at Crotone; *Annibale* at Isola Capo Rizzuto.
Donnici-Cosenza *Hotel Aquila & Edelweiss* at Camigliatello Silano;
Il Setaccio and *Pantagruel Vecchia Rende* at Rende.
Pollino *Alia* at Castrovillari.
Savuto-Lamezia-Scilla
Taverna Kerkyra at Bagnara Calabra; *Marechiaro* at Gizzeria Lido; *Approdo* at Vibo Valentia.

Sardinia *Sardegna*

Off by itself in mid-Mediterranean, Sardinia has every reason to be the most idiosyncratic of Italian regions and its wines express the island's character to the letter. Several varieties are unique in Italy, brought by Phoenicians, Carthaginians, Romans, and, in particular, Spaniards. But over centuries, the peculiar, idiosyncratic climate and soils of the Mediterranean's second-largest island (after Sicily) and Sardinian palates gradually changed their nature. Sardinians once craved intense, alcoholic wines – the stronger the better – maybe drunk "cut" with water. Then the all-important tourist industry fed a complete turnaround and lightness, freshness, and quaffability was the order of the day. Recently, though the island is still a source of strong blending wines, there has been a greater desire among producers to look further than its coastline and, in line with the rest of Italy, maximize the potential of their native grapes. A more diverse range of more concentrated, more interesting wines has been the result. Cooperative wineries still dominate production here more than elsewhere in the south, but that has happily not put a brake on developments.

Of the nineteen DOCs many represent old-style Sardinia and are strong in constitution whether sweet or dry, for example: Malvasia di Bosa, Nasco, and Girò di Cagliari, the rich Moscato of Cagliari and Sorso-Sennori, and the sherry-like Vernaccia di Oristano. But these are now made in limited quantities. It is the island's four main varieties, red Cannonau and Monica, white Vermentino and Nuragus that dominate production. The star is Vermentino, which when grown in the Gallura of the northeast is DOCG. Cannonau, Sardinia's emblematic red, is at its best in the heights of the remote easterly province of Nuoro. Nuragus, introduced by the Phoenicians and possibly named after the *nuraghe*, the island's prehistoric round stone towers, flourishes on the extensive Campidano plainlands north of Cagliari – as do most of the wines with a region-wide (di Sardegna) or province-wide (di Cagliari) denomination. Monica is a light, cheerful red. A further bright point comes from Torbato, grown mostly around Alghero.

Most of Sardinia's DOCs cater for single varietals. For blends producers use IGT designations. There are fourteen of them plus the region-wide Isola dei Nuraghi and all will be seen on labels. Sardinia is famous for its beach resorts, particularly the chic Costa Smeralda near Olbia. Visitors who wander into the wooded hills of the Gallura Peninsula will find the vineyards of Vermentino picturesque. But the entire island is wine country of uniquely scenic splendour. The *Antica Enoteca Cagliaritana* at Cagliari has a wide choice of the island's wines.

Recent Vintages

There are few Sardinian wines that require any amount of substantial ageing, but among the ones that do Vernaccia di Oristano and other strong dessert or apéritif style wines can last for some years. The recommended vintages for wines appear with each entry.

Wines

ALGHERO *DOC*

The area around the town on the northwestern coast has long been known for wine on the island, although it took the presence of the high-ranking Sella & Mosca company to bring it to wider attention. As well as the Cabernet version, from a mix of Cabernet Sauvignon, Cabernet Franc, and Carmenère, there are now also singly varietal versions from Cabernet Sauvignon, Cabernet Franc, and Carmenère.

Bianco *w dr (s/sw) (sw) (fr) (sp)* ☆☆ *DYA* Can come from any locally approved non-aromatic variety; may be *frizzante* (dry or sweetish), sparkling, or sweet *passito*.

Rosato *p dr (fz)* ☆☆ *DYA* Can come from any locally approved variety.

Rosso *(s/sw) (sw) r dr (sp)* ☆☆→☆☆☆ *94 98 99 00 01 02* Can come from any locally approved red variety. May be *novello*, sparkling, or *liquoroso* from semi-dried grapes fortified to 18% alcohol, a desert wine developing garnet-brick colour after 2 to 3 years in barrel and 5 or more in bottle, with a heady bouquet of berries and spices, and warm, lingering elegance. Age: 3 yrs, *riserva* 5 yrs.

Cabernet *r dr* ☆☆→☆☆☆☆ *99 00 01 02* This comes from Cabernet Sauvignon or Franc or Carmenère, and can develop a wide array of enveloping aromas with round, alluring flavours.

Cagnulari *r dr* ☆☆→☆☆☆ *99 00 01 02* Local variety makes a unique red of great individuality and personality.

Chardonnay *w dr (sp)*

Sangiovese *r dr*

Sauvignon *w dr* ☆☆ *01 02* Can be well fruited and cleanly fresh.

Torbato *w dr (sp)* ☆☆→☆☆☆ *00 01 02* From a vine of Spanish origin, this has straw-green colour, a flowery fragrance, and well-rounded fruit with a crisp, clean finish.

Vermentino *w dr (fr)* ☆☆ *00 01 02* This classy variety is a little subdued but still stylish and attractive here.

ARBOREA *DOC*

Lightweight varietals from throughout the plains and low hills of westerly Oristano province.

Sangiovese *r p dr* ☆→☆☆ *00 01 02* Pale red, which can be tasty, or rosé.

Trebbiano *w dr s/sw fz* ☆ *DYA* Trebbiano Romagnolo/Toscano make vinous lemonade.

CAMPIDANO DI TERRALBA OR TERRALBA

DOC r dr ☆→☆☆ *00 01 02* Ruby-crimson wine based on Bovale grapes grown across the northern Campidano, south of Oristano. Good fruit and structure.

CANNONAU DI SARDEGNA

DOC r (p) dr s/sw sw ☆→☆☆☆ *97 98 99 00 01 02* Red Cannonau is Sardinia's emblematic grape; the one Sardinians consider "theirs", whose wines inspire the highest of regard, or great nostalgia, and where others seek that elusive wow factor. In fact, the wine comes in a jumble of styles but the strongly alcoholic, often sweet or fortified types that once dominated are now seen far less often than the standard dry version, of greater or lesser intensity and personality. The DOC covers the whole island, although Cannonau best thrives in the remote uplands of Nuoro where there are sub-zones Oliena (or Nepente di Oliena) and Jerzu for grapes grown around these villages. It also thrives in the southeast corner (where 4 communities comprise the sub-zone Capo Ferrato), and in the Anglona hills and plains above Alghero in the northwest. The pale garnet to mahogany colour can be deceptive, for even the dry red and rosé pack a punch. As the richer and more muscular *riserva* ages, it takes on warmth and roundness. The *liquoroso* may be dry (18% alcohol) or *dolce naturale* (16% alcohol, 3% residual sugar). Age: *riserva* 2 yrs, *liquoroso* 10 mths.

CARIGNANO DEL SULCIS

DOC r dr (sw) (p) (fz) ☆→☆☆☆ *95 96 97 98 99 00 01 02* The Spanish/French grape variety Carignan is prominent in Italy only in the vineyards of Sulcis, Campania's southwest promontory, and adjacent islands. Although it can make strong wines for blending, it can also be a distinguished red, grapey when young but sturdy enough to mellow with several years of age when *riserva* or *superiore*. The modest *rosato*, which may be *frizzante*, is best young. There are also *novello* and *passito* versions. Age: *riserva* 2 yrs.

GIRÒ DI CAGLIARI

DOC r s/w sw (dr) ☆☆

The rare Girò, of Spanish origin, can come from almost anywhere in Cagliari and Oristano provinces. It resembles ruby port. The smooth *dolce naturale* (14.5%) is easy on the palate, though the richer *liquoroso riserva* (17.5%) has more intense flavours. Age: *liquoroso riserva* 2 yrs.

MALVASIA DI BOSA

DOC am dr s/sw sw ☆☆ 95 96 97 98 99 00 01 02

Of Italy's many wines from Malvasia this from the sub-type Malvasia di Sardegna grown on the steep, chalky slopes of the Planargia south of the port of Bosa is one of the most *recherché*, especially in the pale-golden *secco* version with 15% alcohol and flavours recalling dried hazelnuts and green olives. But little is made. *Liquoroso* and *dolce* versions are bolder but less distinctive. Age: 2 yrs.

MALVASIA DI CAGLIARI

DOC am dr (sw) ☆☆ 93 94 95 96 97 98 99 00 01 02 Slight production of this golden to amber Malvasia is centred in the Campidano. Its tenuous bouquet and almondy flavour show best as a dry apéritif. *Dolce* and *liquoroso secco* and *dolce* (17.5%) versions are also allowed. Age: *liquoroso riserva* 2 yrs.

MANDROLISAI

DOC r p dr ☆→☆☆ 98 99 00 01 02 Mandrolisai sits in the barren Barbagia hills at the centre of the island. Bovale Sardo blends with Cannonau in pleasant enough light reds and rosés, mostly for drinking young, though *rosso superiore* can last a few years. Age: *superiore* 2 yrs.

MONICA DI CAGLIARI

DOC r sw (dr) DYA

This red from Monica grapes may be dry but is nearly always sweeet, concentrated by growing on low vines, when growers bother, that is. Age: *liquoroso riserva* 2 yrs.

MONICA DI SARDEGNA

DOC dr (s/sw) (fz) ☆→☆☆ 00 01 02 This is one of Sardinia's most popular and best-value, easy-drinking reds, though it may come from anywhere, most of the grapes are planted in the Campidano, where they usually make dry wine, soft, and fairly light in body, and winningly fruity when youthful. Age: *superiore* 1 yr.

MOSCATO DI CAGLIARI

DOC w sw ☆→☆☆

Dessert wines from the Campidano, some fortified (*liquoroso*). These are golden in hue with Muscat aroma, and a rich texture. Age: *liquoroso riserva* 1 yr.

MOSCATO DI SARDEGNA

DOC w sw sp ☆→☆☆ DYA The DOC for this sweet *spumante* is region-wide, though most come from the north, where Gallura and Tempio Pausania (or Tempio) may appear on labels for wines from those zones. This delicately aromatic wine with fruity sweetness has great appeal and quantities though small, are growing.

MOSCATO DI SORSO-SENNORI

DOC w sw

Low coastal hills make Sassari's traditional Moscato, honey-coloured, sweet, and often strong, but production is almost non-existent.

NASCO DI CAGLIARI

DOC w am dr s/sw (sw) ☆☆ DYA Nasco grows only in Sardinia.

This ancient, unique variety makes pale-golden to light-amber wines of exquisitely subdued personality, but is often overlooked. It can also be distinctive as a sweet fortified wine with traits reminiscent of tawny port. Age: *liquoroso riserva* 2 yrs.

NURAGUS DI CAGLIARI
DOC w dr (s/sw) ☆→☆☆ *DYA*
It seems that Nuragus can always reflect the style of Sardinia. In the days when good meant heavy and powerful Nuragus was amber-coloured, potent, and harsh; at the time when light, crisp nonentities were in vogue, Nuragus was just that; now that the emphasis is on bringing out the personality of indigenous varieties Nuragus is less ubiquitous but generally more concentrated and characterful, with greater breadth of aroma and fullness of flavour, even though it is never likely to set the world alight.

SEMIDANO SARDEGNA
DOC w s/sw sw (dr) (sp) ☆→☆☆*DYA*
The Semidano vine, exclusive to the island and grown mainly in central Sardinia, makes occasionally dry but usually lightly sweet to sweet golden wines, most notably south of Oristano around Mogoro, which is a sub-zone.

VERMENTINO DI GALLURA
DOCG w dr ☆☆→☆☆☆☆ *DYA*
A vine of Spanish origin, Vermentino apparently arrived via Corsica, but it rates native status in the wooded hills of the Gallura, where it is DOCG. Its lively, fleshy roundness rarely disappoints and with careful handling it can develop into a richly flavoured white of great character.

VERMENTINO DI SARDEGNA
DOC w dr (s/sw) (sp) ☆→☆☆☆ *DYA*
This regional DOC has been gaining prominence as demand for Vermentino increases. The wine may also be sweet and/or sparkling, though the dry versions are the most impressive, sometimes on a par with Vermentino di Vallura.

VERNACCIA DI ORISTANO
DOC am dr (sw) ☆☆→☆☆☆☆ *71 80 85 88 90 91 93 94 96 97 98 99 00 01 02*
This most Sardinian of wines comes from the unique and local vine called Vernaccia trained low in the Tirso River flatlands near Oristano where grapes soak up heat from the sandy soil, acquiring strength and flavour. Once very ripe, they are made into wine of high natural alcohol, aged in small barrels in brick buildings with apertures to let in air and sunlight. Since barrels are never full, a veil of yeast known as flor forms over the wine, preventing spoilage and influencing development of bouquet and flavour. Since the same technique is used to produce sherry, it is not surprising that there is a sherry-like character to Vernaccia. But differences in grapes and climate give a Vernaccia its own style. Truest to type are the unfortified versions, particularly the long wood-aged *superiore* and *riserva* of 15.5% alcohol, with nuances of toasted nuts, spices, and faded flowers that heighten with ageing as the sharp, bitter edges disappear. *Liquoroso* types, whether dry or sweet, are richer but less distinctive. Age: 29 mths, *superiore* 41 mths in wood, *riserva* 48 mths.

Producers

Provinces: Cagliari (CA), Nuoro (NU), Oristano (OR), Sassari (SS).

Antichi Poderi di Jerzu, Jerzu (NU). Cannonau in all sorts of shapes and sizes.

Argiolas, Serdiana (CA). One of Italy's most dynamic small estates with fine Sardegna Cannonau (Costera), Vermentino (Costamolino), and Monica (Perdera), and Nuragus di Cagliari (Selegas). Highly acclaimed IGT Turriga (Cannonau/ Carignano/Bouale), Argiolas (Vermentino and others), Korem (Bouale/Carignano), Cerdena (Vermentino), and sweet white Angialis (Nasco/Malvasia).

Attilio Contini, Cabras (OR). The leading producer of Vernaccia di Oristano by a long chalk, with *riserva* dating back to the 1970s and a special blend of vintages called Antico Gregori. Also Vernaccia DOC and IGT and IGTs from Nièddera, a dry, strong but smooth and scented red.

CS di Dolianova, Dolianova (CA). Reliable DOC Vermentino, Monica, Cannonau, Nuragus, Moscato, and IGT blends of indigenous grapes.

CS di Dorgali, Improving Cannonau-based reds.

CS Gallura, Tempio Pausania (SS). Admirable Vermentino di Gallura (Canayli, Mavriana, Piras, Gemellae), Moscato di Tempio Pausania; IGT include unusual reds based on Nebbiolo and rare local varieties.

CS Giogantinu, Berchidda (SS). Three styles of Vermentino di Gallura, IGT Vermentino Passito, and good red blends.

CS Il Nuraghe, Mogoro (OR). Emphasis on the often overlooked Semidano grape.

CS di Oliena, Oliena (NU). Cannonau Nepente di Oliena in 2 styles.

CS di Santadi, Santadi (CA). Model co-op, with acclaimed Carignano del Sulcis (Rocca Rubia, Crolta Rossa, and, especially, illustrious Terre Brune). Also late-harvest Nasco called Latinia, IGT Araja (Carignano/ Sangiovese), Villa di Chiesa (Vermentino/Chardonnay), DOC Moinca, Vermentino, and Nuragus.

CS Santa Maria La Palma, Alghero (SS). Reliable range of DOC Alghero and popular Sardegna Vermentino (Aragosta), Cannonau (Le Bombarde).

CS della Trexenta, Senorbi (CA). Sound quality in DOC Monica, Moscato, Vermentino, Cannonau, and Nuragus, IGT Tanca Su Conti (Cannonau/Carignano).

CS del Vermentino, Monti (SS). Vermentino di Gallura (Aghiloia, Funtanaliras, S'Eleme), and di Sardegna, including sparkling and *passito*, and a range of IGT blends.

Andrea Depperu, Luras (SS). Excellent Vermentino di Gallura.

Ferruccio Deiana, Settimo San Pietro (CA). Promising DOC Cannonau, Vermentino, Monica; IGT indigenous/international blends.

Giuseppe Gabbas, Nuoro (NU). Impressive DOC Cannonau and IGT Cannonau-based blends.

Alberto Loi, Cardedu (NU). Various styles of DOC Cannonau, IGT Cannonau-based blends.

Pedra Majore, Monti (SS). Very good Vermentino di Gallura (I Graniti, Hysonj), di Sardegna (Le Cronche).

Piero Mancini, Olbia (SS). DOCG Vermentino di Gallura (Cucaione, Saraira), DOC Cannonau, IGTs using international/indigenous blends.

Giovanni Maria Cherchi, Often impressive Vermentino di Sardegna (Vigna Tuvaoes, Pigalua, Boghes), Alghero Cagnulari (Soberanu); IGT Luzzana (Cagnulari/Cannonau).

Gianvittorio Naitana, Magomadas (NU). Rare, traditional, high-quality Malvasia called Murapiscados from IGT Planargia.

Pala, Serdiana (CA). Up-and-coming DOC Vermentino, Nuragus, Monica, Cannonau; IGT S'arai (Cannonau/Carignano/Bovale), Entemari (Vermentino/ Chardonnay/Malvasia).

Sardus Pater, Sant'Antioco (CA). Revived winery working mainly with DOC and IGT Carignano.

Gigi Picciau, Cagliari (CA). Lively, characterful indigenous varieties: Sardegna Cannonau, Semidano, Vermentino; Cagliari Malvasia, Nasco. Also, unique in Sardinia, IGT Pinot Bianco.

Josto Puddu, San Vero Milis (OR). Vernaccia di Oristano and wines from Vernaccia, Monica, Cannonau, Nieddera.

Sella & Mosca, Alghero (SS). The vast I Piani estate north of Alghero, turns out an admirable range of wines, led by the highly rated Alghero Cabernet (Marchese di Villamarina), Rosso Tanca Farrà (Cannonau/ Cabernet), and Liquoroso (Anghelu Ruju), along with Bianco Le Arenarie (Sauvignon), *rosato* (Oleandro), and the long-admired Torbato (Terre Bianche). Also Sardegna DOC Vermentino (La Cala) and Cannonau; Nasco *liquoroso* and more.

Tenute Dettori, Sennori (SS). Rare Moscato di Sorso-Sennori plus good white from Vermentino, reds from Cannonau.

Tenute Soletta, Florinas (SS). Sardegna DOC Cannonau (Firmadu) and Vermentino (Soletta), Moscato *passito*.

Meloni Vini, Selargius (CA). Huge range of sound wines from most of the island's most popular DOCs and varieties.

Villa di Quartu, Quartu Sant'Elena (CA). Excellent dessert wines from Malvasia, Moscato, Nasco, all di Cagliari.

Vitivinicola Su Baroni, Masainas (CA). Emerging Sulcis estate. Reds from Carignano/Syrah blends; white from Vermentino.

Wine & Food

Though the island's population has shifted from the hills to the coast in modern times, the "real" Sardinian cooking is that of the back country: pork, lamb, kid, soups of fava beans, and barley, the ravioli-like *culingiones*, the piquant Pecorino Sardo cheese and, most of all, the breads. It has been said that every Sardinian village has a bread of its own. The most sung about is *pane carasau*, also known as "music paper", because, unleavened, it is that thin. Fish is a relatively recent exploitation of a source that has always been there in the deep waters off the island's rocky coasts. Almost every Mediterranean species can be savoured, sometimes together in the lavish fish soup known as *cassòla*.

Wines to accompany each dish are suggested below in italic.

Agnello con finocchietti Lamb stewed with onion, tomato, and wild fennel. *Carignano del Sulcis*

Aragosta arrosta Rock lobster grilled. *Vermentino di Gallura*

Bottarga Dried mullet eggs sliced thin on toast or in salad. *Vernaccia di Oristano superiore*

Favata Rich stew of fava beans and pork. *Monica di Sardegna*

Malloreddus Tiny gnocchi of semolina, dressed with meat or tomato sauce and grated Pecorino. *Cannonau di Sardegna*

Porceddu Sucking pig spit-roasted slowly on an open fire. *Turriga*

Sebadas or **seadas** Pastry with cheese and bitter honey. *Anghelu Ruju*

Su farru Soup of the ancient grain called *farro* (spelt) with mint. *Torbato di Alghero*

Restaurants

Recommended in or near wine zones:

North *La Lepanto* at Alghero; *Gallura* at Olbia; *Da Franco* at Palau; *Sappentu* at Porto Torres; *Il Senato* at Sassari; *Canne al Vento-Da Brancaccio* at Santa Teresa Gallura.

Centre *Sa Funtà* at Cabras; *Su Gologone* near Oliena; *Il Faro* at Oristano.

South *Antica Hostaria*, *Dal Corsaro*, and *Lillicu* at Cagliari; *Al Tonno di Corsa* at Carloforte; *La Ghinghetta* at Portoscuso; *Hibiscus* at Quartu Sant'Elena; *Terrarancio* at Villa San Pietro.

Wine Areas

1   Faro
2   Contea di Sclafani
3   Menfi
4   Santa Margherita di Belice
5   Contessa Entellina
6   Regaleali
7   Sambuca di Sicilia
8   Eloro
9   Delia Nivolelli
10 Sciacca

Sicily *Sicilia*

Vines have flourished on the Mediterranean's largest island since the dawn of history, yet Sicily's millennial aptitude for wine has been more industriously exploited for quantity than quality. And although there is now a noticeable shift in the other direction and the field of admirable premium wines is growing, DOC production still represents only about three percent of the total. Overall, Sicily's wines are the most reliable of Italy's south, and it is generally acknowledged that there is still huge potential for greatness that has only just begun to be tapped. Indeed, wine companies from the north are keen to invest in a region whose natural attributes, first among them sunshine, are a virtual guarantee of fine quality.

Perhaps the most significant development in Sicily has been the revival of marsala, the once famous fortified wine that was left behind during the rush for the light and bright. Yet while critics smeared it, in Sicily's soul it remained its pride and joy. On a smaller scale, the sweet and *passito* wines made on Pantelleria from Moscato, and on the Aeoilan islands from Malvasia, have reinspired interest in this once unfashionable category.

Although the island boasts nineteen DOCs, several of which have been approved or modified quite recently and many of which appear to give ample span to the creative ingenuity of producers, DOC is frequently ignored in favour of IGT, be it the region-wide Sicilia or one of six others.

Sicily bears the stamp of Greeks, Arabs, Normans, Spaniards, and so many others. Major Greek ruins are at Siracusa (Syracuse), Agrigento, Segesta, and

Erice – all near wine zones. Palermo, the capital, and nearby Monreale, have the Alcamo and Contessa Entellina zones at their heels, while the volcano of Mount Etna has Etna DOC curving round its lower slopes. The volcanic Lipari or Aeolian Islands are justifiably noted for sweet Malvasia. At Marsala, Florio's vast cellars and wine museum are worth visiting for wine-lovers.

Recent Vintages

Sicily's temperate to torrid climate permits fairly consistent harvests, although drought can be a problem in non-irrigated areas. High-altitude vineyards have climatic conditions similar to northern regions with the advantage of more sunlight. Recommended vintages appear with each entry.

Wines

ALCAMO

DOC w dr ☆→☆☆ *DYA*

A large hil-clad zone of north western Sicily, intensively carpeted with vines. Most production is the Catarratto-based white but the numerous varietals permitted are gaining an ever firmer presence.

Bianco *w dr (s/sw) (sw) (sp)* ☆→☆☆ *DYA*

Based nominally on one or more sub-varieties of Catarratto but style may be determined by the other, often more characterful, grapes permitted at up to 40%. May be *vendemmia tardiva* or sparkling.

Bianco Classico *w dr* ☆→☆☆ *DYA*

Grapes from the heartland around Alcamo growing at over 250 metres (820 feet) high. The two main sub-varieties of Catarratto account for at least 80%, giving this *classico* a more traditional slant than the standard white.

Rosato *p dr (sp)* ☆→☆☆ *DYA*

From any or all of 8 varieties, vinified off their skins, including indigenous and international grapes. May be sparkling.

Rosso *r dr* ☆→☆☆ *99 00 01 02*

Entirely or principally from Nero d'Avola with optional Frappato, Sangiovese, Perricone, Cabernet Sauvignon, Merlot, and/or Syrah. Also *novello*. Age: *riserva* 2 yrs. The single-varietal versions, all dry, are from Catarratto, Inzolia (or Ansonica), Grillo, Grecanico, Chardonnay, Müller-Thurgau, Sauvignon (white), and Nero d'Avola (or Calabrese), Cabernet Sauvignon, Merlot, Syrah (red).

CERASUOLO DI VITTORIA

DOC r dr ☆→☆☆☆ *98 99 00 01 02*

Dark cherry-red wine from Nero d'Avola and Frappato grown around Vittoria in southeast Sicily. The more Frappato there is (40% minimum), the lighter, zippier, and more vibrantly fruity the wine, but the trend is to give it more presence, weight, and ageing with Nero d'Avola capacity. Both styles have much to offer.

CORVO

Brand name used by Duca di Salaparuta (*see* page 207) .

CONTEA DI SCLAFANI *DOC*

This appellation covers a large zone around Sclafani Bagno and other communes in the hills of central Sicily, straddling the provinces of Palermo and Caltanissetta. Varietal whites are Inzolia, Chardonnay, Damaschino, Grecanico, Grillo, Müller-Thurgau, and Sauvignon. Varietal reds, all of which have a *riserva* requiring 2 years of ageing, are Cabernet Sauvignon, Calabrese (or Nero d'Avola), Merlot, Nerello Mascalese, Perricone, Pinot Nero, Sangiovese, and Syrah. The other types are as follows.

Bianco *w dr (sw)* ☆→☆☆ From Catarratto, Inzolia, and/or Grecanico.

Rosato *p dr* ☆→☆☆ *DYA* Nerello
Mascalese is the base of this rosé.

Rosso *r dr* ☆→☆☆ *99 00 01 02* Nero
d'Avola and Perricone are the
base of a red that can be *novello*
or *riserva*. Age: *riserva* 2 yrs.

Dolce *w sw* ☆→☆☆ *DYA* Any of the
white varieties from the list above
may be used here.

Spumante *w (p) sp* ☆→☆☆ *DYA* Any
of the varieties may be used.

Vendemmia Tardiva *w s/sw sw* ☆→☆☆
DYA Any of the white varieties
may be used here.

CONTESSA ENTELLINA *DOC*
Small zone around the town of
the same name in the high Belice
valley south of Palermo. Varietals
are white Inzolia (also as sweet
vendemmia tardiva), Chardonnay,
Grecanico, and Sauvignon. Reds
are Cabernet Sauvignon, Merlot,
and Pinot Nero. All reds may be
riserva (age: 2 years).

Bianco *w dr* ☆☆ *DYA*
Inzolia with any of 8 other varieties.

Rosato *p dr* ☆ *DYA* Nero d'Avola
and/or Syrah form at least 50%
of this rosé.

Rosso *r dr* ☆→☆☆ *99 00 01* From the
same grapes as the *rosato*.

DELIA NIVOLELLI *DOC*
Zone in the southern part of
the Marsala area covering
lands between the southern
coast and Salemi southeast of
Trapani. Varietals must contain
85% of the grape named. Varietal
whites, which may also be
spumante, are Inzolia, Chardonnay,
Damaschino, Grecanico, Grillo,
Müller-Thurgau, and Sauvignon.
Varietal reds, all of which have a
riserva requiring 2 years of ageing,
are Cabernet, Merlot, Nero d'Avola,
Perricone or Pignatello,
Sangiovese, and Syrah.

Bianco *w dr (sp)* ☆☆ *DYA* Based on
Grecanico, Grillo, and/or Inzolia.

Rosso *r dr* ☆→☆☆ *00 01 02* Any or all of
the red varieties may be used in this
red, which may also be *novello*.
Age: *riserva* 2 yrs.

Spumante *w dr (sp)* ☆→☆☆ *DYA* From
any or all of Grecanico, Chardonnay,
Inzolia, Damaschino, and Grillo.

ELORO *DOC*
Zone for reds (and a pink) only of
good style in the southeast corner
of Sicily, around the towns of Noto,
Pachino, and Rosolino, once noted
solely for strong blending wines.

Rosato *p dr* ☆☆ *DYA* Nero d'Avola,
Frappato, and/or Pignatello make
up this heady rosé.

Rosso *r dr* ☆☆ *99 00 01 02* The same
varieties as the *rosato* make a
tasty red.

Frappato *r dr* ☆→☆☆ *01 02*

Nero d'Avola *r dr* ☆☆→☆☆☆ *99 00 01 02*

Pachino *r dr* ☆☆→☆☆☆ *96 97 98 99
00 01 02* This is a sub-zone, at the
heart of the area around Pachino,
also famous for its tomatoes.
The wine from at least 80% Nero
d'Avola is full, ripe, rich, powerful,
and long-lived.

Pignatello *r dr* ☆ *01 02*

ETNA *DOC*
The soil around active volcanoes is
believed to be excellent for vines
and Etna's wines were once held in
high esteem. But somehow they
lost their spark and have only
recently emerged with new flare.

Bianco *w dr* ☆→☆☆☆ *00 01 02*
Carricante, native to Etna,
sometimes with Catarratto
and others, gives a firm, flinty
wine of character. A *superiore*
version comes from a sub-zone
around Milo.

Rosato *p dr* ☆☆ *DYA* Made from
Nerello, like the *rosso*, this rosé is
light and easygoing.

Rosso *r dr* ☆→☆☆☆ *98 99 00 01 02* This
red from two types of Nerello can
be firm and tasty in its early
years, yet can age with
considerable grace.

FARO
DOC r dr ☆→☆☆☆☆ *96 97 98 99 00
01 02* This red, grown in a zone
around Messina extending to the
lighthouse *(faro)* at the top of the

Straits has just one producer, Palari, keeping it alive. He makes it from Nerello Mascalese with Nerello Cappuccio, Nocera, and Calabrese although small amounts of others are permissable.

MALVASIA DELLE LIPARI

DOC am s/sw sw ☆☆→☆☆☆ 95 96 97 98 99 00 01 02

The slim production of the distinctive type of Malvasia brought to the Lipari or Aeolian archipelago to Sicily's northeast by the Greeks, comes, in theory, from any of the 7 small, volcanic islands but in practice is almost all on Salina. There are 3 types, naturally sweet, *passito* (more lusciously sweet), and the rare, strong (16%), fortified *liquoroso*. These alluring golden to amber wines have a beguiling bouquet reminiscent of ripe apricots with citrus and the herbs and flowers that abound on the island's volcanic soil.

MARSALA *DOC*

Marsala is one of the world's 4 great fortified wines, alongside Sherry, Port, and Madeira, but infrequently recognized as such since memories of flavoured versions (with egg, cream, chocolate, banana, and other horrors) and "cooking marsala" stashed in a kitchen cupboard remain. Yet Marsala, developed for the British market in 1773 by John Woodhouse, has a heady wood-and-caramel bouquet and luxuriantly rich, smooth, slightly burnished flavour, that, whether bone-dry or richly sweet, evince, a breed far from culinary concoctions – especially with the longer-aged *superiore* and *vergine* wines. It is made principally from Catarratto, Inzolia, and Grillo (the more Grillo the better), grown across much of Trapani province in western Sicily and, commonly, the base wine is sweetened and fortified with concentrated must or *cotto* (cooked-down must) plus grape alcohol or, better, *sifone* (or *mistella*: must muted with wine alcohol) before ageing in large wooden barrels. Most marsala of old-gold or amber colour may be labelled as *oro* or *ambro*. The rules, oddly, also permit the use of red Perricone, Nero d'Avola, and Nerello Mascalese and these more ruby-hued wines are called *rubino*. Most marsala is made by largeish companies based in the port of Marsala.

Marsala Fine *am (r) dr s/sw* ☆→☆☆ *NV* The simplest masala, 17% alcohol and made using *cotto* and grape alcohol rather than the superior *sifone* is still often better, and better value, than most base-level fortified wines. The old tag Italy Particular (IP) may still be seen. Age: 1 yr.

Marsala Superiore *am (r) dr s/sw* ☆☆→☆☆☆☆ *NV* This is the most variable category. Blended by house formulas it can be barely superior to the fine or superb and last for decades. The sweet can be rich and luscious. The dry very dry with aromas of wood, nuts, citrus, and spices, and a velvety yet austere flavour. The aged *riserva* is most elegant. The tags Superiore Old Marsala (SOM), London Particular (LP) and Garibaldi Dolce (GD) may still be seen. Age: 2 yrs; *riserva* 4 yrs.

Marsala Vergine or Soleras *am (r) dr s/sw* ☆☆→☆☆☆☆ *NV* This lightly fortified marsala of 18% alcohol is the most prestigious. Dry to bone-dry, it contains neither *sifone* nor *cotto* and is blended from wines aged in barrels for different lengths of time – often by the *solera* system of topping up the old with younger vintages. With its hues of amber and infinity of scents, it has the breed, tone, and complexity to stand alongside the world's great apéritif wines, in particular the long-aged *stravecchio* or *riserva*. Some especially like it with strong or sharp cheeses. Age: 5 yrs; *stravecchio* or *riserva* 10 yrs in wood.

MENFI *DOC*

Zone around the town of Menfi on the southwest coast, would seem to have been created specifically to embrace the output of the huge Cantina Sociale Settesoli which dominates production here. But Settesoli's wines remain IGT despite similar characteristics.

Bianco *w dr* Mostly from Catarratto, Chardonnay, Grecanico, and/or Inzolia.

Rosso *r dr* Mostly from Nero d'Avola, Sangiovese, Merlot, Cabernet Sauvignon, and/or Syrah. Age: *riserva* 2 yrs.

Feudo dei Fiori *w dr* Sub-zone near Menfi for white from Inzolia and/or Chardonnay.

Bonera *r dr* Sub-zone also close to Menfi for red from any or all of the same 5 varieties as the *rosso*. Age: 1 yr, *riserva* 2 yrs.

Vendemmia Tardiva *w s/sw sw* From Chardonnay, Catarratto, Inzolia, and/or Sauvignon grapes semi-dried on the vine. There are also varietal versions of white Chardonnay, Grecanico, and Inzolia (or Ansonica), and red Nero d'Avola, Sangiovese, Cabernet Sauvignon, Syrah, and Merlot.

MONREALE DOC

Zone in the hills above the splendid village of Monreale, overlooking Palermo, whose wines have yet to make much impact. There are *superiore* versions of all the whites and *riserva* versions of all the reds. Age: *superiore* 6 mths, *riserva* 2 yrs.

Bianco *w dr (s/sw)* Based on Catarratto and/or Inzolia. Also a sweet *vendemmia tardiva* version.

Rosato *p dr* From Nerello Mascalese, Perricone, and/or Sangiovese.

Rosso *r dr* Based on Nero d'Avola and Perricone. Also *novello*. Varietal versions are from Catarratto, Chardonnay, Grillo, Inzolia, and Pinot Bianco (white), and Cabernet Sauvignon, Merlot, Nero d'Avola, Pinot Nero, Perricone, Sangiovese, and Syrah (red).

MOSCATO DI NOTO

DOC w am s/sw sw (sp) ☆☆ *DYA*
Made from Moscato Bianco grown around Noto in southeast Sicily, this infrequently seen dessert wine comes in 3 styles. The standard and sparkling versions are semi-sweet and fragrant, to drink young. The fortified type of 16% is rich and aromatic.

MOSCATO DI SIRACUSA

DOC wam sw
After years in which this once-prized Moscato was not made by anyone, there have been attempts to repropagate the few vines still remaining and production, albeit very limited, of this gracefully sweet wine is underway once more.

PANTELLERIA

The island of Pantelleria off the coast of Tunisia is Italy's most remote area, renowned for sweet Moscato from Zibibbo (Moscato d'Alessandria) grapes grown low on bush-trained vines in the black volcanic soil to protect them from the winds that constantly assail the island. A recent and bitterly fought battle to tidy up the nomenclature of the island's DOCs has now resulted in the names Moscato di Pantelleria and Passito di Pantelleria being restricted to its most classic styles and the catch-all denomination Pantelleria being applied to everything else.

Moscato di Pantelleria *w sw* ☆☆→☆☆☆
97 98 99 00 01 02 This fragrant, softly sweet wine contains a proportion of *passito* (semi-dried) grapes

Passito di Pantelleria *w am sw*
☆☆→☆☆☆ *90 91 92 93 94 95 96 97 98 99 00 01 02* From sun-dried grapes, this *passito* version is richly perfumed, powerful, mouthfilling, and very sweet but without cloying. Alcohol exceeds 14%. Age: 1 yr.

Pantelleria DOC *w am dr s/sw (fr) (sp)*
☆→☆☆☆ *00 01 02* This may be straight *bianco* (more or less dry),

Bianco Frizzante, Zibibbo Dolce, Moscato Spumante, Moscato Liquoroso, *passito liquoroso*, or Moscato Dorato, this latter being a strong, sweet fortified product – in short these styles cover dry and sweet, still and bubbly, fortified and non-fortified wines, from fresh and semi-dried grapes.

RIESI *DOC*

Emerging area in central southern Sicily for modern and more traditionally styled wines. The white, which can be sparking or sweet *vendemmia tardiva*, is based on Inzolia and/or Chardonnay; the rosé on Nero d'Avola with some Nerello Mascalese and/or Cabernet Sauvignon; the red (also *novello*) comes from Nero d'Avola and/or Cabernet Sauvignon. There is also a red *superiore* style, solely from Nero d'Avola. Age: *superiore* 2 yrs, *superiore riserva* 3 yrs.

SAMBUCA DI SICILIA *DOC*

Small area around the town of Sambuca in the west of Agrigento province. Age for all reds: *riserva* 2 yrs.

Bianco *w dr (sw)* From at least 50% Inzolia. In the *passito* version Grillo and/or Sauvignon must make up the rest; in the dry version the field is left clearer.

Producers

Provinces: Agrigento (AG), Caltanissetta (CL), Catania (CT), Enna (EN), Messina (ME), Palermo (PA), Ragusa (RG), Siracusa (SR), Trapani (TP).

Abbazia Sant'Anastasia, Castelbuono (PA). Accomplished modern-styled wines: Litra (Cabernet Sauvignon) with Montenero (Nero d'Avola/Cabernet Sauvignon/Merlot), Gemelli (Chardonnay/Sauvignon), Baccante (Sauvignon), and Biancodi PAssomaggio (Inzolia/Chardonnay/Sauvignon).

Rosso and **Rosato** *r p dr* From at least 50% Nero d'Avola. There are also varietal versions from Inzolia, Chardonnay, and Grecanico (white), and Cabernet Sauvignon, Merlot, Nero d'Avola, Sangiovese, and Syrah (red).

SANTA MARGHERITA DI BELICE *DOC*

Another small area, near Sambuca di Sicilia in the Belice valley. The white comes from Catarratto and/or Grecanico with Inzolia; the red from Sangiovese and/or Cabernet Sauvignon with Nero d'Avola. There is no *rosato* but 5 varietals, white Inzolia, Catarratto, Grecanico, and red Nero d'Avola and Sangiovese.

SCIACCA *DOC*

Zone around the coastal town of Sciacca, west of Agrigento. The 11 types include the novel Riserva Rayana, a dry, golden wine from Catarratto and Inzolia grapes grown in a special sub-zone. The wines, so far not evident on the market, can't be assessed. The white comes from Inzolia, Catarralto, Greciano, and/or Chardonnay; the red from Merlot, Cabernet Sauvignon, Nero d'Avola, and/or Sangiovese; the rosé from any of these 8 red and white grapes. The same varieties, Catarralto excepted, can be produced as single varietals.

Also good varietals from Nero d'Avola and Inzolia.

Avide, Comiso (RG). Ever-improving Cerasuolo di Vittoria IGT Herea (Frappato), 3 Carati (Nero d'Avola), Sigillo (Cabernet Sauvignon/Nero d'Avola), white Herea Vigne d'Oro, and sweet Lacrime Bacchi (all Inzolia).

Baglio Hopps, Marsala (TP). Stylish Grillo.

Barone La Lumia, Licata (AG). Highly admired Signorio and Cadetto Rosso (Nero d'Avola); also good Signorio and Cadetto Bianco (Inzolia).

Barone Scammacca del Murgo,
Santa Venerina (CT). Decent
Etna, IGT Tenuta San Michele
(Cabernet Sauvignon), Lapilli
(Chardonnay/Carricante).

Barone di Villagrande, Milo (CT).
Stylish wines from Etna and
delicious Malvasia delle Lipari.

Benanti, Viagrande (CT). Powerful Etna
wines, plus Passito di Pantelleria
and a good range of varietals.

Calatrasi-Accademia del Sole,
San Cipirello (PA). The Terre di
Ginestra wine shows class in
Catarratto and Nero d'Avola;
the D'Istinto range gives lively
indigenous-international blends;
Accademia del Sole are single-
estate wines from Tunisia and
Puglia as well as Sicily; the Terrale
varietals are simpler. High
standards throughout.

Cantine Rallo, Marsala (TP). No longer
owned by the Rallo family but
reliable marsala *vergine* and
range of varietals from Alcamo.

Ceuso, Alcamo (TP). Highly rated
IGT Ceuso Custera (Nero d'Avola/
Cabernet Sauvignon/Merlot);
Fastaia (Nero d'Avola/Cabernet
Franc/Merlot).

Colosi, Messina. Malvasia delle Lipari
naturale and *passita* .

Cooperativa Nuova Agricoltura,
Pantelleria (TP). Moscato and
Passito di Pantelleria DOC.

COS, Vittoria (RG). Easily the classiest
Cerasuolo di Vittoria made,
especially Bastonaca. Superb
single site IGT Nero d'Avola
(Dedalo Labirinto). Also Scyri
(Nero d'Avola), Rami (Inzolia/
Grecanio), and more.

Cottanera, Castiglione di Sicilia (CT).
Modern-directed estate on Etna
with fine IGT Sole di Sesta (Syrah),
Grammonte (Merlot), L'Ardenza
(Mondeuse), as well as more typical
Barbazzale Bianco (Inzolia) and
Rosso (Nerello).

Cusumano, Partinico (PA). Acclaimed
wines from grapes from various
parts of Sicily, most notably Noà
(Nero d'Avola/Merlot/Cabernet
Sauvignon), Sagana (Nero d'Avola),

Agimbé (Inzolia/Chardonnay),
Cubia (Inzolia).

CS di Trapani, Trapani. Reliable,
fruit-rich Forti Terre di Sicilia
range of varietals.

CS Valle dell'Acate, Acate (RG). Lively,
fruit-packed IGT Frappato and
Cerasuolo di Vittoria.

Donnafugata, Marsala (TP). Stalwart
range of Contessa Entellina Bianco
(Chiaranda del Merlo, Vigna di
Gabri), *rosso* (Tancredi,
Milleunanotte), and Chardonnay
(La Fuga). Good IGT blends. Also
passito, Moscato di Pantelleria.

Duca di Salaparuta, Casteldaccia
(PA). The house founded by the
Duke of Salaparuta in 1824, and
owned by the Ente Siciliano per la
Promozione Industriale until 2001, is
now the property of the wine and
spirits group Illva-Saronno (Como),
and is steadily regaining its position
as the region's standard-bearer.
Wines, nearly all IGT, come from
grapes selected in various parts of
Sicily. The simplest fall under the
famous trademark Corvo. The
Ducadi Salaparuta now houses
Colomba Platino (Inzolia/Grecanio),
Terre d'Agala (Nerello Mascalese),
Triskelè (Nero d'Avola, Cabernet
Sauvignon/Merlot), Kados (Grillo),
Megara (Frappato, Syrah), and the
leading Bianca di Valguarnera, and
Duca Enrico (Nero d'Avola).

Elorina, Rosolini (SR). Forward-looking
co-op with admirable Eloro Rosso
and Pachino, Moscato di Noto,
and more.

Feudo Principe di Butera, Butera
(CL). Owned by Zonin (*see page 90*)
and making waves with classy
IGT Deliella (Nero d'Avola), San
Rocco (Cabernet Sauvignon), and
Calat (Merlot).

Firriato, Paceco (TP). International
winemaking team bring a sheen
of class to large range led by
Santagostino Bianco (Catarratto/
Chardonnay) and *rosso* (Nero
d'Avola/Syrah).

Florio, Marsala (TP). The firm founded
in 1833 by Vincenzo Florio and
now owned by Illva-Saronno is

the largest producer of marsala and a leader in its revival with Vergine Baglio Florio and Terre Arse, Superiore Riserva Targa 1840 and Vecchioflorio. Also IGT Morsi di Luce (Moscato).

Carlo Hauner, Salina (ME). Heirs of the late Carlo Hauner continue to make Malvasia delle Lipari, including *passito*; IGT Salina Bianco and Rosso.

Maurigi, Piazza Armerina (EN). Rapidly emerging producer working with international varietals in an area, until now, completely unknown for viticulture – to excellent effect.

Miceli, Palermo. Reliable, good value varietals (Nero d'Avola, Syrah, Cabernet Sauvignon, Inzolia, Grecanico, Chardonnay) from western Sicily; Pantelleria Bianco and Passito di Pantelleria.

Morgante, Grotte (AG). Supremely classy Nero d'Avola (Don Antonio).

Salvatore Murana, Pantelleria (PA). Devoted grower makes authentically fine single-vineyard Moscato di Pantelleria and exquisite, rich *passito* (Khamma, Mueggen and Martingana). Reds too.

Palari, Messina (ME). The only producer of Faro, but an excellent one. Also fine Nerello-based Rosso del Soprano.

Carlo Pellegrino, Marsala (TP). Marsala, including superiore and soleras of good style. Also a proficient range of IGTs and DOCs from all over Sicily.

Planeta, Menfi (AG). Gold-star quality throughout the range of 10 wines from 4 estates in Sicily. IGTs La Segreta Bianco (5-grape blended), *rosso* (Nero d'Avola/Merlot/Syrah) have stormed the world, as has Alastro (Grecanico/Chardonnay) and varietals Nero d'Avola (Santa Cecilia), Fiano (Cometa), Cabernet Sauvignon (Burdese), Chardonnay, Syrah, and Merlot. A classy Cerasuolo di Vittoria is the icing on the cake.

Pupillo, Siracusa (SR). Leading producer of the rare Moscato di Siracusa.

Rapitalà, Camporeale (PA). Vast estate recently acquired by Gruppo Italiano Vini (*see* page 88) makes DOC Alcamo and is aiming at developing other wines.

Regaleali-Tasca d'Almerita, Vallelunga Pratameno (CL). Leading estate in the south with an inspired range of IGT wines sold under the name Regaleali. The basic *bianco*, *rosato*, and *rosso* are complemented by the fine white Nozze d'Oro (Inzolia and the estate's vine called Tasca) and aristocratic Rosso del Conte (Nero d'Avola/Perricone). The size and style of Chardonnay and Cabernet Sauvignon are extraordinary, as is the finesse of *spumante* Almerita Brut (Chardonnay). Others are at similar standards.

Settesoli, Menfi (AG). Leading co-op with huge output of good quality and excellent value IGT varietals and blends under the Mandrarossa line.

Solidea, Pantelleria (TP). *Passito* and Moscato di Pantelleria.

Spadafora, Monreale (PA). Wines that combine great style and drinkability throughout from the Schietto range of varietals (Cabernet Sauvignon, Syrah, Chardonnay) to Don Pietro Rosso (Cabernet Sauvignon/Merlot/Nero d'Avola) and Bianco (Inzolia/Grillo/Catamalto), and more.

Vecchio Samperi-De Bartoli, Marsala (TP). The finest marsala superiore (Oro Vigna La Miccia, Riserva 20 Anni) and Passito di Pantelleria (Bukkuram); Vecchio Samperi, Ventennale, IGT Grappoli del Grillo, Pantelleria Pietranera (dry Zibibbo), and more unique, enthralling wines.

Wine & Food

Sicily is the alleged birthplace of all sorts of good things to eat, among them pasta (unlikely, even if Italy's first such paste may have been formed here), innumerable sweets (including *gelato*, thanks to Etna's year-round snow), and various fish and vegetable dishes. Fairly recent times have also witnessed the rise of the pizza (though Naples takes credit for that) and that other symbol of Italo-American culinary artistry, the meatball. The island's natural endowments of sunshine on fertile volcanic soil combined with the multitude of ethnic influences have left Sicily with an unrivalled heritage of foods. Sadly, many dishes are now neglected. But the basics are as flavoursome as ever: citrus fruit, olives, brilliant vegetables, herbs, spices, lamb, sheep's cheeses, grain for pasta, and a multitude of breads and pastries. Then there's the sea brimming full of fish, offering tuna, swordfish, and sardines, to name but a few. Sicily reigns as capital of Italian sweets, the encyclopaedic array of which culminates in *cassata*.

Wines to accompany each dish are suggested below in italic.

Beccaficu Sardines either stuffed and baked or breaded and fried. *Corvo Colomba Platino*

Braccioli di pesce spada Swordfish fillets wrapped around a cheese-bread-vegetable stuffing and grilled. *Regaleali Nozze d'Oro*

Caponata Aubergine and other vegetables in a rich stew. *Regaleali Rosato*

Cassata The island's pride: opulent array of candied fruit and chocolate on a sponge cake. *Moscato Passito di Pantelleria Extra*

Cùscusu Of Arab origin, couscous-style fish stew with semolina. *Terre di Ginestra Bianco*

Farsumagru Braised veal roll stuffed with meat, cheese, and vegetables. *Cerasuolo di Vittoria*

Pasta con la Norma Spaghetti with aubergine, basil, tomato, garlic, and cheese: an homage to Catania's Vincenzo Bellini and his opera *La Norma*. *Etna Bianco Superiore*

Pasta con le sarde Palermo's classic pasta flavoured with sardines and wild fennel has become an island-wide speciality. *Corvo Bianco di Valguarnera*

Peperonata Peppers stewed with tomato, onion, and green olives. *Bianco d'Alcamo*

Tonno alla siciliana Fresh tuna cooked with white wine, fried anchovies, herbs, and spices. *Planeta Chardonnay*

Restaurants

Recommended in or near wine zones:

Northeast: Etna-Faro-Lipari *Filippino* at Lipari; *Villa Marchese* at Milazzo; *L'Ariana* at Salina; *La Giara* at Taormina.

Southeast: Siracusa-Eloro-Noto-Vittoria *Fattoria delle Torri* at Modica; *Majore* at Chiaramonte Gulfi; *La Pergola* at Ragusa; *Archimede* and *Minosse* at Siracusa.

West: Marsala-Alcamo-Pantelleria *Cortile di Venere* and *Moderno* at Erice; *Il Delfino* at Marsala; *Il Pescatore* at Mazara del Vallo; *I Mulini* at Pantelleria; *Il Mulinazzo* at Villafrati.

Index

Wine-growing areas and wines named after them are indexed together; similarly grape varieties and varietal wines are indexed together. The following abbreviations are used in the index: Coop. Cooperativa; CS Cantina Sociale; K Keller. Kellereigenossenschaft; Prod. Produttori. Page numbers in italic refer to maps.